THE PELICAN LATIN AME[...]
General Editor: Richard Gott

GUIDE TO THE POLIT[...]
OF SOUTH AMERIC[...]

Jean-Pierre Bernard, Silas Cerqueira,
Pierre Gilhodès, Hélène Graillot,
Leslie F. Manigat, Hugo Neira

Guide to the Political Parties of South America

Translated by Michael Perl

Penguin Books

Penguin Books Ltd, Harmondsworth,
Middlesex, England
Penguin Books Inc., 7110 Ambassador Road,
Baltimore, Maryland 21207, U.S.A.
Penguin Books Australia Ltd, Ringwood,
Victoria, Australia

Tableau des partis politiques en Amérique du Sud
published in France by Armand Colin 1969
English translation, revised and brought up to date,
published in Pelican Books 1973
Copyright © Librairie Armand Colin and Fondation
Nationale des Sciences Politiques, 1969
Revised edition copyright © Penguin Books, 1973
English translation copyright © Michael Perl, 1973

Made and printed in Great Britain by
Hazell Watson & Viney Ltd, Aylesbury, Bucks
Set in Linotype Juliana

Contents

List of Figures

Foreword

In politics, as in much else, it is difficult always to be up to date. Since this book was first published in France, there have been military coups d'etat in four out of the ten countries whose political parties are discussed here. Anyone misguided enough in the early 1960s to see South American politics developing along European or Anglo-Saxon lines must have been sadly disappointed, for in practice political developments there have proved almost impossible to analyse with tools useful in other contexts and continents. All party political activity in South America takes place in the shadow of the military which even where, as in Chile and Uruguay, it is rarely exercised directly provides a firm guide-line beyond which the politicians cannot step. Fortunately the French and South American writers responsible for producing this composite work have all taken note of the political impact of the armed forces, and their comments for the most part remain as relevant today as when they were first written.

In preparing this collection of essays for publication in English, I have taken the liberty of deleting some now irrelevant sections and updating others. At the end of each chapter a brief section has been added with new information. In this editorial work, I gratefully acknowledge the assistance of Alexandre Addor, Alan Angell, Malcolm Deas, Michael

Elmer, Elizabeth Finch, Richard Moseley-Williams, Christopher Roper, Ray Sentes and Percy Shelley.

RICHARD GOTT
February 1972

Figure 1. Political Map of South America

LESLIE F. MANIGAT

Introduction

America to the south of the Rio Grande, as Fernand Braudel
has written, seems already 'to have adapted itself to the
epithet of "Latin" applied to it' barely a century ago. At first
sight, the temperament, the main personalities and the history of South America's political parties do, indeed, appear
'Latin'. But whereas this 'Latinity', a favourite and common
theme of eloquent politico-journalistic panegyrics, exists to
prove an undeniable kinship, Central and South America,
multiple yet one, changing yet immutable, have in fact developed a highly original system of party institutions within
a geographical, economic, ethnic and social context utterly
different from that of the European world.

The various essays collected in this volume are intended
to give an overall picture of modern political parties in South
America. The essays are individually signed by their authors,
members of the Latin American section of the Research
Centre for International Relations, part of the French
National Foundation for the Political Sciences, and these
authors therefore take individual responsibility for the views
expressed. Each essay tries to give a picture of the party set-
up within the political life of one South American country.

To say that this undertaking, like any pioneer enterprise
in a field that has not yet been fully explored, contained
potential hazards may help to explain why its authors considered it less rash but still useful – or at least so they hope –

to limit their aims to offering a 'documentary' study of the Latin American political parties, rather than a general theory of these parties. Each of us has kept firmly in the forefront of his mind, while compiling the data on which these monographs are based, Russel H. Fitzgibbon's judicious warning against any premature synthesis of Latin American political parties.[1] This introduction shares that concern with the individual monographs following it.

However, it goes without saying that a picture of Latin American political parties could never be purely descriptive. Each writer has endeavoured to give the widest, most varied and most truthful account possible, well aware that party realities are all the more complex because Latin American political life is turbulent. To this end, maps, statistics and graphs have been used to link up, clarify and expand the political analysis wherever the documentation could give concrete and precise illustrations. For everyone grappling with material apparently so intractable to analysis, the problem has not been one of knowing what simplifications to introduce to make the facts fit his interpretation, but rather how to expand and perfect his interpretation so that it accurately reflects a highly varied, tortuous and often at first sight disconcerting reality.

In fact, the very word 'party' began, after its journey across the Atlantic, with a very different meaning from that ascribed to it in Latin America today. Armed factions built up around one man, then political groupings around a leader, then a group organized for the conquest of power. The acceptance of the word has been defined and has developed together with the transformations of the economic and social structures of each of the countries in the region. The existence of a party system presupposed a minimum respect – not always granted

1. Fitzgibbon, Russel H., 'The party potpourri in Latin America' in Martz, John D., edr, *The Dynamics of Change in Latin American Politics*, Prentice Hall, Englewood Cliffs, New Jersey, 1965, pp. 212–13.

– for the rules of the political game. It did not always prove easy to recognize the proper functions of opposition, and it was always difficult to depoliticize the traditional pre-party or extra-party forces, namely the Army and the Church, which regarded themselves as a matter of course as the parties' mentors. The very fact that the parties operate therefore constitutes a victory for democracy, which is in any case continually threatened in many, if not all, of the South American countries by the return of dictatorship, or by the recourse to armed revolt as a means of settling the fierce struggle for power. As a result, contemporary party politics, the product of a troubled history, are themselves still troubled, The delicacy of the matter under review thus required prudence and discretion from everyone, without, however, any sacrifice of the need for patient elucidation of the truth without prejudice and also without complacency.

Historical Sketch of Latin American Political Parties: Three Generations of Parties

Without going so far as to reduce the history of Latin American political parties to the simple shadow of economic and social realities, it may be said that the opportunities for political action and the expectation of life of the party political system have fluctuated with the development of social relationships and in strict correlation with that development. Each blossoming, each thrust forward of the party system marks an attempt at the renewal of politics by the advent and active participation of a new social category in the political life of the country. There are thus successive generations of parties corresponding to progressive stages in national integration, and each generation leaves some residual witness of its period; these witnesses are responsible, by their survival, for the infinite gradations of the party political rainbow in Latin America. Nevertheless, great issues have arisen to polarize conflicts and correct the heterogeneity of the party system : yesterday, these were universal suffrage, separation of Church from State, nationalism, nativism; today, agrarian reform, anti-imperialism, communism, Castroism, etc. The overall plan, so complicated at first sight, becomes simpler, and the apparent abundance of parties can finally be rendered down into two, or at the most three, main trends or tendencies : the classical division into right, centre and left, defined as a function of local conditions and in terms of local problems.

The development of political parties in Latin America as it emerges from the brief historical sketches contained in the essays that follow provides a good illustration of the various stages of political democracy's painful struggle for the right to exist and the weary march towards national integration, while at the same time explaining the original aspects of modern Latin American party life.

PREHISTORY OF THE PARTIES: CAUDILLISM AND CACIQUISM

The parties may be said to have a 'prehistory', during which *caudillos* reigned, with the authority of local *caciques*. This prehistoric period, of differing duration depending on country, far from being buried in the past, has proved capable of resurgence, of re-emerging as a real political force, as most of the essays published in this volume will demonstrate. A system of this type, autocratic by nature, left no place nor even any prospect for political parties, 'since everything, from top to bottom of the ladder, rested on personal power'.[2]

Caudillism and caciquism, which were the general rule after independence, were only apparently destroyed on the

2. Chevalier, François: 'Caudillos et caciques en Amérique' in *Mélanges offerts à Marcel Bataillon par les hispanistes français*, Féret fils, Bordeaux, 1962, p. 46.

emergence of true political parties. In fact these were initially often simply groups gathered around one man, and the changeover from personal leadership to institutional leadership, from a party of patronage to a party of ideology, from a local party to a national party was hardly instantaneous. Moreover, this threefold transition has not been completed to this day in every part of the continent, as the national monographs constituting this survey will testify.

At all events, this prehistory has left two distinctive marks on the life of Latin American political parties that will immediately be noticeable from most of the essays here presented. These are, firstly, the persistence of the cult of personality, and secondly the survival of regionalism. Examples of the former that spring immediately to mind are Peronism in Argentina, Velasquism in Ecuador, Battllism in Uruguay, Getulism in Brazil. Certainly these are the most obvious. But even in the parties upholding the ideals of 'representative' democracy, the party institutions are deeply marked by the cult of personality. Is the rise of Acción Democrática in Venezuela really conceivable without the personality of Rómulo Betancourt? Neither do the 'ideological' parties escape this fate: in Bolivia, the left-wing parties are dominated by individuals who exercise a powerful personal charisma, and in Brazil a large part of the history of the Communist Party is identifiable with the life of its greatest leader, Luis Carlos Prestes. As for regionalism, it is just as discernible in Argentina, where certain local parties are more powerful in their home regions than the national parties, as in the vast, unequally developed expanses of Brazil. It is not far below the surface in Venezuela, where the Andean states have highly idiosyncratic ways of going about things by comparison with the Federal District of Caracas, or in Colombia, where the Caribbean zone does not breathe at the same rhythm as the rest of the country, and it puts its stamp on the life of the parties and regulates the balance of forces between them in Peru, in Ecuador and in Bolivia.

THE FIRST GENERATION OF PARTIES: THE 'HISTORIC PARTIES'

The first generation of Latin American political parties includes those which are termed the 'historic parties': the conservatives and liberals. They form the *ancien régime* in the history of Latin America's parties. The appearance and practical operation of these 'parties of bosses', inspired chiefly by local dignitaries, seems to have corresponded almost everywhere with the emergence as a ruling political class next to the old landed aristocracy (the *hacendados*) of a new middle class of commercial, intellectual and professional origins, and even of an industrial middle class in places, such as Bolivia with its tin mines, where mineral resources were beginning to be exploited.

The principal axis of debate between the parties from this time on was the political problem of freedom and emancipation versus the absolutist tradition, under pressure from the development of a market economy. The claim for political liberty guaranteed by a Constitution was, in the hands of this 'conquering middle class', a weapon for gaining a share in political power. Clearly, the doctrinal inspiration comes from the eighteenth-century philosophy of enlightenment, which found political expression in the French revolutions of 1789, 1830 and 1848, while the 'model' is contributed by Anglo-Saxon political institutions, greatly admired for their smooth operation. This bipartite struggle between conservatives and liberals gives South American politics a Manichaean style. Where they have survived, as in Colombia, they have maintained a style of political life copied from western Europe in the nineteenth and the early twentieth centuries.

This first generation was to see the political landscape

complicated by the appearance, to the left of the liberal parties, of radical parties placing emphasis on the extension of suffrage, if not universal suffrage, the struggle against clericalism, and even on some tentative social measures on behalf of the labouring classes – all this in faithful imitation of the European model. The effect of the emergence of the radicals was to produce either a reconciliation between yesterday's enemies against the newcomer, or the substitution for the old two-party system of a new three-party system, which in turn resulted in subtle tactical alliances between the parties and skilful manipulation of the polls and the electoral system.

THE SECOND GENERATION OF PARTIES: THE 'MODERN PARTIES'

A second generation, emerging between the wars, brought with it new parties concerned chiefly with social justice. Born of the extension of suffrage and the rise of new social classes, these parties were from the start modern in outlook and structure. This was the advent of the 'mass parties', the sign that the middle and lower classes had now burst on to the political scene, borne by the current of industrialization and the expansion of state responsibilities, encouraged by the achievements of the Mexican revolution of 1910 and the more distant reverberations of the Russian revolution of October 1917, incited by the zealots of the Third International, and deeply stirred by the traumatic effects of the great world economic crisis of 1929. Their appearance led the 'historic parties' to draw closer together, and only the memory of earlier fierce conflicts restrained them, in some cases, from amalgamating altogether.

At all events, the centre of gravity of the debate between the parties shifted towards problems such as social protest against inequality, and the refusal to identify with the interests of any foreign boss, ancient metropolis or paternalistic power. The rise of the European socialist parties stimulated aspirations towards a more equitable distribution of the national income in favour of the underprivileged classes, and Washington's policy towards its southern neighbours provoked a reaction in the form of a combined move towards protection of the national interest and redefinition of the national character. Thus the new lines of ideological demarcation were drawn between socialism and nationalism: socialism or its milder form of social reformism faced by a nationalism often accompanied by its socio-cultural twin, cultural nationalism. It was at this time that APRA appeared in Peru, Acción Democrática in Venezuela, and later the MNR in Bolivia. With certain chronological, geographical and social differences, Argentine Peronism and Brazilian Getulism, both movements with populist tendencies, belong to the same general trend.

This second generation, which ushered in the modern era of South American political party history, also had to face a resurgence of caudillism, in the form of military dictatorships set up by decree. The struggle between the parties also took on a multi-dimensional character, with the split of the socialists into social democrats and communists. This split, originating in Europe, redistributed the pieces on the political chess-board, splintered the forces of the left, and gradually shifted the political centre of gravity as the passionate struggle between these hostile kinsmen progressed.

THE THIRD GENERATION OF PARTIES: THE 'CONTEMPORARY PARTIES'

The third generation, which came into being in the 1950s and 1960s, bore signs of the influence of the distant Chinese revolution, and of that nearer home, in Cuba. These had a truly shattering and traumatic effect in Latin America, especially, of course, the Cuban. This 'contemporary period' in the history of Latin American political parties is strongly conditioned by the political and economic consequences of the Second World War and the difficult post-war years.

The new sensitivity to international affairs can doubtless be attributed to the emergence, against heavy odds, of a new ruling class of the technocratic variety, similar in outlook to the positivists of the last century, and professionally interested in the international struggle against underdevelopment. However, this new trend has been enlivened by the example of the Chinese and Cuban revolutions, which have demonstrated the dormant but massive political strength of the peasantry in the revolutionary cause. Moreover this new social dimension to party activity has not failed to have an effect on certain sectors of the Church, stimulated by the new departure undertaken by Pope John XXIII and the Second Vatican Council, on the Army, where certain officers have been tempted by the example of Nasser (even though their attitude is a minority one, doomed to failure or at best transitory successes), or indeed on the United States, where President Kennedy tried to get his philosophy of an Alliance for Progress accepted in the hope of advancing the development of Latin America. The central problem has become the struggle against underdevelopment, and the new demarcation line is drawn as much between different tactical approaches as between opposing ideologies: is it to be economic development under the guidance of technocracy, or revolutionary war in the name of anti-imperialism? The new parties, all claiming mass support but with an active membership in fact largely drawn from the 'professional' classes, can be defined by their attitudes to the burning questions of the day: internally, agrarian reform and nationalization; externally, the position of the United States and the Cuban revolution.

The political landscape is complicated by a double split. Firstly, the political forces based primarily on Catholicism can be divided into a traditionalist branch, loyal to the conservatism of yesteryear, or at any rate to the traditional line of caution in social matters; and a progressive, even revolutionary branch, with its roots in social Christianity and preaching Christian socialism. Secondly, and more important, serious disputes between the rival factions have been provoked by the schism in the communist community between those faithful to the Soviet Union, reputedly more realistic and more flexible but lacking in 'political sex-appeal', and the supporters of the new, allegedly harder Chinese line, who hope to see the revolutionary peasantry storm the bastion of power currently held by the urban privileged classes. In fact, these two hostile groups do not necessarily espouse the cause of one or other of the great rival powers in the socialist camp, despite the second's regular denunciation of the first for 'revisionism'. The truth is more subtle. It is the opportunity for armed struggle – and more precisely guerrilla warfare – and the lack of such opportunity that actually divides revolutionary Marxists into traditional communists, basing their activity on the working class and its well-tried methods of struggle, and the new style of communist, who places the emphasis on the peasantry and on immediate revolutionary war.

Thus the area covered by party political life in Latin America and the depth of the system's roots can be ascribed to two developments: a historical process going back to the nineteenth century, and cumulative in its effects; and a political environment born of the recent post-war period that is multiplicative in its effects.

Characteristics of Latin American Political Parties

The studies which follow will show both that there are differences between party political set-ups that are not merely a matter of deeper or lighter shades but of genuine divergences, and at the same time that there are a certain number of convergent features common to all the national party systems in Latin America. Whereas these common denominators, when applied to a field in which every country seems unique, do not in the present state of knowledge give sufficient grounds for the construction of a general theory, they do nevertheless contribute the first essential elements of such a theory and above all throw light on the highly original characteristics of party life in the southern part of the western hemisphere.

1. First of all, *the existence of political parties should not foster any illusions as to their actual place and true significance* in political life, of which, generally speaking, they are by no means the sole expression. In fact, the main sources of political dynamism frequently lie elsewhere. The Army, the Church, sectional interests, pressure groups, trade unions and universities all constitute powerful forces which have a decisive impact on political activity, to such an extent that they may render institutions ineffectual. The influence of the United States is likewise a powerful factor, in the face of which the workings of the party system may prove impotent to determine the nation's political destiny. The exception of Chile – which is in any case disputed – and the singularity of Uruguay do not invalidate this almost invisible law governing political trends, which prevents the Latin American parties from taking on and expressing the necessary dynamism in the struggle to win, use and successfully preserve political power.

At best, extra-party forces act as the mentors of the parties, like the Church for the conservative parties of Colombia and Ecuador or the labour unions for the Peronist parties in Argentina. Political life is therefore much richer than inter-party relations can possibly indicate. These extra-party forces may intervene openly, even spectacularly, to block the proper functioning of the party system: the Peruvian Army has never allowed Haya de la Torre to reap the fruits of his party's electoral success; in Argentina these forces successfully prevent the reintegration into political life of Peronism, which they contrive to thwart of its victories at the ballot box.

2. *Latin American political parties depend very considerably on personalities:* the leader is the pivotal point of the party, and sometimes the only reason for its existence, at least initially. To apply Duverger's felicitous expression, it may be said that in these countries the chief is an institution. The charismatic individual is often exalted in almost identical terms in the various parties. One man's personal aura, the radius of his fame, is coextensive with the party's following, and its recruits are taken from among the leader's personal clientele. This polarization around one man, a survival of caudillism, is assisted by the presidential system common to the whole continent. Thus an ideological party with a structure like that of APRA in Peru is just as much consubstantial with its founder Haya de la Torre as an *ad hoc* association such as the Popular Democratic Front in Venezuela is with Larrazabal, or a group like UDELPA in Argentina with General Aramburu.

3. In actual fact, *these parties are not, for the most part, able to create a strong, well-articulated and permanent party organization.* They come into prominence mainly at election times, and lead an episodic existence, with the hot periods of intense activity associated with electoral campaigns succeeded by intervals of calm, during which their metabolism seems to slow down, as if in a state of hibernation. At these times, only the party officials ensure institutional continuity,

and the party apparatus plays a key part in the orientation and development of the party.

There are no doubt well-structured parties with large and active memberships, but they are exceedingly rare. In general, the small number of permanent, card-carrying members, paying regular subscriptions and acting as pillars of their local ward organizations, only represent a tiny fraction of the party's electoral support. Here, far more than in Europe, the number of a party's supporters, and above all the number of its sympathizers, far outweighs the number of militants. The explanation of this phenomenon may doubtless be sought in the low level of incomes and the precariousness of the material foundations for existence, in illiteracy where it still exists, the political ignorance of the rural masses, the vulnerability of the urban mob to the temporary appeal of flashy demagogues, and the obstinate persistence of the rule of patronage. However, it should be said that this is a field where documentation is sparse, and where systematic research would no doubt permit a better and more accurate assessment of the true state of organization of the parties, so that one could judge the relative flexibility or rigidity of the average party organization and suggest reasons. There are therefore still enormous areas open to new research, notably so far as the articulation of the parties is concerned, the nature and extent of member participation, relations between parliamentary deputies and the leadership, the true extent of the latter's authority, decision-making procedure, the enforcement of discipline, financing electoral campaigns, and the renewal mechanisms of the 'inner caucus' at the highest level. This can already be seen from the example of APRA in Peru and Acción Democrática in Venezuela, which are without doubt the most closely observed of the South American parties, with a form of organization which has enabled not only the study of the statutory powers of the party's various organisms at every level of the hierarchy, but also the analysis of the operation and functional efficiency of these organisms and tests of the rigorousness of a vertically and horizontally centralized system.

4. *This almost universal absence of a highly-articulated direct structure expresses, in fact, another related problem affecting party political life in Latin America: the parties' lack of cohesion and homogeneity.* They are under continual threat of breakaways by dissident groups. This 'fractionalism' seems to be encouraged by various factors: Latin individualism, the priority given to ideological discussions at the higher levels of the parties, and the deepening gulf between the generations, with the hot-blooded and revolutionary impatience of the young on the one side, facing the tactical cunning and conservatism of their elders – the passionate expression of a renewed but permanent dispute between ancient and modern. Doubtless the lines of the break seem more complex, but a careful analysis will often show behind the conflicts of men, generations, classes or tactical attitudes the eternal problem of doctrinal orthodoxy challenged by a rash of heresies. But this is only part of the natural progress towards ideological parties.

The result of this splintering tendency is that the new dissident parties, after a tentative and stumbling start, have to define their position in relation to the 'parent group' which gave them birth. This 'propagation of the species', as if by mitosis, is a major conditioning factor affecting the complexity of the political chess-board in Latin America. Argentina, Brazil, Peru and Venezuela are notorious for providing the most characteristic illustrations of a disease which in reality affects party political life over the whole of the South American continent.

5. To examine the phenomenon more closely, *this tendency to disintegration only thinly veils a general trend within the Latin American party system, called in that part of the*

world sinistrismo. This 'slide to the left' takes place in a somewhat original manner, since the left wing of one period becomes the right wing of the next. Of course similar phenomena have occurred in western Europe, but the evolution from liberal parties to radical parties to socialist parties to communist parties has taken a century or more. In Latin America the whole cycle has been completed in the space of a couple of generations, accompanied by the advent of universal suffrage and the succession of simultaneous internal and international crises by which the twentieth century has been marked. *Sinistrismo* is therefore the more striking because it takes place at a much faster rate. It expresses an accelerated development towards mass parties, or at least the passionate desire to move away from 'specialist parties' towards 'totalitarian parties'. This leftward flight is today placing the traditional communist parties themselves in a difficult position, since they are being overtaken by new Marxist parties which may well make them appear the outdated representatives of the moderate left: hence the advanced position of the new MIR parties, representing the new revolutionary left.

Because of this, left-wing labels, including the label 'socialist', sometimes – in Argentina, for example, or in Bolivia or Ecuador – relate to actual party positions which in Europe would unhesitatingly be classified as centre. What has happened is that the old-guard left has retained its denotation, and often its vocabulary and part of its original following as well, while the actual content of its policies and the essential tendency of the positions it adopts on domestic and international issues strongly indicate a movement to the right, as is manifestly the case of APRA in Peru and Acción Democrática in Venezuela.

6. The difficulty of determining the authenticity of party labels caused by *sinistrismo* is aggravated by a further

complication : the *multi-class structure of the parties*. In fact the party system in Latin America exhibits no coincidence between parties and social classes. This social heterogeneity means that most of the major parties are assemblages rather than class parties as elsewhere, despite the ideology proclaimed in each party's programme. Even the socialist and communist parties do not manage to avoid this fate, since their officials and party workers are frequently drawn from the intellectual petty and middle bourgeoisie, the liberal professions and the upper middle classes, while a significant proportion of their natural working-class clientele and the majority of the peasantry still in fact support either conservative parties, as in Ecuador, or movements of the nationalist and reformist type, as in Peru, Bolivia, Uruguay, and Venezuela, not to mention Brazil. A typical case is the Peruvian Unión Nacional Odrista, with its dual popular and middle-class support, and another is the National Democratic Front in Venezuela, with its threefold middle-class, proletarian and peasant support.

The 'multi-class' party is reinforced by the vestiges of regionalism, which transcends class differences and leads the inhabitants of a given region to vote in the majority, if not *en bloc*, for one party, whatever their own social origins. It is further reinforced by racial distinctions, since the racial demarcation line does not always correspond to class boundaries in the so-called native sector of Latin America. Thus the conservatives in Ecuador enjoy the support of practically all the whites (about 10 per cent of the population); APRA in Peru has made efforts to win, and has to a large extent obtained, the support of the country's Amerindians. Finally, the 'multi-class' party is reinforced by the surviving remnants of the neo-feudal system, under which, thanks to the strength of personal loyalties and the preservation of rule by patronage, the parties of the traditional oligarchies are assured a certain mass support. Regional, racial, class and even the vestiges of caste differences form the stuff of South America's social complexity, and their interplay, combined with the conditions in which the parties came into existence and have developed, has resulted in the 'multi-class' nature of party politics in Latin America.

7. In these circumstances, *the prevalence of multi-party systems is hardly surprising.* The result of the cult of personality and of fractionalism, the product of traditional social and political hostilities overlaid with ethnic animosities, the reflection of conflicts which project international rivalries into the internal party political system, the multi-party system is still, in some South American countries, nourished by the multiplier effects of proportional representation. The one exception among the countries studied here is Paraguay, where there is one dominant, dictatorial party. This party, the only effective party in practice, tolerates the existence of opposition parties under certain conditions of limited collaboration but without any real independent participation in political life. Parties unwilling to accept these conditions are forced to operate in exile. Everywhere else, the multi-party system predominates, either behind the mask of an apparent or institutional two-party system, as in Colombia or Uruguay, or openly, where all parties compete with each other, and in the struggle for power make electoral pacts or create inter-party fronts.

As a further point, the multi-party tendencies of the right in Latin America should be noted; it has been said that these provide sufficient material on their own for a full-blown theory of small parties. At all events the permanent minority parties, such as those that look after the interests of the Peruvian oligarchy, Venezuelan conservatism or the Brazilian aristocracy, never manage to amalgamate into a larger party of 'order' as opposed to 'change'. At the other end of the scale, the left-wing parties vie for the support of the urban and rural masses, and likewise fail to present a united front of social revolution in the political battlefield. In some extreme cases, the proliferation of parties reaches such a stage that they positively pullulate; this complete atomization makes it impossible to follow the individual destiny of each tiny unit, except within the framework of an overall analysis.

8. However complicated and changeable the political game may be, it is never dull. The situation is in constant ferment, the balance of forces is continually changing, alliances are formed and broken; all this makes for an inbuilt *instability of regime, if not of the system,* and to Europe and North America gives an impression of political immaturity. In Latin American party politics, the 'continual process of disintegration and disappearance of some, the birth and development of others' is endemic, with parties and governments following one another in a swift merry-go-round interrupted by military coups. Hence the frequency of provisional regimes well versed in exercises of every kind of political arithmetic.

One man's actions may take an unexpected turn, as in the case of Carlos Lacerda in Brazil, or a party leader like Domingo Alberto Rangel in Venezuela may change party three times in less than five years. Parties enter the government and leave it again, are recognized today and banned tomorrow. The example of the URD and the FND in Venezuela, which take turns at being members of the government coalition and members of the opposition, is not an isolated one in Latin America. On the one hand the opposition may become so sweet and reasonable as to suggest complicity with those in power. On the other, it may swing right out of the normal institutional channels and respond to the *de facto* violence of power by revolutionary violence of its own; in this case the party system ceases to exist, and is replaced by the simple and brutal confrontation of material forces. In short, this complex and heterogeneous situation means that the political party system in Latin America may be considered a veritable kaleidoscope.

9. Nevertheless, if one considers the scene not at the level of national unity, but on a continental scale, *the outline and trends of great political movements that extend beyond national frontiers may be discerned.* Latin American politics may be divided into three large spiritual families: conservative parties who feel solidarity with one another, though active in different states, the fellowship and mutual support of the dictatorships, and the chain of Castroist parties. These continental tendencies have been consciously and deliberately developed in the case of a party like APRA in Peru, which was the first to define itself as a Latin American party, not merely Peruvian. Its political ideology was one that embraced the whole of the continent, not just the fatherland of Victor Raúl Haya de la Torre.

In practice, a veritable 'international' of the democratic and reformist left had been in operation for some time, including, besides the Peruvian APRA, Acción Democrática in Venezuela and a number of Central American parties, such as José Figueras's Party of National Liberation in Costa Rica, Muñoz Marín's Popular Democratic Party in Puerto Rico, the Dominican Revolutionary Party led by Juan Bosch; these parties used to publish a joint journal, *Combate*. The Bolivian MNR and the Febrerista Party of Paraguay may be included in the same family. The Communist International in Latin America, part of a greater whole, has always acted more or less in concert, with the support of the Marxist unions. Finally, the Democratic or Social Christian Parties' International, encouraged by the victory of Eduardo Frei's party in Chile in 1964, also began coordinating its activities on the continental scale. Its headquarters were in Santiago de Chile, and its influence was exerted through the medium of its fraternal parties and the Latin American Confederation of Christian Trade Unions. A new kind of International has also reared its head – the Military International that has to all intents and purposes been set up since the Brazilian and Argentinian coups d'etat, in 1964 and 1966, and which expressed its outlook in the Brazilian theory of ideological frontiers and the Argentinian insistence on renewing the proposal to set up an Inter-American Peace Force.

10. In fact, *having now entered upon the international scene, Latin America has become more directly and immediately sensitive to international realities.* Up to now, she only felt the effects of great world, European or American controversies in erratic bursts: separation of Church from State, positivism, nationalism, reformism, socialism, and even fascism. Today she finds herself at the very centre of the great controversies that shake the contemporary world. She was not represented at the Bandung Conference; the Tricontinental Conference on the other hand was held actually in Latin America. It was also in Latin America that the social Christianity of John XXIII and the Vatican Council found its boldest political expression: the case of Camilo Torres in Colombia – a priest and guerrilla fighter at one and the same time – is an extreme example of the revolutionary Christianity that is currently causing upheavals in many countries of Latin America. Also, the Sino-Soviet controversy within the international communist movement was initially fought out most passionately in South America.

*

To evoke the originality of Latin American history and sketch a few of the more striking characteristics seemed the best way to introduce the reader to the still emergent phenomenon referred to in the title of this work, *Guide to the Political Parties of South America.* The history does not, indeed, reveal any fixed pattern or regular succession of phases in all the countries covered, but it makes it possible to follow the main strands involved in the establishment of the foundations of a political system. The features of party political life that are characteristic of this part of the world are, among other reasons, striking for the fact that they may be entirely missing in one place and very strongly marked in another, but in any case they differ somewhat from country to country. However, they do enable us to trace an outline and understand the role of one actor in the political scene : the political party.

It may be that this study will give the impression of a very strong left-wing movement in Latin America. This impression is doubtless not a false one, as regards the political parties as a whole. The main thing, however, is not to forget that whereas the parties have been, and still are, a factor working for change, 'order' and 'movement' still find their most powerful advocates in political forces that are independent of the parties. Who will win? The stakes are high. Socially, the forces of order are endeavouring to keep the urban and rural masses under their control, while the forces of movement wish to win them over and mobilize them. Economically, the forces of order proclaim that they wish to bring about harmonious and integrated development under their banner, while the forces of movement claim that this will only be possible under their auspices. The various essays which follow aim to foster an understanding of the nature, the role and the weight of modern political parties in the southern half of the western hemisphere, and at the same time perhaps to give a glimpse, through the individual destinies of these parties, of the complexities, uncertainties and general direction of political life itself.

July 1966

HÉLÈNE GRAILLOT

Argentina

Although Argentina won her independence in 1816, it was
not until the second half of the nineteenth century that her
political and economic transformation into a modern state
began. Until then, apart from the Andean region, only the
area around Buenos Aires had shown any signs of dynamism;
the development of the rest of the country was severely
hindered by the small population (about four hundred
thousand), inadequate communications, and the incessant
private wars between various *caudillos* in the interior. In
1816 there was absolutely no political structure able to give
any semblance of unity to this vast territory, and until 1860–
80 fierce battles were fought between the centralists (mainly
from Buenos Aires), who advocated a centralized state, and
the federalists (mainly from the interior), who desired a very
flexible form of federation.

The end of this first period of Argentine history coincided
with the collapse of Juan Manuel de Rosas's dictatorship
(1829–52); paradoxically, this *caudillo*, who belonged to the
federalist camp, deserves the credit for laying the foundations of national unity by subjecting all his rivals to his
authority.

From the second half of the nineteenth century the considerable increase in European immigration, combined with
agricultural, industrial and commercial progress, brought
about major changes in both the social and the political

life of the country. The rapid growth of the middle and working classes threatened the political hegemony of the ruling oligarchy which had held power since the foundation of the Republic. The more dynamic elements in these classes set up new parties (the Socialist Party and, even more important, the Radical Party). The oligarchy soon found itself forced to accept a change in the electoral system. The Sáenz Peña law of 1912 was the result. This measure substituted for the previous single-ballot, absolute majority, full-list poll a selective list of candidates, designed to ensure that the minority was automatically represented; registration on the electoral roll was made conditional upon the production of a military service certificate; the secret ballot was introduced, and voting was made compulsory. Ballot-rigging was thereby made slightly more difficult, and electoral abstentions were greatly reduced (the number of voters rose from about two hundred thousand before 1912 to seven hundred thousand in that year. Thanks to this reform, the largest sectors of opinion were able to make themselves heard, and even to take power. It may therefore be said that this date marks the point from which the conditions necessary for the operation of a representative democracy began to be met.

In some respects, Argentine political organization resembles that of the United States – nor is this entirely accidental. The state is constructed on federal lines. Under the Constitution of 1957,[1] the President was elected by universal suffrage on an indirect ballot (although for six years). The lower house was also elected by universal suffrage, with half the seats coming up for election every two years. Nevertheless, the resemblance was more formal than real. In particular, the two-party system operating in the United States has not succeeded in establishing itself in Argentina, which has a very

1. Superseded by the Charter of the Argentine Revolution and other decree-laws proclaimed by the military regime which came to power in June 1966.

large number of political parties (more than two hundred presented candidates at the polls of March 1965). This proliferation of parties is not a recent phenomenon, although it became more marked in the years after 1955.

The reasons for this state of affairs are complex and depend on the interaction of numerous factors – principally those that one might call structural factors, i.e. the federal structure of the state and the electoral system. The continuation of provincial particularism and the existence of a number of parties that are very firmly established at the provincial level but with no organization whatever at the federal level have meant that the various electoral systems have been unable to produce any reduction in the number of political groupings. Thus the ballot based on a selective list instituted by the Sáenz Peña law of 1912 and the Hondt system of proportional representation adopted in 1963 ought, in principle, to have favoured the large parties, but did not in fact succeed in stimulating the regrouping that would have been necessary. The effect of these electoral devices is further weakened by the fact that well-structured parties are rare in Argentina and do not command a large electoral following. The large parties are in fact generally organized on the basis of local or provincial committees, which often results in a multiplication of the number of electoral lists presented.

Since the fall of Perón in 1955, a further 'in-built' factor has contributed to and indeed accelerated this breaking up process: the existence of the Peronist movement. The divergent attitudes towards this movement taken by adherents of other parties have in fact led to frequent splits. This internal fragmentation was no longer kept in check by electoral considerations when the adoption of proportional representation gave even the smallest parties the hope of obtaining some parliamentary seats.

In political life, however, the effects of this proliferation of parties are greatly diminished; what in fact happens for the most part is a kind of bipolarization of opinion and parties with respect to the two major subjects of national controversy : the state of the economy, and the problems arising from the fall of the Peronist regime.

The Argentinian economy's continuing state of crisis and stagnation, which has lasted since about 1949, helps to explain the prominent place given to economic considerations in the political parties' programmes. The various possible methods of remedying this situation have divided opinion and contributed to the instability of political life; whether the development of agriculture and stock-rearing should be given priority, or the development of industry, and whether development policy should lay emphasis on domestic efforts or on requests for foreign aid (in the fields of planning, financing, or exploitation of national resources) are problems which are not always considered from the strictly economic point of view, but are rather conditioned by political considerations.

There is another matter which has helped to limit, to some extent, the proliferation of parties : the fate of Peronism. As the number of Perón's supporters remains considerable, despite all the efforts made to divide and weaken his movement, the other parties as a whole have divided into two camps : one of intransigent opposition to the Peronists, whose participation in the political life of the nation it wishes to restrict; and one which, either through a concern for justice or for interested reasons, practises a 'hand of friendship' policy towards them and demands that they be reintegrated into the national life without any restrictions.

It should be added that since no party is strong enough to impose its will on the others, and because the executive and legislative powers have been progressively weakened, some groups outside the party system (the army and the unions, notably) increasingly tend to exert *direct* influence on the executive power, thus provoking frequent political upheavals.

This tendency, accentuated bp the weakness of the Illía

government, by persistent economic difficulties and by the likelihood of Peronist victories in the projected elections of 1967, culminated in the assumption of power by the military in June 1966. All political parties were banned and their property seized. The Congress was dissolved and legislative powers were vested in a President named by a junta of commanders-in-chief of the three armed services.

One of the declared objectives of the Argentine revolution was to overcome the political impasse by means of a prolonged period of military rule. However, the presidencies of Onganía (June 1966 to June 1970) and Levingston (June 1970 to March 1971) showed that this was not a viable solution. The widespread strikes and demonstrations of 1969 in Corrientes, Córdoba, Rosario and other cities marked a turning-point. The consolidation of a strong political front against the government, including the Peronist and Radical parties, militant trade-union opposition, the polarization of political currents and the spread of political violence, as well as changes in the balance of political forces within the military, diminished the influence of military and civilian advocates of prolonged rule by the armed forces. After over five years of existence this had not contributed to long-term economic or political stability. Incapable of finding a viable political formula to sustain a military government, and unwilling to resort to more authoritarian measures, military groups increasingly yielded to pressures for an acceleration of the promised return to civilian democratic rule.

In 1971 President Lanusse announced that general elections were to be held in March 1973. Proposals for a new constitutional structure were debated, and for an electoral system which, it was widely agreed, should consist of a modified version of the Sáenz Peña law. Proscriptions on the political parties were raised. The re-emergence of parties showed that, while there had been some realignments and probable changes in relative strengths, the patterns of political allegiance established prior to 1966 substantially remained.

The absence of any clear dividing lines between the Argentine political parties makes any attempt at classification difficult. It is nonetheless possible to distinguish, within the political spectrum, a number of different positions ranging from conservatism to the extreme left wing. The difficulty is where to fit the Peronist movement into this framework: its ideological ambiguity and the multiplicity of political trends in the movement defy strict definition. It therefore seemed justified to start this essay with a study of Peronism, especially in view of the fact that, despite being restricted almost to the fringes of political life, it in fact occupies a central position, such that all the other parties are obliged to define their own positions by reference to it.

Peronism

ORIGIN AND EVOLUTION UP TO 1955

The Peronist victory of 1946 may be explained by the coincidence of a large, politically uncommitted sector of the Argentinian electorate with the emergence of a leader able to mobilize and organize this electorate.

Since 1930 Argentina had undergone a profound economic and social transformation, but the traditional parties had shown themselves incapable of adapting to these changes. The inter-war crises and the Second World War had forced the country to try to become self-sufficient, and therefore to speed up the rate of industrial development. The period after the First World War witnessed a considerable growth in the urban population, which was reinforced after 1930 by a massive exodus from the land towards the towns, especially Buenos Aires. These new levels of the urban population, deprived of any well-defined social status, and without any experience of modern politics, remained attached to the system and values of the traditional society from which they sprang, and were therefore more than likely to attach themselves to a *caudillo*, the authoritarian and paternalistic leader who would provide an adequate substitute for traditional authority.

Even after the military coup d'etat of 1943, these uncommitted masses were not integrated into the traditional parties, which never grasped, or understood too late, the real nature and extent of their claims: while the working class was demanding social reform first and foremost, the political parties continued to demand a return to normal democratic processes and respect for individual rights.

At the same time, an equally unattached potential clientele arose at the other end of the social scale: that of the new industrial and commercial bourgeoisie that had profited from the war. The aspirations of this group were to effect the final transformation of Argentina into a modern industrialized state, less dependent on the outside world; but they were not as yet sufficiently powerful to effect the necessary changes themselves.

There thus grew up in the population as a whole, although for various reasons, a tendency favourable to the establishment of an authoritarian, nationalist government. Argentina was hoping for a strong man who would be able to embody the national aspirations which had become dominant among public opinion. That man was Colonel Juan Domingo Perón.

After participating in the military coup of 1943, Perón was made director of the Departamento Nacional de Trabajo y Previsión (National Department of Labour and Social Planning), which he subsequently succeeded in raising to the status of a ministry. This post was his springboard to power; he quickly won considerable popularity with the working class by a series of social measures, and he undertook the reform of the trade-union movement. He was powerfully assisted in this enterprise by a propaganda campaign launched by Eva Duarte, subsequently his wife, who was later to become the object of a positive cult with a large sector of the Argentinian population.

A history in depth of the Peronist movement would go beyond the terms of reference of this essay; we shall therefore confine ourselves to an examination of its more characteristic features, which throw light on the present-day Peronist movement.

Perón was elected President of the Republic in 1946 thanks to the support of the urban and rural proletariat, the lower middle class and part of the new industrial bourgeoisie. The Partido Peronista was founded in 1947, replacing the Partido Laborista and demonstrating by its very name the highly personal nature of the party and the regime. Reorganized in 1949, the Peronist party still remained more of a movement than a properly structured party, to the extent that the strength of Peronism resides principally in extra-party groups (trade unions, youth movements), highly organized and directly dependent on the ruling power. The regime that was progressively establishing itself in Argentina may be described as populist – a combination of demagogy, nationalism, opportunism, paternalistic socialism, and fascist dictatorship.

In foreign policy, Perón attempted to win the leadership of Latin America for Argentina, to the exclusion of the United States; rejecting an alliance with either of the two major power blocs, he adopted what would nowadays be called a neutralist position (*la tercera posición*) and attempted to revive the old viceroyalty of La Plata to Argentina's benefit. He also wanted to make his country economically independent, and above all modern – hence the absolute priority given to industrial development and the communications network, often to the detriment of agriculture. To achieve this, he had to be assured of the active support of all or part of the bourgeoisie and the proletariat by offering them certain benefits in exchange – hence his policy of 'social justice'. The industrial working class, which was initially only one of the factors on which Perón's power rested, progressively became its most solid base and the principal beneficiary of the regime. When a new military coup overthrew the Peronist regime in 1955, the victors found themselves faced with an irreversible situation : a working class conscious of its strength, organized in powerful trade unions, and determined not to be deprived of its newly acquired rights.

PERONIST AND NEO-PERONIST PARTIES: POLITICAL WEAKNESS

Deprived of its leader in September 1955, and hence greatly weakened, since it revolved entirely around the leader's personality and its formal structure was rudimentary, the Peronist Party was dissolved by decree in December 1955.

From that date on, the Peronists attempted to regroup and form a new party, but their attempts at reorganization met with major difficulties from various sources. The biggest obstacle lay in the hostility of the ruling power : no government, on pain of being overthrown by the Army, could allow the Peronist Party to reconstitute itself freely or participate without hindrance in elections. (President Frondizi was deposed by the Army following the Peronist successes in the partial elections of March 1962.) Moreover personal rivalries, tactical disputes and factional differences (orthodox Peronism versus Neo-Peronism) within the movement made the task of reorganization very arduous. The internal situation was further complicated by the attitude of Perón himself, who had no scruples about intervening from his place of exile to discredit the Peronist leaders best placed to succeed him as leaders of the party; his strategy seems to be to play off one group against another so as to remain the supreme arbiter of the movement. This position, which he has succeeded in maintaining up to now, has nevertheless enabled the Peronists to present a united front to the other political parties.

A group of Peronists formed a Movement for Justice Co-ordinating Committee under the leadership first of Raúl Matera and then, after 1963, of Delia de Parodi. In 1963 Perón decided to assemble into a single party the various Peronist and related groups (Peronists, Neo-Peronists and the Peronist unions), appointing to this end a commission of seven members, including A. Iturbe, A. Framini, and A. Vandor. In July 1964 the first organizing convention of the Justice Party was held; the party was strongly structured, with a national congress, a national executive council, and a political bureau integrating political and trade-union Peronist groups at every level. Since this party had great difficulty in getting itself legally recognized, Peronism continued to be represented in Parliament by the Unión Popular in particular, and the neo-Peronist parties (Partidos Populares Provinciales).[2]

Attempts to unite the movement and to structure the party after 1964 were hindered by major differences within orthodox Peronism itself. While declaring themselves Peronists, Augusto Vandor and the majority of the Peronist unions sought autonomy from the party leaders and, increasingly, from Perón himself. This independence was expressed in the attitudes adopted by Vandorist union leaders towards governments both before and after the 1966 coup d'etat. The conduct of Vandorist sectors of the movement in the elections of March 1965 and, later, the contacts which took place between Vandor and army officers in the gestation of the 1966 revolution were occasions when Vandor acted at variance

2. On the parliamentary level, at least, these parties succeeded in uniting: in March 1965 they combined in a single group, the Unión Popular, under the chairmanship of the ex-labourer Paulo Niembro.

with Perón's own wishes. The split inhibited attempts to structure the party, but reached organizational expression with the division in 1965 of the Peronist unions into rival federations, headed by Vandor and José Alonso. Most of the Peronist politicians, including those on the left wing of the movement, aligned themselves behind Alonso.

As he had been able to do on earlier occasions, Perón attempted to take advantage of the division to assert his personal authority. This time, however, he was in a weaker position because of the importance of the Vandorist unions and the widespread personal support which Vandor commanded. This was suggested by the largely unsuccessful attempt to displace Vandor made by Perón in 1964–5, when Perón's wife, Isabel Martínez de Perón, visited Argentina with the aim of reasserting vertical lines of command within the movement. Paradoxically, the restoration of Perón's influence within the movement was an indirect effect of the policies of the military governments.

The Unión Popular

This was the biggest of the Peronist parties before 1966. It was founded in 1955 by J. Bramuglia and led successively by R. Tecera del Franco and Enrique Rocca (1963). The electoral court granted it legal recognition at the federal level in March 1963. A decree issued the following month by the provisional (Guido) government forbade it, however, to present candidates for executive posts (President of the Republic and provincial governorships) or for the Senate. The party could therefore only participate in elections to the lower house (the National Chamber of Deputies), provincial assemblies and local councils. This party owed open allegiance to Perón, and represented orthodox Peronism. Its party programme set out three basic objectives: to establish social justice, safeguard political sovereignty and ensure the economic independence of the nation. It therefore advocated social reforms in favour of the workers and peasants, and was very hostile to the oligarchy, the Army and foreign capital.

The Unión Popular's cohesion was threatened by disagreements among its leaders on the choice of tactics for achieving power: should the party follow legal channels, or take the revolutionary road? Supporters of the 'hard line', Hector Villalón and Andrés Framini, left the party to create the Movimiento Revolucionario Peronista, which represented the extreme left wing of the Peronist movement; however, its support was very limited.

The Other Neo-Peronist Parties

The parties collected under this label represented the attitude of 'Peronism without Perón'. Supporters of the policies of the ex-head of state, they rejected his leadership and constituted the right wing of the Peronist movement. Moderates and nationalists, they rejected both communism and capitalism, representing themselves as the defenders of democracy and enemies of oligarchy. While supporting the demands of the workers and peasants, they were firmly opposed to direct action against the government and sought legal ways of participating in the political and electoral life of the country.

Their strength noticeably increased in the early 1960s, especially in the provinces of the interior, where, despite the instructions issued by the movement's leadership, the Peronist electorate preferred to vote for neo-Peronist candidates rather than record a blank vote; as a result these parties won 7 per cent of the votes in the elections to the legislature held in 1963. However, they were still much weaker than the Unión Popular: in the elections of March 1965 (when part of the seats in the lower house came up for re-election) the latter won 29 per cent of the votes, as against 6 per cent cast for the Neo-Peronists.

This part of the Peronist movement was chiefly represented by the bloc called Partidos Populares Provinciales, led by Juan Alejandro Luco. The names of the parties collected in this federation varied from province to province (Partido Blanco, Tres Banderas, etc.). They were most firmly established in the provinces of Salta, Jujuy, Neuquén, Río Negro, and San Luis, where they often challenged the Unión Popular.

The Peronist parties' chief electoral support comes from the urban and rural working class and the lower middle classes (minor officials, etc.) with a generally low level of education and whose political behaviour is usually conditioned by largely emotional considerations. It should however be pointed out that whereas these classes form the mainstay of Peronist support, this has spread to other groups, and more or less devoted supporters may be found among the bourgeoisie and even in the Army. Moreover, it seems likely that the splits that occur within the movement are in part due to the petty bourgeoisie and to the elite of the working class, for both groups show a distinct tendency to support the Neo-Peronist wing.

TRADE-UNION STRENGTH

Despite the size of these parties, the true source of Peronist strength lies in the trade-union movement, the General Confederation of Labour (CGT), which is the spokesman for organized labour as a whole but is increasingly tending to act like a political party. It is very largely thanks to their trade unions that the Peronists have been able to preserve a structure and a degree of cohesion that the disbanding of the party had seriously compromised.

The CGT was founded in 1930 by the federation of a number of unions. Then firmly apolitical, it based its claims solely on social and trade-union questions. Internal dissensions and the hostility of the government and employers prevented it from being a powerful force in politics. It was Perón who, as Minister of Labour and then as President, turned it into one of the most powerful political labour movements in South America (while at the same time exercising strict control over it). From the fall of Perón to 1961, the CGT was practically under the control of the government.

In 1963 the CGT had a membership of two and a half million workers. These may be divided into three main groups: the Peronists; the independents; and the communists.[3] In the elections to the leadership in 1963 the three factions were represented as follows: sixty-two Peronist unions, thirty-two independent unions (principally white-collar workers, printers and railwaymen), and nineteen unions belonging to the Movimiento de Unificación y Coordinación Sindical (MUCS), which is communist in allegiance. (In fact it seems that the Peronists were in an even more powerful position than the figures suggest.) The independents were opposed to a hard-line policy by the CGT and to its use for political ends. In protest against the adoption of a 'fighting plan'[4] in 1964, they resigned from the federation, which was therefore left under the complete control of the Peronists, supported by the MUCS.

Under Peronist leadership, the CGT increasingly neglected purely social demands in order to embark on a political offensive. The importance of the part played by the 'Sixty-two' is demonstrated by the fact that their main leaders in the mid-1960s, Augusto Vandor, Andrés Framini and José Alonso, provided a significant proportion of the leaders and officers of the *political* Peronist movement. This explains why the

3. At that time the Peronist unions organized more than a million workers, the independents 650,000 and the Communists 350,000.

4. The 'fighting plans' consisted of a series of measures to be introduced successively if the government did not accept the workers' demands: selective stoppages followed by full-scale strikes and, finally, by a general strike.

differences observed between the various Peronist parties also appeared within the trade-union sector of the movement. This sector, which for many years supported orthodox Peronism (under the leadership of José Alonso), was divided between the hard-liners and a more moderate wing.

The hard-line policy found most of its support among the representatives of the smaller unions, which were hardest hit by the economic crisis, especially in the provinces of the interior. These placed themselves under the direct leadership of Perón; they were opposed to any attempt at conciliation, and were ready to pursue the trade-union struggle to the bitter end in order to realize their claims. In fact this branch of the movement sought to transform Peronism into a revolutionary movement relying on violence to seize power. The chief exponents of this group before 1966 were Andrés Framini (head of the Association of Textile Workers) and José Alonso.

The moderate wing included the strongest and best-organized unions. It had fairly close ties with the main sectors of the Neo-Peronist movement. Under the leadership of Augusto Vandor it proved more reformist and more inclined to reach agreements with other organizations, while still firmly supporting the workers' demands. Despite its public pronouncements, it seemed to hope that Peronism would dissociate itself further from Perón himself. Through the medium of this wing of the movement, the trade-union sector of Peronism endeavoured to adapt itself to the existing regime.

Through their domination of the CGT, the Peronists possess a powerful lever through which to exert pressure on the government, and they may force it either to make concessions or to harden its own position. In either case there are advantages to be gained. The country's very parlous economic state is not improving, and the workers are nostalgic for a regime about which they remember nothing except the prosperity of its early years.

PERONISM IN NATIONAL LIFE:
ITS ELECTORAL STRENGTH

The Problem of the Vote

Since they have not been able to nominate their own candidates for election (except in 1962 and 1965) the Peronists have only had two ways open to them of making their presence felt electorally: by registering a blank vote or by supporting representatives of other parties.

The blank vote was used for a long time by the Peronist leadership as a means of protesting both at the policies of the government of the day (witness its withdrawal of support from Frondizi in 1960) and at the proscription of the party. In general, Peronist supporters were recommended to record blank votes chiefly in elections to the chamber of deputies. On the other hand, this tactic was not used so systematically in the case of elections to the presidency or of provincial governors, where the Peronists tended rather to follow a policy of support for the candidate best disposed towards them.

There were certain direct consequences of the electoral tactics adopted by the Peronists. First of all, they became the arbiters of national political life. In 1958, for example, Frondizi was elected to the presidency largely thanks to their votes; in 1957 the UCRI only won 21 per cent of the votes cast; in 1958 they won 42 per cent while the abstentions fell from 24.5 per cent of the total votes cast in 1957 to 8.8 per cent in 1958. (See graph on p. 101.) Furthermore, the other parties, greedy to win this great mass of voters, tended to revise certain points in their programme; these overtures to the Peronists provoked a series of splits in all the other parties.

After 1961, the Peronist electorate seemed less willing to obey orders to spoil their ballot papers, as shown by the results of the three elections in which the Peronist leadership recommended this course (1957, 1960, 1963). In 1957 and in 1960 the percentage of blank votes represented 24·5 per cent and 24·9 per cent of the votes cast, respectively; in 1963, however, the figure fell to 17·5 per cent.

Together with this fall in the blank vote, there was a noticeable rise in the votes collected by the Neo-Peronist parties; in 1963 these obtained 7 per cent of the total votes cast as against 2·4 per cent in 1957 and 1960.

Electoral Results

A comparative study of the elections held between 1957 and 1965 reveals a fairly steady increase in the Peronist electorate. Since the results achieved by the other parties over the same period (especially the Radicals) remained practically stable, it would seem that the Peronists were the main beneficiaries from the increase in the electorate between these two dates.

The results of the 1958 election are only apparently an exception, since the blank votes were not cast by the majority Peronist faction; in fact in deference to Perón's own instructions, the Peronists that year voted for Frondizi's UCRI, which thus gained twice as many votes as in 1957 and emerged victorious.

It may also be observed, moreover, that when the Peronists were allowed to present their own candidates at the polls (1962 and 1965) they won an appreciably higher percentage of the votes. Their victory in the 1962 elections (when they won forty-one of the ninety-six seats contested compared with thirty-eight won by the party in office, and took eleven provincial governments of the nineteen up for election) brought about Frondizi's fall and federal intervention in five provinces, including Buenos Aires.

The elections of March 1965 were a repetition of the 1962 success. The Peronists once again overcame their adversaries, winning such major provinces as Buenos Aires and Córdoba;

Electoral Results of the Peronists and Blank Votes 1957–65

Elections to the legislature (National Chamber of Deputies)	Blank papers[5]	%	Unión Popular	%	Neo-Peronists	%
1957	2,132,806	24·5	—	—	208,659	2·4
1958	808,651	8·8	—	—	247,797	2·7
1960	2,228,014	24·9	—	—	196,526	2·4
1962	262,913	2·8	1,592,446[6]	16·9	1,406,700[6]	14·9
1963	1,668,170	17·5	—	—	665,376	7
1965	364,296	3·7	2,835,093	29·4	550,000	5·7

Except for the elections of 1965, these figures and percentages and those that follow are taken from Snow, Peter G., 'Parties and politics in Argentina; the elections of 1962 and 1963', *Midwest Journal of Political Science*, February 1965, pp. 1–36. The figures for 1965 are taken from the official results: Ministerio del Interior, Departamento electoral, *Resultados electorales 1965*, Buenos Aires. The author himself has also used the official results published by the Departamento Electoral del Ministerio del Interior in *Resultados electorales comparativos* and *Elecciones generales del 7 de julio de 1963*, Buenos Aires, 1963.

5. A comparison of blank ballot papers and the number of votes obtained by Peronist candidates when they took part in the elections leads to the conclusion that almost all the blank papers were cast by Peronists (see Figure 4, p. 101). However, other parties do sometimes adopt the same tactic, e.g. Solano Lima's Popular Conservative Party in 1963, and the Frondizi faction in the UCRI.

6. For the 1962 elections, Peter G. Snow only gives the overall votes obtained by the Peronists, i.e. 2,999,146 votes (31·9 per cent of the total votes cast). The distribution of the votes between the two groups has been reconstituted on the basis of the provisional results published by *La Nación*. The considerable increase recorded by the Neo-Peronists is due to the fact that the Unión Popular only presented candidates in the federal capital and in the province of Buenos Aires, while the Neo-Peronists divide up the rest of the country amongst themselves.

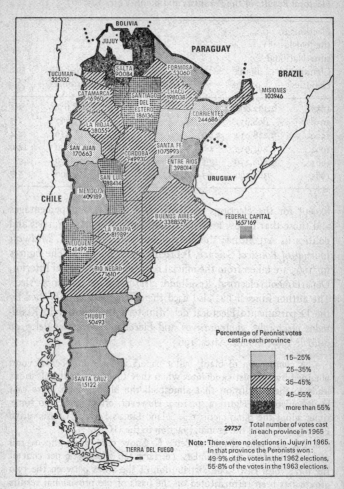

Figure 2. Distribution of Peronism in the 1965 Elections

thirty-six deputies of the Unión Popular entered the chamber to join the sixteen Neo-Peronist deputies elected in 1963. Together they controlled fifty-two seats out of one hundred and ninety-two.

The results of these elections clearly demonstrate the Peronists' electoral strength; the Unión Popular was the biggest national party, beating the radicals. The Peronists and Neo-Peronists together commanded more than a third of the Argentine electorate.

Regional Strength

The Peronist electorate is distributed more or less evenly over all the provinces. The biggest Peronist vote is nevertheless found chiefly in the industrial provinces with a large working population, such as Córdoba and above all Buenos Aires. Therefore although the Peronists are well ahead of the Radicals in the province of Buenos Aires, which has a very large working-class population, the reverse is true of the federal capital,[7] where the composition of the electorate is somewhat different (the tertiary sector predominates, and the working-class population is smaller).

However, the Peronist electorate is not confined to the towns and industrial areas. There are also supporters in many rural provinces, especially where there is a high proportion of agricultural labourers and seasonal workers. Previously conservative, these regions were won over to Peronism following the social laws passed by the Perón regime (extending the right of association to the *peons* and granting statutory protection to seasonal workers). The resultant politicization of the countryside thus chiefly benefited the Peronists. They

7. The federal capital is the town of Buenos Aires; the capital of the *province* of Buenos Aires is the town of La Plata. Therefore Buenos Aires here means the *province* of Buenos Aires.

have had major successes in the north-western provinces; at the last elections the Peronists and Neo-Peronists actually came top or second in the poll in the majority of the interior provinces.

It would be wrong to attempt to draw a clear distinction between the Peronist and Neo-Peronist electorates; it would seem however that the Unión Popular was much better organized and more firmly entrenched in industrial areas and the most densely populated provinces (Buenos Aires, the federal capital, Córdoba, Santa Fe), while the Neo-Peronists found most of their support in the agricultural provinces of the interior (Mendoza and the north-west: Salta, Jujuy, Tucumán, the Chaco; also Neuquén and the Río Negro).

*

Despite the exile of their leader, the Peronists have not let themselves be absorbed into the other parties, and remain one of the most important political forces in the country. Compared with the level it reached under the Peronist regime (5,000,000 votes in the 1954 elections) their electoral strength has certainly fallen off; the two and a half million or so electors lost have in the main returned to their old party allegiances. However, because of the dispersal of votes due to the multiplication of parties after Perón's fall, these defections hardly altered the actual balance of political forces and the Peronists, who in 1965 could call on one third of the electorate, still represent Argentina's largest political organization.

Some people claim to see signs of the weakening of Peronism in the rivalry between orthodox and Neo-Peronists. The factional disputes and leadership struggles that broke out in full view of the public in both the political and trade-union sectors of the party have tended to give credence to this view. Aware of the great advantages to them of a split in the Peronist movement, and thinking that it would be easier to re-inte-

grate the Neo-Peronists into the national life than a mono-
lithic movement led from outside the country by Perón, the
government and the Army have not stood aside from the conflict and have given more or less direct support to the Neo-
Peronists.

It would be unwise to attach too much importance to this
supposed division, however. Disagreements within the movement can often be traced to tactical disputes or personal rivalries between leading figures, about which the mass of Peronist
electors are largely ignorant. Although apparently contested
by the Neo-Peronist leadership, Perón's authority over the
whole of the movement remained absolute. Moreover the vertical form of organization and the extremely rigid structure
of the Peronist parties make it all the easier for leadership
to be exercised from a distance.

Of all the Argentine parties, Peronism probably benefited
most from the period of military rule after 1966. The movement was reunited, and Perón's personal authority was established again, if temporarily. In addition, the relative strength
of Peronism probably increased. This was largely an indirect
result of government policies. The banning of all parties for
the first time placed all political organizations on an equal
footing but Peronism, because of its authority in speaking for
a majority of Argentina's working class and because of its
organizational foundation in the union movement, came to
occupy, with the government, the centre of the political stage.
Moreover, complex earlier alignments increasingly tended to
be replaced by the dichotomy of those for and against the
government. The spread of opposition to the policies of the
military regime which, under Onganía and Levingston, had
progressively alienated most major sectors of society, reinforced Peronism as the sole viable alternative of the time.

Within the movement itself, the influence of Neo-Peronism, already diminished by electoral reverses in 1965, dwindled
as Peronism moved after 1969 to a united position behind its

leader in opposition to the government. Many Neo-Peronists, such as Felipe Sapag of Neuquén, compromised with the regime. The assassination of Augusto Vandor in 1969, the discrediting of the policy of negotiation with the military which was associated with him, and, in general, the proscriptions on political activities, also tended to reassert Perón's influence over his movement. The role of Perón's personal representatives in Argentina – successively Alberte, Remorino and Jorge Paladino – increased after 1966, although they still found it necessary to negotiate with Peronist union leaders who, more than ever before, assumed the representation of the movement at the political level.

While the decline of Neo-Peronism and the central part played by Peronist-organized labour caused Peronism to become a more homogeneous, working-class movement, personal, tactical and ideological differences remained within it. The right wing of Peronist unionism, although it lost influence with the discredit of Vandorism, was still a strong current under men such as Rogelio Coria of the Construction Workers' Union. There also emerged, for the first time, a widespread left wing within the movement. Within organized labour this was largely associated with Raimundo Ongaro and the CGT de los Argentinos, founded in 1968, which grouped a number of smaller unions, particularly those in declining industry and those in the cities of the interior, as well as rank-and-file members of larger organizations who were dissatisfied with moderate leadership.[8] A few leading Peronists outside the unions were attracted towards the left, but radical Peronism drew most of its strength from the base of the

8. The following figures were given in June 1968 for the relative strengths of the rival union groupings: Vandorist unions, organized in the CGT with its headquarters in Azopardo, a street in Buenos Aires, 785,00 affiliates; those led by Ongaro, in the CGT de los Argentinos, 650,000 affiliates; 'participationalists', or those outside the CGT organizations which sought to collaborate with the govern-

movement and from youth groups, particularly in the provinces. Organizationally it was represented by local and regional committees in many parts of the country, and – on the extreme left – by small urban guerrilla groups such as the Fuerzas Armadas Peronistas (FAP). Many of these Peronist groups were associated with the left wing of the Radical party, with radical Christian organizations and with Marxist elements. This reflected the fact that the Peronist left consisted of a bewildering spectrum of ideologies from radical nationalist and Christian positions to various shades of Marxism. An additional source of weakness was that the left wing could not count on Perón's support and was unable to win important allies in leading Peronist circles.

The return to legality in 1971 and the need to organize a new party, which was to be called the Justice Party, raised questions about leadership and programme which once more put strains on the unity of the movement. The left wing feared the loss of their gains should Perón move to a more moderate position, which would respond to Perón's own inclinations and which might be the price for military countenance of a future Peronist government. They attempted to prevent the return of the pre-1966 Peronist politicians to control the party or, at least, to conserve the autonomy of their organizations within the new structure of the movement. Peronist union leaders were again divided over their attitudes to the party. A large proportion of them under José Rucci sought to turn the Justice Party into a labour party dependent on the unions, which gave rise to major differences between Rucci and Jorge Paladino. Other unionists, led by Rogelio Coria, attempted to turn the CGT into an apolitical body.

---

ment, 350,000 affiliates; and a few non-aligned unions which represented 140,000 members. By 1970, however, this picture changed with the reconstitution of a sole confederation under the new secretary-general, José Rucci. The previous alignments remained, but most were now reflected in the committees of the new CGT.

Once again Perón was forced to conciliate between the different factions. Paladino announced the decision that the new party would be loosely organized in order to accommodate all Peronist currents. One major source of conflict was thus postponed, but dissension was likely to recur when future decisions were required on the specific party programme and, more important, on the lists of candidates to be presented by the party in the projected elections of March 1973.

Other questions which remained unresolved in 1971 concerned the attitudes towards Peronism of the military and of the traditionally anti-Peronist parties. There were some indications, however, that many groups within the armed forces had become less intransigent towards Peronism. The support which President Lanusse obtained for his commitment to holding free elections suggested that many officers – at least within the Army – were now prepared to allow some form of Peronist government. Similar changes seemed to have taken place in the thinking of many non-Peronist political leaders. The Unión Cívica Radical del Pueblo, the second largest political party, had been the most powerful anti-Peronist force from 1955 to 1966. Under the military regime, however, they made common cause with the Peronists in opposition, and in November 1970 their leadership entered into an alliance for limited ends, called the Hora del Pueblo, with the Peronists and other smaller parties.

The rapidly changing political situation after 1971 made the future development of the Peronist movement exceedingly difficult to predict with any confidence. One major question mark was placed against the political future of Perón who was now 76 years old. One thing was certain, however; Peronist electoral strength was likely to have been preserved and, if anything, increased. There was no doubt that Peronism would again prove a decisive factor for any future civilian government.

The Conservative Parties

ELECTORAL WEAKNESS

In Argentina the concept of conservatism is highly ambiguous: it is not characterized, as it is in continental Europe, by the conflict between order and agitation, or at least not entirely. Whereas the Argentine conservative is often stubbornly opposed to any change in economic and social structures, he is cosmopolitan in spirit and welcomes new ideas. The conservative parties therefore tend to correspond rather to a party like the old Liberal Party in Britain. They generally represent the interests of the large landed proprietors and of that sector of the upper middle class that has chosen to ally itself with them; they support free trade and economic liberalism (after a brief flirtation with economic planning in the 1930s), and are opposed to any significant state intervention in the economy.

Between 1870 and 1880, under Avellaneda's presidency, conservative concepts in the economic and political fields began to be more clearly defined. The conservative oligarchy held power until 1916, the year that the young Radical Party walked away with the presidential election. The coup d'etat of 1930 enabled it to govern the country once more, until 1943, when the Army again intervened, largely as a reaction against the abuses and too obvious malpractices of which the conservatives had been guilty.

Since the fall of Perón, the conservatives have not been able to recapture power; however, they make their influence felt in the political field, as they maintain close relations with certain important sectors of the economy (the Sociedad Rural, the banks and insurance companies), so that although it seems unlikely that they will in the near future be able to govern the country directly again, they do constitute a major political and economic pressure group.

Although the conservatives exhibit a certain degree of unity in their organization and electorate, there is not, in fact, *one* conservative party, but a large number of local parties, often very different from one another. In order to defend their position against more homogeneous parties, the conservatives have made several attempts to unite (Unión Nacional in 1912, Concentración Nacional in 1922, Partido Demócrata Nacional from 1931 to 1958, at which date it was succeeded by the Federación Nacional de Partidos Conservadores, the FNPC). Each of these was a failure. Because the parties wishing to embark on this union were somewhat disjointed, unification could only come about as a result of concessions to local programmes, which at once compromised the projected unity of structure and action. As a result, even recently there was not one of the provincial conservative parties that had lost its local peculiarities, despite the efforts of the modern FNPC. There were two other parties that took a broadly conservative line: the Partido Demócrata Conservador Popular, and the Unión del Pueblo Argentino (UDELPA).

The Federación Nacional de Partidos Conservadores (FNPC)

The FNPC, chief mouthpiece for the country's conservatives, came into the category of the traditional parties, the parties of the executive and managerial classes. It had a very weak party structure, represented a conglomeration of local interests, and only acquired a degree of cohesion and discipline on rare occasions, chiefly at the time of a presidential election. The party's basic unit was the local committee. The FNPC did not levy subscriptions from its members, and therefore obtained its financial resources by 'patronage'.

Until the establishment of the Peronist regime, conservative leaders were coopted; since the party's reorganization in 1956 (when it was still the Partido Demócrata Nacional), a system of internal elections has been set up, but was not able to eliminate paternalism in the most hidebound of the traditionalist provinces (San Luis and Corrientes). From that time on, future leaders of the party had to be men who had made their careers within it. However, because of the party's poor chances of success in the electoral field, there were no 'professional politicians' in the FNPC. The party's chairman in 1966 was Emilio J. Hardoy. Of the most important conservative personalities, it is also worth mentioning Emilio Olmos and Emilio Joffré, who were the FNPC's presidential candidates in 1963, Carlos Aguinaga, and Oscar Vicchi.

The FNPC did not have a newspaper of its own, but the two biggest dailies, *La Nación* and *La Prensa*, may both be considered party mouthpieces to a certain extent.

Although they do not possess a political programme in the ordinary sense, the conservatives have a clear position on two points: unshakeable opposition to Peronism, and a desire for strict control of the trade unions. The FNPC's attitude was much more clearly defined in the economic field: it supported economic liberalism and free enterprise, and was very hostile to any excessive state intervention in the economy. For example, it opposed the system of price ceilings, state control of agricultural exports, and exchange control; it wanted some state-controlled enterprises to be returned to the private sector; it wanted priority to be given to the development of agriculture, and emphasized Argentina's 'historic agrarian and pastoral calling' at the expense of industry. It goes without saying that it was violently opposed to 'the alleged need for agrarian reform', which was the main reason for its hostility to certain international organizations which refer to this subject a little too often for their taste (the FAO in particular).

Electoral results. In the elections of 1951 and 1954, under the Peronist regime, the Conservative Party (then still called the National Democratic Party) was the third biggest national party, but with less than two hundred thousand votes fell far behind the Peronist Party and the Radical Party. Since the elections of 1957, the conservatives on average polled between five and six per cent of the votes (about 500,000 votes), but the absolute number of votes cast for it progressively decreased after 1960. Nevertheless, the FNPC remained the most important of the second-rank parties before 1966, coming a long way after the Peronists and the Radicals.

The conservatives are represented in every province, but they are most strongly entrenched in the province of Mendoza and the adjoining provinces (especially San Luis); equally strong in the province of Corrientes, they are in a minority in the province of Santa Fe and in the federal capital. To summarize, it may be said that the FNPC's potential support, bound up with agrarian and cattle-farming interests, is recruited principally in the agricultural provinces of the interior; in the more industrialized regions, on the other hand, voters with conservative leanings would be more likely to support the Radical Party.

The weakening of the Conservative Party has been further accentuated by internal dissensions. The most serious crisis occurred in 1956, when supporters of an understanding with the Peronists, under the leadership of Vicente Solano Lima, came up against the solid opposition of the conservative majority, and left to found their own group, the Popular Democratic Conservative Party.

The Partido Demócrata Conservador Popular

The only difference between this party and the FNPC lies in its attitude towards the Peronists. The Popular Conservatives have demanded that the latter should be permitted to participate freely in the political life of the nation, and have tried (without success) to get some sectors of the Peronist electorate to join their own party. In 1963 Solano Lima even tried to establish a united front with the Unión Popular and Frondizi's Radical Party on the occasion of the presidential elections; this manoeuvre failed. In 1970 the Popular Conservatives again showed their willingness to associate themselves with the Peronists when Solano Lima joined with Radicals, Peronists and others in the Hora del Pueblo alliance to press for a return to civilian rule.

The Popular Democratic Conservative Party has been further weakened by a fairly large number of internal splits. It commands an extremely limited sector of the electorate, and does not even contest elections in every province. It wins, on average, a hundred thousand votes, and its electoral support is declining.

The Unión del Pueblo Argentino (UDELPA)

UDELPA is the very model of the personalized party. It was created in January 1963 for the sole purpose of supporting General Pedro E. Aramburu's candidature for the presidency. The memory of his spell as President of the Republic under the provisional government (1955–8) ensured the support of a number of conservatives, while many electors saw in him a 'strong man' capable of restoring order.

UDELPA's programme was not specified until after the 1963 elections; at first, Aramburu was content to leave his electoral platform somewhat vague, knowing that the electors would vote for his person rather than for his ideas. He thus confined himself to championing the cause of anti-Peronism, order and authority (party slogan: *Orden en todos los órdenes*). Like the conservatives he preached the development of agriculture as a priority over industrial development.

After the elections, and during the preparations for the 1965 electoral campaign, UDELPA proved more sensitive to social problems, while remaining hostile to the CGT's policy of wage claims (it was opposed to the 'fighting plan'), and opposing the principle of a single trade-union confederation. Although it supported some degree of flexible planning and general orientation of the economy by the state, this party continued to uphold the principles of free trade and was against nationalization and direct state control; it demanded the return of the petroleum industry and the railways to the private sector. It really regarded itself as a kind of technocratic right-wing party.

In 1966 UDELPA was dissolved, as were the other parties, but Aramburu continued to gain support among conservative groups disaffected with the military regime. By 1970 there were rumours that Aramburu might emerge as the presidential candidate of a future centre-right coalition, but his assassination in May of that year shattered the hopes of wide sectors of moderate conservative opinion.

Electoral results. In the first elections in which UDELPA took part (1963) its candidates won 6.8 per cent of the vote (656,124 votes) and took fourteen parliamentary seats; its presidential candidates (Aramburu with A. Etchevehere for Vice-President) won 7.7 per cent of the vote. These results put the party in third place in the national table.

However, the March, 1965 elections did not live up to this early promise: UDELPA won fewer than 200,000 votes. These were only legislative elections, though, not coupled with the presidential election as in 1963. It is not to be wondered at that a party organized almost entirely around a single personality should experience a spectacular drop in its electoral support when its leader's own candidature is not directly involved. UDELPA's best results were in the federal capital and in the province of Buenos Aires.

Together with this party, we can consider the Partido Republicano Argentino (PRAR), created in April 1964 by Julio Cueto Rúa. Its founders were ex-members of the Unión Conservadora (of Buenos Aires, affiliated to the FNPC), expelled for their opposition to collaboration with the Illía government. This party was more concerned with economics than politics, the main plank of its platform being an increase in the role of private enterprise in every sector of the nation's development. Its electoral support was insignificant, but it had some influence on the attitudes of industrial circles in the capital.

Another party, the Partido Cívico Independiente, may also be associated with this neo-liberal tendency; its virtual leader was Alvaro Alsogaray, an advocate of economic liberalism. Its status as a party of executives and managers enabled it to ignore its electoral weakness and exert an immediate influence on the handling of the country's economic affairs. The PCI was an active supporter of the coup d'etat of 1966 and made its influence felt on economic policy during the early stages of the Onganía government. At this time several men of this tendency – notably Alsogaray and his brother, Lieutenant-General Julio Alsogaray – were appointed to political or diplomatic posts.

Right-wing Nationalists

To the extreme right of the conservatives floats a small constellation of nationalist groups of negligible electoral significance. Except for the Unión Federal, led by Pablo Pardo and Mario Amadeo, they were more leagues than parties, on the pattern of the old French nationalist leagues, with names like the Liga Republicana, Alianza Nacionalista, Legión de Mayo, Legión Cívica.

POLITICAL STRENGTH

Generally speaking, it is difficult to measure a party's strength strictly in terms of electoral results. This observation is especially true of the conservative parties. In fact the conservatives do not seem to regard their party as the organization most likely to bring about the victory of their interests; their political influence is generally exerted through extra-party intermediaries.

Consequently if the Argentine conservative parties are studied by reference to their electoral results, the apparent conclusion would be that their political role has not ceased to diminish since 1943. Nothing could be further from the truth. The conservatives continued to exercise considerable influence over the nation's political life, despite the weakness of their parties and the fact that few of their leaders held political posts of any importance. The conservatives possess great cohesion as a group, although not as a party. Their direct and personal method of political action is based on the social prestige of their leaders; even so, the main reason why they are influential in politics at all is because of their economic strength, expressed through pressure groups representing the main branches of activity in the national economy (Sociedad Rural, Unión Industrial, the commercial stock exchange, banks and insurance companies).

The role of the conservatives in political life is also increased indirectly by the intervention of two extra-party forces, the Army and the Catholic Church, whose policies, deliberately or otherwise, frequently coincide with the conservatives' interest. In fact the Army's various incursions into politics have often had the result, if not the object, of reinforcing the conservatives' position. Moreover the importance of the support given to them, at least until recent years, by the ecclesiastical hierarchy can only be fully appreciated if one considers the special position of the Church in Argentina and the close ties that exist between the hierarchy and the government.[9]

9. The Constitution of 1853 makes Catholicism the official religion of the country, and grants the Catholic Church state financial aid. Article 86, Section 8 of the Constitution provides that when an episcopal see falls vacant, the new Bishop shall be appointed by the

While their economic strength enables the conservatives to exert indirect influence in the political sphere, their electoral weakness precludes them from taking power by any normal means. However, the cohesion of their group and its economic power have enabled them to win the confidence and support of the armed forces. They have therefore always found themselves in a favourable position to reap the fruits of any intervention by the Army, which generally calls on them whenever the seat of power falls vacant.

This occurred to some extent under the military regime since 1966, and notably under the presidency of Onganía. Conservative opinion was, however, divided. Most felt able to support a programme of economic stabilization, but many considered that the policy of extreme economic liberalism associated with Alsogaray and Krieger Vasena went too far, particularly when measures taken by the Onganía government, such as those affecting rural production, hurt their interests. The traditional conservatives were also increasingly alienated by the government's political policies, and came to press for a rapid return to civilian rule. They were alarmed by the influence of right-wing corporatist thinking on the Onganía regime, by the repeated occasions when they were not consulted on legislation which affected them, and, in general, by the polarization of opinion and the growth of political violence which, it was felt, came partly as the consequence of repressive policies.

The most positive right-wing political support for the 1966 revolution came initially from nationalist groups, notably those connected with the periodical *Azul y Blanco*, edited by Sánchez Sorondo, who had many sympathizers within the

Head of State from a list drawn up by the Senate. If strictly applied, this provision would turn bishops into actual civil servants; in practice, however, the apostolic nuncio puts forward a candidate for the executive power's approval, the granting of which is in effect a mere formality.

military. They hoped that military dictatorship might make possible the establishment of a form of corporate state. But the Nationalists were divided and few in number, and soon fell out with Onganía over the liberalism of the government's economic programme.

Partido Demócrata Progresista (PDP)

Origins of the Party

Of all the Argentine parties, the Partido Demócrata Progresista is perhaps the one that has been most strongly marked by the personality of its leader – to the extent that it might almost be said that its history is inextricably bound up with the biography of its founder, Lisandro de la Torre, one of the most attactive political figures of his age.

Lisandro de la Torre was one of the first militants of the Radical Party; he broke away from it in 1897, through opposition to the policy of electoral abstention and subversion practised by the new leader of the party, Hipólito Yrigoyen. In 1908 the Liga del Sur was created, a movement to defend regional autonomy, practically restricted to the south of the province of Santa Fe; this league, the expression of the struggle being fought by the capitalist petty bourgeoisie of the interior against the provincial oligarchy, demanded the democratization of political institutions. Lisandro de la Torre rapidly became its spokesman, and was even elected to the provincial parliament in 1911. The ideas that he expressed during this period were subsequently to provide the basis for the Democratic Progressive Party's political programme, since this group was to be born of the amalgamation of the Liga del Sur with a number of small provincial parties with a similar outlook.

When he founded the PDP in 1916, the year of the presidential elections, Lisandro de la Torre hoped to create a centre movement able to hold its own against the Radicals over the whole country. In its programme and membership, the PDP could be described as aligned with the European movements of the centre-left, like the French Radical-Socialist Party. In the political sphere, the PDP considered that only increased autonomy for the provinces and district councils could guarantee the free play of constitutional liberties; a secular party, it demanded the separation of the Church from the State.

However, the party's programme was most clearly defined in the economic sphere. It supported Argentine interests against the inroads of foreign monopolies, and attacked the official policy which tended to favour the trusts to the detriment of the middle and lower middle classes (small farmers and tradesmen). It supported state intervention in the running of the economy, and even went so far as to advocate the nationalization of public services. One of its chief claims related to the country's agrarian structures : dismemberment of the large estates, land taxes and penalization of absentee landlords. In brief, the PDP's chief aim was to protect the interests of the small cattle men of the interior against the big landlords and the monopolies of the refrigeration industry owned largely by British interests.

The Democratic Progressive Party was in its day the representative of authentic radicalism, and perhaps the most generous and disinterested of all Argentine parties. Yet it has never succeeded in winning an important place on the political stage. In contrast to the Radical Civic Union it never became a mass party; its biggest difficulties stemmed from the heterogeneity of the various groups and interests it represented and of which it was composed, and in particular from the fact that a large number of conservatives were connected with it from the start.

The PDP's Position in the Life of the Country

Lisandro de la Torre's death in 1938 practically sounded the death-knell of his party, which was never able to find another leader of his stature. The PDP has not been able to adapt to the changes in conditions in Argentina, and the conservative elements in its ranks have increasingly tended to predominate. In the presidential elections of 1963, the PDP even made an alliance with UDELPA, and its general secretary, Horacio Thedy, agreed to stand as General Aramburu's running mate.

Initially the party, as has been said, represented first and foremost the interests of the farmers of the interior as against the interests of Buenos Aires. In recent years it has seemed to attract mainly intellectuals and members of the liberal professions in the region of Santa Fe.

The PDP is a party with no very great strength at the national level. Even during the lifetime of Lisandro de la Torre, it was unable to gain a foothold in every province, and never managed to organize itself properly except in the province of Santa Fe. This situation has hardly altered: the party is not represented in every province, and has tended to concentrate on the coastal region,[10] especially the federal capital, where it recently made considerable progress (in the elections of March 1965 it came third, after the Radicals and the Unión Popular, with 84,500 votes, as against a little over half a million for each of the other two parties). It nevertheless continued to win its biggest successes in the province of Santa Fe. It held first place in that province for many years, but seemed to lose ground to the Radicals and the Unión Popular. But in 1965 this province still provided 60 per cent of its total votes.

10. The area referred to as the coastal region includes the provinces of Buenos Aires, Santa Fe, Corrientes, Entre Ríos and the federal capital.

The PDP was unable to increase its parliamentary representation after its foundation. In 1932 it had fourteen deputies, in 1962 twelve. Since the fall of the Peronist regime, it has obtained about 3 per cent of the total number of votes cast.

The alliance with UDELPA in 1963 proved a successful electoral manoeuvre for the PDP, however, and won it a new lease of life. This improvement was likely to be temporary, and may have been entirely due to the UDELPA candidate's personal prestige. The results obtained by the party in 1965 did not follow up the improvement recorded in 1963 : the PDP once again received only 3 per cent of the total vote (or 291,546 votes), compared with 5·8 per cent in 1963 (555,991 votes).[11]

As the PDP was reconstituted in 1971 there were few indications that the party had been able to win greater support in the years after 1966. Aware of his party's continued electoral weakness, it was likely that Horacio Thedy would again attempt to seek favourable political alliances for future elections.

The Radical Parties

All the present-day radical parties – the Unión Cívica Radical Intransigente (UCRI), the Unión Cívica Radical del Pueblo (UCRP), and the Movimiento de Integración y Desarrollo (MID) – have sprung from the same parent party, the Unión Cívica Radical (UCR).

11. This figure relates to the parliamentary elections. At the presidential elections, which were held at the same time, the PDP actually improved on its performance : 619,471 votes, or 6·5 per cent of the total. Which goes to prove that the growth in its electoral support was principally due to its support of General Aramburu's candidature.

HISTORY OF THE RADICAL CIVIC UNION

Formation of the Party

The acceleration in Argentina's economic development that took place between 1874 and 1880 led to major changes in society. These were not however followed by a corresponding modernization of political structures. In fact, political power stayed in the hands of the old ruling oligarchy, which by this time was not even the chief repository of economic power. The Constitution of 1853 had proclaimed the principle of universal suffrage, but electoral manipulation and fraud deprived the elections of all significance, and corruption reigned throughout the administration. The Unión Cívica Radical was born in 1891, the result of a protest movement against this state of affairs, led principally by Leandro N. Além and A. del Valle, and then later by Hipólito Yrigoyen, whose powerful personality was soon to dominate the party and determine its main characteristics. Radicalism was thus an offshoot of moralism, identifying itself with the struggle of Good against Evil; its victory, as it proclaimed, would be the victory of 'the Cause' over the corrupt 'regime'. This cause was to be identified with that of the nation, for the UCR never considered itself a class party, but a union of all citizens. The arguments it uses against the other parties tend therefore to be expressed in exclusivist terms.

After its foundation, the radical movement suffered from a number of limitations, which were to prove lasting, particularly as regards its programme and its potential areas of support. The party's programme in fact limited itself entirely to claims intended to ensure the participation of the majority of the population in the exercise of political power; freedom to vote, administrative honesty, and abandonment of the officially approved system of centralism in favour of greater provincial and local autonomy were the only points on the

UCR's programme. The only thing the party's future electors had in common therefore was their desire to take part in political and economic decision-making. The vague nature of the radical democratic credo did not favour the establishment of a close-knit organization. The main nucleus of the UCR electorate consisted of those sectors of urban society most intimately concerned with the process of economic expansion, the middle classes and the emergent proletariat, which were still in a state of dependence. In contrast, the ruling elite of the party, while it did not as yet participate directly in the decision-making process, was much closer to the conservatives in its political attitudes and economic interests.

The only factor common to all these groups was therefore the fact that they were still out in the cold, politically speaking. The great differences in employment, economic and social status, and even in political attitudes between the different sectors of the radical party's support were ultimately to produce fatal splits in the very heart of the party the moment it had succeeded in winning reform of the electoral system, and especially once it had actually achieved power (1916–30). It may be said, therefore, that in these circumstances the Radical Party was from the start fated to remain a centre party, oscillating between the left and the right according to the particular problems of the day.

After the 1916 elections, when it won 45·9 per cent of the vote, the Unión Cívica Radical became the Argentine's biggest political party. Although its numerical support fell off under the Peronist regime, it still remained the major opposition party (especially in the federal capital and the province of Córdoba):

Elections	Peronist Party	UCR
1951	4,740,000	2,400,000
1954	5,000,000	2,500,000

The Break-up of the Unión Cívica Radical

The first signs of the impending split became visible as early as 1922. Under the leadership of the radical Alvear, an internal struggle broke out in which Yrigoyen and his supporters were opposed by a right-wing minority calling itself 'anti-personalist' (or Alvearist) which favoured a rapprochement with the conservatives. This struggle led to an actual split in 1924; this was not the end of the conflict, however, and it broke out again in 1945. Once again, two opposing tendencies confronted one another. A movement calling itself 'unionist', led by Zavala Ortiz and hostile to the Peronist regime, called for an electoral alliance with all the other opposition parties. The 'intransigents', more to the left, rejected any electoral compromise, especially with the conservatives; they were less hostile to collaboration with the regime, and even surpassed it in reformist ardour. This faction gave birth, in April 1945, to the Movimiento de Intransigencia y Renovación (MIR), which under the leadership of Ricardo Balbín and Arturo Frondizi soon became the majority group in the UCR. Its programme was defined by the Avellaneda Declaration of 1945 and a document entitled *The Bases of Political Action*, drawn up in 1947 by Moisés Lebensohn, Gabriel del Mazo and Arturo Frondizi, which called for the nationalization of the power industry, the public services and foreign monopolies, for the definition of workers' rights and for the economic and political sovereignty of the nation.

On the fall of Perón the opposition between these two hostile tendencies did not disappear – quite the contrary. The moderate 'unionists' supported the provisional government, while the 'intransigents' fought it and tried to win over the Peronist section of the electorate. The breach finally came over the choice of candidate for the presidential elections. At the Congress of Tucumán, at the end of 1956, the majority group put forward Frondizi's candidature, which was accepted. Ricardo Balbín, who was unhappy about the rapprochement with the Peronists and angry that Frondizi was preferred to himself, left the party, followed by the majority of the Buenos Aires branch of the MIR, by the unionists and by the Córdoba branch of the intransigents; in March 1957 these opposition groups founded a new party, the Unión Cívica Radical del Pueblo (UCRP), while the majority faction in the UCR became the Unión Cívica Radical Intransigente (UCRI). At the elections to the constituent assembly held in 1957, the radical movement went to the country divided for the first time.

THE PRESENT-DAY RADICAL PARTIES

The Unión Cívica Radical del Pueblo (UCRP)

Programme. Institutionally, the People's Radicals wanted to abandon the system of proportional representation and return to the system laid down by the Sáenz Peña law. The result of this would be the artificial expansion of the larger parties' parliamentary representation. It has been calculated, for instance, that if the selective-list system had still been in force, the UCRP would have won one hundred and thirteen seats in the 1963 elections instead of seventy-two, thus obtaining an absolute majority in the Lower House.[12] In domestic policy, it should be noted that despite its marked anti-Peronism the UCRP was quite liberal, even to the extent of permitting the Peronists to take part in the elections of March 1965.

In economic affairs the People's Radicals held a liberal viewpoint, although they were prepared to accept a certain degree of planning. This attitude was probably due largely to the precarious state of the economy, which forced the government to take account of the views of CEPAL and the International Monetary Fund. The UCRP placed its hopes for

12. Snow, Peter G., op. cit., p. 27.

stimulating production on private enterprise. It also advocated the development of agriculture and cattle-farming to obtain the foreign exchange necessary for the industrialization of the country.

Under the Frondizi government the UCRP suddenly became the champion of 'economic nationalism'. There is some ground for thinking that this slogan, which had never appeared in the party's programme, was adopted from electoral considerations. The party then conducted a campaign for the annulment of 'illegal oil contracts' and the revision of Frondizi's agreements with the IMF which 'jeopardized national independence'. However, the UCRP took good care not to go too far in this direction, and welcomed the entry of foreign capital into the country.

Factions within the UCRP. The old antipathies that existed in the Radical Civic Union lived on in the UCRP. There were three main factions:

the Unionists, led by Miguel A. Zavala Ortiz and Carlos Perette. Very close to the conservatives. However, they modified their position in recent years to advocate the setting up of a social democracy. In organization they resembled the middle-class parties. Unionism is well represented in the federal capital and the provinces of Entre Ríos and San Juan;

the MIR; represented the intransigent faction led by Ricardo Balbín. Carried on the tradition of Yrigoyen, under which the party structure is dominated by the leader, and policy is formulated pragmatically, not according to a preconceived programme. It took a centrist position and is the strongest faction in all the provinces where the old UCR was most powerful;

the MIN (Movement of National Intransigence), formed by A. Sabbattini, was a radical faction practically restricted to the province of Córdoba. The former President of the Republic, Dr Arturo Illía, belonged to this group.

Party organization. The People's Radical Civic Union has retained the same form of organization as the old Radical Civic Union. In the provinces in which radicalism was most firmly entrenched, the UCRP has in fact taken over the UCR party apparatus. The party's basic unit is still the local committee. The party's chain of command is weak, as the provincial associations enjoy a large measure of autonomy and the party leadership's control over the rank and file is severely limited. The UCRP has tried to create a national executive on which all areas in the country are equally represented.

The leadership is elected democratically, except sometimes in the case of appointments made at local level (parish or ward committees) in some regions where traditions of paternalism and caudillism have survived. Appointment to senior positions in the party hierarchy is dependent on the candidate's having made his career in the party. The UCRP's top leadership consists of 'professional politicians'.

Electorate. The UCRP does not, any more than the UCR, aim to represent the middle classes; it claims to represent the whole nation, and to be a mass party. It does not seem quite to have achieved this status, however. According to a survey conducted in 1962 in the federal capital,[13] the social composition of the party was as follows:

Upper middle classes	33 %
Lower middle classes	44·5%
Working classes	22·5%

Moreover in its study of the electoral motivation of UCRP voters, the inquiry reached the conclusion that their voting habits had relatively little to do with political or economic

13. Imaz, José Luis de, *Motivación electoral*, Buenos Aires, Instituto de Desarrollo Económico y Social, 1962. (Sixth Conference of the IDES, 1962.)

considerations, and were chiefly determined by reference to the traditional moral values represented by the party and its leaders.

Election results. (See Table, p. 82.) The UCRP electorate remained practically constant after 1957; the proportion of hard-core support was estimated at about 83 per cent of the total votes received by the party.

As a result of the split in the UCRI, the People's Radical Civic Union became in the mid-1960s the second largest political organization in the country, after the Peronists; it is therefore liable to gain a large number of anti-Peronist votes in future elections.

Areas of support. The UCRP is especially strong in the federal capital, where thanks to its large women's vote it has up till now always beaten the Peronists. It has also obtained excellent results in the provinces of Córdoba, Entre Ríos, Buenos Aires, Santa Fe and Santiago del Estero, that is to say mainly in the biggest provinces of the coast and the interior.

As the Peronists were permitted to take part in the elections of March 1965, the UCRP was beaten by the Unión Popular, but the difference in the votes was fairly small – about one hundred thousand.

The UCRP was to some extent discredited by its failure in government under Illía, and there was widespread indifference to the military intervention even among many supporters of the party. As on earlier occasions in its history, the UCRP showed the resilience of radicalism in times of adversity and proscription. Together with the Peronists, the UCRP took a leading part in the movement against the military dictatorship. It was likely to emerge once more as the second largest party in any future elections.

The dissolution of the party from 1966 to 1971 left the national leadership of the UCRP largely in the hands of

Ricardo Balbín, but it was clear that older divisions remained inherent in the movement. Conservative-minded leaders such as Zavala Ortíz were alarmed by Balbín's move towards a more left-wing programme, and by the agreement with the Peronists which Balbín negotiated in the name of the party in November 1970.

The Unión Cívica Radical Intransigente (UCRI) and the Movimiento de Integración y Desarrollo (MID)

In studying the Intransigent Radical Civic Union, two separate periods have to be distinguished: before and after 1964. By contrast with the UCRP, the UCRI was not ultimately able to maintain its unity. In 1964, the minority faction broke away to form a new party, the Movement for Integration and Development (MID), although the UCRI continued to exist; however, this UCRI of 1964 had very little in common with the UCRI founded in 1957, of which the MID is the true successor.

The UCRI before 1964. As we have seen, the UCRI was born in 1957 of a dispute that centred on the person of Dr Arturo Frondizi. The party was to be the vehicle of his accession to supreme office. During the election campaigns of 1957 and 1958, Frondizi tried to conciliate both of the two irreconcilable hostile camps – the Conservatives by presenting himself as the only political force able to prevent the return of the Peronists, and the Peronists by claiming to continue the work begun by Perón.

Frondizi drew up his programme outside the framework of the party, with the aid of a team of technocrats of no party allegiance, the chief of whom was Rogelio Frigerio. The programme of government put forward by the leadership of the UCRI during the election campaign is striking for the priority given in it to economic considerations. In the political field, in fact, apart from a few promises included to placate the Army and the Church, it was content to make pious remarks about the need for national reconciliation and the drafting of an amnesty. Some hostility can also be detected to the institutions set up by the Bogotá Charter or by UNO, which the party accused of infringing the country's national sovereignty.

The whole of the UCRI's economic programme revolved around the notion of 'development' and the winning of economic independence. Two methods of achieving these aims were recommended : nationalization of natural resources (especially petroleum), and industrialization. To achieve the latter, the Frondizi team prescribed a limited form of planning (control and canalization of investment and credit) which would still give plenty of scope for free enterprise, and the establishment of a system of protection for national industries.

However, political and economic realities prevented Frondizi from putting this programme into practice once he had acceded to the presidency. On the political plane, he was obliged to attempt to reconcile two antagonistic forces; elected with the support of the Peronists, he knew that he could not maintain his position at the head of the country without the support of an army which tolerated rather than accepted him, and which he therefore had to handle with circumspection. The precarious situation of the Argentine economy, the legacy of the preceding regime, did not give him a very wide margin for manoeuvre. Frondizi was therefore forced to bend with the wind in order to retain power. Consequently he had to renounce his intentions of nationalizing the country's natural resources in July 1958 : he signed contracts with Standard Oil and facilitated the entry of foreign capital. The end of the abortive experiment in economic planning was then marked by the appointment of Alvaro Alsogaray, a fervent believer in economic liberalism, to the direction of economic affairs. The admiration for North America professed by the ruling clique, internal pressures and the deterioration in the international situation (notably the Cuban crisis of 1962) also provoked major modifications in the government's foreign policy. Argentina thus aligned herself with the United States and offered no resistance to integration in the inter-American system, thus abandoning dreams of the revival of the 'Third Force' policy so dear to the Peronists.

This succession of reversals of policy brought about the disaffection of a large part of the UCRI's electoral support. The growing deterioration in the economic situation and the resultant increase in the cost of living also caused considerable discontent in various quarters, especially the trade unions. The withdrawal of their support meant that the government had lost a major counterweight that might have enabled it to resist the growing pressure of the Army, which was increasingly interfering in the conduct of affairs. But it was the Peronist victory in the 1962 elections which administered the final blow to the government: the Army intervened to 'ward off the threat to the social order', and overthrew Frondizi.

Up till then the UCRI had managed to maintain its unity, but from now on two opposing tendencies emerged: that of Frondizi, who wanted to form a national front including the Peronists, and that led by Oscar Allende (chairman of the party's national executive), which rejected this plan. The conflict grew steadily sharper during Dr Illía's presidency, and finally resulted, in April 1964, in a split. The minority group in the UCRI, led this time by Frondizi, then founded the Movimiento de Integración y Desarrollo (MID), all reference to radicalism being dropped.

Like the UCRP, the UCRI retained the organizational structure of the old Radical Civic Union; the basic unit of the party was the local committee.

Apart from questions of policy and programme, the great

difference between the UCRI and the Popular Radicals, at least until the 1964 split, lay in their respective areas of support. As has been seen, in the places where the old party apparatus was most strongly entrenched, the radical party organization was taken over by the UCRP. Frondizi's intransigence and Peronist sympathies contributed to the alienation of the local radical party bosses. The UCRI therefore started life to all intents and purposes a new party, without any ready-made organization in the regions. Although recruited for the most part from the ranks of the middle classes, its support lacked cohesion, since different sectors followed Frondizi for different reasons, which in the long run proved irreconcilable. One of the biggest groups of Frondizi supporters consisted of the 'radical old guard'; out of loyalty to the old traditions of the party, these supported the majority faction, though without any great enthusiasm. Side by side with this conservative faction, there was in the UCRI a left-wing movement composed of intellectuals, young dissidents from the communist and socialist parties, and a group calling itself the 'national left' (or 'national Marxist movement') led by Rodolfo Puiggrós and Jorge A. Ramos. The UCRI attracted these groups by its programme of national economic development and its readiness to establish good relations with the Peronists. For similar reasons, a number of Peronist intellectuals and businessmen were moved to support Frondizi's party. The UCRI electorate's voting habits therefore tended to be guided more by economic and political considerations than those of the Popular Radicals, though the purely routine vote cast by traditional radical supporters did not disappear.

Electoral Results of the UCRI. Between 1957 and 1964 national elections showed constant swings of the radical electorate between the UCRI and the UCRP. (See table, p. 82.) The difference in the number of votes cast for the two parties has always been fairly small; the notable exception of the 1958 election is due to the fact that Frondizi won the support of the Peronists (which he was never able to do again). It may be said, therefore, that up to 1964 some degree of equilibrium existed between the UCRI and the UCRP, between which the radical electorate was more or less evenly divided.

After 1964: the UCRI and the MID. In 1964, however, the split in the UCRI brought this situation to an end and completely altered the balance of forces between the two great representatives of Argentine radicalism. The figures are quite unequivocal on this point. The electoral results obtained by the two parties in 1965 show, by comparison with 1963, that the UCRP managed to maintain and even slightly to increase its electoral support, while the UCRI vote collapsed completely (see table opposite); the 400,000 votes received by the latter party only represented a quarter of the figure for 1963, so that it moved from third to fifth place immediately behind the MID and the Conservatives.

Right from their very first contest at the polls, the MID managed to beat the UCRI. This victory can doubtless partly be put down to Frondizi's personal magnetism. However, it is interesting to compare the electoral support and the programmes of the two rival groups.

It is hard to say which part of the old Frondizist UCRI electorate went over to the MID; however, it seems likely that the section termed the 'national left' and part of the progressive electorate joined forces with the new party. On the other hand, it seems that the traditional radical support preferred to stick with the majority and stay in the UCRI. This party thus retained the more conservative elements of intransigent radicalism; this is confirmed by the fact that in recent years the party programme had little in common with that of the old Frondizist UCRI. Purely political questions took precedence over economic considerations. The party's attitude was only vaguely defined: thus in the political field its programme was content with presenting the UCRI as a force for unity and reconciliation. On the economic plane, it was chiefly noted for its opposition to planning; it emphasized the need to do away with controls and give free rein to private enterprise.

By contrast, the MID's action programme continued to repeat the main points of the proposals put forward by Frondizi in 1957–8, and remained centred on the problem of developing the country. The party also continued the policy of rapprochement with the Peronists.

Electoral Results of the Three Radical Parties Compared (1957–65)

Elections to the Chamber of Deputies		UCRP Votes	%	UCRI Votes	%	MID Votes	%
Constituent	1957	2,016,929	23·2	1,847,583	21·2	—	—
General	1958	2,229,224	25·4	3,778,561	41·8	—	—
Partial	1960	2,119,094	23·7	1,832,248	20·6	—	—
Partial	1962	1,875,587	19·9	2,301,397	24·5	—	—
General	1963	2,419,269	25·4	1,541,902	16·2	—	—
Partial	1965	2,734,940	28·1	418,270	4·3	606,872	6·2

NOTE: The Radical Civic Union had 2,415,000 votes in 1951; 2,493,000 votes in 1954.

Major changes took place after 1966 which were likely to reflect on the electoral strength of both the UCRI and the MID. Notable among these was the support given by Frondizi to successive military governments. Frondizi adopted a critical attitude – for example, his public criticism was one reason for the fall of Onganía in 1970 – but his influence probably diminished within the radical movement. He also lost potential allies among the other parties. But while most disagreed with Frondizi's own political position, the policy of

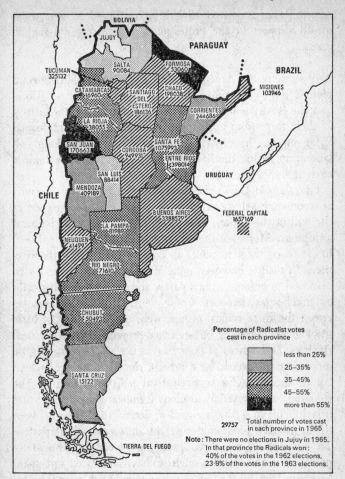

BOLIVIA

JUJUY

PARAGUAY

TUCUMAN
325132

SALTA
90084

FORMOSA
53060

BRAZIL

CATAMARCA
116960

SANTIAGO
DEL
ESTERO
186136

CHACO
198038

MISIONES
103946

LA RIOJA
38055

CORRIENTES
244686

SAN JUAN
170663

CORDOBA
949931

SANTA FE
1075993

SAN LUIS
88414

ENTRE RIOS
398014

MENDOZA
409189

URUGUAY

LA PAMPA
81980

BUENOS AIRES
3388529

FEDERAL CAPITAL
1657169

NEUQUEN
41499

CHILE

RIO NEGRO
71610

CHUBUT
50493

**Percentage of Radicalist votes
cast in each province**

less than 25%

25–35%

35–45%

45–55%

more than 55%

SANTA CRUZ
15122

29757   Total number of votes cast
in each province in 1965

Note : There were no elections in Jujuy in 1965.
In that province the Radicals won :
40% of the votes in the 1962 elections.
23·9% of the votes in the 1963 elections.

TIERRA DEL FUEGO

*Figure 3. Distribution of Radicalism in the 1965
Elections**

* The 'family' of radical parties is represented here, i.e. the URCP,
the UCRI and the MID.

desarrollismo associated with him continued to win wide-spread support in the professional and managerial middle class.

*

Any study of the Argentine radical parties would be incomplete if limited to a simple analysis of their differences. Moreover this is why so much emphasis has been laid on the history of their formation; apart from immediately obvious formal antagonisms, these parties inherited from their long collaboration within the Radical Civic Union a certain number of common features.

Like the old UCR, they continued to take an exclusivist attitude, each being convinced that it was the incarnation of the will of the nation, to the exclusion of all other political groupings. Moreover their Manichaean notions of political life inclined them to reject all compromises with other factions. In reality, however, none of them, despite their efforts, managed to become a mass party, and all depended basically on middle-class support. Consequently the divergences between the three radical groups were not the result of basic ideological differences, but stemmed principally from personal rivalries. Differences of policy or tactics were frequently no more than an excuse for a breach, the real causes of which lay in the struggles between rival political *caudillos*. The secondary role played by ideology is indicated by the fact that it is difficult to establish any clear demarcation lines between the legislative programmes of the different radical parties. To summarize, all three groupings were fundamentally parties of the centre; this ought to have facilitated agreement between them, all the more so since together they represented a majority of the electorate. The few tentative moves that were made towards reconciliation failed, however.

In 1971 it was impossible to estimate the future of the Radical parties with any confidence. One major question among many was whether there would be a continuation of the bipolarization of political life in Argentina which was seen before 1966. The alliance between the UCRP and the Peronists suggested that a change had taken place. This alliance was, however, merely a short-term agreement reached between the leadership of the two movements, and not a basis for an electoral coalition. Given strong anti-Peronist feeling in the UCRP, particularly at the local level, it was difficult to imagine the party retaining its unity in a coalition with the Peronists. For this and other reasons, Popular Radical leaders might again be tempted, as in 1965, to try for a majority as the only viable non-Peronist alternative.

Partido Demócrata Cristiano (PDC)

Formation of the Party

The PDC was first organized in 1954, but it did not make an official appearance on the political scene until July 1955. It originally modelled itself on European examples, and its leaders were Lucas Ayarragaray (candidate for the presidency in 1958), Manuel Ordóñez and Francisco Mejía.

The PDC enjoyed a certain measure of success from the very first elections in which it took part, since in 1957 it gained 419,630 votes, which made it the fifth largest national party. The following year it even moved up a place, despite the fact that it only gained 327,744 votes, apparently because part at least of its supporters had decided to vote for the Frondizi-Peronist coalition. Like most of the Argentine parties, the PDC soon fell a prey to dissension between the supporters and opponents of cooperation with the Peronists. The two tendencies confronted one another at the 1961 party congress in Rosario, the one faction led by the younger party leaders, who favoured a rapprochement with national and popular sectors, the other led by Ayarragaray and Mejía, who opposed this policy. For once, the victory of the former faction did not lead to a split; Horacio Sueldo was elected party chairman, while his opponents refrained from breaking away, although they did submit their own list of candidates, the *lista verde*, at some elections.

Once embarked on this new course, the PDC attempted to combine with Frondizi's UCRI, the Peronists, and Solano Lima's Partido Demócrata Conservador Popular to form a national popular front for the 1963 presidential elections. However, it soon gave up the idea and to everyone's surprise invited Raúl Matera, a notorious Peronist leader, to stand as the party's candidate. The Army vetoed this move, and the party eventually adopted Horacio Sueldo and Francisco Serra as its team.

Party Organization and Programme

The PDC started life as a party of the centre, and apparently moved to the left in the course of its development. The most significant feature of this evolution was the efforts it has made to woo the Peronist electorate. In election campaigns its own programme seemed closer to the Peronist position of the 1943–55 period than that of even the Unión Popular. When this policy did not produce the desired results it was abandoned, or at least considerably modified.

In the political field, the Christian Democrats have supported legalization of the Peronist parties. In foreign affairs, they have taken up the Peronist idea of the 'third force', and consequently support their country's independence of the United States and campaign vigorously for the formation of a Latin American bloc. Without harbouring too many illusions as to the success of a pan-American union, they hoped that the Latin American countries might at least succeed in arriving at a common foreign policy. In the social field, the PDC pressed for further reforms to the benefit of the working class (workers' participation in company management, tying wages to the cost of living index, increase in government expenditure on the welfare services).

The party's economic programme can be expressed by three principal guidelines: nationalism, planning, and reformism. The PDC came out in favour of annulling the petroleum contracts and control of the economy 'by the nation itself' (hence the attacks the party occasionally made on Argentina's ties with the International Monetary Fund). It recommended the adoption of a flexible planning system and the establishment of state control over a number of activities (exchange, credit and trade). Finally, it emphasized the need for agrarian reform and even went so far as to propose that the large landed proprietors be expropriated.

Party leaders have been chosen democratically, elected by the entire membership. It seems that initially, at least, one of the criteria for recruitment of many of the party leaders was militant activity in a lay Catholic organization. Next to Horacio Sueldo, one of the chief personalities in the PDC was Enrique de Vedia.

The party is financed mainly from individual subscriptions.

Electoral Results and Future Prospects

The PDC is one of the few Argentinian parties to be organized over the whole country. The results recorded in successive elections do not augur well for its political future; in fact its vote has steadily declined since its creation:

1957	419,630	4·8%
1958	327,744	3·6%
1960	347,316	3·9%
1962	212,605	2·3%
1963	436,935	4·6%
1965	251,675	2·6%

The exception of 1963 is probably due to the attraction of the PDC's then revolutionary economic programme for voters reluctant to follow Frondizi's and the Peronists' counsel to register a blank vote.

Analysis of voting patterns reveals that the party's electorate has a large majority of women voters, who constitute almost 70 per cent of its support, and this despite the PDC programme's apparently revolutionary nature.

However, the Christian Democrats have not been able to win over the electorate of the so-called traditional provinces; this is especially clear in Mendoza, where conservative votes are cast for the FNCP or the UCRP and opposition votes are divided between the Peronists, the MID and even the Socialist Party. Generally speaking, the PDC has been unable to gain a strong foothold in the provinces with a large electorate; this is especially true of Buenos Aires and the federal capital, and to a lesser extent of Córdoba and Santa Fe.

The Christian Democratic ideology has enjoyed some considerable increase in popularity in Latin America in recent years, more particularly in Chile and Venezuela. Why, then, the relative lack of success of the Christian Democrat Party in Argentina? It seems that the chief obstacle to the PDC's success is the lack of any specific area of support or group on which it can rely. The Christian Democrats might have been able to siphon off some of the votes of the Catholic centre and right. This did not occur for two reasons. First of all, the ideological attraction which this party could have exercised on the Catholics played practically no part, because religious questions have long ceased to be a subject of political controversy; moreover the senior ecclesiastical hierarchy, disquieted by the progressive nature of the party programme, has been unforthcoming. Secondly, and above all, the PDC itself made no effort to attract this audience, deliberately turning instead towards the left and the Peronists. Its efforts do not seem to have aroused much of a response from the radical left-wing or socialist electorate. Moreover its attempts to win votes from the Peronists have utterly failed. Its programme was not enough to detach the labouring classes from Peronism, as they remained convinced that Perón's own party was alone capable of solving their problems. Thus the PDC's only hope of recruiting working-class support is in the so-called 'independent' trade-union sector. Given these facts, the party's future prospects are hardly bright. Even if it manages to preserve or improve its position, it is unlikely to make a dramatic advance like its sister parties in Chile or Venezuela, unless some major upheaval should intervene.

The Socialist Parties

THE SOCIALIST PARTY UP TO 1958

European immigration played an important part in the creation of the Argentinian Socialist Party. In the capital immigrant workers started out by forming apolitical trade-union organizations (the German workers' Vorwärts, the Italian Fascio dei Lavoratori, the Spanish Agrupación Socialista and the French Les Egaux). They subsequently began to recreate, in their new homeland, parties analogous to the socialist parties set up in Europe between 1840 and 1860. The founder of the Workers' Socialist Party (PSO) was Juan B. Justo, and this new party's inaugural congress was held in 1896. By 1904 it had one deputy in Parliament, Alfredo Palacios.

The Workers' Socialist Party soon found itself in difficulties: despite the increase in its parliamentary representation, it was weakened by several splits; between 1899 and 1930 there were five, including that in 1920 which led to the formation of the Communist Party.

After 1920 the Socialist Party was the undisputed leader of

the trade-union movement; nevertheless, astonishingly, it never succeeded in establishing itself as a mass party. This failure may be explained by the fact that its areas of support are limited, both geographically and socially. The Socialist Party only managed to become firmly entrenched in the main areas of immigration, especially the large coastal towns undergoing industrial expansion; it completely failed to penetrate the agricultural areas of the interior. Moreover its support continued to be drawn primarily from the ranks of organized labour (a minority of the working class), mostly immigrants or sons of immigrants. When, after the great migratory movements of the 1930s, considerable numbers of landless labourers from the hinterland moved into the towns to swell the urban proletariat, the Socialist Party proved unable to take advantage of the situation. It was unable either to perceive or to express the needs of these masses, nor even to place them in context. What is more, the workers belonging to the PSO sometimes exhibited some hostility towards these newcomers – the worker's defence reaction against cheap labour threatening to undermine a hitherto privileged position. At first regarded as revolutionaries, the Socialists were rapidly 'bourgeoisified', especially once middle-class elements joined the party and began to play an increasingly large role.

For all these reasons, the Socialist Party suffered more than others from the emergence of Peronism, which deprived it at a stroke of the working-class support which up till then it had still enjoyed in spite of everything. The PSO then passed through a period of internal crisis which resulted in July 1958, at the Rosario Congress, in a new split: the Workers' Socialist Party broke up into two distinct formations – the Social Democratic Party (PSD) and the Argentine Socialist Party (PSA).

THE SOCIALIST PARTIES SINCE 1958

Party Programmes and Leaders

The Social Democratic Party. The PSD defined itself as 'left-wing humanist, rationalist and anti-clerical'. In reality, like its predecessor the Workers' Socialist Party, it took rather a moderate line, to the extent indeed that many of its positions on specific issues bear a close resemblance to those adopted by the UCRP. It preached gradual social reform by democratic methods; in this context it may be interesting to note that in 1964 the PSD opposed the 'fighting programme' adopted by the CGT, aligning itself with the UCRP and the conservatives. Also like them, it is hostile to the Peronists and the Communists.

The main leaders of the party are Américo Ghioldi and, until his death, Nicolás Repetto (the 'old guard' of the Socialist Party). The PSD also publishes a newspaper called *La Vanguardia*.

The Argentine Socialist Party. As has been seen, the PSA was born of the crisis that gripped the Workers' Socialist Party during and after the Peronist regime. The younger men in the party, who provoked the split (and who were the majority faction, be it noted), found their party too timid. Their aim was to adapt socialist claims to a society undergoing social reform, and to re-establish their party on a mass footing. In opposition to the 'old guard' of the Socialist Party, they therefore wanted to try making overtures to the Peronists. This attempt seemed at first as though it might be successful, since they won the support of the Communist Party and of the left wing of the PSD and PDP, creating a kind of union of the left which enabled them to win a seat in the Senate in 1961 (Alfredo Palacios for Buenos Aires).

In contrast to the PSD, the PSA advocated violent methods

to force the government to grant social reforms (and it therefore supported the CGT's 'fighting programme' of 1964). The party's programme contained a number of radical points: workers' participation in management, bank nationalization, establishment of a state monopoly in foreign trade, total dismemberment of large estates without compensation, and cuts in the Army budget.

In fact, although further to the left than the PSD, this party was far from being as extreme as it pretended, and succeeded neither in frightening off its bourgeois voters nor in winning over the working classes. A single example will suffice to demonstrate the purely theoretical nature of the PSA's revolutionary ardour: in 1961, to take advantage of the wave of apprehension caused by Castro's revolution, the Peronists gave it out that unless their movement were legalized they might find themselves obliged to resort to revolutionary measures. To prove as much, they actually voted for the Argentine Socialist Party in a number of local elections. At this point the leaders of the PSA, who little relished the prospect of becoming the front line of Peronism and the revolutionary left, prudently back-pedalled; they even refused to make an electoral alliance with the Justicialista Front in 1962. This about-turn provoked another internal crisis, the extreme left wing of the party breaking away to join two new groupings: the National Left – a nationalist, Trotskyist and pro-Peronist movement led by Jorge A. Ramos and R. Puiggrós – in 1961; and the Argentine Vanguard Socialist Party (PSAV) in 1962. The latter won several thousand votes in the federal capital and in Buenos Aires province in 1962 and 1963, but remained a minority party confined to these two areas.

Leaders of the PSA in recent years have been Carlos Sánchez Viamonte, Alicia M. de Justo and Ramón Muñiz. Until the beginning of 1965 the party was led by Alfredo Palacios, one of Argentina's first militant socialists.

Organization

The two socialist parties have a highly centralized organization based on the federal capital, where most of their leaders, who are elected internally, come from.

The PSA and the PSD have a rigid structure with a strong chain of command. Until recently, the leading groups in both were fairly stable. Only men who have made the party their career are elevated to responsible posts in it, which obviously does not make for a rapid turnover among its leadership. Party funds are obtained by individual membership subscriptions.

Election Results: Areas of Support: Electorate (See table, p. 95.)

Although the results obtained by the socialist parties have fluctuated considerably from one election to the next, it would seem that the long-term trend is downward. This discouraging trend has become most marked since the split between the two parties became effective in all the provinces, that is to say since 1963.[14]

A study of election results gives rise to a number of observations. First of all, in every election the socialist vote seems to vary in inverse proportion to the results obtained by the Peronists. Between 1958 and 1965 every drop in the socialist electorate coincided with the participation of the Peronists in the election (i.e. 1962 and 1965). Conversely, as in 1960 and 1963, the Peronist blank vote is accompanied by a rise in the number of votes cast for the socialists. Of course there may be no causal connection, but it seems likely that in these two cases the socialists were temporarily able to attract a small

14. In 1960, the PSA and the PSD only put forward separate candidates for election in the federal capital and the provinces of Buenos Aires, Santa Fe, Entre Ríos, Tucumán and San Luis; these were joined in 1962 by Córdoba and Mendoza. Over the rest of the country, they kept the name 'Partido Socialista' until 1963.

percentage of the Peronists' support. This interpretation is especially persuasive where the Argentine Socialist Party is concerned; its support varies much more noticeably between elections than does that of the PSD (see table, p. 95). This phenomenon emerged quite clearly at the time of the 1965 elections, when the two socialist parties fell victim to the polarization of votes around the People's Radicals and the Peronists; there are indications that some of the votes that had previously gone to the PSD went to the UCRP, while in the PSA the displacement of the electorate was more to the advantage of the Peronist parties.

A more detailed study of the votes cast shows that in general elections socialist candidates for seats in the national or provincial parliament win more votes than candidates of these same parties for the national presidency and vice-presidency. The adoption of proportional representation in 1963 enabled the two socialist groups to win a parliamentary representation such as they had not enjoyed for many years.

In contrast to the Christian Democratic Party, which is in fact a younger party, the socialist parties do not submit candidates for election in all the provinces – in fact candidates are only presented in just over half the country. Their main areas of support are the big urban centres, which also coincide with the original areas of European immigration and are in the provinces which have been industrialized longest. The socialists have most success in the federal capital; in 1965 the PSA won 4 per cent of the votes there, which puts it in fourth place after the UCRP, the Unión Popular and the Progressive Democrats. The electorate in the province of Buenos Aires is less well-disposed towards them: in 1965 the PSD won 2·8 per cent of the votes in that province, and the PSA 2·5 per cent.[15] In the provinces of Mendoza, the

15. The federal capital and the province of Buenos Aires together account for just over four fifths of the electorate of each of the smaller parties.

Chaco and Misiones they are equally well represented and, to a lesser extent, in Córdoba and Santa Fe.

The two parties draw their support mainly from intellectuals and minor officials; the socialists play a very small part in trade-union organization at the moment.

If the socialist parties – parties of intellectuals – exert any influence at all, it bears little relation to their electoral strength, and is due principally to the prestige of their leaders and the respect they have been able to win in the country.

Electoral Results of the Socialist Parties

	PSO Number of votes cast	%	PSA Number of votes cast	%	PSD Number of votes cast	%
Elections						
1957	524,311	6·1	—	—	—	—
1958	520,830	5·7	—	—	—	—
1960[16]	746,432	8·4	—	—	—	—
1962[16]	426,134	4·5	—	—	—	—
1963	—	—	310,739	3·3	306,650	3·2
1965	—	—	184,779	1·9	170,362	1·7

Partido Comunista (PC)

Origins and Development

Like the European Communist parties, the Argentine Communist Party was born out of socialism at the end of the First World War. At that time, the opposing tendencies which had long existed within the Socialist Party came into serious conflict. In 1918 the minority internationalist faction was expelled from the PSO and gave birth to the International

16. In the elections of 1960 and 1962, the official publications only give the overall figures obtained by all the socialist parties (PSA, PSD and PSO, which continued to exist in a few provinces). For purposes of comparison, here are the results obtained by the different

Socialist Party; on the occasion of its first congress two years later, the latter finally adopted the name of Communist Party.

The PC thereafter endeavoured to become the party of the working class. However, the development of nationalist feeling in Argentina during Yrigoyen's presidency temporarily put a brake on the party's expansion; its 'internationalist' label only earned it suspicion, and it was regarded as a foreign product. It was also weakened by internal struggles (Trotskyist opposition). Moreover it was several times banned: in 1936, under Justo's presidency, up to 1946; allowed once again to take part in elections during the Peronist regime, it continued to play a recognized part in political life under the provisional government (1955–8). However, it was once again debarred from taking any political action or engaging in propaganda under Frondizi; it was finally declared illegal under Guido's presidency, since which time it has been unable to reintegrate officially into the political scene. However, it is not so closely watched as to be unable to disseminate propaganda more or less as it wishes, or to make pronouncements on this or that political issue. It was even allowed, in some provinces, to present candidates for provincial parliamentary and Senate seats (Tucumán, 1965) and for seats in the provincial parliament and on local authorities (Chaco, 1965).

The Argentine Communist Party has followed the same course of development as its sister parties in Europe; after a period of intransigent revolutionary opposition, which lasted up to the 1930s, it shifted its policy to one of joining in popular fronts, of which it became the most ardent proponent: the Frente Popular of 1936, the Democratic Union

socialist groups: they are taken from the provisional results published by *La Nación*, and give some indication of orders of magnitude: in 1960: PSO 76,000, PSA 333,000, PSD 295,000; in 1962: PSO 17,432, PSA 136,609, PSD 251,269 in 1945 with the UCR, the PDP and the socialists, left-wing fronts in 1961 and 1962 with the socialists and the Peronists. The party even debated whether to support or oppose the governments of Perón and Frondizi; at first opposed to Perón, whom it denounced as a fascist, it soon realized that this attitude could harm its image with the masses attracted to Peronism. In both cases it decided to collaborate, with reservations, until it finally ended up in opposition once more.

Party Programme and Organization

In principle, the ultimate aim of the Communist Party is to establish the dictatorship of the proletariat. Meanwhile, it is ready to throw its weight behind any move to detach Argentina from the western bloc and above all the United States; as a result, it adopts slogans which are at the same time nationalist (with regard to petroleum, for instance), isolationist, and neutralist (against the Organization of American States and for peaceful coexistence). Since it pursues a policy of friendship towards the Peronists, it naturally also supports their social demands; it advocates radical agrarian reform (expropriation without compensation, and distribution of the land to peasant cooperatives).

The Argentine Communist Party, however, is less concerned with internal questions than with international policy and the position of the Soviet Union with regard to them. The majority of the party supports Moscow in the Sino-Soviet dispute.[17] The Argentine Communist Party's con-

17. Differences between Cuba and the USSR on the question of revolutionary strategy in Latin America had more serious repercussions in the Argentine Communist Party. Several members of the FJC, the Argentine Young Communists' organization, were expelled or resigned from the party because of their favourable attitude towards the OLAS conference, and founded the Movimiento Comunista Revolucionario.

siderable dependence on the USSR often comes into conflict with the feelings of nationalism instilled in the people by the Peronist regime, and is a further obstacle to the party's establishment in the working class.

The leaders of the Argentine Communist Party are mostly intellectuals. After its foundation the party was led by Vitorio Codovilla until his death in 1970, when the leadership devolved on G. A. Alvarez. Other important members of the Central Committee include Alcira de la Peña and Rodolfo and Orestes Ghioldi (brothers of the PSD leader). Until his death in 1964, Víctor Larralde also played a major role in party affairs.

The organization of the Argentine Communist Party is just as rigid as it is in all other countries (central committee, executive committee, plenum); it controls a whole range of subsidiary organizations, such as the Communist Youth Federation, the Union of Argentine Women, and a number of cultural associations (popular theatre groups and the like). The party makes deliberate efforts to infiltrate every sector of national life.

The party also controls a substantial press network, which although small in circulation is very wide-ranging, since all the Communist organizations and associations publish their own journal. *Nuestra palabra* is the official organ of the party, *Nueva era* (which had been edited by Codovilla) is the Central Committee's journal.

As it is a working-class party, the Argentine Communist Party is naturally closely interested in the trade-union movement. After the fall of the Peronist regime, the party had hopes of retrieving at least in this field some of the ground it had lost. In fact the opposite happened. The Peronists were able to maintain themselves and reorganize in the political field largely thanks to their dominant position in the trade-union confederation. Their strength grew with the years, instead of diminishing. Nevertheless, the party was assured of representation in the CGT thanks to the MUCS (Movimiento de Unidad y Coordinación Sindical), called the 'Group of Nineteen'. The three most important communist unions are those of the building workers, the chemical workers and the hotel staffs. One of the most prominent MUCS leaders was Rubens Iscaro, general secretary of the building workers' union and member of the Communist Party Central Committee.

However, the part played by the 'Nineteen' in the confederation seems comparatively small. For one thing, the communists have never been able to get elected to the leadership of the confederation; and besides, the MUCS was in something of an embarrassing position : it wanted to uphold the claims of the workers, but was afraid to take too hard a line, which might have antagonized the government and irremediably compromised the liberal legislation for which the Communist Party so ardently hoped. Finally, it would seem that the balance of forces within the CGT has tipped fairly drastically against them and in favour of the Peronists.[18]

It should be emphasized that there are other Marxist parties in Argentina. They do not, however, act in concert with the Communist Party in any way, since they disagree with it both on ideology and on tactics : in practice, they favour close collaboration with the Peronists. The most important of these groups are the Partido Socialista de la Revolución Nacional, a breakaway group from the Socialist Party led by Enrique Dickmann, and the National Left mentioned earlier, led by R. Puiggrós and Jorge Abelardo Ramos. The latter had also founded the Movimiento Comunista Trotskysta in 1946, a

18. With regard to the groups who share control of the CGT, reference is still made to the blocs of 62 (Peronist), 32 (independent) and 19 (communist). However, many observers consider that this distribution, which reflects the CGT's situation at the time when it was under government control (1955–61), has now been superseded; according to some sources, the true figures in 1966 were closer to 76, 53 and 6.

movement of similar political tendencies. The strength of these parties is very limited, and is more or less confined to the federal capital and the province of Buenos Aires.

The Party's Role in National Life

The bias of most sources of information and the fact that the PCA has been out of electoral competitions since 1958 make it difficult to give a realistic assessment of its strength in recent years. In 1920 it had 2,000 members; in January 1959 it claimed 76,000. In the elections in which it was allowed to take part, it has succeeded in increasing its voting strength quite considerably: in 1951 it won about 71,300 votes; in 1954 the figure was 89,000. During the constituent elections of 1957 it won 228,800 votes, or 2·6 per cent of the total votes cast. In 1958 its vote dropped to 192,000 votes, which is largely accounted for by the fact that the Communist Party withdrew most of its candidates in order to support Frondizi. The best guess at the moment is that it would win something like half a million votes.

Overall, the Communist Party's areas of support correspond roughly to those of the Socialists. Up to 1958 the party had only acquired significance in the province of Buenos Aires, where it controlled about 2·6 per cent of the electorate, and in the federal capital (4 per cent), where it held seventh place. It had no success in the conservatively inclined provinces of the interior, or in Patagonia or the new provinces, where it was in many cases not represented at all (only in Neuquén did it win 2·6 per cent of the vote). In 1965 it won 1·1 per cent of the votes in the elections to the provincial parliaments of Tucumán and the Chaco.

Despite the PCA's repeated efforts to win over the Peronists there are no signs that it has met with the slightest success. Moreover this situation is unlikely to change in the near future.

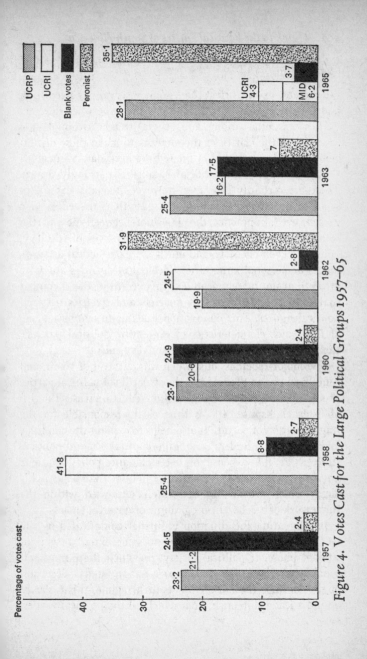

Percentage of votes cast

Figure 4. Votes Cast for the Large Political Groups 1957-65

UCRP
UCRI
Blank votes
Peronist

Conclusion

At the end of this brief study, some reservations need to be added with regard to the distinctions drawn between different parties of similar origins and general trend. Although it is essential to the clarity of the analysis to make these distinctions, there is a risk that in the light of everyday political life they may appear too artificial because too strongly drawn. There are certainly cleavages; however, in many cases they seem to be more a legacy of the past than the effect of a present need. In practice, the opposition between these parties is based only very superficially on differences of ideology, policy, or even clientele, and much more on tactical disagreements or personal animosities. Ideological disputes are more often than not merely a pretext invoked to justify a conflict that is in fact the result of quarrels and rivalries between political figures. This observation leads us to emphasize one of the major characteristics of Argentine political parties: their continuing penchant for personality cults.

The major repercussions which this survival of traditional caudillism has on the role and the structure of political parties should on no account be underestimated. It increases the risk of internal disputes and is thus partly responsible for the fragmentation of parties. It also helps to explain the emphasis laid by political leaders on questions of tactics and political strategy at the expense of doctrinal and policy matters. Loyalty to a leader is often a stronger motive than belief in his ideas (which are in any case rarely expressed within the framework of a coherent programme of government).

In Argentina the situation is further complicated by the fact that the country finds itself to some extent in a transitional phase. If political society, in which the purely personal factor plays such a major part, has suffered a succession of shocks since the fall of the Peronist regime, this is partly due to a leadership crisis from which all the political parties, with the exception of the Peronists, have suffered. The absence of leaders able to move the electorate goes a long way towards explaining the failure of the so-called ideological parties (the PDC and the Socialist and Communist Parties), and even the gradual weakening of Radicalism, which has never again found a *caudillo* with the power and appeal of Yrigoyen. By thwarting the people's need to idolize a leader, the political leadership crisis has actually accentuated the evil effects that had earlier resulted from such personal idolatry.

All this tends to show that the main obstacle to the normal functioning of a parliamentary regime in Argentina lies in the failure of the party structures to provide the forms of organization that a modern society entails. There have been hardly any effective attempts to renew or adapt them to meet these needs. As a result, the parties have witnessed their own inexorable exclusion from the decision-making process, and even from the power to question the decisions that are arrived at. Because of their inability to find a solution to the economic crisis and the problem presented by the continued existence of the Peronists, the parties gradually lost the initiative in guiding political events to extra-party forces: pressure groups, trade unions, and, above all, the Army.

The Army, despite its official protestations of being apolitical, has thus increasingly come to assume the proper role of a dominant party. Directly or indirectly, it controls and directs the operations of government, frequently imposing a brusque veto on proposed measures that it considers unacceptable. The Army's intrusion into the political arena is of relatively recent date,[19] but the frequency with which it has intervened in political affairs has accelerated in recent years.

19. 1930 (the overthrow of President Yrigoyen) marked the end of a period of Army indifference to politics which had lasted for three-quarters of a century, and the collapse of the system for electing civilian governments. Since that time, the Army has been directly instrumental in the fall of four constitutionally elected Presidents:

Generally speaking, Argentine Army coups are justified in the name of 'efficiency' [20] and 'defence of national values' of which the Army regards itself as the repository and the guarantor. After the beginning of the Cold War, the appearance of the notion of internal subversive warfare has served to stiffen military resolve in this respect.

The Army's advance to the front of the political stage has also resulted in a progressive crystallization of the opposing tendencies which had long existed within it. [21] After Frondizi's fall, two factions disputed the ascendancy: the Colorados (alternatively dubbed the 'Reds' or the 'Gorillas') and the Azules (the 'Blues' or 'Legalists'). These two tendencies had in common the fact that they were nationalist and right-wing. However, the Colorados, led by Admiral Rojas and two generals, the brothers Torranzo Montero, and with a membership recruited largely from the Navy, were convinced that civilian government was doomed to failure, and therefore wanted to set up permanent military rule to restore stability and liquidate once and for all the Peronist threat. The Azules

---

Castillo (1943), Perón (1955), Frondizi (1962) and Illía (1966). Of the seventeen Presidents between 1930 and 1971, only six were civilians, and, of these, four were not permitted to complete their term of office.

20. Inefficiency is the reproach made against most of the civilian governments overthrown by the Army; a growing tendency towards technocracy is discernible in the Army, encouraged by the fact that senior officers are often put in charge of major economic or administrative departments.

21. The appearance of conflicting groups is not new. The army first began to come into prominence and interest itself in politics from the time of Alvear's presidency (1922–8). This new interest expressed itself in the proliferation of political groupings and the creation of secret military lodges, like the General San Martin and especially the Grupo de Oficiales Unidos (the GOU, to which Perón belonged), celebrated for its part in the 1943 coup d'etat. Political differences subsequently hardened into internal rivalries between the various corps, especially between the Army and the much more conservative Navy.

(Generals Onganía, Rattenbach, Rauch and Villegas) on the other hand preached a rapid return to civilian government; they proved less intransigent towards the Peronists, and attempted to solve the problem by bolstering up the neo-Peronists at the expense of the movement's 'orthodox' sections.

It is a curious fact that the Army's progressive elimination of the political parties has taken place almost without a struggle; political leaders have of course openly condemned the military coups but the lack of anything more than a verbal reaction gives rise to a suspicion that most of them have accepted these interventions with equanimity, if not relief.

This *de facto* military government has forced the civil power and the political parties to take a back seat. Even when it does not exercise power directly, the Army arrogates to itself the right to vet government policy. In addition, senior Argentine officers have for some years shown a tendency not to content themselves with intervening in the internal affairs of their own national community, but in common with their Brazilian counterparts to try and extend their control to neighbouring countries which in their opinion are threatened by 'subversion'. It remains true, however, that the prime concern of the military and the chief motive of their intervention in politics is to settle the Peronist question once and for all. There is thus little hope for an improvement in the workings of the Argentine political system as long as political life is dominated by the antagonism of two such irreconcilable forces as the Army and the Peronists.

*

After five years of military governments it was, in 1972, still too early to tell whether lasting changes in political alignments had taken place. There were indications that there had been shifts in the relative strength, composition and ideology of several parties, notably the Peronists but also, to a lesser extent, the UCRP. But no new major organization or front emerged which did not consist of alignments of existing parties. The parties reconstituted in 1971 were for the most part those founded before 1966, and it was possible that future civilian rule would mean a return to the politics of 1955 to 1966. Continued inflation and economic difficulties made it questionable whether the Argentine revolution had had any lasting effects. Nevertheless, there were signs that antagonism between the armed forces and Peronism had moderated. The military was divided on the issue, but President Lanusse won wide support within the Army for his commitment to free elections. There remained deep suspicion of Peronism, particularly within the Navy. But the changed attitude of several officers, as well as of many previously anti-Peronist politicians, suggested that there was at least a possibility that Peronism might be allowed to participate in political life without restrictions.

1966: revised 1972

JEAN-PIERRE BERNARD

Bolivia

General Characteristics of Bolivian Political Life

Since the Chaco War of 1932–5, Bolivia has been engaged in a gradual process of national integration. In recent years she has also been directing her efforts towards economic development. This means that this vast, under-populated territory (with just over four million inhabitants) is tackling a number of problems simultaneously, some of them a legacy from the colonial era and the early independence period, others more recent in origin.

Bolivia has no access to the sea. Internal communications are poor. The population is largely rural and illiterate, living as it were on the margin of the country, earning a meagre living on lands ill-suited to agricultural development, at the edge of immense unpopulated areas. Industry is embryonic. The country's reserves of foreign exchange are obtained almost entirely from the sale of tin ore (78 per cent[1]), the production of which has steadily fallen over the past few years. The country possesses no national capital assets. Somewhat overwhelmed, perhaps, by the magnitude and urgency of the problems to be solved, the political parties large and small engage in disputes and polemics with considerable bitterness, all the more so since even on the Left personalities count for more than ideology.

1. Bolivian Government Statistics Department.

A cursory glance at the history of the country shows that the biggest political decisions are almost invariably taken by those who happen to be in possession of the means of coercion at the time – army or police, or else revolutionary militias. A kind of system of arbitration has thus been established, the need for which, though sometimes painful, is still more or less recognized by the parties themselves. However, Bolivian experience seems to indicate that this 'arbitration' creates more problems than it solves.

Towards the end of the last century the military oligarchy, allied to the large landed proprietors, was obliged to open its ranks to admit the new owners of the fortunes made in tin-mining. This 'liberal revolution' presided over the birth of the modern Bolivian state, but gave it a very limited social and political framework, since it clearly never occurred to these 'liberals' to integrate the indigenous peasant masses into the national life. By concentrating their efforts for economic progress on the production of tin ore, with the aid of English and later American capital, they in fact increased Bolivia's economic dependence, while the control of this industry and its profits was almost entirely beyond the reach of state interference. The economic strength of the big mining enterprises, with Patiño in the lead, rapidly became the source of real power behind the political throne.

The tutelage exercised by the mining oligarchy was first called in question when it became clear, at the time of the Chaco War, that the state was in fact exceedingly feeble, despite appearances, and that a Bolivian nation did not as yet exist. But the military governments which followed, either nationalist or even neo-social-revolutionary in outlook, put the still considerable strength of this oligarchy to the test. However, they were to witness and sometimes to help in the appearance of new elements on the political scene. Below the closed circle of the bourgeoisie that had sprung up in the wake of the major fortunes created by mining, a small urban middle class of relatively modest means began to appear. Aware of the new currents of political ideas, Marxism, Aprismo[2] or fascism, this new class hoped to become the successor to the oligarchy in power. It needed to compensate somehow for its numerical and economic weakness, and so helped to set up working-class political movements, which it needed as allies. At the same time, the first stirrings of the native peasantry, most of which lived in a state of near-serfdom, could be detected.

Faced with these new arrivals – or hopeful travellers, rather – the parties of the oligarchy tended to turn for support to the Army (which had reverted to its natural conservatism) to maintain structures that became increasingly fossilized as they were overtaken by reality. This was the troubled period from 1946 to 1952 known as the *sexenio*.

This hardening of the political structure masked a serious weakness. In 1951 serious difficulties arose in finding a market for tin ore. The social unrest engendered in the towns and the mining communities by growing inflation, and further heightened by a propaganda that official repression had only made more virulent, finally spread to the countryside. The combined assault was too much for the property-owning oligarchy and its foreign backers; the Bolivian *ancien régime* was brought crashing down. The revolution of 1952 brought about a profound change in the conditions of political life. The old oligarchy was thrust aside, the power of the Army was temporarily broken, the trade unions were liberated, the peasant masses were finally granted a voice in political affairs, and for a dozen years power rested in the hands of the radical nationalist petty bourgeoisie represented by the Revolutionary Nationalist Movement (MNR).

2. From the Peruvian APRA, American Popular Revolutionary Alliance – *Translator's note.*

Table of Political Parties

This table is only intended to provide a general, almost diagrammatic picture of the political parties up to 1965. The problems facing them and their development in 1966 will be considered in the third section of this essay. It goes without saying that the presentation is fairly arbitrary. The parties are grouped in major families, but this does not, of course, exclude major differences or powerful animosities between parties of the same family.

		Date founded	Leader (1965)	Characteristics
The 'traditional' right	PL	1883	E. Montes ⎫	Successor or remnant parties
	PURS	1946	E. Hertzog ⎭	of the old regime.
	PSD	1946	L. A. Siles	Group of moderate intellectuals.
The Marxist parties	PIR	1940	R. Anaya	Now shrunk to a small ideological clique
	POR	1934	G. Lora (and others)	Trotskyite party, currently divided.
	PCB	1950	M. Monje (and others)	Communist party, currently divided.
Parties of the nationalist revolution	MNR	1941	V. Paz E. (and others)	Architects of the 1952 revolution.
	PRA	1960	W. Guevara A.	Right-wing breakaway group from the MNR.
	PRIN	1964	J. Lechín O.	Left-wing breakaway group from the MNR.

		Date founded	Leader (1965)	Characteristics
'Confessional' parties[3]	FSB	1937	M. Gutiérrez	Falangist party on the model of the Spanish movement of that name.
	PDC	1954	R. di Natale	Christian Democratic.
	MPC	1964	H. Bozo A.	The 'official' party supporting the Junta.

THE PARTIES OF THE 'TRADITIONAL' RIGHT

The Partido Liberal (PL)

Formed before the turn of the century in opposition to the old conservative party, it took power at the time of the Federalist Civil War (1898). The strong personality of I. Montes at first fired the party with his own dynamism. The party marked the arrival among the ruling oligarchy of the new rich, people who had made their fortunes in tin mining, and the triumph of La Paz over the legal capital Sucre – a

3. None of these three parties, of course, is or has been subjected to Church direction, and only in the case of the PDC is the index of practising Catholics higher than that found in the MNR, the 'traditional' parties, or for that matter even the PCB in some towns. The PDC alone possesses a corpus of specifically Christian-derived political doctrines.

Today (1972) neither the PL nor the PURS has any electoral significance. The PL, which has not yet come to terms with the fact of the 1952 Revolution and its three basic reforms, is essentially a political club for the dispossessed *gente decente*. The PURS is socially less exclusive than the PL and recently has been used to advocate the advantages of military rule in Bolivia. This apart, it has no political significance.

first step towards modern urbanization. It represented a group of powerful families with a bond of common interest. Its supporters, though not numerous, were relatively influential in the civilized centres of the country: professional people, especially barristers, company executives, engineers, in short the upper echelons of the middle classes. The party moved rapidly to the right, and, retaining its alliance with the landed proprietors, on the eve of the revolution it was still able to command 5 per cent of the total vote for its candidate, Tomas Manuel de Elio. It was hard hit by the anti-oligarchic policies of the MNR, and under its present leader Eduardo Montes is now only a shadow of its former self. It still enjoys a certain amount of social prestige, but no longer has any real political power. Nonetheless since 1960 it has been able to express many of its ideas through the medium of the powerful right-wing press, *El Diario* and *Ultima Hora*. The salient features of its ideology are defence of property and of democratic freedoms, and a trenchant anti-communism.

Partido de la Unión Republicana Socialista (PURS)

The PURS is the direct descendant of the Republican Party founded in 1914. It is connected principally to land-owning and urban property interests more hostile to the Liberal Party's power than to its ideology. It was created in 1946 by the addition to its avowed republicanism of a moderate 'socialist' tendency. At the close of the experiment in nationalist government under the leadership of Villarroel, between 1943 and 1946, the PURS hoped to rally conservative and democratic opinion, and quite naturally assumed the mantle of the old oligarchic governments. It drew its support from the same sectors of society, expanded by the urban economic progress associated with overseas trade. After it came to power in the 1947 elections, the rigid right-wing policy it pursued at a time of political and economic crisis alienated not only the working classes but also the lower middle classes that were clamouring for change. Although it emerged on top in the 1951 elections, its candidate Gabriel Gosálves only obtained 30 per cent of the votes cast (official figures). Toppled violently from power in the revolution of 1952, it made a discreet come-back towards 1960, but in a state approaching that of the Liberal Party – greatly weakened and very much on the defensive. However, it would seem that some of its members have been won over to the service of the present junta in a private capacity as technical advisers.

In the absence of its chief, ex-President Enrique Hertzog, who lives in Argentina, the PURS is led by a deputy, Constantino Carrión.

Partido Social Demócrata (PSD)

This party first appeared on the political scene between 1944 and 1946 in the shape of a group of intellectuals and well-known university lecturers gathered around Roberto Arze. It represents a small sector of the urban middle class that is inclined towards moderate social reform. However, its position was quite clearly conservative when compared with that of the MNR, which utterly wiped it out between 1952 and 1960.

This sector of opinion has never yet been able to try its hand at the exercise of power. In numerical terms it is, in fact, insignificant. However, in a country like Bolivia, which is very poor in skilled manpower, the level of its members' professional training gives it a relatively important place in the political scale, in which respect it resembles the PURS.

Though only organized in the cities of La Paz and Sucre, the PSD still has some importance. It represents the reformist left of the old pre-Revolution elite and commands the support of a number of prominent Bolivian intellectuals and men of letters. It had a brief period of prominence in 1969 when, after the accidental death of General René Barrientos, a PSD member, Dr Luis Adolfo Siles Salinas, became President. His brief presidency brought the party some respect for its honesty and constitutional concern, but it convinced most observers that the party was more concerned with the legalistic problems of nineteenth-century French politics than the political problems of twentieth-century Bolivia. The PSD can be expected to support the essentially military government of President Hugo Banzer, and to exert a certain pressure, on humanitarian grounds, for a lessening of political repression.

THE MARXIST PARTIES

Partido de la Izquierda Revolucionaria (PIR)

The Party of the Revolutionary Left, an independent Marxist party founded in 1940 by the sociologist J. A. Arze, contains various groups of intellectuals from the middle and lower middle classes who had been won over by the general crisis following the Chaco War. Having won a degree of support among the miners and industrial workers between 1940 and 1946, it succeeed in gaining control of the Bolivian Workers' Trade Union Confederation. However, its power was gradually eroded by competition from the MNR under Villarroel, and the MNR's ally the Federation of Mineworkers' Unions (FSTMB).

The PIR had an extremely radical programme based on the great causes that the revolutionary left had been proclaiming ever since the Chaco crisis. Doubtless the MNR also took its inspiration from the PIR programme, though toning it down somewhat : anti-imperialism, economic independence, nationalization of the mines, agrarian reform. However, the party's actual tactics were opportunist, and it participated in or supported regimes connected with the oligarchy. It was therefore widely discredited between 1946 and 1952, the years of the *sexenio*. The younger section of the PIR clung to its radical views, and broke away from the ruling caucus in 1950 to found the Bolivian Communist Party. Then, after 1952, its trade-union officials in turn began to break away from the party and were caught up in the orbit of the MNR's revolutionary government.

Since the revolution, the PIR's support has been reduced to small groups of urban intellectuals and progressively minded petty bourgeois, and the party has led a precarious existence oscillating between temporary dissolution and resurrections that proved no less ephemeral. It is now less of a party than a group of neo-Marxist opinion with no direct links with the working class. Its ideological influence, once considerable, seems to have diminished greatly, even among students. Even so, a large proportion of works on Bolivia's political and economic problems owe their existence to the pens of onetime or current members of the 'Piristas'. Since the death of J. A. Arze in 1956 the PIR has been led by Ricardo Anaya.

The PIR won 4 per cent of the vote in the 1951 elections. In 1956, the Piristas joined electoral forces with the communists, but the two together only managed to win 1 per cent of the vote. As a working-class party, it had been completely eclipsed by the MNR.

The PIR is now (1972) reduced to a small elderly group of self-styled 'intellectual revolutionaries' who are only to be found in any number amongst the ranks of university teachers. It exerts virtually no influence on the student age group, which is apt to regard it as an essentially opportunist group. There is some evidence to support this accusation in that the PIR, or at any rate prominent members of it, have allowed themselves to be used by authoritarian military regimes as window dressing to give a spurious impression of ideological pluralism.

Partido Obrero Revolucionario (POR)

Founded in 1934, in the middle of the Chaco War, as the 'avant-garde' of the proletariat, the POR had in 1940 to detach itself from the over-personal leadership of the writer Tristan Maroff (Gustavo Navarro). It started off as a party of leading intellectuals, but these were soon outweighed by trade-union officials. The MNR had compromised itself with the Villarroel government and the POR took advantage of this in an attempt to win over J. Lechín's FSTMB (the Pulacayo programme). Persecution by the governments of the *sexenio* forced it underground and into alliance with the MNR. It won a modest victory in 1952, side by side with the MNR, hoped for a time to dominate the Bolivian Trade Union Confederation, but lost control to the MNR in 1953. Some POR trade-union leaders joined the MNR in 1954 (Edwin Moller, among others).

From this time on, two clear factions began to emerge in the party. The first was a group of intransigent ideologues gathered round Guillermo Lora, whose views were expressed in their monthly journal *Masas*. The other group, under the leadership of the party's general secretary Gonzáles Moscoso, was a trade-union wing, more moderate in its criticisms of MNR policy, that published a weekly called *Lucha Obrera*. The POR propounds the classic Trotskyist thesis of the permanent revolution working towards the establishment of a workers' and peasants' government. Its chief demands were total nationalization of land, agrarian reform which would entirely liquidate all medium and large estates, nationalization of the mines without compensation, and workers' control of factories and business concerns.

Election results show that the POR is a party of generals without an army: it won about 0.3 per cent of the vote in 1956, 0.15 per cent in 1960 and did not take part in 1964. Some intellectuals managed to win some sympathy for the party among the mining unions and some groups of peasants in the region of Cochabamba and North Potosí between 1950 and 1954. Their main function at the time was to foment revolution.

One of the most active personalities in the party was the trade-union leader Filemón Escobar, a miner.

Partido Comunista Boliviano (PCB)

This party was formed in 1950 following a breakaway by the PIR's youth sections. It was a party consisting principally of students and teachers, under the leadership of José Pereira. It gradually gained a foothold in the towns, and won some sympathy among factory workers and miners. In contrast to the PIR, it is not worried by the MNR, with which it probably has secret ties. In the 1956 elections it won 1.5 per cent of the total vote – with the support of the Pirists, it is true – and in 1960, when it stood alone, it obtained 1 per cent of the vote. In the elections of 1964, the PCB was the last party to decide on abstention in protest against the re-election of Paz Estenssoro.

The main themes of the Party's propaganda are anti-imperialism, economic development through the establishment of relations with the eastern bloc countries, support for the Cuban revolution, opposition to the dictatorships of the MNR and the junta, defence of democratic and trade-union liberties, and, currently, working-class unity.

The party machine is controlled by Mario Monje Molina, Jorge Kolle Cueto and Ramiro Otero Lugones. But this group, loyal to the Moscow line, is bitterly attacked for its authoritarian tendencies and its compromises with the ruling power by the party's hardliners, Alfredo Arratia, Raúl Ruiz González and others, who tend towards the Chinese viewpoint. The two groups reciprocally expelled one another from the party in March 1965.

THE PARTIES OF THE 1952 NATIONALIST REVOLUTION

Movimiento Nacionalista Revolucionario (MNR)

The MNR took twelve years to fight its way into power. During these twelve years, it underwent some profound transformations, and it would be useful to trace its history.

The party was set up in 1941 by a group of university lecturers and journalists, veterans of the Chaco War, around the personalities of Victor Paz Estenssoro, Hernan Siles Zuazo and Carlos Montenegro. Drawing its inspiration partly from the Peruvian APRA and influenced by European fascism, which had a number of highly active emissaries in Bolivia, the MNR declared its intention of winning power from the oligarchy, which was 'the puppet of foreign interests', for the benefit of a 'national' urban petty bourgeoisie. After the defeat of the Axis powers, it removed all traces of fascism from its ideology, and based its programme on the following principles :

– abolition of the oligarchical structures of 'feudal' society;

– anti-imperialism, economic liberation through nationalization of the three big mining companies and state control of foreign trade;

– agrarian reform, to integrate the peasant masses into the nation (the precise details of this reform were never clearly explained). However, it retained from its early years the principle, once in power, of fusing with the state the dominant mass party that it had now become.

The MNR had the good fortune to win a certain amount of support at the beginning of 1943 among the miners at the expense of the independent Marxist party, the PIR. It then used its position in the Villarroel government (1943–6) to extend its influence in the mines by founding or giving its support to trade unions, especially the Bolivian Mineworkers' Trade Union Federation, from which emerged the future miners' leader, J. Lechín Oquendo. With the oligarchy once again victorious, the MNR was persecuted and forced to organize and strengthen itself underground. Its agrarian policy became more radical. Reinforced by the support of some of the trade unions, it did not hesitate to seek allies among the Trotskyists and young Stalinists. It prepared to seize power by force. Perón's Argentina backed it, but without giving it much material assistance.

It won a major victory in the 1951 elections (probably more than 45 per cent of the 126,000 votes). But it was robbed of the fruits of this victory by the Urriolagoitia government, which shortly handed over to an 'anti-fascist' and 'anti-communist' military junta. Shortly afterwards, however, an internal revolt by the cavalry corps of the Army enabled the MNR and its working-class allies to make another attempt to overthrow the regime. This was at the beginning of 1952. Armed intervention by the miners ensured the victory of the revolution.

The MNR at that time was a party of intellectuals and young middle-class nationalists, hardened by the struggle into a truly radical force. They carried with them the small urban middle class, and were the *de facto* leaders of the labouring classes, either directly or through the medium of their left-wing allies. Yet they still had very few connections with the peasants. Following the victory of April 1952, the trade unions, which had themselves been sorely tried by the repression exercised by the previous regime, quickly reorganized around the MNR. Likewise the peasant masses, aroused from their torpor by the crash of the oligarchic regime, rallied almost spontaneously to the revolution. These were somewhat unlikely alliances, formed either with a view to conquering power or immediately after it had been won, and the actual exercise of power was gradually to dissolve them.

The MNR's left wing, under the influence of the Trotskyism of Lechín and Nuflo Chávez, seemed at first to be winning the upper hand over the moderate faction. This was the heady epoch of the revolution's great 'conquests':

17 April 1952: *Creation of the Bolivian Workers' Confederation*, the COB, whose original objective was to participate in the power of the revolution and to exercise 'workers' control' over the factories.

21 July 1952: *Universal suffrage*. The vote was granted to the illiterate masses, mostly peasants, and to women.

31 October 1952: *Nationalization of the three great mining companies* (Patiño, Aramayo and Hochschild), to be administered by a state agency, the Comibol.

2 August 1953: *Agrarian reform*, the main aim of which was to destroy the political and economic power of the large landed proprietors, and liberate at one stroke the Indian peasants from their condition of semi-slavery, rather than to promote agricultural progress.

Meanwhile the MNR grew rapidly, because it was in power and was also a party based on the support of the people. For the first time in Bolivian history, a political party extended the tentacles of authority into almost every realm of political and economic life: into the administration, state enterprises, political commissariats for supervision and control, workers' and peasants' trade unions, urban militias and militias in the mining communities and the villages. These militias were substituted for the regular armed forces, dismantled immediately after the revolution. Besides the state apparatus itself, the MNR, having quickly brought the remaining press to heel, controlled a newspaper of its own, *La Nación*, and a whole string of radio stations.

Nevertheless, internal dissensions became increasingly serious. Between 1952 and 1956 the party chairman, Paz Estenssoro, succeeded in his efforts to arbitrate between the conflicting parties. Siles Zuazo, his successor, was unable to avoid a direct confrontation with the left wing of the party.

The revolution had very soon been obliged to accept financial and economic aid from the United States. Before long the country was overtaken by galloping inflation. The economy was in a state of total disarray. The government soon found itself obliged to impose a stabilization plan, which the Americans were asked to draw up. The idea was not to allow the country to founder in 'chaos' and 'anarchy'. With the support of the party's right wing and the trade unions associated with the regime, Siles Zuazo triumphed, though not without difficulty, over the COB and the revolutionary unions, and the operation was successful. But at the head of the left-wing opposition, Juan Lechín was on the verge of revolt. Paz Estenssoro at this point made a come-back, and under his influence the party presented the team of Paz-Lechín, symbolizing the embattled revolutionary alliance, for the 1960 presidential elections. In response, the right wing of the MNR, led by Walter Guevara, broke away from the party to form the PRA, the Authentic Revolutionary Party.

Lechín's vice-presidency was not enough, in the eyes of the left wing, to compensate for the 'slowing-down' of the revolution: the progressive diminution of the COB to the simple function of an organization for collective bargaining, the division of working-class forces between the pro-government unions (e.g. the railwaymen) and those of the opposition (e.g. the miners), the rejection of loans from the eastern countries, a new code governing petroleum, and subsequently mining, opening up the country to western investment and economic planning on a pattern devised by the United States. The immediate cause of the left wing's break from the MNR was the need to put in order the management of the nationalized tin mines, which were running at a loss. During the run-up to the 1964 elections, the left wing reconstituted itself as the PRIN, under the leadership of Lechín.

Despite a highly centralized structure governed by the National Political Committee and its permanent bureau, the

MNR had permitted the development within the party itself of a whole range of organized factional groups, from the very moderate socialist sector, or the armed forces lobby, to Lechín's 'leftist' sector. The government still retained control of the NPC by means of judicious purges at moments of crisis, but it was not able to restrain local or provincial organizations, the commissariats and their own militias, from coming into occasionally violent conflict. The party began to find it increasingly difficult to maintain the balance between the authoritarian tendencies of the upper echelons and the 'democratic' representation of local interests or personalities. Moreover the departure of the small moderate faction in 1960 and the very large left-wing sector in 1964 deprived the MNR of a number of its best administrative and trade-union personnel. Over the same period, between 1952 and 1964, the top officials of the party were almost entirely replaced through the progressive elimination within the political bureaux of the architects and leaders of the revolution. The party's membership also underwent a change, with 'new rich' merchants and businessmen replacing the progressive intellectuals of the party's early days.

By 1964 only Paz Estenssoro was still able to keep in hand a complex and much criticized government apparatus, and a party greatly weakened by schisms and threatened with further dislocation. To do this, he was obliged to rely on the support of the Army. This force had quietly been building itself up again after 1956, thanks to American aid, to provide a political counter-weight to the miners' and peasants' militias. Gradually, and especially after 1961 during Paz's second presidency, it assumed a more important role on the political scene as an arbiter in conflicts where force was resorted to, particularly in the country areas, where General René Barrientos succeeded in winning some degree of popularity. As a result Paz Estenssoro chose Barrientos as his official running-mate for the 1964 elections, despite growing opposition from certain quarters in the MNR (Siles Zuazo, notably) and in the face of abstention by all other political groupings including the recently formed PRIN (J. Lechín). Paz's electoral campaign emphasized the urgent need for economic development, which entails political stability and industrial discipline. Paz Estenssoro won easily, not surprisingly, since he had no rivals for the office, and the conduct and form of the elections immediately sparked off a storm of protest from the entire opposition.

During the middle of 1964 public disturbances began to take an alarming turn : there were strikes on the left, terrorism on the right. Paz Estenssoro had to resort to force to deal with school-teachers, students, the press and the miners, which only hardened the resolve of the newly created movement against his re-election. The armed forces then decided – not without some hesitation – to supplant a party which was no longer in control of the country and assume power themselves. They claimed to have the support of all sectors of the opposition in deposing Paz and eliminating his supporters. Such was the 'revolution' of November 1964, undertaken by forces of the centre and left but led by the military, represented by General René Barrientos Ortuño and Alfredo Ovando Candía, with the assent of the Pentagon. Through its inability to preserve its own internal cohesion, the MNR had lost power.

It is very difficult to assess its current strength. What was left of the old trade-union and political officers of the party were for the most part obliged to go into exile, but persecution stopped there. Undoubtedly, a large number of peasants and a considerable proportion of the lower middle class in the towns and the industrial workers remain true to the MNR in their hearts, but not with sufficient fervour to come out into the open and give the lie to the official campaign of vilification of the fallen regime. Besides all this the MNR, deprived of Paz's immediate leadership, is faced with all the difficulties of a painful and uphill reorganization. It no longer has access to the financial resources of the state, nor the propaganda weapons it had forged for its own use while in power.

During 1965, the first steps were taken towards regrouping by a number of men such as F. Alvarez Plata, M. Díez de Medina, L. Sandoval Morón and others, who set up an emergency national command, while at local level some of the old party cells managed to reconstitute themselves. Paz Estenssoro, despite the bitterness that his name aroused and the isolation of his exile in Lima, continued to be regarded as the party's leader. Unfortunately he is more of a divisive than a uniting force. V. Andrade Uzquiano, rebelling against this sterile attachment, broke away from the national command and on his return from secret negotiations with the United States founded a faction which was to seek recognition, at the beginning of 1966 when elections were impending, both by the militant grass-roots MNR support and by the junta. In response, in order to frustrate this schismatic tendency and other personal ambitions, V. Paz and H. Siles Z. became the referees for the policies of F. Alvarez Plata's National Unified Command. But the disorientation persisted, and the junta was easily able, with the help of Andrade, to prevent this new incarnation of the MNR from growing in strength. Unless Paz and Siles are reconciled, a resurgence of the MNR seems extremely improbable. However, there does seem to be some trend towards rapprochement between them, and also with J. Lechín and the PRIN.

The MNR, if led by Victor Paz, the man known to the Indians as 'Tatu Paz', and who they believe personally gave them the land, could probably win any 'free' election by about 60 per cent of the vote. However, today (1972) the MNR has been reduced to its urban elite strata and any attempt to raise its latent mass backing would result in heavy repression. This is something that the party is psychologically unprepared to face as a result of the virtually continuous persecution since 1964.

Partido Revolucionario Auténtico (PRA) (sometimes called MNRA)

This group originated in the breakaway of the right wing of the MNR to support the candidature of its leader, W. Guevara Arze, in the 1960 elections against the re-election of V. Paz and his alliance with J. Lechín. The party received about 14 per cent of the votes, as against the MNR's 70 per cent. Initially, its support was drawn mainly from small businessmen with a stake in economic development. Anti-imperialist in word, the PRA nevertheless accepted the foreign capitalist tutelage essential to progress. It is attached to property, and critical of the grosser abuses of agrarian reform, but without ever going back on the principle. It even managed to win the support of the peasants' unions in a few areas in the early days, contrasting with the MNR's penchant for politicking and demagogy. It opposed the preponderance of the unions and 'workers' control', and claims to be simply democratic. On these grounds it vigorously opposed the bureaucratic dictatorship of the Paz-Estenssorist faction in the MNR.

This group has apparently suffered a continuous decline since its formation, partly because of the MNR's policy of harassment towards it and partly because of the growth of right-wing opposition outside the MNR. It abstained in the 1964 elections, and was decisively beaten on the occasion of Paz's third election to office. It does not have its own mouthpiece in the press. It is a party with small grass-roots support, mainly coming from the middle and lower middle classes of the provincial capitals and, to a lesser extent, La Paz. However, it has made strenuous efforts to win over the workers, and has shown that its internal structure is very highly organized.

Partido Revolucionario de la Izquierda Nacionalista (PRIN)

This party was formed by the breakaway of the 'left sector' of the MNR at the beginning of 1964, to support the presidential candidature of its leader, Juan Lechín Oquendo, against the Paz-Barrientos partnership. Together with all the opposition parties to the MNR it boycotted the elections in the end in protest against their undemocratic nature. It drew its support at the time from the majority of the trade unions, especially the miners, but some others as well – compositors, textile and petroleum workers – and the Trade Union Confederation, the COB. The party officials, trade-union leaders who had orginally been influenced by Marxism or Trotskyism, moved gradually to a more moderate position as a result of the fact that they had grown up in the shadow of the ruling party. Although the 'left sector' from which the PRIN had sprung aspired to take power, its tactics, departing somewhat from its ideology, placed increasing emphasis on trade-union claims of a strictly industrial nature : the defence of the workers' standards of living, trade-union freedom, workers' participation in management. Its anti-imperialism is in practice somewhat muted. It does not hide its sympathies with Cuba, but rejects over-close ties with the countries of the east.

Before the junta crippled the miners' opposition in May and September 1965 by sending soldiers to occupy the mines and exiling a large number of trade-union leaders, the PRIN controlled a number of local papers, and especially some popular radio stations – for the mines, Radio Catavi and Radio Huanuni, for the textile industry Radio Continental. It also controlled an armed miners' militia, which the junta has not entirely succeeded in disarming. It can also count on the active support of a number of students and young university teachers.

It is probably fairly strong in the mining areas (Catavi,

Siglo XX) and in towns with any degree of industrialization (La Paz). It suffered a severe blow in the 'restoration' of November 1964 and by the military occupation of the mines in May 1965, so the party has not really had enough time to organize itself as such. It is based principally in the trade unions, where personal ties play an important part. Its leader, Juan Lechín Oquendo, is more of a tribune of the people than a party leader, and needs to be able to work in the open to recover the working-class audience that the PRIN seems partly to have lost since its creation.

PRIN still has an important following in La Paz and more importantly in the Siglo Veinte and Catavi mining area. It is however split, and though the majority group is at present united behind Juan Lechín it would probably not hold together after his death. When this happens, and Lechín is now in his seventies, some sections might well join the MNR.

THE 'CONFESSIONAL' PARTIES

Falange Socialista Boliviana (FSB)

This political group was founded in 1937 in Chile by exiles, on the model and sharing the principles of the Spanish Falange. It did not make its formal entry on the political scene until 1964, through a series of 'anti-Communist' demonstrations organized by groups of young men of good family who had decided upon direct action. This was the expression of an economic malaise (inflation) and political weakness (oligarchic control with the aid of foreign capital) affecting the middle class and the petty bourgeoisie. The party's 'charismatic' leader until his death in 1959 was Oscar Unzaga de la Vega. The FSB had some success in the 1951 elections, when it supported the candidature of General Bilbao, a party sympathizer, winning 11 per cent of the votes cast.

When the MNR took power in 1952, the FSB naturally managed to collect around its dynamic party structure (it was organized on the basis of cells) a very large proportion of those members of the bourgeoisie who had been victims of the revolution – dispossessed landowners, professional people who had worked for the now nationalized mining companies, Army officers transferred to provincial commands – and also had some success in attracting white-collar workers and sixth-formers. The party engaged in incessant and unsuccessful conspiracies against the new regime until 1956. In that year, it won about 15 per cent of the votes cast in the election. However, it was weakened by the reconstitution of the Army around the MNR, by Unzaga's death and by competition from the PRA, so that by 1960 it only managed to gain 8 per cent of the vote.

The FSB's programme may be summarized as follows : a strong one-party state, discipline and hard work to achieve economic development, defence of property. The twin pillars of the fatherland are the Church and the Army. The party's slogan calls for 'a soldier to defend, a priest to preach, a master to teach'. Anti-Communist and anti-Castroist, the party also, paradoxically, claims to be anti-imperialist. Today, similarly, it claims to be basically democratic and 'of the left'. The FSB's present leaders are Mario Gutiérrez and Gonzalo Romero. Some differences of opinion have emerged between the two leaders on questions of tactics, but they do not seem to have compromised the party's unity, and the party structure, highly authoritarian, is also very robust.

During the summer of 1964, the FSB organized a number of guerrilla groups in the low eastern plains, no doubt to 'sound out' army opposition to Paz Estenssoro. It also believed, in November 1964, that it could gain credit by associating itself with the military junta's victory. These hopes were disappointed.

Having to all intents and purposes failed to win over the peasantry (its efforts in this direction were concentrated in the region of Cochabamba), the FSB is firmly entrenched in the towns (especially La Paz and Santa Cruz) where it is able to provide a counterweight to the strength of the MNR.

The mainstream of the party, led by Mario Gutiérrez, is at present (1972) in government operating as a civilian 'helper party' in what is essentially a military regime. Since the party's ideology coincides closely with that of the dominant rightist group in the Bolivian Army it seems likely to maintain its position for some time to come.

Partido Demócrata Cristiano (PDC) (Formerly Partido Social Cristiano, PSC)

The Christian Social Party was founded in 1954 by Remo di Natale. Around a core of university professors, it gathered a group of opinion responsive to the relatively progressive attitudes found in a small section of the bourgeoisie. The party claims to go beyond both capitalism and communism, hopes to unite employers and workers in a cooperative-style community, and is basically democratic in outlook. In the face of the abuses of power, it vigorously defends trade-union liberty. Having failed to ally itself with the other 'confessional' formations, notably the Falange, it seems to be turning towards the working class in an attempt to expand its support in that quarter, which is at the moment still rather limited. It operates an intelligent policy of training trade-union officers, both among the miners and among the peasantry. This work may, in the long run, be rewarded by mass support, when the workers tire of the demagogy of official trade unionism.

After Frei's victory in Chile, the PSC took the name Christian Democratic Party, chiefly to prevent Barrientos using it for his MPC. Party activists are drawn mainly from the student population, especially those from the new middle class. R. di Natale is the party's leader. Other important personalities in the PSC include Rafael Gumucio and Benjamín Miguel.

The Christian Democrats split in May 1970, the mainstream continuing as the PDC and the minority left-wing group renaming itself the Revolutionary Christian Democratic Party (PDCR). In July 1970 the leaders of the PDCR, who totally rejected any intermediate third position between socialism and capitalism – considering themselves Christian revolutionaries – led an abortive guerrilla campaign (Teoponte) in which some seventy men lost their lives. The remnant of the PDCR is now in exile in Chile.

The mainstream PDC continues as a reformist democratic left party which is unique in that it is the only progressive force not to have been attacked by President Banzer. It enjoys neither great support nor prospects, but is protected to some extent by its membership of ODCA – the Christian Democratic International.

Movimiento Popular Cristiano (MPC)

This party appeared late in 1964 to drum up support for the candidature of Air Marshal René Barrientos, joint president of the junta, in the elections promised for the end of the year. Led by the Commander of the Air Force H. Bozo Alcócer, it in fact consists of a number of party officials who left the MNR on the fall of Paz Estenssoro in November 1964 to join forces with the victor. Its chief aim is to polarize the great mass of floating voters in the towns and, in particular, to capture the peasant masses. In this it had some success, at least in the region around the Cochabamba valleys, where Barrientos already enjoyed real personal popularity even before the coup d'etat.

Throughout 1965 it made strenuous attempts to become the spearhead of and give political direction to the CNTC, the National Confederation of Agricultural Workers, whose leaders were J. Solis and L. Zurita. But it soon became evident that the peasant unions would only give their support to the MPC in so far as the latter represented the personality of

Barrientos, whom they looked up to as their leader. The MPC, which had entertained hopes of becoming the Bolivian agrarian party (MPCA), was forced to beat a retreat.

Will the MPC, whose whole reason for existence up till the 1966 elections was to provide an electoral vehicle for Barrientos, be able to survive and turn itself into a proper party? Its clientele, which is the same as that of the ruling group, is hardly homogeneous. Its aims and programme are identical with those of Barrientos himself: to create a national democratic union and promote economic development. The MPC therefore remains a somewhat artificial formation. It can now hardly be said to exist as its fortunes coincided with those of the late General Barrientos.

The Balance of Political Forces after the Elections Held on 3 July 1966

1. The above inventory of Bolivian parties in 1965 is by no means exhaustive. A number of more or less insignificant political groupings have been deliberately omitted, including the UDP (People's Democratic Union), led by M. Morales Davila; the ABD (Bolivian Democratic Action Party), led by T. Almaras Mendoza; and the ARU (University Revolutionary Alliance), led by J. Reyes Merida.

These groups, and others created to meet special circumstances or out of personal ambition, are destined to lead an ephemeral existence. They spring in the main from ill-defined sections of the middle class, and practically all support the junta's policies. At the other extreme of the political spectrum, there is also a number of Marxist groups with no popular support, such as the Espartaco Revolutionary Movement.

Mention should also be made of a number of civic groups, with more of a moral than a political basis; their main function is to act as stimuli to public opinion, at election times for example. The most important of these are the associations of veterans of the Chaco, which are very numerous and widely distributed. The best known are the Chaco Veterans Bloc led by Angel Telleria, and the Confederation of Chaco Veterans. It goes without saying that they are generally well disposed towards military governments which have tended to increase pensions.

2. However, even with these additions, the list does not give any clear idea of the *true political forces*. It includes parties which are often purely nominal, or else quite incapable of mobilizing on their own a fraction, however small, of public opinion; and on the other hand it leaves out institutions which, although not themselves parties, often exert a decisive influence on Bolivian political life: the trade unions and the Army, for instance.

(a) *The political strength of the peasantry* is entirely the creation of the revolution. In 1951, there were only about two hundred thousand electors, nearly all of them townsmen. By introducing universal suffrage in 1952, the MNR quintupled the number of electors; the vast majority of the peasants, or about 75 per cent of the population, now vote, despite the fact that a majority is still illiterate. Their weight is therefore decisive. The country vote today swamps that of the towns.

Between 1956 and 1964, the peasants voted for the MNR, for four main reasons:

– the peasant's gratitude towards the MNR and to 'Tata Paz', who freed him from serfdom and gave him his own land;

– a tough and oppressive pro-MNR trade-union organization, which suppressed any attempt at opposition, by force if necessary;

– the MNR's militant campaign to mobilize the peasant

masses, and intense radio propaganda, which became increasingly effective as ownership of wireless sets grew in 1959–60, especially on the High Plateau;

– finally, and perhaps most importantly, the Indian peasants' traditional submissiveness towards the established power.

All this explains why the MNR did not need to resort to violent pressure or systematic fraud, at least in the country, in order to win all the elections from 1956 to 1964 by impressive majorities. The violence practised for example in Cliza (1957–61) or in Achacachi (1959–62), two centres of peasant unrest, although not entirely transitory, was largely vicious infighting amongst *campesino caciques* seeking to maintain their fiefdoms.

A brief analysis of the 1966 elections would show that the peasants accepted on the whole the idea that General Barrientos was the heir to the revolution, and gave him the support and the votes that his personal campaign and the orders issued by the peasant unions demanded.

The National Confederation of Agricultural Workers, an umbrella organization covering departmental federations, provincial unions and local branches, is the orly trade-union organization created by the revolution that the junta has not only maintained but actively encouraged. This organization, which includes practically all Bolivian peasants, fulfils two basic functions: it acts as a hierarchical intermediary between the central power and the peasants, and it organizes the latter politically. If the current seems stronger or more intense as it flows towards the junta than in the opposite direction, the reason is that the leadership of the unions, from the provincial level up, has only produced, or has only kept in its ranks, men of mediocre ability, more interested in their own careers than in the improvement of the peasant labourer's conditions of life. The trade-union hierarchy, having failed to become the driving force for development in the countryside, now seems to have become a kind of artificial growth, an excrescence. The roots from which it draws its life seem to be less in the peasantry itself than in the power-centre on which it is dependent. Its political role has been in decline for several years, except at election time. There is a possibility that some regions might return to the MNR to escape the sterility of a corrupt officialdom; or the eventual solution to the crisis that is just beginning to develop may perhaps be the creation of a peasant party. Three groups have made tentative efforts to establish themselves, for the purposes of the 1966 elections: the NIC, the Inca Community Centre; the PIK, Kollasuyo Indians' Party; and the PIAK, Aymara and Quechua Indian Party. These names indicate a return to a pre-colonial tradition, and the more or less total exclusion of the 'whites' in the formation of a peasant organization independent of the centres of power. The peasant is 'Indian'. Under present conditions, these attempts are doomed to failure. No peasant party could set up shop in opposition to, or even outside the orbit of General Barrientos. But they do indicate a trend which might perhaps become significant if times were to change.

(b) *The non-agricultural unions* have, for their part, been placed under severe pressure during the period of junta rule, from 1964–6. Although relatively muted at the moment, they still remain one of the most dynamic forces in Bolivian politics.

Their present disorganization and disorientation are doubtless partly a hangover from the 1962–4 period, during which the MNR precipitated a number of crises and setbacks among the poorer working class. They are even more the immediate fruit of the junta's policy, which first attacked the vanguard of the Bolivian working-class movement, the miners. In an effort to streamline the big nationalized tin mines, the governing board of the mining industry, Comibol, dismissed about five thousand redundant workers in April 1965. Under the leadership of the PRIN and the forces of the left, acting through the trade unions, the mineworkers' reaction was not long in making itself felt, and immediately took a violent turn. But the junta did not hesitate in sending the Army in to take over the rebel mines. This move, effected without spilling much blood, threw the left opposition completely off balance and forced it to recognize its own impotence. The junta immediately followed up this victory, and announced the dismantling and reorganization of all trade-union organizations above factory level, at the same time deporting a large number of the more active leaders. Many were forced into exile, including Juan Lechín, leader of the PRIN and the miners. The factory workers', miners', railwaymen's and teachers' trade-union organizations were decapitated at one stroke.

(c) Before we come to the Army, it may seem strange that no consideration has been given here to the *Church*. By contrast with many Latin American countries, the Church is not a major political force in Bolivia. The Church had been fought and almost broken by successive liberal and republican governments since the beginning of the century, and had accepted the revolution of 1951, though not its excesses. It does not directly support any political party, not even the Christian Democrats, let alone the MPC. The La Paz daily paper *Presencia* represents the Church's general line, a very cautious progressivism. The clergy, which is in any case not very numerous, includes a large number of foreigners (four fifths) who are far and away the most dynamic of its members. This long political eclipse, the trend towards religious revival, and the long-standing tradition all help to make the Christian values an ideological point of reference that is fairly widely shared, for it is after all extremely vague.

(d) Reconstituted after 1956 as an integral part of the forces of the left, and sent into the Cochabamba countryside on a campaign of pacification in 1961, the *Army* there laid the foundations of a peasant alliance constructed around the person of General Barrientos. Faced with the collapse of the MNR party structure at the beginning of 1964, Paz Estenssoro found himself obliged to call on the Army's support on the eve of his third term. He placed the Army in the saddle. The military were not slow to take advantage of the situation, and in November seized the reins of power. The size of the armed forces at this time was still a modest 9,000 men, but the number quickly swelled to reach 20,000 in 1965, a highly efficient, well-armed, well-equipped force, with United States advisers. In the same period the obsolete arms of the revolutionary militias had either been seized by the authorities or had become unusable. They had rusted in their cubbyholes, or lacked ammunition. The balance of forces had tipped in favour of the Army, as the left was to learn to its cost in May 1965.

In November 1964 the Army thus changed its role of arbiter for the direct exercise of power. Apart from the outburst in May 1965, this did not result in any serious conflicts. It is true that the fall of Paz Estenssoro and the collapse of the MNR produced a sort of political vacuum which has yet to be filled. The two joint presidents of the junta, Generals Ovando and Barrientos, took advantage of this, the first to take over the effective government of the country, the second to conduct an untiring campaign, especially among the peasants, to ensure his future election to the presidency. Neither of these two men has made any open attempt to reverse the social changes that have taken place since 1952, but their actions and their programme, broadly directed towards the restructuring and development of the Bolivian economy, in effect favour the interests of the upper middle classes at least in the short term. A number of prominent figures in the old regime, exiled by the MNR, have returned; some of them once again occupy important posts in the public service or the economy. Economic progress is moreover probably slower than the rate of population growth, and dreams of Bolivian independence seem to be receding into a fantasy-world of the future.

(e) What was the political picture that emerged from *the elections held on 3 July 1966?*

These elections were at first promised for 1965, but throughout that year the junta took the agitation of the miners or alleged plots by the MNR as a pretext for asserting that public order was not sufficiently well assured to permit a truly democratic consultation of the electorate. At the end of 1965 it felt itself to be sufficiently master of the situation, lifted the state of emergency and decided that elections would take place in June, and then finally in July 1966. It thus signalled the official opening of an election campaign that had in effect started at the beginning of 1965. That was the time when General Barrientos undertook a series of tours through the provinces. He visited the most important areas in the republic as well as some of the most obscure, showing himself everywhere as the leader of the peasant movement, as head of the Army, and as joint president of the junta. Popular opinion therefore naturally regarded him as the next constitutional President. His programme, not noted for its clarity of detail, revolved around the following points: 'restoration' of the revolution, national unity over and above party differences, administrative honesty and efficiency, economic development, renewal of the inflow of foreign capital, industrial discipline and, in the field of foreign affairs, alignment with the policies of the United States.

At first the parties did their best to protest at this kind of campaign, conducted directly by the ruling power; as a result they were themselves a little slow in defining their own attitude with regard to the promised elections and to Barrientos. They thus entered the election campaign around December 1965 with a handicap, aggravated by the fact that they were extremely short of funds with which to finance it. Barrientos seems never to have had any worries of that kind. To facilitate his trips through the Andes he even had at his disposal, apart from all his official vehicles, a private helicopter, flown in direct from the United States. Apart from the men of the MPC, who were able to count on assistance from the junta, what politician was able to call on funds or vehicles other than his own, if he possessed any?

The first electoral alliance to emerge in December 1965, after a gestation period of a few months, was the Front for the Bolivian Revolution (FRB), set up around General Barrientos. It consisted of the MPC, still a largely artificial party, the peasants' trade-union organization, which was in fact to operate almost as if it were a political party, the PRA faction from the MNR, the Marxist PIR, the small middle-class PSD and a league of Chaco veterans. The cohesion of this incongruous collection rested solely on the person of Barrientos and the support he enjoyed from the junta; which was as much as to say that he was practically assured of victory.

Against this FRB front, the opposition parties attempted to form a civilian front of their own. But how to unite yesterday's mortal enemies, the MNR and PRIN on the one side and the FSB on the other? The PDC hoped for a time to hold the balance and act as arbiter between the two 'colossi', but the scheme came to nothing. Conscious of their inability to amalgamate and outclassed in mobility and funds by Barrientos's personal campaign, which in any case had a head start on them, these parties and the other small opposition groups tried to apply delaying tactics. The junta refused to put off the date of the elections. Public opinion, however, did not seem convinced that they would take place at all. No party, and no political front, succeeded in shaking the general mood of apathy. Even Barrientos, despite his triumphant tour of the countryside, gave the impression of floating in a void. It seems possible that part of the Army was reluctant to follow him in his steady march towards the plebiscite. So he stopped short. To rally the Army behind him, and to rouse an indifferent electorate, he withdrew his candidature three months before the election, at the end of March, followed by his running-mate, L. A. Siles Salinas of the PSD, who had been campaigning for the vice-presidency. The vacuum left by this manoeuvre made it imperative that Barrientos be persuaded to return, and he was soon restored to his position amid much pomp and circumstance and general rejoicing.

While this was going on, differences between the parties became more acute. Within the official front, relations between the PRA and the PSD became strained. The bone of contention was the situation of the peasants under the forthcoming legislature. Within the ranks of the opposition, the MNR failed to unite. Already divided between its old leaders, V. Paz Estenssoro and H. Siles Zuazo, placed under strain by younger aspirants such as Alvarez Plata wishing to replace them, the party was further split by the action taken by V. Andrade U., who carried yet another faction with him. The junta viewed this new split with some satisfaction; it was the only breakaway group that the electoral court authorized to stand for election under the initials MNR. At once a group of young MNR supporters, loyal to Paz Estenssoro, founded for purely electoral purposes the MRP, the Paz-Estenssorist Revolutionary Movement. The POR remained divided into two or three factions, the PC was split into two hostile camps, the PRIN was paralysed by the chaos in the trade unions and the proscription of its leader J. Lechín O., who was forced to conduct his political activities largely underground. The FLIN, the National Liberation Front, tried to rally the extreme left; it only had limited success. The PDC, the pro-Chinese faction of the PC and the PRIN decided on a boycott. But the FSB, which had previously decided on the same course, did a volte-face and decided, all of a sudden, to take part in the elections as the 'Christian Democratic

Community'. This manoeuvre, probably thought up on the spur of the moment, put the party in a favourable position. In fact the junta, abolishing the practice of the 'electoral quota' brought into disrepute by the previous regime, announced its decision that the victorious coalition would share out four fifths of the seats among its member groups, while only the immediate runner-up in terms of votes would have the right to the remaining fifth of the seats to be filled in the various provinces. At this, all the MNR groups except Andrade's and the extreme left threatened a boycott. But they did not carry public opinion with them. The die was cast, and the junta held its elections.

Before giving a figure of the election results of 3 July 1966, which are in any case not official, it would be useful to give a brief summary of the results of earlier elections.

Electoral Results of the Various Parties Between 1947 and 1966

1. *Elections held under restricted suffrage*

	Voters	Abstentions	PURS	PL and PIR
1947[4]	?	?	43,581	43,302

	Voters	Abstentions	PURS	PL	PIR	FSB	MNR	ACB[5]
1951[6]	126,123	37%	39,940	6,441	5,170	13,180	54,049	6,559

1956 General presidential and parliamentary elections. No data available on numbers of registered electors. 15 per cent

4. Source: Smith Arinez, edr, *Veinte años de revolución en Bolivia*, Lima, Raíz, 1960, p. 28.

5. ACB (Bolivian Civic Action), an ephemeral electoral alliance under the patronage of C. V. Aramayo, proprietor of a fairly powerful mining company and of the newspaper *La Razón*.

6. Source: Penalosa C. (Luis), *Historia del Movimiento Nacionalista Revolucionario*, La Paz, 1963.

2. Elections by universal suffrage

a) Before the military coup d'etat in November 1964

	Voters	FBA[7]	UCN[7]	FSB	PRA	MNR	PSC	PC	POR
1956	958,016			130,669		787,202		12,280	2,333
1958	472,377			56,952		391,537	2,950	6,911	1,994
1960	987,730			78,963	139,713	735,619		10,934	1,420
1962	1,068,512			74,734	44,291	887,534	19,825	20,494	278
1964	1,297,249	12,245	11,142	613	92	1,114,717	228	74	16

b) After the military coup d'etat of November 1964

Voters' antecedents:		PURS PL	FSB	CDC	AID	FRB	PRA MNR	MNR	MNR MRP	MNR blank votes	Far Left FLIN
	Voters–Abstentions										
1966	1,099,525 20%				11,389	137,001	677,445	88,358	60,505	63,709	33,437

7. The FBA, Bolivian Anti-Communist Front, and the UCN, National Civic Union, were short-lived electoral alliances which in 1964 attracted a certain amount of traditionalist and other right-wing support.

abstentions. Source: Corte Nacional Electoral, *Informe*, undated, duplicated.

1958 Partial parliamentary elections; three out of the nine provinces excluded from the election: Potosí, Chuquisaca and Santa Cruz. No data given on number of electors registered or abstentions. Source: Corte Nacional Electoral, *Informe anual*, La Paz, September 1958.

1960 General presidential and parliamentary elections. No data given on number of electors registered or abstentions. Source: Corte Nacional Electoral, *Informe al Honorable Congreso Nacional*, La Paz, July 1960.

1962 General parliamentary elections. No data on numbers of electors registered or abstentions. Source: Corte Electoral, *Cómputo de votos de las elecciones de 3.6.1962.*

1964 General presidential and parliamentary elections. No data given of numbers of electors registered or abstentions. Source: Comité Político Nacional Del MNR, *Bolivia, triunfo del voto universal*, 1964.

1966 General presidential and parliamentary elections. Number of registered voters not given. Source: As the official figures have not yet been published, reference has been made to *El Diario* of 17 July 1966, with the corrections published in *El Diario* for 3 August 1966 for the province of Pando.

The military coup of 4 November 1964 and the electoral campaign of 1966 brought about a profound change in the political landscape. The FRB, Front for the Bolivian Revolution, was a collection of different old and new political organizations that had joined together to promote General Barrientos's candidature: the MPC, PRA, PIR and PSD, not to mention the National Confederation of Agricultural Labourers and an ex-servicemen's organization. The MNR, on the other hand, broke up. Its votes were divided between the FRB, on the one side; and on the other side the dissident MNR faction led by V. Andrade, and the MRP, the Paz-

Estenssorist Revolutionary Movement, set up in 1966 and led by M. Diez de Medina. The blank ballot papers returned in 1966 were mainly in obedience to instructions issued by H. Siles Zuazo and the MNR Unified Command.

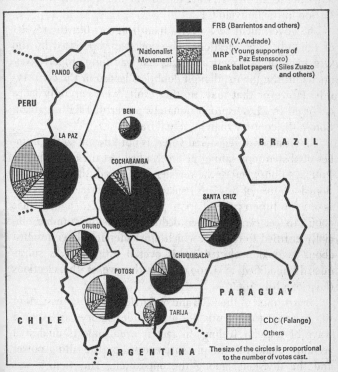

Figure 5. Results of the July 1966 Elections

On the Right, the AID (Democratic Institutionalist Alliance) is a new incarnation of the old PURS and PL. The CDC, Christian Democratic Community, was the name taken during the elections by the FSB, in combination with two temporary organizations, the ANPD, National Association of Democratic Officers, and the ADR, Revolutionary Democratic Association.

On the Left, the PSC boycotted the elections and the FLIN, led by M. Miranda Pacheco, attracted votes from the left wing of the MNR, from the PRIN and from the Moscow faction in the Bolivian CP.

The government took over a month to sort out the results of the July 1966 elections. The poll was supervised by the Organization of American States and was quite properly conducted in the towns, though doubtless less so in the countryside. However that may be, the results were certainly more distorted by the disproportionately powerful FRB organization in the country than by actual fraud.

The number of registered voters is not known, so the number of abstentions cannot be ascertained. At the beginning of June, 48 hours before the register was closed, the press mentioned a figure of 851,228 registered voters (*Presencia*, 2 June 1966). On June 15 the *Diario* reported 1,160,450, adding that about 10 per cent had been deducted from the number officially entitled to register, which must therefore have totalled about 1,300,000 electors. This overall estimate was subsequently modified to 1,200,000 on the eve of the elections (*Diario*, 3 July 1966).

The triumph of the FRB and of Barrientos – 61·6 per cent of the national total – was not a landslide victory carried on a wave of popular feeling. In fact it even appears modest if account is taken of the pressure exerted by the ruling power and the divisions among the opposition. The victory was crushing in Cochabamba, the General's personal fief, and clear in Chuquisaca, Beni and Santa Cruz, all of which were areas undergoing major transformations and which looked to the government for aid. But it was a lot less convincing in the mining areas of the High Plateau, especially Oruro, and in Tarija, an area which had despaired of help to drag it out of its isolation and backwardness. Besides this, Barrientos's votes came for the most part from rural areas. The FRB won 65·7 per cent of the votes in the provinces, but only 44·4 per cent in the provincial capitals, the only towns worthy of the name. This points to the conclusion that the person of Barrientos and the peasant union organizations did more for the success of the official front in the countryside than the MPC, the PIR, the PRA or the PSD – all groups actuated by opportunism – managed in the towns.

It may, moreover, seem arbitrary to group together the votes cast for Andrade's MNR, Díez de Medina's MRP and the blank votes recommended mainly by Siles and the Unified Command. However, it is interesting to give an overall assessment of the MNR's strength and classify the MNR electorate in a single bloc, on the hypothesis that the internal divisions, deliberately exacerbated by the junta, in fact only affect the party officers and career politicians of the movement. Looked at like this, MNR electors accounted for 25 to 30 per cent of the votes on the High Plateau and in Tarija, while in Cochabamba and the low-lying areas of the north-east the MNR was crushed, being kept down to less than 10 per cent. The MNR vote was more or less equally distributed between the towns and the country, despite a relative weakness in the rural areas of Cochabamba, Santa Cruz and Chuquisaca, where the party had been supplanted by the Barrientist peasant unions.

The CDC or Falange, on the other hand, is much stronger in the towns than in the country, and its vote was especially limited in Cochabamba and Chuquisaca, the provinces largely dominated by the Official Front. Winning 12·5 per cent of the national vote, i.e. hardly more than half that won by the MNR in all its manifestations (19·3 per cent), the CDC still managed to win the biggest share of opposition votes, owing to the divisions in the latter movement.

The AID, the new party of the traditionalist right wing, is confined to the towns, and its strength is practically negligible

(1 per cent of the national total). But the FLIN, with 3 per cent of the votes, achieved a total never before obtained by the PC or the POR, even if both are taken together. The extreme left was no doubt reinforced by votes that would have gone to the MNR, but were changed through the electors' weariness with the dissensions and prevarications of the organizations claiming membership of the Movement. The extreme left's natural territory is around the mining and industrial centres of the High Plateau.

Developments since 1967

During the interim presidency of Dr Luis Adolfo Siles Salinas in 1969, a journalist asked a prominent Bolivian politician which, in his opinion, was the strongest political party. 'The Armed Forces' was the unhesitating reply.

The primacy of the armed forces has been the key fact in Bolivian politics during the last five years, a period which has seen the constitutional presidency of General René Barrientos (1966–9), the short-lived caretaker regime of Siles Salinas (April–September 1969), the 'left nationalist' governments of General Alfredo Ovando Candía (1969–70) and General Juan Jose Torres (1970–71), and now the basically right-wing nationalist rule of Colonel Hugo Banzer Suarez (1971–   ).

The earlier part of this quinquennium was for most of the important parties at worst a period of active repression, at best a time of enforced hibernation. The Army, rebuilt in the years immediately following 1956, was used time and again to repress sections of the Indian peasantry, the principal base of the MNR, and to break up the unions – particularly the tin-miners' FSTMB (the base of Juan Lechín's PRIN) – as well as the parties of the Marxist left.

During his three-year rule, Barrientos's power rested on four main supports: the armed forces, sections of the urban business-oriented middle class, the United States embassy, and the myth of widespread Indian peasant backing. The first and last of these were cleverly used by Barrientos to counter-balance each other.

It has often been alléged that the Barrientos regime rested upon the strong support of the peasantry. In fact, though, his only real backing lay among the Quechua-speaking peasants of the Cochabamba valley (where Barrientos was born), and was not reflected elsewhere to any great extent – certainly not among the Aymaras of the Altiplano.

The sudden death of Barrientos in a helicopter crash in April 1969 changed the political scene overnight. Union and party activity that had been suppressed by Barrientos soon erupted during the honest but weak rule of Siles Salinas. The left, which had been persecuted by Barrientos and deeply humiliated by the failed guerrilla campaign of Che Guevara in 1967, began to reorganize, as did the MNR. For the first time since the army coup of November 1964, parties other than small groups of Barrientos-helpers in the FRB began to operate openly.

The rejuvenation of these atrophied political forces took place so rapidly that it soon became clear that the commander-in-chief, General Alfredo Ovando, could have little hope of winning a constitutional victory at the polls – scheduled for 1970. Consequently in September 1969, General Ovando ousted President Siles in a bloodless coup.

Once in power, Ovando organized the Acción Nacional Revolucionario (ANR), a completely new political party led by Mario Rolon Anaya. It fulfilled much the same functions as had the FRB under Barrientos. But Ovando lacked the charisma to forge the ANR into an effective political instrument, and it foundered long before his own fall in October 1970.

Under Ovando the new springtime for political parties was not to last for long. Indeed for the MNR it could hardly be said to have begun. The Ovando generation in the armed forces have a lasting dislike and distrust for the MNR as the party that tried to destroy the army as an institution. Repression of the Marxist left parties and the PDCR became necessary as these groups opposed the continual rightward drift of the Ovando regime – itself under pressure from the rightists in the Army who disliked the economic decline consequent upon Ovando's nationalization of the American petroleum firm, Gulf Oil, in 1969. These parties were not repressed because they represented a real threat – they had not had time to reorganize properly – but because failure to do so would have made an internal coup from the Army rightists more probable.

When he took power, Ovando had immense prestige within the armed forces. But the Gulf debacle and the ensuing economic crisis so dissipated his support that when he appeared to be taking a soft line over the guerrilla uprising by the Christian Democrat radicals at Teoponte, the rightists, led by General Miranda, attempted to stage a coup.

Badly planned and poorly executed, Miranda's coup was a failure. The indecisive situation allowed General Juan Jose Torres, whose support within the armed forces was far less than that of Miranda, to seize power – aided by the trade-union movement led by Juan Lechín and some units of the air force.

President Torres paid heavily for Lechín's support. An 'Asamblea Popular' was organized, theoretically representing all working-class and peasant elements in the country. In practice it was based on the tin miners organized by PRIN and the Moscow group of the Communist Party. The assembly was to function almost as an alternative government, with the declared intention of setting up a socialist republic. Had the rightists in the Army been totally defeated, the popular movement might have stood some kind of chance. In fact, the rightists had remained intact, and they became particularly concerned when the Asamblea Popular began to voice its intention of setting up a militia. It is almost a law of Latin American politics that every attempt to install a counter-balancing force weakening the Army's monopoly of arms will catalyse the most divided Army into action.

In August 1971, Colonel Hugo Banzer organized a new coup. Once it got under way there was never much hope of successful resistance. The involvement of the FSB in the coup and the subsequent government was hardly surprising. Unexpected was the participation of the MNR and the return of Victor Paz Estenssoro from his exile in Lima. His decision to join was partly a reaction to the years of continuous repression suffered by the party which encouraged opportunism, and partly a naive belief in his own political ability. He apparently felt that the MNR's political expertise would enable it to take control from within. This can now be seen to have been a serious miscalculation. The MNR is easily the weakest partner in the coalition supporting Banzer, and it has been reduced from a peasant party with a mass base to one operating exclusively at an urban elite level.

With the FSB and the MNR trapped into unequal co-operation with the armed forces, and the remaining opposition groups (PRIN, POR, PS, PDCR, and PCB (Moscow and Peking)) squabbling in their Chilean exile – where they have constituted an anti-imperialist front – the outlook for the Bolivian political parties appears dim. All this leaves the statement that the Army is Bolivia's strongest, and in a sense the only effective, party truer today than when it was first formulated.

1967: *revised 1972*

SILAS CERQUEIRA

Brazil

Introduction

Brazil is the biggest country in Latin America and the fifth
biggest in the world in area – 3,286,487 square miles. It
also has the largest population of any Latin American country: in 1964 there were almost eighty million inhabitants,
with an estimated annual growth rate of 3·4 per cent.
According to the preliminary results of the 1970 census, the
population had increased to 94·5 million inhabitants; the
growth rate had been 2·9 per cent a year in the 1960s (thus
smaller than the 3·4 per cent a year predicted earlier).

The magnitude of these basic statistics gives them a quali-
tative as well as a quantitative significance. The five geographical regions of the country – the north, the north-east, the
east, south, and centre-west – may from the economic, social
and electoral point of view be regrouped into three principal
regions: centre-north, north-east, and south.

The historical foundation of the Brazilian nation also dis-
tinguishes it from the other countries in South America,
although Brazil shares with them a number of fundamental
determining factors, notably its *latifundia* and economic dependence on foreign capital.

The single, vast colony of the Portuguese crown in
America, Brazil retained her territorial unity on gaining independence – hence the continental scale of the country. This

unity was the result of a number of objective factors: the semi-feudal monopoly ownership of land, combined with a highly commercialized exporting monoculture; the use of slave labour and the centralized state that such a social system entails; and racial inter-breeding. The political factor, however, is the decisive one. Brazil's transition to independence was peaceful – having said which, one immediately has to modify that statement and admit that the period immediately preceding independence was troubled by social conflict and uprisings. Independence was in fact a compromise, indirectly hastened by Napoleon's scheme for a continental blockade, which led to the Portuguese court's taking up temporary residence in Brazil. The first Emperor of independent Brazil was a Portuguese prince. The big landowners (sugar, cotton, livestock, coffee) and merchant exporters who dominated Brazil thus freed themselves from the Portuguese commercial monopoly, only for it to be replaced by English hegemony. The tendency to compromise, to rub off the corners, to blur contradictions, has continued into our own time. The object has always been to avoid and prevent the political participation and radicalization of the great mass of the people by means of ultra-conservative political alliances. This kind of tactical approach makes use of a myth, as the historian Honorio Rodrigues has shown, and has the same force: at the time of the last military coup d'etat, the sector of the Army that remained loyal to the President of the Republic offered no resistance to the coup 'to avoid bloodshed'.

Not only did Brazil achieve independence peacefully, it was also one of the last South American countries to become independent, the last to emancipate the slaves (1888), and the last to have a republican regime (1889). This retarded development helped to avoid fragmentation and preserve the unity of this continent-sized country. It is a factor that has left its mark on Brazilian political history, which is characterized by the 'attempt to adapt colonial modes of production to commercial capital, similarly colonial methods to capitalism, and semi-colonial methods to imperialism'.[1]

Brazilian society originally sprang from a fairly homogeneous agrarian base – the sugar-planting *latifundia*. It was shortly to branch out, with resulting economic and social contradictions often made manifest in friction between regions or states, Brazil being at that time nothing more than a 'conglomeration of areas of production'. The hegemony of sugar-planting *senhores de engenho* (north-east) was succeeded from about 1840 by that of the coffee-planting *fazendeiros* (São Paulo and Rio de Janeiro) who fought against slavery, under the protection of their English patrons. The establishment of the republic in 1889 was an expression of this internal and external alliance, and the power system was reorganized on the basis of a 'policy of the governors'. Under this system, each State was given over to its regional oligarchy of 'colonels', and the federal power was shared alternately between the candidates of the two most powerful oligarchies, São Paulo (coffee) and Minas Gerais (cattle farming).

An industrial bourgeoisie, originating from a sector of the coffee-merchant class, began to emerge during the First World War, and was strengthened by the world economic crisis of 1929, which weakened the coffee sector, centred on São Paulo. This group came to power in alliance with the cattle ranchers of Minas Gerais and Rio Grande do Sul, represented and led by Getúlio Vargas. The 1930 revolution struck a serious blow at the power of the local oligarchies, but without overthrowing them. Getúlio Vargas tried to operate a policy of industrialization and economic independence (growing state participation in economic development, creation of a national steel industry, etc.), at the same time winning for his policies and his person the support of the 'middle classes' and, despite

1. Werneck Sodre, Nelson: *Historia da burguesia brasileira*, Rio de Janeiro, Editora Civilização brasileira, 1964, p. 296.

his repression of the left wing of the labour movement, that of a large sector of the new urban working class. At the same time, Vargas attempted to play off American and German influence against that of the British.

Once the Second World War had intervened, such a policy could not long be sustained. Getúlio Vargas, who had embarked on the democratization of the regime at the end of the war, was overthrown by a coup d'etat encouraged by Adolf Berle, the United States ambassador. General Eurico Dutra was elected President of the Republic. His economic policy, in contrast to Vargas's, enabled the establishment of American economic hegemony in Brazil. When Vargas, who never lost his popularity, was re-elected President of the Republic on a free vote in 1950, he made still greater efforts to push through his earlier policy of industrialization and economic independence. It was at this time that the Brazilian nationalist movement formally came into existence, with the campaign for the nationalization of oil and the creation of Petrobras.

During this period, the forces that shared power in the Brazilian state were heterogeneous; they were principally the commercial bourgeoisie, the industrial bourgeoisie, and the big landowners. The balance of power within this coalition was unstable, and distorted by the fact of American domination. Getúlio Vargas's suicide on 24 August 1954 was a political gesture directed against the adversaries of Brazilian economic independence, and was to provide a point of reference and a dividing line in the political life of the nation. However, this should be taken merely as a pointer to the changing play of forces, since Vargas was himself a transitional figure, straddling two contradictory epochs.

The period following Vargas's second term was punctuated by numerous attempted coups; President Juscelino Kubitschek was able to continue in office from 1956 up to 1960, but President Jânio Quadros was forced to resign in 1961 and

President João Goulart was overthrown by the military coup of 1 April 1964. During those ten years, the political struggle was carried on between basically the same forces that confronted one another at the time of Vargas's suicide, although some people changed camp, and new forces, problems and points of dispute emerged, particularly in the fields of agrarian reform and foreign policy. The two camps, neither of which presented an entirely united front, were the *nacionalistas* opposed to foreign (and specifically American) economic and political domination, and the *entreguistas*, who welcomed it. This division was observable within practically all the political parties.

The government of Marshal Castelo Branco, spawned by the coup d'etat of 1 April 1964, while endeavouring *a posteriori* to build itself a reputation for moderation and to preserve for a while the exterior forms of democracy, struck a savage blow at political and trade-union liberty. All political parties were banned. A change of regime was in fact effected by the progressive installation of the juridical and institutional forms typical of a right-wing military dictatorship. Its foreign policy, its economic and financial policy of 'austerity' and 'deflation', of reliance on foreign capital, and restriction of credit, precipitated the denationalization of the Brazilian economy. This was true both of private and state-owned industry, and was made manifest by the very substantial concessions made to foreign capital, like that of the enormous iron-ore deposits of Minas Gerais to the American Hanna Mining Corporation.

Since 1930, and especially between 1950 and 1963, the Brazilian economy experienced a major industrial expansion, so that the volume and structure of the national product shifted radically in favour of industry, the value of which now exceeds that of agricultural production.

Possessed of immense natural resources, Brazil's rate of growth has been the fastest in Latin America. The overall average between 1947 and 1961 was 5·8 per cent (industrial growth : 9·6 per cent); the most impressive period was 1957 to 1961, when the rates reached 6·5 per cent and 7 per cent, with peaks of up to 9 per cent (industrial growth : 12·7 per cent). Foreign capital has adapted to this irreversible process of industrialization, and attempted to turn it to its own advantage. More devious methods of taking control have been developed; foreign investors no longer confine themselves to mineral extraction or the commercial exploitation of agricultural products, but have penetrated manufacturing and processing industries (primarily the motor industry). This was the period of the *desenvolvimentismo* under Juscelino Kubitschek's presidency : development and industrialization was preached – as it was by the nationalists – but in contrast to the latter, the idea was to rely chiefly on foreign capital for this development, so that foreign capital in fact became the principal beneficiary.

This brusque and unbalanced capitalist form of economic take-off came into collision with the archaic agrarian and social structure, with the traditional relationship of subservience to the United States, and with the political structure itself. The Brazilian parties reflect this new departure, and are only a very incomplete representation of the realities of national life.

Very powerful and influential interest groups coexist, or rather carry on a bitter struggle for mastery in Brazil's vast territories. Brazil has been called an 'archipelago of oligopolies',[2] in which the following broad groupings may be distinguished :

a) *The big landowners*, planters growing staple agricultural products for export (coffee, cocoa, sugar cane), who have an

2. Duarte Pereira, Osny, *Qué é a Constituição?*, Rio de Janeiro, Editora Civilização brasileira, 1964, pp. 78–89, 279, 317. On the part played by the other social classes, notably the working class, see below, p. 182 ff.

interest in maintaining a low level of industrial development, and are dependent on the big American monopolies controlling foreign trade.

b) *The wealthy urban and national industrial bourgeoisie,* partly connected with foreign capital but eager to free itself from this bond. Unable to compete on the international market, this group presses for moderate agrarian reform which would raise the peasants' purchasing power, although it is opposed to higher wages for urban workers. It hopes to establish commercial relations with the socialist countries.

c) *Exporters* (middle-men) and *foreign monopolists who import or produce raw materials* concerned, like the big landowners, to keep export prices down and devalue the cruzeiro (examples include the American trusts Hanna and Bethlehem Steel, who import Brazilian iron and manganese; Sanbra and Anderson Clayton, importing coffee, cotton and cocoa; and Rockefeller, who import iron and petroleum).

d) *Importers* (middle-men) and *foreign monopolists selling industrial products* (cars, electrical goods, pharmaceuticals, etc.); this group is favourable to the fairly moderate programme of reforms proposed by the Alliance for Progress, in order to increase the national purchasing power and expand the internal market. These corporations (Ford, Morgan, General Motors, etc.) have started to invest and manufacture in Brazil itself.

e) *The cattle ranchers,* a group of big landowners and members of the wealthy rural middle class. Thanks to their special situation, these people have on frequent occasions been able to act as arbiters in disputes and conflicts between other interest groups, and hence to hold power with a certain amount of popular support. They are opposed to the foreign monopolies controlling the international meat market – Armour, Swift, Anglo, Wilson – and also to the planters, since the cattlemen favour a kind of agrarian reform; they are allied to the industrial middle class on this latter point, but disagree with it to the extent that they favour a policy of increasing workers' wages, which in turn leads them to seek the support of the unions, since it is in their interest to expand the urban meat market. Getúlio Vargas, João Goulart and the latter's brother-in-law Lionel Brizzola belonged to this group.

The institutional framework is defined, or rather was defined, in the Brazilian Constitution of 18 September 1946, the result of prolonged haggling between opposing democratic and conservative forces, with national and foreign pressures coming into play. Although this constitution was the most democratic of all the Brazilian constitutions, each article that proclaimed far-reaching social and political rights was balanced by others limiting its application. As a result the programme of 'basic reforms', i.e. structural reforms, put forward by the nationalist forces and President Goulart also included constitutional amendments. For example, the clause requiring compensation in cash in advance for any expropriation effected in the course of agrarian reform was to be suppressed, the right to vote was to be extended to illiterates and all electors were to be granted equal electoral status. Curiously enough, it was the right-wing groups of *entreguistas* that had accused President Goulart of trying to abolish constitutional legality who ended up by amending and finally abolishing the Constitution and setting up the military dictatorship.

Since this study concerns Brazilian political parties which are at present banned, we shall refer here to the institutional framework as it existed between 1945 and 1964, before the coup d'etat. The situation from 1964–7 is discussed briefly on pp. 221–9 and from 1967–71 on pp. 229–35.

According to the 1946 Constitution, Brazil was a federal republic comprising twenty-two states, four territories and a federal district, Brasilia, the capital. This still reflected the old colonial division of the country into vast *capitanias* and *lati-*

fundia. The present-day states were subdivided into enormous *municípios* (parishes). Within the limits defined by the Federal Constitution of 1946, each state had its own constitution, and elected its own governor directly – this official had something of the powers of a 'president' of the state. The *municípios* were free to choose their own mayor – the *prefeito* – who was elected by popular suffrage, as were the *vereadores* (local councillors). They were also autonomous in matters of taxation and administration (i.e. under the 1946 Constitution). It is at this level, the level of the *municípios,* that the economic, social and political power of the big landowners (the 'colonels') is most keenly felt, although their national role is declining as a result of the nationwide crisis in farming.

At the apex of this structure was the federal state machine with its separation of executive, legislative and judicial powers. In fact, very great power is concentrated in the hands of the President of the Republic, elected (before the coup d'etat) for a five-year term by 'popular' suffrage on a secret and direct ballot. Federal ministers are appointed by the President of the Republic, and he sanctions, promulgates and publishes all laws; he has the right of veto, is the supreme commander of the armed forces, etc. In the case of Brazil, the supremacy of the executive power, in the person of the President, is the result of a highly complex development of the balance of forces within the unitary framework of the federation, as between centralizing and decentralizing forces. The relative simplicity and homogeneity of the Brazilian colonial economy found a political parallel in the strong unitary central power exercised by Portugal. After independence, when the diversification, conflict and unequal development of various economic interests in Brazil occurred historically on a regional basis (each region having its own dominant group or oligopoly), this diversification was expressed politically by a federal rather than a parliamentary system. Today, however, the capitalist modernization of the south of Brazil, the growing interpenetration of regional economic groups, the domination of the others by the most powerful of them (those supported from abroad), all tend to reinforce the centralizing and unitary tendency. Hence the political importance of the presidential elections.

The history of the Brazilian political parties has been powerfully conditioned by this general evolution.

In 1823, Brazil was independent, but still monarchical and highly centralized. The constituent assembly was divided into a majority – magistrates, higher Church dignitaries, aristocrats – and a minority: the lower clergy, and small rural landowners. From these two groups were later to emerge a Conservative Party, the party of the rural aristocracy, and a Liberal Party (1831), loosely connected with the urban petty bourgeoisie. In practice there was hardly any difference between the two parties, and oddly enough some of the more radical measures were taken while the Conservative Party was in power – notably the laws providing for the progressive abolition of slavery. Other, more radical, branches were to spring from the Liberal trunk: the Progressive Party (1882) and the New Liberal Party (1869) of Joaquím Nabuco, which pressed for political reforms, the improvement of the conditions of the workers, progressive emancipation of the slaves, free trade and free enterprise.

The Republican Party, a party of the urban middle class, was founded in 1870 in São Paulo. However, it played no fundamental part in the republican revolution of 1889. During the 'Old Republic', from 1889 to 1930, no political parties of national significance emerged. In reality there was only one party, operating under a variety of names in the different states: Conservative Republican Party, Liberal Republican Party, Federal Republican Party, and so on. In fact these parties were controlled by the ruling oligarchies in the great states, especially São Paulo, Minas Gerais and Rio Grande do

Sul, which, as we have seen, took turns to nominate the President of the Republic.

This system – called the 'rule of the governors' or alternatively the *politica do cafe-com-leite* (milky coffee) since the presidency went alternately to a governor of São Paulo (coffee) and of Minas Gerais or Rio Grande do Sul (dairy farming) – was founded on regionalism and *coronelismo*. The 'colonels' were big landowners promoted to this more or less honorary rank in the national guard. These men not only held all the economic power, but also practically controlled the political and legal power at municipal level, completely dominating the rural community, which was further bound to them by personal ties. *Coronelismo* resulted from the introduction of 'representative government' into this archaic social structure, which produced the *voto de cabresto* – the control by the 'colonel' of a 'herd' of electors who voted as he wished – accompanied by corruption and fraud. At state and federal level, arrangements negotiated between the local powers and the central power provided advantages and support for both. The true dominant party was the party of the land-owning class.

After the armed insurrections of the *tenentismo* (an anti-oligarchic movement led by young army officers) and the victory of the 1930 revolution which brought Getúlio Vargas into power, little had apparently changed. The new Constitution of 16 July 1934 was the result of a compromise reached with the 'colonels'. In fact, however, profound changes in the socio-economic structure brought about a distribution of power between the landed gentry and the rising bourgeoisie. Getúlio Vargas went back on an agreement signed with the landowners in 1934, repeated his coup d'etat, and on 2 December 1937 suppressed all political parties with his Order in Council No. 37[3] : Brazil was to live under the centralizing

3. The urban middle class did not favour elections, since the social structure of Brazil ensured that the results could only favour the

dictatorship of the corporatist *Estado novo* until 1945. Under Vargas, for the first time, a serious blow was struck against regionalism and *coronelismo*; industrialization and urbanization proceeded apace. The objective conditions were thus created for the renewal of Brazil's political parties, despite their prohibition, and for more participation in political life by the people.

With the end of the war in 1945 the parties were once again free to organize; the Communist Party became legal once more, other parties were set up and attempted to establish a national organization. Even though Vargas had been overthrown by a coup d'etat, his influence was still great. The new-found political equilibrium in the country was largely the result of his influence and that of the structures which he had helped to create. Two of the new-born parties attached themselves directly to him: the Social Democratic Party (PSD), a 'classic' conservative party closely bound to landed property and to the 'colonels', and the Brazilian Labour Party (PTB), a 'populist' party, urban and reformist, connected with the industrial bourgeoisie and one of the fruits of Vargas's paternalism towards the working class. The more or less anti-progressive alliance between these two currents was violently opposed by the National Democratic Union (UDN), an extreme right-wing party supported by big land-owning interests, the financial and commercial bourgeoisie, and American interests.

Proportional representation was adopted as the electoral system in 1945, and elections were held for the legislature by direct ballot and for the executive (*prefeitos*, state governors, President of the Republic) on a simple majority ballot. However, the system of representation soon became seriously dis-

---

landowning class. Vargas popularized the slogan 'the vote will not fill your belly'. The dictatorship also served to control the labour movement and repress any left-wing movements by methods derived from Mussolini.

torted by the progressive and abnormal growth within this electoral system of the phenomenon of electoral pacts; joint lists were drawn up with the sole object of sharing out the leftovers in each state, lists that bore no relation to any actual political coalition or parliamentary group.

The franchise was also appreciably restricted by the fact that illiterates were not permitted to vote, and they still accounted for about 60 per cent of the Brazilian population. So-called universal or popular suffrage in Brazil is in fact still very limited.

No party could legally register in 1945 unless it had a minimum of ten thousand electors in each of at least five states. Law 1174 of 24 July 1950 made it easier for small parties to register since it only required one elected candidate, or fifty thousand votes, and a national programme and statutes. But after the coup d'etat of 1 April 1964, a law was promulgated (15 July 1965) which laid down conditions of ineligibility, on the pretext of an electoral reform, that struck a blow at the small and medium parties, these being the most likely to provide a platform for protest movements. Under this law, such parties were automatically disbanded if they could not produce at least five members of parliament at federal level plus 5 per cent of the vote in elections.

This paper will consider the big national parties: the Social Democratic Party (PSD), the Brazilian Labour Party (PTB), the National Democratic Union (UDN), and the Brazilian Communist Party (PCB); and the smaller parties or regional parties that have played a part in the political life of the nation will also be mentioned: the Social Progressive Party, the Republican Party, the Brazilian Socialist Party, the Christian Democratic Party, the Liberationist Party, the Popular Representation Party, the Social Labour Party, the National Labour Party, the Labour Movement for Renewal and the Republican Labour Party. It should be remembered that all these parties are at present banned.

Finally, in the descriptions of the various parties which follow, reference will be made to the nationalist movement, which is of fundamental importance in political life, and to

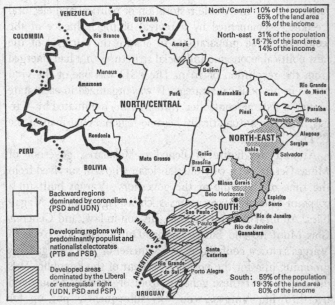

Source: Jaguaribe, H., 'Las elecciones de 1962 en el Brasil', *Desarollo económico*, January-March 1964, pp.607-30.

Figure 6. Distribution of the Major Political Groups in the 1962 Elections

organizations such as the trade unions and institutions like the Army and the Church, since they not only condition the behaviour of the parties but often, in Brazil, take the place of parties, as is currently the case.

Partido Social Democratico (PSD)

Origins and Evolution

The PSD was founded in 1944–5 by Getúlio Vargas, President of the Republic. At the end of his dictatorship Vargas, faced with the inevitable restoration of political and electoral freedom, accompanied by a revival of the influence of the 'colonels', made preparations to ensure the survival of the new political, economic and social structures that had emerged from the revolution of 1930. The PSD was one of the vital pieces in his political strategy. It was organized in each state around a federal 'controller' (*interventor*) nominated by Vargas, and who automatically became regional chairman of the PSD.

Around the figure of Benedito Valadares, governor of Minas Gerais and a wily old politician who still survived from the time of the 'rule of the governors', Vargas built up a corps of federal *interventores* such as Agamemnon Magalhães, Admiral Amaral Peixoto, his son-in-law, and Generals Gois Monteiro and Eurico Gaspar Dutra. The latter was in Vargas's closest confidence, and Minister of War. Vargas was grooming him for the post of President of the Republic. This did not prevent these generals from organizing a coup and overthrowing Vargas, who was subsequently put up for election to the legislature by the PTB in seven constituencies and by the PSD in his home state of Rio Grande do Sul. He was elected in every one, and chose the mandate of PSD senator for Rio Grande do Sul.

Class or Social Group, Party Interests

The PSD was the party of the big landed proprietors of the interior (the men of the *latifundia* and rural associations) and wealthy industrialists (in metallurgy, mechanical engineering, chemical industries, and industrial federations in Rio and São Paulo) who favoured an economic and financial policy based on export of primary products; at the same time, however, they favoured industrialization aided by the foreign monopolies and foreign investments, and based on inflation. The PSD had links with the rural *coronelismo* of the pre-1930 period, but also based itself on a kind of urban form of *coronelismo*.

Organization and Type of Party

The party was an electoral machine with a strictly oligarchical internal structure, having close ties with the administration and the state apparatus. The chief personalities and leaders of the party include Admiral Amaral Peixoto, ex-ambassador to Washington; Juscelino Kubitschek, ex-President of the Republic (1956–60) who stood again as presidential candidate before the coup, ex-'coordinator' also of the Alliance for Progress; Tancredo Neves, one-time prime minister, and ex-majority leader (PSD and PTB) in the federal parliament; and Martins Rodrigues, PSD leader in parliament.

The officials and representatives of the PSD, its local chiefs at the level of the *municípios* or the states, were primarily big landowners from the interior (the 'colonels'), professional people (lawyers, doctors, etc.) and businessmen.

The mass of the party's electoral forces, controlled by *cabos eleitorais* ('corporals' or election agents), was composed of poor or landless peasants living on the big estates as tenant farmers or share-croppers; agricultural labourers; peasants recently emigrated to the towns; and finally the lower strata of the middle classes.

The Party's National Role and the Extent of its Support

The PSD was a party with nationwide support, indeed Brazil's biggest political party in terms of numbers so far as candida-

ture in all the state elections is concerned. Of Brazil's dominant classes only the big landowners organized themselves
as a group in political parties; the parties were also used to
some extent by industrialists, but less systematically. The
PSD's influence was identical with that of the big propertied
interests and their electoral clientele. For twenty years the
PSD was the national party of the ruling class, representing
the social *status quo* and political (but not economic) conservatism.

Over this period its electoral strength tended to decline.

The PSD's results in elections to the federal legislature were
as follows: [4]

2 December 1945 : 151 deputies elected on a proportional
ballot : 42·7 per cent of the votes (2,531,944 votes out of
5,924,600); 26 senators elected by simple majority;

3 October 1950 : 112 deputies elected on a proportional
ballot : 32·7 per cent of the votes (2,501,800 votes out of
7,662,200); 30 senators elected by simple majority;

3 October 1954 : 120 deputies elected on a proportional
ballot : 33·9 per cent of the votes (3,127,200 votes out of
9,228,200); 22 senators elected by simple majority.

3 October 1958 : 115 deputies elected on a proportional
ballot : 32·3 per cent of the votes (3,653,045 votes out of
11,333,826); 22 senators elected by simple majority.

7 October 1962 : 122 deputies elected on a proportional
ballot; 22 senators elected by simple majority.

Results in presidential elections:

2 December 1945 : General Eurico Gaspar Dutra, PSD
candidate, elected with 3,251,507 votes (about 50 per cent of

4. The total number of seats (which, according to the 1946 Constitution, was based on the number of inhabitants in each state) was 286
in 1945; 304 in 1950; 326 in 1954 and 1958; and 409 in 1962.

the electoral college, which did not exceed 16·22 per cent of the population and 55 per cent of the total poll);

3 October 1950: the PSD candidate, Cristiano Machado (who got 21·5 per cent of the total poll), heavily defeated by Vargas (candidate of the PTB);

3 October 1955: the PSD candidate, Juscelino Kubitschek, elected with 3,077,000 votes, or 36 per cent of the total poll; there was an electoral pact with the PTB (João Goulart became Vice-President);

1960: the joint PSD and PTB candidate, the 'nationalist' Marshal Teixeira Lott, with 28 per cent of the poll, was beaten by Jânio Quadros (UDN + PDC, etc.); but the candidate of the PTB, João Goulart, was elected Vice-President and became President after Quadros's resignation on 25 August 1961, until the coup d'etat of 1 April 1964.

The party's activity and organization extended over the whole country. In order to define the zones where the PSD's influence was strongest, different trends within the party would need to be distinguished, elections at federal level would have to be compared with those in each state and in the municipalities, and distinctions drawn between elections to legislature and executive – the most revealing being the executive elections at federal and state level (state governorships).

The PSD was entrenched in all the rural areas, notably in the hinterland in the east and south (Bahia, Minas Gerais, Espírito Santo, Rio de Janeiro, Guanabara), the new areas of the centre west (Mato Grosso, Goias, Roudônia) and, in the south, in São Paulo, where it had an alliance with the Social Progressive Party (led by Ademar de Barros), and Rio Grande do Sul in alliance with the UDN.

Ideology and Programme

The PSD was in practice an electoral machine with the strategic objective of maintaining the social *status quo*. Tactically, it formed an alliance with the PTB at federal level, both in the executive and the legislature, although up to the coup d'etat the alliance was torn by constant and increasingly bitter wrangling in Congress, with each side concerned to squeeze the maximum advantage from the alliance and neutralize the other. In several states they were hostile opponents. Under Brazilian law all parties were obliged to submit a programme, but this did not necessarily have any real significance.

To the extent that the PSD had any ideology, it was that of the established order. Under Juscelino Kubitschek's presidency, the theme of development – the ambiguous ideology of the *desenvolvimentismo* – appeared in juxtaposition to the traditionalism of the 'colonels'. In fact the strange mixture of agricultural and industrial interests that the PSD represented, and its diverse social base (landed gentry, wealthy middle class, but also labouring peasants), made this party an ideal battleground for various opposing personalist and regionalist factions. These factions were to acquire a primarily political significance in the course of the confrontation, and inevitably led to the break-up of the PSD under the impact of structural transformations, growing industrialization and urbanization, and currents of popular opinion that demanded agrarian reform and economic independence of the North American stranglehold. The ultimate tendency of this process was to clarify the interplay of political forces in Brazil, and to lead to a greater harmony between the political parties and social realities.

After 1953, a new current appeared within the PSD, opposed to collaboration with the PTB and in favour of closer links with the UDN. This was at the time when Getúlio Vargas was assuming a more nationalist position towards the United States. Even under Eurico Gaspar Dutra's presidency, from 1946–51, the much more 'logical' alliance of PSD and UDN had been the one to work best in practice. The PSD was if anything opposed to the basic reforms put forward by its partner in the government, the PTB. Juscelino Kubitschek, who was 'presented by the Rural Labour Party' as presidential candidate in 1965, avoided committing himself on this problem, and clearly tried to act as a brake on the Goulart government to keep it on a centrist and non-nationalist course. Kubitschek hoped to go into the 1965 presidential elections as the chief rival to Carlos Lacerda. But his old ambassador and counsellor, Augusto Frederico Schmidt, the moving spirit behind the 'pan-American operation', was opposed to the alliance between Kubitschek and the PTB which had brought Kubitschek to power in 1956.

Before the coup d'etat, there had been a joint project on agrarian reform drawn up by Doutel de Andrade of the PTB and Viera de Melo of the PSD, but the PSD was hostile to the scheme. It was opposed to the creation of special tribunals empowered to short-circuit litigation arising out of the Agrarian Reform Act; it was divided on the question of paying expropriated landowners compensation in securities instead of in cash, which would require an amendment to the Constitution. Senator Moura de Andrade, one of the leaders of the PSD faction opposed to the basic reforms, had been elected Leader of the Senate by a PSD–UDN alliance, defeating the PTB candidate. In parliament, deputy José Maria Alkmin, who was to become Vice-President of the Republic after the coup d'etat, was another leader of the anti-reform element in the PSD, who were known as 'Democrats' (members of the Parliamentary Democratic Action Group) or sometimes 'Herodians'. On the other side, forty PSD deputies, known as the 'Aggressives', were advocates of an alliance with the PTB to carry through the basic reforms. They accepted the moderate formula of a 'front of support for the basic reforms' put forward by an ex-minister, Santiago Dantas, to embrace – or to take over from – the existing Parliamentary Nationalist Front in a wider alliance with a narrower programme of a few minimum reforms, to be achieved by parliamentary means. The 'Aggressive' faction had the tacit support of three PSD ministers in the Goulart government: Abelardo Jurema, Oliveira Brito and Expedito Machado. The group represented a new generation of PSD members, which had begun to press for a policy of economic independence as early as Juscelino Kubitschek's presidency, but still remained very much a minority force within the party. The majority of the PSD either helped to prepare or went along with the coup d'etat of 1 April 1964.

União Democratica National (UDN)

Origins and Development of the Party

The Democratic National Union was founded in 1945. Initially, it represented itself as an 'association' or 'front' based primarily on the Paulist Democratic Party – anti-*coronelista* and anti-*Estado Novo* – in combination with bourgeois liberals and intellectuals linked to the American ambassador Adolf Berle, plus members of ex-President Artur Bernardes's Republican Party and the moderate socialists of the Democratic left. Its leader, the Air-Force General Eduardo Gomes, who had taken part in the *tenentismo* movement, demanded the restoration of 'all power to the judiciary' – which meant the dismissal of Vargas. The UDN very soon emerged as the political instrument of American pressure against Vargas, i.e. of the forthcoming military coup. The Republican Party and the Democratic Left withdrew from this multicoloured coalition, but continued to support the UDN's presidential candidate, Eduardo Gomes, who was popular with the urban middle class. The Democratic Left later became the Brazilian Socialist Party. Initially liberal-conservative in tendency, the UDN was to move steadily to the right, and finally to the neo-fascist extreme right.

Class or Social Group, Party Interests

The UDN was also a party of wealthy landowners, like the PSD, but dominated primarily by the big commercial and financial bourgeoisie. Its interests did not lie in the growth of national production and the national market or in industrialization, but in the export of agricultural products and raw materials (e.g., coffee, cocoa, iron, manganese), chiefly to the North American market. The interests of these large-scale specialized producers, bankers, and rich merchants were therefore opposed to the interest of the industrialists. Whereas the latter supported a policy of subsidies to industry, financial protectionism and tariff barriers, the wealthy importing and exporting merchant class pressed, through the medium of the 'rural and commercial associations' of Rio de Janeiro and São Paulo, for free exchange, free rein to foreign investment, financial austerity, devaluation of the cruzeiro, and low wages. The UDN was the most faithful and loyal supporter of American interests in Brazil.

Organization and Type of Party

The UDN was born out of the Paulist Democratic Party, founded earlier by bourgeois liberals and lawyers from São Paulo, which in turn was modelled on older European counterparts. The UDN saw itself as a party independent of the state, uncompromisingly hostile to *coronelismo* and the heritage of the *Estado Novo* and the virtuous upholder of legal and electoral order.

Owing to the relatively few contradictions or conflicts between the rank and file and the leadership – in contrast to other parties – the UDN leadership could permit itself a higher degree of 'internal democracy' (a new party chairman elected every two years, for example), while party discipline in matters of voting and political action was more strict.

Of the party leaders, mention should be made of General Eduardo Gomes, twice unsuccessful candidate for the presidency of the Republic; one of the UDN's ex-chairmen is Herbert Levy, member of parliament for São Paulo; the chairman at the time of the coup d'etat was the deputy Bilac Pinto, one of the civilians most actively involved in preparing the coup; the leader of the UDN in the Federal Parliament before the coup was the deputy Pedro Aleixo; the best-known figures in the party were the banker Magalhães Pinto, governor of Minas Gerais, and Carlos Lacerda, governor of the State of Guanabara.

The UDN recruited its officials chiefly from among professional people, businessmen and the big landowners. The UDN's electoral support and membership was drawn from the upper middle class – professional people, higher civil servants – and from the urban and village petty bourgeoisie – clerical workers, small rentiers, intellectuals – haunted by the fear of economic crisis and of communism, and generally adherents of a liberal conservatism.

The Party's National Role and the Extent of its Support

The UDN was the party of systematic conservative opposition, opposed to agrarian reform and the other 'basic reforms', to export control, exchange control and restrictions on the transfer of profits, to nationalization and other measures to achieve Brazilian economic independence, and also to the policy of *desenvolvimentismo*. The UDN was a minority party exerting pressure on the PSD to break with the PTB and form a new UDN alliance. Up to the coup d'etat in 1964, the UDN played practically no part in the exercise of power.

The UDN's rural electorate was of similar composition to that of the PSD. In fact, when the PSD organization was being set up by Vargas's federal 'controllers' in league with the dominant *coronelista* oligarchy, the other, non-governmental sector of that same oligarchy was providing support for the UDN. At local and regional level, the rural electorate was shared between the UDN and the PSD, so that local alliances between the two parties were very common, and local dignitaries quite frequently switched parties.

In federal elections to the legislature the UDN's results have been as follows:

2 December 1945: 77 deputies elected on a proportional ballot: 26·6 per cent of the votes cast (1,575,375 votes out of 5,924,600); 10 senators elected by simple majority;

3 October 1950: 81 deputies elected on a proportional ballot: 24·9 per cent of the votes cast (1,909,900 votes out of 7,662,200); 13 senators elected by simple majority;

3 October 1954: 74 deputies elected on a proportional ballot: 20 per cent of the votes cast (1,884,800 votes out of 9,228,200); 13 senators elected by simple majority;

3 October 1958: 70 deputies elected on a proportional ballot: 19·9 per cent of the votes cast (2,237,608 votes out of 11,333,826); 19 senators elected by simple majority;

7 October 1962: 94 deputies elected on a proportional ballot; 15 senators elected by simple majority.

The UDN's electoral strength has perceptibly declined, for the total number of deputies in 1945 was 286, in 1950 it was 304, in 1954 and 1958 it was 326, and in 1962, 409.

In presidential elections the UDN almost always put up or supported a losing candidate:

2 December 1945: General Eduardo Gómes polled 2,259,372 votes (35 per cent); defeated;

3 October 1950: General Eduardo Gómes polled 2,342,384 votes (29·7 per cent); defeated;

3 October 1955 : General Juarez Távora polled 2,610,462 votes (30 per cent); defeated;

3 October 1960 : the UDN basically supported Jânio Quadros's successful candidature (48 per cent of the total poll); however, he was not the official candidate of any party. He won with 5,636,623 votes, but João Goulart of the PTB was elected Vice-President with 4,547,010 votes;

1965 : before the coup d'etat two party leaders disputed the UDN candidature for the presidency, Carlos Lacerda and Maghalhães Pinto, the latter the more moderate of the two; after the coup, Carlos Lacerda's candidature was finally approved, but the whole proceedings were rendered futile by the progress of the military regime, which first extended the mandate of Marshal Castelo Branco, and then imposed the candidature of General Costa e Silva. Lacerda meanwhile dissociated himself from the new regime, which he criticized with increasing bitterness.

The UDN was established in the north-east, the centre west, and the south, with strongholds in the sugar-growing region of the north-east, the state of Ceará, the extensive cattle-ranching areas of the centre west, the state of Guanabara, and the south, notably the hinterland of Santa Catarina, Paraná and Rio Grande do Sul.

The main newspaper always to support the UDN and its policies is the *Estado de São Paulo*, the aggressive mouthpiece of the São Paulo coffee magnates and one of South America's best-known journals. Its proprietor, Julio Mesquita Filho, was one of the architects of the coup d'etat, although like Carlos Lacerda he has since become highly critical of the military regime. The *Estado de São Paulo* has consistently defended the UDN viewpoint, and continues to do so; at the time of the coup it supported the candidature of the UDN leader, Carlos Lacerda. The great majority of Brazil's supposedly informative press, supported by advertising from big American firms, and practically all the country's radio networks had much the same line. The most notable examples include the extreme right-wing daily *O Globo* (Rio), the *Diários Associados* chain owned by Assis Chateaubriand, and Carlos Lacerda's own paper, the *Tribuna da imprensa* (Rio).

Ideology and Programme

The UDN ideology started as a mixture of liberal, conservative and vaguely reformist ideas, but it has followed a pattern familiar in Latin America and slid towards the extreme right, its favourite theme being anti-communism. The UDN also proclaimed a 'fight against corruption' and against 'the system', i.e. the heritage left by Getúlio Vargas (labourism, the PTB, the unions, etc.), defence of 'representative democracy', of 'God, family and property'. Carlos Lacerda had tried to win a measure of popular support by emphasizing these themes and presenting himself as an 'efficient and honest' administrator.

The UDN fully supported United States policy in Brazil. Its tactics in opposition consisted of continual harassment of the PSD; it operated a policy of blackmail designed to disrupt its enemies' alliances, or failing that to obtain political concessions. The UDN – and Carlos Lacerda in particular – were largely responsible for initiating Brazil's major political crises, brandishing the threat of a military coup whenever serious differences arose between the Brazilian government and the United States; the results were Vargas's suicide, Jânio Quadros's resignation, and finally the last coup d'etat, when the ultimate threat was finally carried out.

The UDN was divided into two factions, particularly where the choice of candidate for the presidential elections was concerned: the dominant ultra-conservative faction, to which Carlos Lacerda and Bilac Pinto, the party chairman, belonged; and a 'moderate', or 'realist' group, which wanted to put forward Magalhães Pinto, a banker and governor of the state of Minas Gerais, for the presidency (although this gentleman was not too moderate to help Carlos Lacerda organize the coup d'etat). This minority faction, given the nickname *bossa nova*, included deputies like José Carlos Guerra (Pernambuco), José Sarney (Maranhão), Ferro Costa (Pará), Seixas Doria (governor of Sergipe). The adherents to the *bossa nova* faction understood that the most intelligent and effective way to minimize the effects of the reforms and to alter their content and political significance was to upset the balance of power within the nationalist coalition by creating an alliance between UDN 'moderates', the PSD, and PTB 'conciliators'. The choice between the two factions proved such a difficult one that the UDN convention to choose the presidential candidate had to be adjourned.

Partido Trabalhista Brasileiro (PTB)

Origins and Development of the Party

The PTB was founded in 1945 by Getúlio Vargas, who remained its chairman until his death. The refurbished *coronelismo* represented by the PSD was no longer adequate to meet the needs of Brazil's new economic, social and administrative structure. The Brazilian Labour Party presented itself as the nucleus of a 'mass party' of a type hitherto unknown in Brazil, a 'populist' party. It took advantage of the prestige acquired among the recently urbanized masses by Getúlio Vargas, the social measures associated with the 'New State', and its considerable body of labour legislation. The PTB was based on a trade-union machine controlled by Ministry of Labour officials. Curiously, the foundation of the PTB by Vargas – who had also organized the PSD – drove the latter body to stage a coup d'etat. After Vargas's dismissal, *getulismo* remained a powerful force within the Brazilian trade-union movement, with which the PTB kept up strong ties. However, the PTB shortly exhibited more radical tendencies and moved towards trade-union autonomy.

Class or Social Group, Party Interests

Contradictory interests coexisted within the PTB. Whereas its social base was firmly anchored in the people, it represented the interests of various social groups, and in particular of two sections of the national bourgeoisie. The first was that of the big cattle-ranchers, to which Getúlio Vargas himself belonged, together with João Goulart and his brother-in-law Lionel Brizola (all of whom came from Rio Grande do Sul). This group's primary concern was with agrarian reform that would not affect pasture land but would raise the standard of living and the meat consumption of more than thirty million very poor peasants. For the same reason, the cattle-men were in favour of increasing the purchasing power of the urban working class. The other national middle-class group represented by the PTB was that of the industrialists forced to accept association with foreign monopolies and interest groups, but opposed to the concentration that the latter wished to impose; they were in favour of limited nationalization, and also hoped for agrarian reform to increase purchasing power on the national market, but opposed any increase in urban wages. A small section of the petty bourgeoisie (students, intellectuals, low-ranking army officers) also supported the PTB. Since they wielded no economic power, they hoped to ensure the hegemony of the mass movement through propaganda and political agitation, relying on the nationalist slogans to which they were themselves responsive. These groups were thus all concerned to defend Brazilian economic independence against penetration by the United States, to establish trade relations with the socialist countries and to introduce 'basic reforms'.

It goes without saying that not all the PTB's members of parliament were nationalists. Given the diversity of political shadings in each of the Brazilian parties and the different local alliances they set up from state to state, the Parliamentary Nationalist Front consisted of parliamentarians of all parties (principally the Labour Party and the Social Democratic Party, but some from the UDN, the PDC, and others as well). Likewise, the Parliamentary Democratic Action group – a parliamentary coalition of right-wing deputies or *entreguistas* – also included members of all parties. Political thought and action in Brazil was polarized between these two major currents: nationalist and *entreguista*.

Organization and Type of Party

The PTB was a party of the populist type, with close ties with the trade-union world and drawing its support principally from the towns.

The chief leaders of the PTB were Getúlio Vargas (who remained chairman of the party until his suicide on 24 August 1954), João Goulart, who succeeded him (also a big cattleman, a disciple of Vargas, he came into politics via trade unionism), Doutel de Andrade, PTB leader in the Federal Parliament, and Artur Virgillio, PTB leader in the Senate.

Of the party's other leading figures, mention should be made of Francisco Santiago Dantas, ex-Minister of Foreign Affairs and of Finance; Lionel Brizola, a deputy, one-time governor of Rio Grande do Sul, also a cattleman and brother-in-law to President Goulart; Almino Afonso, a deputy, ex-leader of the PTB parliamentary party, ex-Minister of Labour; and finally, Pasqualini, the party's leading theorist.

The PTB's party officers and politicians were mostly drawn from a bourgeois elite (businessmen and big landowners) allied to trade unionists, one-time leaders of student movements, and civil servants. Most of the party's militants were master craftsmen, white-collar workers, small shop-keepers and students; there were very few manual workers among them.

The PTB's electoral support was basically urban, and consisted chiefly of recently urbanized proletarians of rural origin.

The Party's National Role and the Extent of its Support

Although the PTB was a national party, its support in the countryside was weak; its development and the increase of its electoral strength accompanied the urbanization of the country.[5]

In the Vargas government of 1951, the PTB only had one minister; in the government formed on 20 June 1963 it had four – more than any other party.

Calling itself a party of the left, it opposed the conservative parties (the UDN and the PR) while at the same time allying itself with a centre party that was just as conservative, the PSD. It acted largely as a force for conciliation, but over the years it gradually became a nationalist and 'ideological' party – though still retaining its original weak structure. The first phase of this transformation of the PTB occurred during Vargas's presidency (1950–54) under the influence of the popular nationalist movement, which led to the creation of the state petroleum monopoly in 1953. The second phase, which took place under the presidency of Goulart, comprised the campaign for 'basic reforms' and reform of the Constitution. The growing participation of the urban

5. The population of the state capitals rose from 5·8 million inhabitants in 1940 to 8 million in 1950 and to 13 million in 1960. The total urban population in 1964 was 40 million. By 1970 the population of the state capitals had risen to 20·5 million, and the total urban population was 52·9 million or 56 per cent of the entire population.

and even the rural masses in these political and social conflicts forced the PTB to evolve; however, it was still far from becoming a progressive and coherent party of the masses.

In federal elections to the legislature, a steady increase in the percentage of votes won by the PTB and in the number of deputies representing it in Parliament may be observed:

2 December 1945: 23 deputies elected on a proportional ballot: 10.2 per cent of the votes cast (603,500 votes out of 5,924,600); 2 senators elected by simple majority;

3 October 1950: 51 deputies elected on a proportional ballot: 18.1 per cent of the votes cast (1,389,300 votes out of 7,662,200); 5 senators elected by simple majority;

3 October 1954: 56 deputies elected on a proportional ballot: 19.5 per cent of the votes cast (1,799,600 votes out of 9,228,200); 18 senators elected by simple majority;

3 October 1958: 66 deputies elected on a proportional ballot: 19.8 per cent of the votes cast (2,237,608 votes out of 11,333,826);

7 October 1962: 109 deputies elected on a proportional ballot; 17 senators elected by simple majority.

In presidential elections the PTB has almost always supported the candidature of the eventual winner:

2 December 1945: the PTB supported the candidature of General Eurico Gaspar Dutra, the PSD candidate, who was elected with 3,251,507 votes;

3 October 1950: Getúlio Vargas, the PSP and PTB candidate, was elected with 3,849,040 votes (44 per cent[6] of the total cast); vice-president was João Café Filho, the candidate of Ademar de Barros's Social Progressive Party, elected with 2,520,790 votes;

6. Vargas secured 48.7 per cent according to Skidmore, T. E., *Politics in Brazil, 1930–64: An Experiment in Democracy*, Oxford University Press, 1968.

3 October 1955 : the PTB presented a vice-presidential candidate of its own, João Goulart, standing as the running-mate of the PSD's presidential candidate (Kubitschek); both were elected;

3 October 1960: the PTB put up a vice-presidential candidate, João Goulart, as running-mate of the PSD's presidential candidate General Teixeira Lott; Goulart was elected vice-president, but Lott was defeated; Jânio Quadros was elected President. When he resigned on 25 August 1961, Goulart became President (the last before the coup d'etat).

The PTB recruited its members chiefly in the coastal towns of the north east – Pernambuco – and the centre east – Rio de Janeiro, Guanabara, and to some extent Bahia and Minas Gerais.

The PTB possessed no daily paper of its own. It was supported in a general fashion by *Ultima Hora*, a daily sensationalist paper with a very large circulation (200,000 copies), which had its headquarters in Rio, regional offices in Brasilia, São Paulo, Curitiba, Santos, Campinas, Rio Grande do Sul, Minas Gerais, and produced a special edition for the north east at Recife. The paper was nationalist in general line, and received financial support from João Goulart.

It is worth mentioning two other nationalist newspapers, weeklies and both independent but relatively favourable to the PTB: *O Semanário* and *Política e negócios*, both published in Rio. There was also one solitary nationalist radio station, the station of Mayrink Veiga, which was not directly connected with the PTB, but belonged to the Labour deputy, Leonel Brizzola.

Ideology and Party Programme

A number of different components may be distinguished in the PTB's ideology: there is a 'social', pro-labour strand, going back to Vargas's dictatorship before the PTB was founded; a nationalist strand which became prominent during Vargas's second presidency after 1950, based on a true mass movement for the public ownership of the oil wells, *o petróleo é nosso*; a strand of *desenvolvimentismo* which regarded industrialization with the aid of foreign investment as the miracle drug that would cure all Brazil's economic disorders (this trend came to the fore during Juscelino Kubitschek's presidency); and finally a 'reformist' strand, manifested in the campaign for the 'basic reforms' programme.

The reform programme put forward by João Goulart was intended to ensure a degree of development in Brazil that would benefit the national bourgeoisie and could be controlled by them, using the mass of urban and agricultural workers as the spearhead of the struggle against the big landed proprietors and American interests. This was a complex strategy, for all the interests represented by the PTB were at once interlinked and contradictory. The party therefore adopted tactics which oscillated between conciliation of these conflicting interests and a direct demagogic appeal to the masses.

Correspondingly, there were at least three factions in the PTB. These factions disagreed, for example, on the type of agrarian reform that should be carried out (with or without cash compensation, which would require an amendment to the Constitution), or on the forms of action the party should engage in or the alliances it should make. The left-wing tendency represented by Leonel Brizzola hoped to win political supremacy for the mass movement, claiming to be socialist or even 'Marxist', calling for violent revolution on the Cuban pattern and rejecting alliances such as that proposed by Santiago Dantas (the Parliamentary Front for support of the basic reforms), and criticizing the indecision of João Goulart. Goulart's own faction, the 'unconditionals' such as Doutel de Andrade, represented the majority of the party : their tactics were to manoeuvre their members into key posts in the government and administration, and to pursue the mirage of the 'basic reforms' without coming into violent conflict with foreign interests and the big landowners. A further faction consisting of intellectuals sympathetic to Marxism, such as Almino Afonso (variously known as the 'compact group' and the 'ideological group') criticized both Goulart's indecisiveness and Brizola's extremism, preaching instead mass action as a means of exerting pressure to get the reforms accepted.

'Labourism' and the Trade-union Movement

Since 'labourism' has become a key word in the Brazilian political vocabulary since the rule of Getúlio Vargas, a brief mention should be made of the Brazilian trade-union movement, which has participated in the political struggle much more directly than the European trade unions.

It should be pointed out that this reference to Brazilian trade-unionism is included in the section on the PTB merely for the sake of convenience, and that there are other currents than that represented by the Labour Party in the Brazilian trade-union movement. These other influences and other currents that have grown up in the working-class and trade-union movement include, principally, that of the Communist Party, and the influence of the Church has been almost as strong.

Getúlio Vargas created a trade-union movement controlled by the state, with a large bureaucracy wielding considerable funds from trade-union levies and social insurance contributions. In 1946, a unified trade-union confederation, the CTB, came into being, in which the Communists played a dominant role; it was banned in 1947. Until the coup d'etat, and even more so after it, the establishment of a national trade-union congress continued to be forbidden; each union had to obtain individual recognition from the authorities, and the only federations or confederations permitted were between unions in the same trades. In 1945 there were more than eight hundred recognized trade unions. In 1959 the number was 1,578 – including white-collar as well as blue-collar unions – with about 1,300,000 members. Trade-union membership steadily increased until 1964.

The ban on these unions' uniting at national level into a single confederation slowed down the development of the trade-union movement and favoured the proliferation of sects and factions. The unions therefore tried – before the coup d'etat, that is – to create special bodies to organize and maintain alliances between the leadership of each individual union. Examples include the Inter-Union Alliance, the Pact for Unity of Action, the CGT (Comando Geral dos Trabalhadores), run by well-known trade unionists such as Clodsmith Riani, Oswaldò Pacheco, Dante Pelacani, Hercules Correia, which was well on the way to becoming a veritable unified national trade-union confederation. These bodies had the drawback that they remained summit organizations, whose policy guidelines might or might not be followed depending on the occasion, since they did not possess a horizontal organization to see that they were applied.

Industrial strikes were very frequent in Brazil, and often crowned with success, especially in the public sector.[7] The trade unions had long since begun to intervene in political life, and played an increasing part in this respect by means of political strikes such as that called in September 1954, after Getúlio Vargas's suicide. The unions also intervened in October–November 1955, during the Kubitschek investiture crisis, and finally called a well-supported general strike after the resignation of Jãnio Quadros, to ensure that legal proce-

7. In São Paulo in 1960, 254,215 workers lost 3,252,069 hours in strikes; in 1961, 150,891 workers lost 3,067,474 hours.

dure was respected and that João Goulart succceded to the presidency.

Under the latter's presidency, since he had himself made his career in the unions and had been Minister of Labour, the trade unions were called upon from time to time to attend meetings with ministers, or even with the President himself; they were asked to collaborate, and to support government policies, which gave them certain advantages, but was also liable to limit their independence. The trade unions' reaction to João Goulart's policies differed according to which faction of the trade-union movement they belonged to: the *pelegos*, unionists connected with the Ministry of Labour since the time of Getúlio Vargas, controlled a few unions, but their influence and numbers were in decline; the strongest and best organized group was that influenced by communism and by the nationalist movement; the 'Movement for Trade Union Renewal', representing a move to launch a Christian or American style of trade unionism of the so-called 'modern', apolitical type, effectively played the UDN's game.

It took many long years before there was any effective agricultural trade union movement to mobilize the vast peasant masses, who were apparently passive.[8] The famous 'labour laws' introduced by Getúlio Vargas in 1943, guaranteeing a minimum wage, social security, etc., were not applied in the countryside until 1963 with the Rural Workers Act. However, under the influence of the communists and other

8. In 1960 the rural population still represented 55 per cent of the total population, or 39 millions, of which 18 millions were in active employment. Of these 18 million, 3 million were landowners – ranging from big landowners to small independent farmers – and the remaining 15 million were landless peasants (small-holders, tenant farmers, share-croppers) and agricultural labourers. The preliminary results of the 1970 census showed that for the first time the urban population superseded the rural one, the latter being 41·6 million, or 44 per cent of the total.

left-wing militants, an agricultural trade-union movement was created after the war: the ULTAB (União dos Lavradores e Trabalhadores Agrícolas do Brasil), rooted chiefly in the states of São Paulo and Rio de Janeiro, and the Peasant Leagues in the state of Recife between 1945 and 1947. The peasant movement and agricultural trade unionism did not really play a very important part in Brazilian political and social life until 1955, and even then they were still numerically weak. The Peasant League movement was revived in the north-east in that year, composed of small landless peasants rather than agricultural wage-earners, and led by the barrister Francisco Julião, later to become a socialist deputy. This movement extended from Pernambuco to Paraíba and Ceará, but was for the most part confined within the frontiers of the north-east, to the region of Agreste, between the coast and the *sertão*. Limited as it was, it nevertheless revived widespread interest in agricultural trade unionism on the part of the Communist Party and the ULTAB, on the part of the industrial unions connected with agriculture (meat packing, sugar refining, dairy products, foodstuffs), and also on the part of the Church.

The promulgation of the Rural Workers Statute in 1963, and the granting – before the coup – of the Ministry of Labour to a Christian Democrat, Franco Montoro, facilitated the organization of numerous Catholic unions of small peasants and landless labourers. Sometimes young priests would assume the leadership of peasant movements and themselves organize takeovers of land, in order to combat the influence of the communists and of Francisco Julião.

Between 1961 and 1964 the number of officially recognized agricultural workers' unions rose from six to more than five hundred. Despite its manifest weakness, the youthful peasant movement – both leagues and unions – caused the big landowners profound disquiet.

Partido Comunista Brasileiro (PCB)

Origins and Development of the Party

The PCB grew out of the major working-class upheavals and strikes that shook Brazil between 1917 and 1920, and under the influence of the Russian revolution of October 1917. The combination of these two factors resulted in the appearance of small local communist groups, and in the signs of sympathy shown for the communist or 'maximalist' ideology by a number of well-known intellectuals, such as the writer Lima Barreto. In Brazil, the Communist Party was not an offshoot of one of the pre-existing socialist parties, as in other parts of Latin America and in Europe, but resulted from a split in the anarcho-syndicalist movement which dominated the Brazilian labour movement from 1906 to 1920. In 1921 the chief anarcho-syndicalist leaders went over to communism, and the first Congress of the Brazilian Communist Party was held from 25 to 27 March 1922, at which it was agreed to accept the twenty-one conditions of entry to the Communist International. The founders were for the most part workers and intellectuals, one of whom, Astrojildo Pereira, was elected General Secretary, a position he retained until 1929. Shortly afterwards a state of emergency was declared in the country because of the increasing social unrest and a number of attempted coups, and the PC was outlawed.[9]

This was to be a more or less permanent feature of its existence: the party was clandestine from 1922 to 1926; legalized in 1927 and banned once more the same year, although using the Workers' and Peasants' Front as an electoral vehicle from 1927 to 1930; subjected to the most severe police persecution after the crushed insurrection of 1935 and

9. Linhares, Herminio: 'O comunismo no Brasil', *Revista brasiliense* 25, Sept.–Oct. 1959, pp. 146–66; 26, Nov.–Dec. 1959, pp. 178–97; 28, March–Apr. 1960, pp. 122–42.

the Vargas coup (1937), but returning to legality, still under Vargas, towards the end of the Second World War; forced underground once again under Dutra's presidency (1947–50); tolerated though still illegal under Vargas's second presidency (1950–54), and similarly under the presidency of Kubitschek; and finally operating almost in the open under the presidency of Goulart. The Communist Party was hoping to be legalized at last when the coup of 1 April 1964 intervened and drove it underground once more. The banning of a political party does not always have the same significance in Brazil as in Europe or elsewhere, particularly where the freedom of the press is concerned. It has, for instance, not prevented the Communist Party from continuing to publish its newspapers and journals. The chief among these were the weeklies *A Classe operária* (1925–49), *A Voz operária* (1949–59) and *Novos rumos* (from 1959 to the coup), and the dailies *Tribuna popular* (1945–8) and *Imprensa popular* (1948–58), and finally the theoretical monthly journals *Problemas* (1947–56) and *Estudos sociais* (1958–64).

The PCB was accepted into membership of the Communist International in 1924; in 1925 the Communist Youth Federation was founded. The party's second congress was held in the same year; the year 1928 witnessed the party's third congress and the foundation of the Brazilian General Confederation of Labour. The party's first national conference was held in 1934, but the second did not take place until 1943, with the election of a Central Committee including Luis Carlos Prestes (then in prison). The fourth party congress was not held until 1954, twenty-six years after the third, and the fifth and last took place in August 1960.

Class or Social Group, Party Interests

At the time the Communist Party was founded, Brazil was a country with a semi-colonial structure. It did not have more than three hundred thousand industrial workers, the main nucleus of which consisted of workers of European origin (Italian, Spanish, Portuguese) and with artisan backgrounds, which helps to account for the strength of anarcho-syndicalist ideas among them. The 1922 founding fathers of the party did not number more than a dozen; in 1928 the party had about five hundred active members, in 1930 more than a thousand; by 1945, at the end of the war, it counted tens of thousands of party members and sympathizers.

Until 1930 the PCB was a small and motley group, composed largely of intellectuals and students from the petty bourgeoisie or skilled working classes. After that date, and especially after 1944–5, it tended increasingly to become, if not a 'mass' party, at least one with a somewhat broader base than before; it became working class in composition and outlook, began to exert considerable influence in the trade-union world, etc. However, even today the party has not succeeded in becoming entirely identified with the working class. The Brazilian working class itself is still growing rapidly;[10] its internal structure is undergoing violent change, and it includes large unstable elements only recently urbanized that tend to be more attracted by a party of the 'populist' type like the Labour Party. Moreover the PCB leadership is to this day for the most part drawn from the intellectual petty bourgeoisie; and, finally, the party's integration in the nationalist movement sometimes tends to blur the distinction between this supposedly working-class party and other nationalist trends of bourgeois origin.

10. In 1964 Brazil had 3,800,000 urban workers, mostly of recent peasant stock and often moved by non-working-class interests. In 1970, the census recorded 5,263,805 industrial workers, or 7·97 per cent of persons ten years old and over, as compared to 2,963,160 in 1960, or 6·08 per cent of persons of ten and over.

Organization, Type of Party

While the Social Democratic Party is Brazil's most powerful political unit electorally, from the point of view of organization the PCB is the only truly national party in Brazil. This does not mean that its support extends over the whole of Brazilian territory, but that it is the only party to view itself as a national party, organized on a national scale, independent of regional rivalry and patronage. On the other hand, compared to the European Communist Parties and even to some Latin American communist parties (notably the Chilean one), the PCB's organization is strongly conditioned by Brazil's social structure and environment: the organization is based on localities, rather than on trades or economic conditions (shop-floor party cells, for example), and regular political business is confined chiefly to the management committees in the big towns and the central committee. It is said in Brazil that the life of the political parties is confined to the *cúpulas* (the summit of each organization). The PCB does not entirely escape this charge. Its organizational weakness was exposed at the time of the coup d'etat on 1 April 1964, to which it was unable to offer any organized resistance when the crunch came. Likewise in 1947–8, the Dutra government had outlawed the party and cancelled the mandates of its representatives in Parliament without meeting any organized resistance, despite the fact that in two years of legal activity the party had grown from 4,000 to 200,000 members.

Astrojildo Pereira was one of the party's founders, one of its leading theoreticians and its first General Secretary. The best-known of its leaders is Luis Carlos Prestes, party General Secretary since 1945. He was in many ways Fidel Castro's spiritual forerunner,[11] and their political careers follow a similar pattern, with suitable variations. Three phases may be distinguished in this political journey. Prestes started his

11. Linhares, Herminio, loc. cit.

career as a young officer of liberal education and joined the *tenentista* movement, a reformist and anti-oligarchic movement of the petty bourgeoisie which was to provide a considerable proportion of the dramatis personae of Brazilian politics for the next thirty years; he took part in the revolt of 1924, and at the head of his 'invincible column' started off on his own 'long march' across the *sertão*. In the second phase, he established himself in the eyes of the people, especially the urban middle class and the peasantry, as a legendary knight-errant. Prestes developed politically, became a radical agrarian revolutionary, anti-latifundiarist and anti-imperialist; towards the end of 1926 he was forced to seek refuge with the remnants of his column in Bolivia; later he left for the Argentine. His prestige grew, to extend eventually over the whole continent. He witheld his support from Getúlio Vargas's revolution of 1930, considering it too moderate, and tried to launch a radical left-wing movement, the League for Revolutionary Action, relying on Communist support which was denied him. Phase three: after an exchange of polemics and a period of negotiation with the PCB, Prestes repudiated *prestismo* as a 'petty-bourgeois and nationalist political viewpoint', and went over to the communists. In 1931 he left for the USSR as an engineer; in 1934 he became an official member of the Brazilian Communist Party, and in 1935 a member of the Central Committee and the Politbureau. In the same year he led the National Liberation Alliance – a popular antifascist, anti-latifundiarist and anti-imperialist front – and organized an insurrection against Vargas, which failed. He was arrested in 1936 and not released until 1945. Hardly was he out of prison than Prestes was elected General Secretary of the party, and representative for the State of Rio de Janeiro in the Senate and the Constituent Assembly. In 1948 he was forced to go into hiding, and did not reappear publicly until 1958, only to return once more into hiding after the coup of 1 April 1964.

During the periods of underground activity, the party's authoritarian methods of leadership soon made themselves felt. The readjustments following the twentieth congress of the CPSU and Prestes's return to legality did not take place without upheavals within the PCB: in 1956–7, after a period of very heated debate, the party's treasurer, Agildo Barata, led a right-wing breakaway group, and around 1958–60 a left-wing split was engineered by Diogenes Arruda, Mauricio Grabois and João Amazonas, all ex-members of the central committee, who in 1962 founded the Communist Party of Brazil, a small pro-Chinese group with little real influence. These splits could hardly fail to weaken the party, even though it increased its influence over the young and the student population, especially in trade-union circles and in the major working-class centres.

The middle ranks of the party hierarchy, often of petty bourgeois origins, are recruited chiefly from among trade unionists and student militants. The militants and the great mass of the party's electors come from the proletariat in the industrialized and highly developed areas. Before being outlawed in 1947, the PCB won more than 500,000 votes in the 1945 presidential elections, including 192,867 votes from the state of São Paulo and 134,709 from Rio de Janeiro. Because of the role played by the PCB in the nationalist movement, it has been able to enlarge its base to include some sections of the urban petty bourgeoisie (mainly intellectuals and students), the rural proletariat and the poorer peasants.

The Party's National Role and the Extent of its Support

Of Brazil's five principal parties, the Communist Party is far and away the oldest, and the only one to survive the dictatorship of the *Estado Novo*, or indeed the present one. The other parties, created in 1945, have already disappeared as formal organizations.

Despite the clandestine existence to which it has been condemned, and which appreciably reduces the number of its members, the PCB has acquired a degree of influence and prestige which belies its numerical weakness. This has been largely thanks to its progressive political programme, modern organization, and the possession of a true band of militants, in the proper sense of the word. Its influence in the trade-union world is very strong. It has been directly or indirectly responsible for initiating most of the major campaigns that have troubled the surface of Brazilian politics from time to time – creation of a national steel industry, agrarian reform, nationalization of oil. It is a debatable point whether it has always been able to maintain its autonomy and stand by its own principles, or even assert its dominance, in these campaigns, or whether its influence, by expanding its field of operations, has become dissipated over the nationalist movement as a whole.

The results of elections can only give a very partial indication of the PCB's influence, since it has very rarely taken part in elections, at least not under its own colours. On emerging from clandestinity, it took fourth place in the federal parliamentary elections on 14 October 1945, out of twelve parties represented in Congress, sending fourteen deputies and one senator to Parliament. In the elections to the state assemblies, held in January 1947, it had forty-six deputies elected, and eighteen councillors on the municipal assembly of the federal district. These successes made the ruling classes nervous, and they had the party banned on 7 May 1947, and cancelled the mandates of its deputies on 7 January 1948. Since then, the PCB has never entirely returned to legality, but known communists have managed to get themselves elected to city councils, state parliaments and the Federal Parliament under different party labels. The other parties made strenuous efforts to win communist votes, especially the PTB, with which the PCB tried to conclude preferential alliances at national level. However, at state and local level the PCB sometimes found incongruous allies – the PSD, the UDN, and once even Ademar de Barros in São Paulo, among others.

In the presidential elections of 2 December 1945, the PCB presented its candidate for the presidency of the republic a little in advance of the other parties; he was Iedo Fiuzza, a non-communist public figure, who succeeded in winning 568,818 votes, or 10 per cent of the votes cast. In the 1950 elections, the PCB supported Getúlio Vargas (elected), in 1955 Juscelino Kubitschek (elected), in 1960 Marshal Teixeira Lott (defeated by Jânio Quadros) and João Goulart as Vice-President (elected).

The strength of the PCB's support in the country is difficult to estimate, for the reasons mentioned above; it is reasonable to place its chief areas of influence in the urban and industrialized coastal regions, notably São Paulo, Rio de Janeiro, Recife and Porto Alegre.

Ideology and Programme

The PCB's political line has oscillated around a certain number of basic problems: assessment of the current chances of revolution in Brazil, the party's attitude towards the national bourgeoisie and the peasantry, what methods of struggle and type of organization to adopt. At its birth in 1922, the minor sect that then called itself the Communist Party enthusiastically embraced as its immediate task the establishment of the dictatorship of the proletariat in Brazil. Subsequently, from 1927 to 1930, the PCB pursued a right-wing policy, and tended to merge with the other elements of an umbrella electoral organization, the Workers' and Peasants' Front. Its attitude towards the bourgeoisie and the Liberal Alliance, the 1930 revolution and the dictatorship of Getúlio Vargas was coloured by the same spirit.[12] After Prestes's conversion to

12. Linhares, Herminio, loc. cit.

Communism, there was a new swing to the left (1931–5) culminating in the National Liberation Alliance, 'the only revolutionary anti-imperialist and anti-feudal front', which combined an extreme left-wing policy with insurrectionist revolutionary methods, approaching the philosophy of the *putsch*. The failure of this attempt at revolution brought about Prestes's arrest, together with a large number of other party leaders, in 1936. After its return to legal existence between 1945 and 1947, the PCB, with its 200,000 members, seemed about to become a mass party; and indeed this prospect led to what Prestes called parliamentarian illusions and reformist deviations. At the onset of the Cold War, the PCB once more became an underground party, prohibited and pretty well isolated. On Vargas's return to power there was a revival of the party's influence, particularly among the trade unions and in the nationalist movement, but it opposed Vargas, whom it accused of being an imperialist lackey, instead of recognizing in him a representative of the national bourgeoisie with which it was trying to establish an alliance. It did not become aware of this tactical error until hit by the powerful repercussions of Vargas's suicide.

From 1956 to 1958, the party was thrown into turmoil by an animated debate on the subject of the twentieth congress of the CPSU. The programme that emerged from the fifth congress of the PCB in 1960 proclaimed the necessity of an alliance with 'the national bourgeoisie, the great majority of which has been led by its own class interests to enter into conflict with foreign monopoly capital' and which was anti-imperialist although 'inconsequential'. The programme defined a peaceful approach to the struggle with the object of installing a 'government which would ensure full economic emancipation of the country, elimination of the backward agrarian structure, the establishment of full democratic liberties and the improvement of the living conditions of the masses'. The problems that were subsequently to exercise the leadership of the PCB no longer concerned the validity of particular political attitudes, but rather their practical application. The party's 1962 national conference criticized the policy of 'conciliation' with the Goulart government, but later, after the coup d'etat, the Central Committee published a severely self-critical analysis: it recognized that it had – in the first instance – carried the fight against conciliation too far, and demanded too advanced measures of the Goulart government without taking account of the unfavourable developments in the attitude of the national bourgeoisie and the petty bourgeoisie; also it had underestimated the dangers of a coup. It subsequently considered that it had fallen into the opposite error, after the beginning of 1964, and placed excessive confidence in Goulart and his military establishment, even encouraging him to embark on an adventurist course. As a result, the coup met with almost no resistance.

In January 1965, the PCB called on all patriots and democrats to join in a great united front for democracy and progress, against military dictatorship. It promised its support to all those who would fight for the application 'of even one of these points: the restoration of democratic freedoms, a political amnesty, defence of autonomy of the various states, revision of wage scales, an independent financial and economic policy, support for Petrobras, an independent foreign policy, the replacement of the present dictatorial regime'. In 1966 the party was agitated by a lively debate on the analysis of the defeat represented by the coup d'etat. Some militants, important men in the party but very much in the minority, possibly influenced by Cuban ideas, called in question the whole of the PCB's political line, particularly the principle of peaceful development, and the current leadership.

The Smaller Parties

The wide diversity of interest groups in Brazil, the complexity of their mutual relationships, the peculiarities of Brazilian electoral law, the nature and oligarchic structure of the big parties all contributed to the multiplication of small parties with a local or highly personality-conscious following.

A Brazilian periodical published in 1958 an ironical summing-up of the nine small parties that between them took about 30 per cent of the electorate's votes: some had ideas but no voters (Liberationist Party, Popular Representation Party, Brazilian Socialist Party, Christian Democratic Party); others had voters but no ideas (Social Progressive Party and the Republican Party); others had neither ideas nor voters (Republican Labour Party, Social Labour Party, National Labour Party, all taking the name 'labour' popularized by Vargas).

Whereas each of these small parties on its own may have had little importance, their role taken together and in relation to the big parties was by no means negligible. They often provided the only means of expression to popular protest by putting up dissident or independent candidates – witness Adhemar de Barros and the Social Progressive Party in São Paulo, Getúlio Vargas's successful candidature for the presidency, the successive electoral victories of Jânio Quadros and that of Miguel Arraes, governor of Pernambuco.

Consequently the decree of 15 July 1965, threatening all the small (and medium) parties with automatic dissolution, far from serving to 'clarify' political representation, as claimed at the time, was actually the prelude to the abolition of all the existing parties, as subsequent developments were to show.

Partido Social Progressista (PSP)

Origins and developments. The PSP was founded in 1947 by
Ademar de Barros, a doctor grown wealthy thanks to his political career, who had been appointed *interventor* for São
Paulo by Vargas but turned against the regime in 1942. At
first a member of the UDN, Ademar de Barros subsequently
created the Social Progressive Party by amalgamating three
smaller parties, the Popular Syndicalist Party, the Progressive
Republican Party and the old Social Progressive Party. The
PSP was to become the largest of the small parties.

Class or social group, party interests. This party was a secondary offshoot of the dominant social groups in Brazil. It had
close ties with business interests in São Paulo, and at the same
time succeeded in establishing a fairly broad social base
among the sub-proletariat and middle classes in that
state.

Organization and type of party. Originally a populist, personalist and regionally based party (centred on São Paulo), it
subsequently managed to become one of the parties in the
government, thanks to the demagogic skill and private fortune of Ademar de Barros. Ademar de Barros was founder,
president, and to all intents and purposes proprietor of the
Social Progressive Party, which he dominated by the force of
his personality. He had had the good fortune to be elected
governor of the state of São Paulo in 1947, thanks to the
momentary support of the Communist Party, the middle
class and the sub-proletariat, and he took full advantage of
the powerful lever that this post gave him in the economic
and political affairs of the country. In his later electoral campaigns, his supporters made the claim, 'He may be a thief, but
he gets things done.' He was defeated by Jânio Quadros in the
1954 elections for the governorship of São Paulo, was subse-

quently prosecuted for corruption and forced to leave Brazil for a time.

The PSP was above all an efficient electoral vehicle; its party officers were professional politicians of every conceivable shade who had decided to join the band-wagon of the PSP's successful leader.

The party's national role and the extent of its support. Despite its title, the Social Progressive Party was one of Brazil's more conservative parties. Its chief centres of support were São Paulo and Rio de Janeiro, but it had one or two deputies from other states. Its importance was entirely due to its leader's acquisition of the post of governor of the state of São Paulo and his participation in the presidential elections.

Thanks to the powerful electoral machine it possessed in São Paulo and Guanabara, the PSP was able to obtain the following results in elections to the federal legislature:

3 October 1950: 24 deputies, 5 senators; 9 per cent of the vote (692,800 votes out of 7,662,200);

3 October 1954: 32 deputies, 3 senators; 11·2 per cent of the vote (1,036,200 votes out of 9,228,200);

3 October 1958: 25 deputies, 7·4 per cent of the vote (827,685 votes out of 11,333,826);

7 October 1962: 22 deputies, 2 senators.

In 1950 the PSP's candidate for the vice-presidency of the Republic, João Café Filho, was elected, polling 5,520,790 votes, and in the presidential elections of 1955 Ademar de Barros polled 2,222,725 votes, 26 per cent of the total, coming third to Juscelino Kubitschek, successful candidate of the PSD–PTB coalition, and Juarez Tavora, the UDN's defeated candidate. Elected mayor of the city of São Paulo in 1957 and failing to win re-election to the governorship in 1958, Ademar de Barros managed to defeat Jânio Quadros and get himself re-elected governor of the state of São Paulo in 1962 – a key position in the run-up to the presidential elections of 1965.

However, he was shortly eliminated from Brazilian politics by his allies in the coup d'etat, which he had himself helped to organize.

Ideology and programme. In order to attract the popular vote and woo electors away from the PTB, Ademar de Barros made lavish use of patronage, made grossly exaggerated promises to the electorate in true demagogue style, sometimes verged vaguely on 'nationalism' but never attacked the established social order.

Partido Democratica Cristão (PDC)

This party was founded in 1945 by Mgr Arruda Câmara, but until 1953 its support among the electorate was practically non-existent, except in the states of São Paulo and Pernambuco. Mgr Arruda Câmara was known, if at all, for his parliamentary tirades against divorce.

The PDC appealed chiefly to the urban intellectual petty bourgeoisie, particularly in São Paulo. In March 1953 a coalition between the Christian Democrat Party and the Brazilian Socialist Party emerged victorious from the São Paulo local elections, against a coalition of all the other parties. Its candidate was Jânio Quadros; he was elected mayor after a vigorous campaign in which his emblem was a broom and his slogan 'a brass farthing against a million'.

One famous convert to the PDC was Marshal Juarez Tavora; however, the party was pretty well limited to a small group of intellectuals with no real influence on the national scene.

In the 1958 elections six PDC deputies were returned to parliament. The party subsequently supported Jânio Quadros's candidature for the presidency of the Republic, and during João Goulart's presidency it was a member of the government coalition. In 1962 twenty PDC deputies were returned and one senator.

Under growing popular pressure for reform and increasing national consciousness, two distinct trends began to appear in the party. One of these, grouped round the party leader, Ney Braga, and Marshal Juarez Tavora, was hostile to President Goulart's reform programme; the other supported the struggle for the 'basic reforms' and took an active part in it. The latter faction included Paulo de Tarso, who became Minister of Education, and Franco Montoro, who became Minister of Labour and encouraged the formation of numerous peasant unions, chiefly Catholic in complexion, in the north-east. This faction was nationalist, and promised the PDC a bigger role in national political life when the coup intervened to cut short all progress in this direction.

Ney Braga and his group accepted the coup d'etat and reconciled themselves to the new regime. Paulo de Tarso and other PDC leaders were obliged to go into exile in Chile.

Christian Democracy never succeeded in becoming a political force in Brazil, and the PDC was never a mass party. Left-wing Christian ideology found expression outside the PDC for the most part, in periodicals such as *Brasil urgente* (banned) and in the action of a few priests who had attached themselves to the labour movement and the peasant unions, and were prosecuted and imprisoned after the coup d'etat.

The Church. The PDC's position in relation to the Brazilian ecclesiastical hierarchy should be defined. The Brazilian Church had been a bastion of conservatism since colonial times, notably in its attitude to such burning problems as national independence, the emancipation of the slaves and the establishment of a republican regime.

The first Republican Constitution decreed the separation of Church and State. Getúlio Vargas, although not a believer himself, reintroduced religious education in state schools. In 1945, the Constituent Assembly once again separated the Church from the State; but the Brazilian Church continued to intervene in political life through the Catholic Electoral League, which recommended certain 'Christian' candidates to all Catholic voters. In the last years before the coup d'etat, such intervention took other forms.

The Church is still very powerful in Brazil. It still owns large estates and controls a large proportion of secondary and university education.

In the days before the coup, the hierarchy was for the most part opposed to the 'basic reforms' programme presented by President Goulart and the nationalist movement. Among the leaders of the most conservative faction were Cardinal D. Jayme de Barros Câmara, Archbishop of Rio, who frequently campaigned against trade links with the socialist countries; Mgr Sigaud and Mgr Proença, both declared adversaries of agrarian reform. In recent years the Catholic University Youth organization, People's Action, and some bishops have shown themselves increasingly conscious of the seriousness of the social and economic situation : Cardinal Motta, Archbishop of São Paulo, Dom Carlos Gouveia Coelho, Archbishop of Recife, Dom Helder Camara, also Archbishop of Recife, Dom Jorge Marcus de Oliveira, Bishop of Santo André, and others. In the north-east and elsewhere, a professor of the University of Pernambuco State, Paulo Freire, together with the National Union of Students, People's Action (a political movement of Catholic students), the Bishops' National Conference, and with the support of the federal Ministry of Education, launched a campaign against illiteracy that provoked a violent reaction from the right. Among the lower clergy, some priests participated – before the coup d'etat – in various popular protest movements, especially in the north-east. Some well-known Catholic intellectuals, such as Alceu Amoroso Lima, gave signs of moving towards an attitude containing some elements of progressive ideas, especially after the coup. Some Dominicans made an active contribution to this current of social Catholicism. One of them, Fra Carlos

Josaphat, published the periodical *Brasil urgente* in São Paulo, which attracted violent attacks from the *Estado de São Paulo* and was banned after the coup d'etat.

Despite all this, it was largely due to the Church and to Catholic organizations that an atmosphere favourable to the coup d'etat against the government was created among the urban middle classes. Since before the 1962 elections, a movement called the Crusade for the Family Rosary had been launched in Brazil, with powerful support; the movement was founded by an American priest, Patrick Peyton, and propagated in Brazil by another American priest, Joseph M. Quinn, and his Brazilian assistant, Father Araújo. This movement, and the women's organizations 'For God and Family', mobilized the religious feelings of the people and the middle classes against the 'communist menace' and organized big politico-religious processions, notably in São Paulo on 19 March, in which 300,000 people took part.

After the coup, the episcopate found itself once more divided in the face of the repression unleashed by the victorious faction of this Army; while some bishops, such as Dom Helder Camara, preached moderation, the majority associated themselves with the successful coup. Nevertheless, as the Brazilian crisis has continued to develop, the Church appears to be realizing gradually how serious the situation has become, and concerned to prepare an alternative solution; some bishops have addressed repeated and increasingly anxious warnings to the authorities, and recently Dom Helder Camara has formulated outspoken and direct criticisms of the regime.

Partido Socialista Brasileiro (PSB)

The Brazilian Socialist Party was set up in 1947 as the independent successor to the Democratic Left (Esquerda Democrática), which had at one time been attached to the UDN.

The PSB's influence on the working class was minimal. It consisted largely of left-wing intellectuals and university teachers, some Trotskyists, and a few liberals from São Paulo, Guanabara and Rio de Janeiro who hoped to see some relatively moderate changes and reforms. It had no organizational structure.

Its electoral debut in 1950 was disastrous, both in the presidential elections in which the party's leader, João Mangabeira, stood for the presidency, and in the legislative elections, in which only one PSB deputy was returned.

Nevertheless, as the nationalist movement progressed the PSB also moved closer to the nationalist position and became more progressive, in particular with regard to problems such as the defence of the state-owned Petrobras corporation, measures to support economic independence, and agrarian reform. Thanks to this development the PSB did for a time manage to win votes in elections: three federal deputies were returned in 1954, nine in 1958, four in 1962.

Partido Republicano (PR)

The first Republican Party had been formed in 1870 in São Paulo. It was a party of the urban petty bourgeoisie, supported by a number of army officers sympathetic to the positivism of Comte, who, after the republican revolution of 1889, endeavoured to apply a policy more favourable to the interests of the commercial and industrial bourgeoisie. Under the 'Old Republic' it was practically the only party, until the 'bourgeois revolution' of 1930, but it nevertheless did not manage to create a national organization since, on account of the revival of the influence of big landowners and the extreme decentralization of the country, there was a republican party in every state of the federation, controlled by the 'colonels' of the local oligarchy. The centralist dictatorship of Getúlio

Vargas put an end to this state of affairs, and the Republican Party lost a good deal of its influence until 1945.

The party's old leader, former President Artur Bernardes, an upright and clear-headed conservative, was able to inject new life into the PR (temporarily integrated into the UDN in 1945) as a traditional centre party, but with some nationalist leanings. The PR became the fifth largest Brazilian party in terms of electoral support, and was most firmly entrenched in the states of Minas Gerais and Bahia. Its results in the elections to the federal legislature were as follows:

2 December 1945: 7 deputies elected on a proportional ballot: 3.7 per cent of the vote (219,600 votes out of 5,924,600);

3 October 1950: 11 deputies elected on a proportional ballot: 4.8 per cent of the vote (364,900 votes out of 7,662,200);

3 October 1954: 19 deputies elected on a proportional ballot: 5.2 per cent of the vote (480,000 votes out of 9,228,200);

3 October 1958: 17 deputies elected on a proportional ballot: 6 per cent of the vote (676,407 votes out of 11,333,826);

7 October 1962: 5 deputies elected on a proportional ballot, 1 senator.

The old President's son, Bernardes Filho, was not able to maintain the direction that his father had been able to impart to the Republican Party.

Partido da Representação Popular (PRP)

The PRP was the rump of the old Brazilian Integralist Action Party, inspired originally by the fascism of Mussolini's Italy and of Maurras, which had enjoyed mass support in Brazil between 1932 and 1937 (600,000). This party was both 'ideological', since it was based on an extreme right-wing doctrine, and personalist, having Plinio Salgado as its chief. The old Integralist Action had initially supported the policies of Getúlio Vargas, and indeed practically acted as the shock-troops of his movement, until a conflict flared up over tactics and power; Getúlio Vargas promptly outlawed integralism, and Plinio Salgado fled to Portugal, where he remained in exile until 1945. After 1945 the PRP, having lost its mass audience and the virulence of its earlier 'integralism', found its influence confined to Rio Grande do Sul, in particular, and to São Paulo, Paraná and Espírito-Santo. In elections to the federal legislature, the PRP had two deputies returned in 1945 and 1950, three in 1954 and 1958 and four in 1962. In 1950 it supported Getúlio Vargas's candidature for the presidency. In the 1955 presidential elections, Plinio Salgado polled more than 700,000 votes (about 8 per cent of the total poll).

The PRP presented itself as an authentically 'nationalist' party – in the Maurrassian sense of the word – and emphasized its attachment to the Church, the Encyclicals, and to corporatism as a system of government and political representation.

Partido Libertador (PL)

The PL had been founded in 1928 in Rio Grande do Sul as an opposition party to the then Republican Party. It supported Getúlio Vargas's 1930 revolution, but at the end of the war it re-emerged as an opposition party, at first temporarily integrated with the UDN.

Once it had broken away from the UDN, it became the private domain of a man living in the past, committed to an 'ideal': Raúl Pila, whose great dream was 'parliamentarianism'. It would, however, be incorrect to suppose that the solitary, brief interregnum of parliamentary rule that contemporary Brazil has known, after the resignation of

Jânio Quadros (September 1961) and during the first period of João Goulart's presidency until the referendum of January 1963, was in any way attributable to the Liberationist Party's influence.

The PL always formed part of the conservative opposition, except in 1960, during Jânio Quadros's presidential campaign, when it gave him its support. Its local base was the state of Rio Grande do Sul; it also had some support in the state of Bahia and, in 1962, in the state of Amazonas.

It had one federal deputy returned in 1945, five in 1950, eight in 1954, and three in 1958 and 1962.

Other Small Parties

Between 1945 and 1964, a number of more or less ephemeral small parties existed, which may be mentioned for the record.

Partido Social Trabalhista (PST). A personalist party under the leadership of Senator Vitorino Freire, who made his name under Dutra's presidency. An offshoot of the PTB with an unstable local base, the PST had nine federal deputies elected in 1950, two in 1954 and 1958, eight in 1962.

Partido Trabalhista Nacional (PTN). Founded in 1945 by officials in the Ministry of Labour, it became the instrument of a small group of São Paulo politicians, notably Emilio Carlos and later Jânio Quadros. The PTN had five federal deputies elected in 1950, six in 1954, seven in 1958, eleven in 1962.

Partido Republicano Trabalhista (PRT). This party also originated from São Paulo, under the leadership of the Methodist pastor Silveira; it sponsored the election to the Federal Parliament of Roberto Morena, a well-known communist and trade unionist, in 1954. The PRT had one federal deputy returned in 1950 and 1954, two in 1958, three in 1962.

Movimento Trabalhista Renovador (MTR). The MTR was founded in 1960 by Fernando Ferrari, a dissident PTB leader, and won some local support in Rio Grande do Sul. It had four federal deputies elected in 1962.

It should be noted that all of these little parties took the name 'Labour Party', thus implicitly linking themselves to Getúlio Vargas and his social policy.

THE BANNING OF THE PARTIES
THE ROLE OF THE ARMY AND OF THE NATIONALIST
MOVEMENT

On 1 April 1964 a military coup d'etat deposed President Goulart and put an end to the 'normal' political life in which the parties had participated. In the wake of the coup, thousands of Brazilians were arrested – trade unionists, students, intellectuals, priests, politicians; the mandates of forty federal deputies were revoked, fifty-eight leading figures and hundreds of other citizens were deprived of their civil rights for ten years. Under cover of an 'Institutional Act' claiming to 'maintain the Constitution of 1946 ... maintain the National Congress ... limit the plenary powers of the revolution', while suspending 'for six months' a number of constitutional guarantees, more or less absolute emergency powers were granted 'for sixty days' to the President of the Republic, Marshal Castelo Branco, in order to 'ensure the economic, financial, political and moral reconstruction of Brazil'.

Eighteen months later, on 27 October 1965, Marshal Castelo Branco signed in Brasilia a second 'Institutional Act' which suppressed presidential and vice-presidential elections by direct ballot, abolished all existing political parties and granted him practically unlimited powers 'until 15 March

1967'. On 5 February 1966, he promulgated a third 'Act' suppressing elections for state governors and vice-governors by direct ballot. President and Vice-President would now be elected by the Congress, and governors and vice-governors by the several states' legislative assemblies. This has remained in force till now, and state governors are in fact chosen by the president and then 'elected' by the respective assemblies.

The Army

The Brazilian Army is fairly highly politicized, although its intervention in political life did not follow the classic pattern of *pronunciamentos*. Its action was indeed more 'political' than had been the rule elsewhere, partly because of the Army's traditions and partly because of its social composition.

As early as imperial times, the Military Club withheld from the Emperor the Army's services for hunting down runaway slaves; the Army helped in the overthrow of the Empire and the establishment of the Republic, for most of its officers were from the petty bourgeoisie. Even today, secondary and higher education in the Military College is open to the sons of humble families. While a majority of the senior officers are still from the more privileged classes, others are the sons of NCOs or working people, like Admiral Candido Aragão, Commander of the Marines before the coup. Moreover, because Brazil is an 'archipelago of oligopolies', each of the local or national oligarchical groups endeavours to recruit and train its own military officers. Consequently although the senior officers are for the most part conservative, the officer corps as a whole embraces a wide spectrum of political attitudes and social origins.

The Military Club at the time of Getúlio Vargas's election in 1950 was the mouthpiece of the 'legalist' faction among the senior officers. Subsequently, the right-wing faction won control of the Club. The non-commissioned officers, organized in their own club, pressed claims for career opportunities and higher pay as well as political claims, particularly eligibility for political office.[13] They proved responsive to the political ideas of the nationalist movement.

Since obedience to the law is made a strict duty for army officers under the Brazilian Constitution, legality may seem to some military men to take precedence over discipline. Recourse to such a principle has on previous occasions legitimized the intervention of one faction in the Army to defend the law or the Constitution against a coup d'etat being prepared by another faction.

In 1955, for example, a coup was being prepared to prevent the legally elected President, Juscelino Kubitschek, and the Vice-President, João Goulart, from taking office; the Minister for War, General Teixeira Lott, used the Army to intervene on 11 November to defend the Constitution. On that occasion, and for the first time, the 'legalist' generals, to ward off the threat to their authority represented by the 'putschist' generals – the *gorilas* – sought the support of the NCOs, which proved decisive. When President Quadros resigned on 25 August 1961 and the Ministers for the Navy, the Army and the Air Force proclaimed to the country their intention to oppose the accession of Vice-President Goulart by force, it was once again the NCOs' refusal to obey the putschist generals' orders that gave the victory to the legalist generals and to President Goulart.

The movement within the Army represented by the NCOs gained in political importance. President Goulart called on them for support on several occasions. In September 1963 a revolt by NCOs in Brasilia, claiming eligibility to stand in parliamentary elections – a revolt organized without the knowledge of the nationalist forces and even against their

13. Since the Constitution was not clear on this point, one NCO had however managed to get his election to Parliament ratified by the courts.

will because of its political inexpediency at the time – won a certain degree of popular approval; it also had the unexpected effect of interrupting an important court case between the Hanna Mining Corporation and the Brazilian Government, which had withdrawn development rights to the enormous iron-ore deposits in Minas Gerais. President Goulart eventually allowed the offenders to be disciplined by the military authorities, as the senior officers had demanded. In contrast, when a thousand sailors mutinied in Rio on 26 March 1964, President Goulart hesitated at first, and then did not discipline the mutineers, thus alienating the officer corps once and for all. It was the spark needed to set off the powder-keg. On 30 March, the President again addressed a meeting of NCOs; in the night of 31 March to 1 April, the military coup took place.

A number of divergent political trends could be observed among the officers and non-commissioned officers at this time:

– *the janquistas*, i.e. those loyal to João Goulart; they composed the President's military entourage, in whom he placed excessive confidence (most of them abandoned him when the coup was sprung, notably General Amaury Kruel);

– *the nationalist officers*, including moderates, such as General Pery Bevilacqua for example, who favoured the defence of legality and of the Constitution, and were therefore opposed to the insubordination of the NCOs; others, in contrast, were progressive, like General Osvino Alves;

– *the officers of the right and the extreme right*, including Marshal Castelo Branco, General Costa e Silva – the 'strong man' of the regime and Castelo Branco's successor as President of the Republic – Jurandir Mamede, Mourão Filho, Cordeiro de Farias, a number of colonels, etc., the youngest and most intransigent faction of whom is known as the *linha dura* (the hard-liners); the *Higher War College*, founded in 1949 in close collaboration with the American Army, has played a

very important part in the higher training of these officers;
– *communist officers*;
– and finally a large fluctuating majority with no political affiliations.

After the coup d'etat and the Institutional Act of April 1964, hundreds of regular servicemen – NCOs, general staff officers, and even one Field-Marshal – were expelled from the Army.

The Nationalist Movement

Among the parties and other social and political forces affected by the coup d'etat, mention should be made of the nationalist movement, which was the common meeting-point for a number of these forces. It cannot be omitted from any description of Brazilian political parties if these are to be fully understood.

Historically speaking, Brazilian nationalism should be seen in the context of a country that has been independent for more than a century, with a powerful sense of national unity, but which only emerged from a semi-colonial situation about thirty or forty years ago.

From the economic point of view, Brazilian nationalism is both a product of and a factor in the high rate of economic growth of the country, and its extraordinary industrial advance in the face of foreign domination, notably by the Americans.

The movement's origins can be traced back to the 1930s and 40s, to the policy of economic independence launched by Vargas, one of whose first concrete achievements was the establishment of a steel works at Volta Redonda in 1943. After 1950, with the powerful popular movement that had built up around the campaign for the nationalization of the Brazilian oil industry and the creation of Petrobras, the nationalist movement became a considerable force that embraced widely varying social classes, professions and political creeds: sectors of the working class, intellectuals, sectors of the national industrial bourgeoisie, the urban middle classes, the student movement which played a leading part in nationalist agitation, the largest and most powerful section of the trade-union movement, a faction within the Brazilian Labour Party and others, the Brazilian Communist Party and a number of army officers and NCOs.

The movement's aims were primarily economic – e.g. nationalization of oil and electricity, reinforcement of state capitalism, building up the national steel industry, control of foreign investment and of the transfer of profits – but also political, affecting both domestic and foreign policy. It was often difficult to achieve unanimity on these different aims.

Heterogeneous in political composition, the nationalist movement also contained ideological differences, since each group gave its own ideological interpretation to nationalist problems and preoccupations. It has been organized and expressed in political fronts that have been fairly changeable: in the House, the Parliamentary Nationalist Front, which included, before the coup, more than a hundred deputies of all parties (and in particular the forty deputies whose mandates were revoked after the coup), notably from the PTB, but also the PSD, the UDN, the PSB and the PDC; outside Parliament, the National Liberation Front created in 1961, and later the Front for Popular Mobilization.

The nationalist movement's weaknesses lay in the absence of any organizational structure, in its very limited support among the rural masses, and the division between contradictory trends within it.

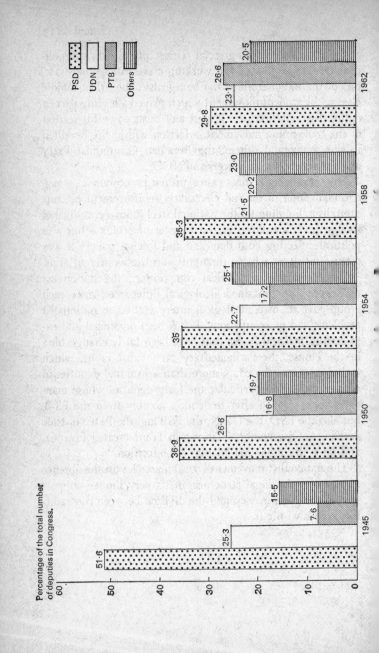

Percentage of the total number of deputies in Congress.

Legend:
- PSD
- UDN
- PTB
- Others

	1945	1950	1954	1958	1962
PSD	51·6	36·9	35	35·3	29·8
UDN	25·3	26·6	22·7	21·5	23·1
PTB	7·6	16·8	17·2	20·2	26·6
Others	15·5	19·7	25·1	23·0	20·5

Conclusion

This guide to political parties of necessity provides only an approximate picture of Brazilian political life. It is in fact a descriptive and somewhat static study of a profoundly dynamic phenomenon. But, in practice, most of the Brazilian parties have played a relatively minor and superficial role in the country's history.[14] Revolution and political changes of direction in Brazil have been carried out and decided by popular movements, currents of opinion and fronts going beyond the scope of the parties.

Despite these reservations, the data contained in this guide indicate certain significant trends and shifts of emphasis in the Brazilian political tapestry.

Most of the Brazilian parties, from their formal inception in 1944–5 to their prohibition in 1964, evolved along conflicting and contradictory lines. Two objective tendencies came together and clashed in the course of this evolution.

Most of the parties represented a variety of interests: oligopolies, different sectors of the same social class, and different social classes. At the same time, however, the influence of the big landowners remained very great in nearly all of them.

Because of all this, the ideological, political and sociological boundaries between the parties were extremely blurred. In-

14. In view of the high degree of personalization of politics, the role of individual personalities is very important. This has only been remarked upon in passing, and only with reference to personalities on the party-political scene: Getúlio Vargas, Luis Carlos Prestes, Juscelino Kubitschek, João Goulart, Carlos Lacerda, Lionel Brizola and others. Other impressive and significant personalities, belonging to no political party, have been left out of the picture – notably Miguel Arraes, who was governor of Pernambuco and without doubt one of the most influential leaders of the Brazilian left.

deed, the true frontiers often cut across party affiliations, dividing different factions, regional groupings, or leaders within the same party. Very few of the parties had any real national structure. Small parties expressing purely local interests were springing up and disappearing all the time. The extraordinary differentiation and volatility of the electoral base of most of these parties, the fragmentation of the electorate between parties representing the same class interests, the lack of any clear correspondence between parties and social classes ended up by producing a very serious anomaly : the multiplication of purely local electoral pacts, highly abnormal in a system of proportional representation and entirely devoid of any community of political attitude. Between one parliamentary election and the next, the number of candidates presented and elected on lists under the *ad hoc* electoral label of a local coalition rose every time. These labels and coalitions lasted no longer than the duration of the elections, served merely to attract votes and divide up the scraps left over from the proportional ballot, and bore no relation to the political loyalties or parliamentary responsibility of those elected.

Distortion of Proportional Representation

	Candidates of political parties as such		Candidates of electoral coalitions (temporary electoral labels)		Spoiled and blank ballot papers
	Votes	Elected	Votes	Elected	
1945	6,188,000	286	0	0	—
1950	6,107,364	—	1,552,636	—	—
1954	6,739,282	—	2,496,501	—	654,692
1958	7,379,403	191	4,140,655	135	1,159,939
1962 [15]	6,276,210	216	5,769,213	193	2,701,798

15. In 1962 the number of deputies rose from 326 to 409.

Elections of 1962: Increase in the Parliamentary Representation of the Parties Thanks to Candidates Elected in Local Coalitions[16]

	Elected under party label	Total number of representatives in Parliament
P S D	79	122
P T B	63	109
U D N	55	94
P S P	6	22
P D C	1	20

To use Maurice Duverger's terminology, we may speak of a fairly profound dual division in Brazil: between the electoral and the parliamentary personae of all the parties; and between the distribution of votes and the true shades of public opinion.

If we add to these distortions of 'representative democracy' the oligarchic nature of many of the parties, the restriction of the electorate (from which illiterates are excluded, so that it includes less than 25 per cent of the total population and less than 50 per cent of adults over eighteen), it is easy to see why many Brazilian intellectuals have rejected Brazil's political parties as utterly devoid of all significance except as regional or personality-centred electoral vehicles.

This, in the author's view, is an over-hasty judgement, betraying a misunderstanding of the dynamics of the phenomena we are discussing. The data and notations given in the table of parties indicate, in contradiction to the evolution traced above, another tendency pointing towards the conclusion that the parties do have some real significance.

16. Source: de Souza, Pompeu, 'Eleições de 1962: decomposição partidária e caminhos da reforma', *Revista brasileira de estudos políticos*, January 1964 (special issue in the 1962 elections), pp. 7–19.

	Urban population[18] (% of the total population)	Total electorate (illiterates are excluded from voting)	Total electorate (% of the total population)	Total electorate (% of the population ag‐ over 18 years)
1945[l]	35	7,460,000	20	35
1950[l]	37.2	11,455,149	22.03	39
1954[l]	40	15,105,000	22.05	42.51
1955[p]	—	—	—	—
1958[l]	42	13,780,000	21.9	42.23
1960[p]	44.2	—	—	—
1962[l]	46.6	18,500,000	24.65	47.54

a Percentage of abstentions swollen by the 'phantom electorate'. Almost 2,000,000 'electors' were still on the register although de‐ceased.

Accompanying the increasingly rapid growth of indus‐trialization and urbanization in Brazil, and the relative decline in the economic and social role of the big landed estates, a whole series of changes and new political phen‐omena have emerged through the medium of, or in spite of, the party system: a shift in the electoral centre of gravity from the countryside to the towns, the increase in the size of the electorate by two and a half times between 1945 and 1964, an increased rate of participation in elections, a tenden‐cy for the electorate to be concentrated around the big parties, a slackening off in the proliferation of small parties, the decline of the traditional conservative parties (UDN, PSD,

17. Sources: *Revista brasileira de estudos políticos*, Censuses of 1950 and 1960, Statistical Yearbooks (IBGE).

18. i.e. population living in centres with more than 2,000 in‐habitants.

19. In 1945: PSD, UND, PTB, PCB + PR. After 1945: PSD, UDN, PTB, PSP + PR.

and Political Trends [17]

Votes cast	Abstentions (% of registered electors)	Votes polled by the traditional Conservative parties (PSD + UDN + PR) (% of votes cast)	Votes polled by the PTB (% of votes cast)	Votes polled by the PCB (% of votes cast)	Votes polled by the five parties with the most votes [19] (% of votes cast)
6,188,000	16.9	73.0	10	9	92.0
7,900,000	20.8a	62.4	18.1	—	89.5
9,890,475	25.6a	59.1	19.5	—	89.8
8,600,000	29.5a	—	—	—	—
12,678,997	18b	58.2	19.8	—	85.4
11,700,000	—	—	—	—	—
14,747,221	20.3	—	—	—	—

b After the purge of the 'phantom electorate'.
l Legislative elections.
p Presidential elections.

PR) and the increased influence of the PTB (see table above). Still more important was the increased and unprecedented participation of large sectors of the urban proletariat, and even of some rural workers, not only in elections but in social and political struggles of much wider significance, in the years between 1954 and 1964, and especially during João Goulart's presidency.

Under these pressures, parties such as the PSD, the UDN and the PTB – which had previously been the instruments of a balance of oligarchical political power that was slowly but surely being left behind by events – found themselves forced to redefine their position and adapt themselves to altered circumstances, or break up and give birth to new parties. This kind of evolution was towards a clarification of political life, towards a system in which the parties corresponded to social classes. Certainly this process took some surprising and baffling turns, such as the apparently 'spontaneous' and 'irrational' demonstrations of 'collective psychic response' represented by the massive popular votes for Jânio Quadros, for example.

Nationalism, although a factor tending to polarize political life, was not enough on its own to provide a clear demarcation between the old or new political formations, for the nationalist movement cut across all class frontiers and the balance of forces within it still presented a confused picture.

In its two years of legal operation, the PCB proved itself to be the only working-class party, and the most homogeneous socially, politically and ideologically of all the Brazilian parties. Its long period of proscription has delayed any precise definition of its strength and its policies, and the lack of contrast has blurred those of its closest rival, the PTB, and of the nationalist movement as a whole.

Nevertheless, the political polarization continued and became more marked, finding expression within the federal Parliament in the formation of two fronts (the Parliamentary Nationalist Front and Parliamentary Democratic Action), which cut across all party lines and were beyond the reach of party discipline. Was this merely one more symptom of the lack of real significance and authenticity of the parties and their representation in Parliament? To the extent that these fronts represented broader and deeper currents of opinion than the currents revealed by elections, this was a phenomenon that helped to compensate for the gulf already described between public opinion, the vote and parliamentary representation. The Brazilian party system was in the process of restructuring itself, and was taking on a new meaning.

A sudden brake was applied to this process by the coup of 1 April 1964. At the same time, the coup must have destroyed – once and for all, it would seem – the institutions of the old political balance, but without being able to eliminate the strong currents running below the surface of Brazilian political life. Everything points to the likelihood that the complete restoration of political liberty in Brazil will be both a conditioning factor and a product of a higher level of popular participation in political life, and a more advanced form of party political organization.

Brazilian Politics 1967–71

On 15 March 1967 Castelo Branco's successor, Artur da Costa e Silva, 'elected' by a purged Congress, took over power, with the promise of 'humanizing the revolution'. This humanization was supposed to comprise two main aspects : a loosening of the squeeze in credit and wages (and thus, consumption) and a softening of repression at the political (and police) level. Economic policy was to be changed, development becoming the paramount goal, instead of the simple struggle against inflation. The credit and wage restrictions adopted by Castelo's Minister of Planning, Roberto Campos, had led to economic stagnation and an increasing control of vital sectors of the economy by foreign enterprises, as these, thanks to Instruction 289, could get credit from abroad and be more competitive than the squeezed Brazilian companies. Industrial and commercial associations had bitterly protested against this situation. From the wage-earners' viewpoint, the situation was not brighter, as the fight against inflation had caused a recession and serious belt-tightening, and trade unions, under government intervention, could not defend their claims.

At the political level, Castelo Branco's government had become increasingly isolated, and even staunch supporters of the 1964 coup were critical of repression and of a foreign policy which uncritically toed the US line. A 'redemocratization' and the abolition of 'exceptional' legislation were among the demands of the most articulate civilian social groups in Brazil : lawyers, university students, intellectuals and priests.

Even within the Army there was some opposition to Castelo: many did not accept the theory of 'ideological frontiers' (which implied subjection to the policies of the leader of the western world); others thought the constitutional framework should be preserved. The professional politicians could not be happy with a regime where their role became ever more marginal.

This was not just Castelo's legacy. Economic stagnation, for instance, had set in during Goulart's government, for GNP, which had grown at 7 per cent a year in 1956–61, grew only 1·6 per cent in 1962–3, that is, less than the population. But now, a serious squeeze and a harsh repression were on, and people did not see the supposed positive results: the control of inflation and the resumption of economic growth. The talk about the victory over 'subversion' and 'corruption' was not enough to satisfy the majority of the people.

Costa e Silva's 'humanization' of the revolution, however, did not take place. At the economic level, the new Ministers of Finance and Planning criticized the policies of Roberto Campos, who was accused of planning for an 'imaginary country'; stronger import controls were considered, as Campos's liberal policies had led to considerable loss of foreign exchange. There were attempts to modernize Brazilian capitalism: tax incentives were granted for investment in the stock exchange. Tax collection was made more efficient, in an attempt to solve gradually the age-old problem of budget deficits. A report on Brazilian industrialization criticized the alleged fact that it had been carried out at the expense of agriculture. One could already see this trend, stated by Costa e Silva at the end of the first year of his government: the main objective was to be economic development; plans were drawn up for the improvement of the economic and social infrastructures – modernization of agriculture, building of new roads, better housing, increased productivity in industry and an emphasis on education.

But, at the political level no serious 'opening' was intended. In the same speech in March 1968, Costa e Silva, repeating the idea put forward by Vargas in the *Estado Novo* ('the vote won't fill your belly'), declared that 'the people are not interested in questions about the form of suffrage'. The trend towards centralization proceeded apace, with liberal sectors protesting against the increasing militarization of the state apparatus, the stiff legislation on 'breach of security', and the *cassação* of the autonomy of the *municípios*. Costa spoke for 'liberty with order', but 'never subversive agitation'. The difficulty here was that subversion, just like its obverse national security, could be interpreted in any way convenient to the military government.

The relations between Church and State became increasingly bitter. Priests were arrested for allegedly helping student agitation or direct participation in subversion, and many of them were badly treated or tortured. Although politically split as to the government, the Church felt that it should defend its own members against repression. At the end of 1967 Brazilian bishops asked the government to recognize the National Union of Students (UNE), outlawed by Castelo Branco, and which had had to remain underground.

1968 was the turning-point of 'post-revolutionary' Brazil. On the one hand, the economy began to pick up again, and by the end of the year GNP had grown 8·4 per cent (and then 9 per cent in 1969 and 9·5 per cent in 1970). On the other hand, all hopes of a political thaw vanished entirely. Let us briefly see why.

In early 1968, the squeeze and inflation were still on; there were demands for the cessation of the use of the Institutional Acts and for direct elections; unions opposed government policies and there was 'growing popular despair'. But the armed forces were united behind the regime. In January Decree-law 348 gave sweeping powers to the National Security Council: the concept of security was very broad indeed.

In order to achieve a balanced budget, severe cuts were imposed on expenditure. Education was the hardest hit: there were universities where lecturers did not receive their salaries for months on end. This situation, plus the government's stated aims of humanizing the revolution and a political 'opening', unleashed a wave of protests and demonstrations all over the country. April began with student mobilization against American influence in education, against cuts in the education budget, bad food in university and secondary school canteens; the killing of a student by the police in Rio brought renewed protests. The government outlawed the Broad Front (Frente Ampla), organized by old politicians such as Lacerda, Kubitschek, and Goulart (the last in exile).

Costa e Silva was under attack from several quarters. The hard-liners (*linha dura*) wanted him to stop subversion and to use his special powers granted by the Institutional Acts; liberal and democratic sectors, especially in the urban centres, demanded that he liberalize the political system. The students got increasingly organized to resist repression; demonstrations resumed in earnest in late June, covering the whole second half of 1968.

The student movement worried the military government, not only as an organized body of opposition, but also because, on account of its very special characteristics – traditional participation in political life; fast mobilization; middle-class origin (at least of most of its leaders), which meant the previous years' repression had harmed it less than the peasants' and workers' movements – it offered a base around which all the inarticulate opposition to the regime could, and did, polarize. The most aggressive sectors of the MDB (see below, pages 228 ff. for a brief discussion of the new political parties) joined in the protest movement, and advocated the creation of 'popular mobilization committees'. Marcio Moreira Alves, an MDB deputy who was to provide the pretext for Institutional Act 5, announced the creation of such a committee in Brasilia in mid-April 1968.

Even among the armed forces there were signs of uneasiness. The 'nationalist' current, led by General Albuquerque Lima, pressed for reforms, mainly an agrarian one. Military manifestoes asked for salary rises; some military refused to work as police during demonstrations; others criticized alleged corruption in government and complained about the estrangement between the military and the people. Some people, including those in the Army, feared Costa e Silva's alleged *continuismo* (intention to remain, to *continue* in power).

In December, more priests were arrested, bringing protests from 200 priests and the National Conference of Brazilian Bishops (CNBB). There was much political mobilization. The government had asked the Congress to withdraw deputy Moreira Alves's parliamentary immunity, in order that he could be tried for a speech allegedly insulting the armed forces. The purged and broken Congress surprisingly resisted the government, and this, for the military, meant a challenge to the 'revolution', an attempt to return to the 'politicking' of the old times. The vote itself (216 against and 141 for the suspension of immunity, with 12 abstentions) showed that even the ARENA, the government party, had been split over the issue, with more than 100 of its deputies joining the opposition. On 13 December 1968 a new Institutional Act (number 5) – still in force today (February 1972) – was decreed. Costa e Silva was given the power to suspend habeas corpus for activities 'endangering national security', to suspend the political rights of any citizen, to suspend Congress, to cancel mandates in any legislative body, to decree a state of siege, to intervene in the states of the Federation and municipalities, to dismiss civil servants and expel people from the armed forces and so on. In the first purge 38 federal deputies, 2 senators and 3 Supreme Court judges lost their positions; a wave of arrests followed. A few weeks later, nearly

100 state deputies and another 3 federal deputies also lost their jobs. Hundreds were dismissed from the public service including dozens of University lecturers. Although it was stated that the punitive phase after Act 5 would be short, and that the special powers would be used to carry out reforms (without the traditional legal problems involved), intermittent waves of *cassaçãoes* have never stopped since. President Médici has made use of special powers in the same way; on the other hand, no really significant reform has taken place to improve the lot of the lower layers of Brazilian society. Minister Albuquerque Lima, the 'nationalist' leader within the Army, resigned his government post early in 1969, in protest against the regime's unwillingness to pass reforms, the impoverishment of the masses and the increasing foreign influence in the economy.

The National Security Council in January 1969 ruled that those who opposed the government would be considered a legitimate opposition, but those who opposed the revolution would be considered subversive, and would be fought with deprivation of political rights and other measures. 1969 witnessed significant growth of armed resistance against the government, which culminated in the kidnapping of the American ambassador in September. The country was then ruled by a military junta formed by the ministers of the three armed services, as Costa e Silva had suddenly been taken ill, and the military did not think it fit to transfer power to the civilian Vice-President, Pedro Aleixo, an old UDN politician elected together with the President. The junta decided to accept the kidnappers' demands, and released fifteen political prisoners in exchange for the ambassador, against the protests of more right-wing officers. In the fifteen months up to the end of 1970 three more foreign diplomats – the Japanese consul in São Paulo, the West German and the Swiss ambassadors – were kidnapped by Brazilian revolutionary groups, and later exchanged for political prisoners, many of whom had been badly tortured. Even if armed struggle against the government was not only a reaction to the new repression following Institutional Act 5 (some revolutionary groups had previously defined their strategy in terms of armed struggle), its appeal grew when it became the only means of meaningful opposition as these groups saw it.

In early October General Garrastazu Médici was chosen by the military, after long consultations, as the new President. Little known outside the Army, he had been head of the SNI (National Intelligence Service, coordinating all security bodies) and since mid-1968 had been for the adoption of the emergency measures contained in Act 5. This time, not to take any chances, the Vice-President was also a military figure, Admiral Radmaker. The Congress was hastily brought back to life, in order to elect the new rulers in late October. Before they took over, the junta carried out a new wave of *cassações* and dismissals.

The military government has consolidated itself under Médici. The economy is doing well, although there are serious problems ahead. Foreign indebtedness has more than doubled between 1964 and 1971 (from under three to about six million dollars). Heavy reliance on the inflow of foreign investment and on export expansion, as well as a liberal exchange policy which cost Brazil 100 million dollars for tourism in 1970, make development particularly vulnerable to foreign factors. Encouragement of mergers with foreign companies in the export sector has the same effect. Income concentration can also reduce consumption, or distort its patterns, and hamper development. Despite all this, GNP grew 10 per cent in 1971, and industrial production 11 per cent. There are doubts whether this can go on for long, but the performance is enough to keep support for the government, at least from those sectors which have benefited most, the upper and middle classes.

At the political level, Congress is as usual well under con-

trol, and the police and armed forces have been quite successful in controlling armed-struggle revolutionaries, whose three
most distinguished leaders were killed by the security forces
(Carlos Marighela in November 1969, Joaquim Câmara Ferreira in October 1970 and Carlos Lamarca in September 1971).
Among the traditional left, the Communist Party policy seems
to have been to keep its organization alive, most probably because of its extremely cautious approach to political activity
in Brazil today, as if it were in hibernation waiting for a
redemocratization 'thaw'. The masses are politically inarticulate, and the armed forces stand solidly behind the government, as far as one can see.

The New Parties

The Institutional Act 2 – which banned all previously existing political parties on 27 October 1965 – began a new period
of party-political life in Brazil. On 20 November Complemen-
tary Act 4 allowed congressmen to form new political organizations, each grouping not less than 120 deputies and 20
senators. They were not to be 'political parties', but 'organizations with political party functions'. These would run for
election in 1966, after which the definitive parties would be
formed. There was at first a deadline of forty-five days for
this reorganization, which had to be extended as the opposition had difficulties rallying a sufficient number of congressmen to make it a political organization according to the law.

The Castelo Branco government wanted to reduce the
proliferation of parties which existed before, which did not
represent either different ideologies or identifiable social
groups and interests (as shown above). Nevertheless, the
social basis of political power, or rather, of the political
power expressed in Congress, was left untouched, especially
in the rural areas. The new laws could not prevent old and
traditional politicians from being elected once again.

In 1966, two organizations with party political functions were created: the Aliança Renovadora Nacional (ARENA – National Alliance for Renewal) and the Movimento Democrático Brasileiro (MDB – Brazilian Democratic Movement), the former for the government and the latter in opposition. But one could not speak of a clear division between the two. Within ARENA, the majority gave uncritical support to the military, but others thought it was high time for the emergency laws to be dropped and for constitutional normalcy to be brought back. In the MDB, two blocks could be distinguished: some thought political mobilization should be used against the government's arbitrary power (those who favoured vigorous, aggressive opposition were called the group of the immature); others (the majority) thought opposition should be carried out within the limits defined by the government. The ARENA liberals and the MDB moderates had thus a lot in common. Referring to the way the parties were now formed, by government decree, the scathing *cariocas* – Rio de Janeiro inhabitants – called them the 'Yes' Party and the 'Yes, Sir' Party.

The November 1966 elections, carried out in an atmosphere of nearly total political control (the government considered many candidates inappropriate, and these could not run, but some criticism of the government was allowed), gave the following results: [20]

Electoral college	Total poll	Valid votes	Annulled and blank votes
22,348,118	17,260,382	13,630,743	3,629,639

In the elections for the Senate – majority ballot: ARENA got 7,719,382 votes, electing 47 senators; MDB got 5,911,361 votes, electing 19 senators. In the elections for the Chamber of Deputies – proportional ballot – these were the results:

20. Source: *Revista Brasileira de estudos políticos*, number 23/24, July 1967/January 1968.

ARENA got 8,731,638 votes, electing 277 deputies; MDB got 4,915,470 votes, electing 132 deputies.

In formal terms, the government got the evidence of support it sought. One should, however, take into account the very high proportion of the non-participating vote: 20 per cent blank and annulled. The controlled vote of the interior was enough to assure the election of traditional politicians, mostly in the government party. The election campaign itself was used by the military as a means of political control. Those candidates more vigorously opposing the government could be (and often were) *cassados* (deprived of political rights) and harassed in their professional and private lives.

In terms of membership, ARENA is mostly composed of former UDN and PSD members, although ex-PTB politicians are not uncommon. Among its leaders are Filinto Muller (ex-PSD and former Chief of Police during Vargas's Estado Novo dictatorship), Raimundo Padilha (ex-UDN and an Integralista – member of the fascist-style Brazilian movement – in the 1930s), Daniel Krieger (ex-UDN from Rio Grande do Sul) and Nei Braga (ex-PDC and former governor of Paraná State).

The MDB is mostly formed of ex-PTB and ex-PSD members, and a few ex-UDN politicians. Many of its most important leaders after the 1966 elections were *cassados*: e.g. Marcio Moreira Alves and Hermano Alves (deputies from Guanabara State), Mario Martins (Senator from Guanabara, former UDN deputy). Its leader today (1972) is deputy Pedroso Horta, from São Paulo, a former 'janista' (supporter of Jânio Quadros) politician. The former chairman of the party, Senator Oscar Passos, tendered his resignation after the disappointing results of the 1970 elections. Other leaders are Senator Ernani do Amaral Peixoto, from Rio de Janeiro State, former PSD; Nelson Carneiro, senator from Guanabara State, ex-PSD, elected rather for his defence of divorce than for more political stands; Senator Aurélio Vianna, from Guanabara State and a former PSB member.

As the government allows no room for effective opposition, the MDB has tended to fall into line with the Executive's policies. Already in 1968, in view of the restrictions on political activity, there were three different positions within the party : the first thought it should dissolve; the second that it should join ARENA, and carry out whatever opposition would be possible from within; the third believed a radical extra-parliamentary movement should replace the legal struggle. The third has died since, and two currents exist today : one, led by Pedroso Horta, thinks the MDB should press for the abolition of the emergency legislation and a return to normal democratic institutions, to constitutional life (reinstatement of habeas corpus, individual and political rights, rejection of repression and torture); the other, led by deputy Adolfo de Oliveira, thinks the MDB should manipulate the existing framework, allegedly the only viable alternative today.

There has recently been some talk that the military would be interested in what is called a 'limited decompression' of the political system, allowing some discussion to influence the decision-making process. But this would not apply only to Congress – or not even chiefly to Congress – but to all the 'living forces' of the nation, such as industrialists, technicians, financiers, possibly the clergy. It seems that political party life as such is not to be emphasized. As was shown before the 1970 elections, which were preceded by mass arrests all over the country, the dictatorship will go on making full use of its power to determine the outcome of any consultation at the polls.

*

Médici's government has been trying to usher Brazil into the 'Great Power' era. This is not only implicit in official statements, but was officially admitted in the Three Year

Development plan for 1972–4, presented in a message to Congress in September 1971. The plan's basic objectives are: (1) to turn Brazil into one of the world's developed nations by the end of the century; (2) to double *per capita* income between 1969 and 1980; (3) to keep the current growth rate (9 per cent or more per year), while reducing inflation to a maximum of 10 per cent a year (it was around 18 per cent in 1971). In order to achieve this, private enterprise should be encouraged; public investment will concentrate on the main national priorities; economic and political decentralization are to be encouraged; more emphasis is put on education, agriculture and health, rather than on industrial growth; there are plans for the integration of the north-east and Amazonia; exports should be expanded.

All this requires a serious political mobilization (political in the sense of the relationship of the people with the decision-making power). But it has not been, and will not be, political mobilization in the usual sense of the word. The government selects what it considers to be the national priorities and then launches massive campaigns through an efficient and all-embracing publicity apparatus. In a country where the level of political consciousness and participation has always been low and where party politics was often considered corrupt and self-interested (and often was so), the people can be expected to support schemes which seem beneficial to themselves and to Brazil as a whole. Expressions like 'national integration' and 'Brasil Grande' (a great Brazil) are now more instrumental in political mobilization and attempts to gain support than the usual party politics.

On the other hand, the two parties keep many of their local allegiances and have not become national parties. The discussion about *sublegendas* (party fractions which allow local alliances to be formed for elections) in the last few years has shown how provincial their outlook and how regional their bases still are. The much talked about third party (led by Pedro Aleixo, Costa e Silva's Vice-President) has been struggling to get off the ground, with the aim of helping the government to take the country back into constitutional legality, but its future is uncertain. There hardly seems to be room for two parties, let alone for a third.

The repressive apparatus is firmly established today. Intimidation or open violence is a permanent threat to all actual or potential opponents of the government, and anyone who thinks about organizing the masses to defend their own interests has to take this into account. Repressive violence has become institutionalized, and the security bodies often seem to lead a life of their own, uncontrolled by the government. Torture, though always denied by the military, is widespread. Médici's purge of some hard-liners in the Air Force in December 1971 might indicate some government interest in reducing violence practised against political prisoners. The existence of the Death Squads (groups of policemen, retired or not, who execute supposed criminals in isolated spots outside the big urban centres), which have claimed over 1,000 deaths in the last few years, seems to go on unchecked: some of the military would regard the moves to disband them and arrest their members, attempted by the judiciary, as a challenge to the ruling dictatorship. Some policemen involved in these Squads have also been efficient servants of the regime combating subversion.

Could economic growth or the new international situation lead to a more liberal political system in Brazil? The possibility exists, but it is not a very strong one. While trying to strengthen capitalism in Brazil (encouragement of stock exchange transactions, of multinational mergers; tax exemptions for investments in poor areas; attempts to increase productivity in industry and agriculture and to improve public services), the military are now as ever obsessed with security. The recently formulated Geisel doctrine, called after the Minister of the Army in late 1971, states that if the needs of development (trade with any country, including the socialist ones) open Brazil outward, security needs must close it inward, to avoid ideological contamination from other peoples. Development, according to the doctrine, requires strict political discipline, which reinforces the idea that Institutional Act 5 is not only a special power against subversion but an institutional instrument of development. International economic cooperation should increase, together with political vigilance.

While the economy grows fast, the military regime is likely to be safe. There are, however, serious economic distortions which might lead to economic troubles and social unrest, as the benefits of growth are concentrated not only socially – in the upper and upper-middle classes – but also geographically : São Paulo State, which accounts for 19 per cent of the total Brazilian population, accounted for 62 per cent of industrial production in 1971 (as compared to 55 per cent in 1970). Another sign of imbalance is that the Three Year Development Plan for 1972–4 foresees an increase of only 3·2 per cent in the number of jobs in the period; as the population is likely to increase by about 9 per cent and GNP by around 30 per cent in these three years, it seems that the already privileged sectors and regions will become even more so.

Until a mass-based popular movement – underground, as no other means is available at the moment – is organized in Brazil, for political freedom and economic emancipation for the people, pleas for human rights are bound to get lost in the wilderness. The MDB leader Pedroso Horta recently protested against the suspension of habeas corpus and the existence of 3,000 political prisoners in São Paulo alone. Political party life gets increasingly unimportant. ARENA is only a sounding-board for the government, and the MDB's opposition, even if full of good intentions, is restricted to well-behaved middle-class moral criticism of the government. The parties can retain some local power, mostly due to the distribution of patronage and favours, but their national role will be uncertain and small.

Meanwhile, a type of corporate state is trying to establish itself in Brazil. With the army and the upper classes as its mainstays; relying on total control of the trade unions, on massive propaganda and control of information (press and book censorship etc.), on physical and also intellectual repression (purges in schools and universities) and psychological intimidation; allowing some participation – mostly advisory – of upper-class groups and technocrats in decision-making; and bandying about the expression 'economic development' and the mystique of 'Brasil Grande', the regime is trying to impose on the people an ideal image of Brazil, drawn up by the Higher War College ideologues and strategists and by capitalist technocrats. Not a dictatorship, the military would say, a democracy certainly, 'but not of a liberal type'.

1966: revised 1972

SILAS CERQUEIRA

Chile

Introduction

Chile occupies an area of 292,257 square miles on the western
edge of the Andean Cordillera, and supports a population of
ten million inhabitants, according to the 1970 census. Only
the central valley containing the big towns of Santiago, Valparaíso and Concepción are relatively densely populated. The
urban population (i.e. that of centres with more than two
thousand inhabitants) represented 73 per cent of the total
in 1970 (66·5 per cent in 1960). It is still growing rapidly;
Santiago now contains just over three million inhabitants.

The country's economy is characterized by big copper ore
deposits, for many years exploited by North American companies : the Chile Exploration Co. (Chuquicamata), the Andes
Copper Mining Co. (El Salvador), and the Braden Copper
Mining Co. (El Teniente). Copper ore represents 69 per cent of
the country's exports in value, and all mineral exports together account for 80 per cent. The copper mines were
nationalized in 1971 by the government of President Salvador
Allende, though the previous administration had also taken
sectors of the mining industry into state control or into mixed
enterprises with the American companies.

Cultivable land was, until recently, mostly owned by a
small number of big landlords; in 1964, 2·2 per cent of the
estates were of more than a thousand hectares, and together

represented 73·2 per cent of the total cultivated land. These big estates were worked on archaic traditional principles by agricultural labourers or small tenant farmers. Agrarian reform, started by the Christian Democrat government of President Eduardo Frei (1964–70) was dramatically accelerated in 1971 by the Allende government. In the six years of the Frei administration about 1,200 farms were expropriated; in the first seven months of President Allende's government over 1,300 farms were taken over. Moreover, rural trade unions, which hardly existed in 1964, were widespread and powerful by 1971, organizing over 150,000 agricultural labourers.

The distribution of income is still very unequal. According to ECLA, 50 per cent of the population earns 15·6 per cent of the national income, 45 per cent receives 59 per cent, and the remaining 5 per cent accounts for 25·4 per cent of that income. The average annual income per head is about 470 US dollars, but the Allende government is pledged to very considerable redistribution of income.

The annual rate of growth of the national product is approximately 3·5 per cent. Export growth is irregular, but a general deterioration in the terms – at least up to the early 1960s – limited Chile's import capacity. After the last war the economy was overtaken by galloping inflation which was not remedied either by the stabilization plan introduced by President Alessandri or the reforms of President Frei, nor yet by the Allende government. The proportion of the GNP attributable to agriculture is only 12 per cent, and the country is an importer of foodstuffs.

These few outline data are reproduced in order to give an idea of the framework within which Chilean political life functions. Chile is one of the Latin American states which appears to the European observer to lead a relatively stable political existence, similar in some ways to French politics. Political parties are permitted, elections take place at the dates fixed for them, and even when a Marxist based Popular Unity government took power the Army still makes a more or less firm rule of political neutrality.

The 1925 constitution, still in force today,[1] established a republican government with separation of powers, the Head of State being elected by universal suffrage on a secret and direct ballot, or else chosen by Congress if no candidate has obtained an absolute majority; he cannot serve two consecutive terms. The Church is separated from the State, but the Constitution recognizes the Catholic religion as that of 'the majority of the population'. Women (since 1952) and men over eighteen years of age are now entitled to vote, though until recently there was a literacy requirement. The electoral system is proportional representation. Members of the armed forces on active service and clergy of all denominations are not entitled to vote. The executive power is vested in the President of the Republic, who is elected for a six-year term; his powers are considerable, although limited by the legislature. A two-thirds majority in both Houses (Senate and Chamber of Deputies) can overrule the presidential veto. Constitutional reforms can now be referred to the people by plebiscite. The Senate and the Chamber of Deputies together constitute the National Congress. The Senate is composed of forty-five members elected by universal suffrage for eight years; half the seats come up for re-election every four years. The Chamber of Deputies consists of one hundred and forty-seven members elected for four years; there is one to every thirty thousand inhabitants or fraction of over fifteen thousand.[2]

1. It has been subjected to some amendments since the election of President Frei, so as to permit certain reforms, notably the extension of the right to vote to the illiterate. President Allende has new proposals to turn the bicameral legislature into a single chamber system.

2. Since constituency boundaries were drawn up on the basis of outdated censuses, there is a serious problem of under-representation of the new working class areas in the cities – especially Santiago – and over-representation of some rural districts.

From the point of view of the creation and development of political parties, Chile's political history may be divided into four periods:[3] from 1830 to 1860 two political currents – conservative and liberal – were discernible, but there were no political parties in the proper sense; in practice the conservatives had the ascendancy. Between 1860 and 1890, the period of liberal ascendancy, political groupings appeared and disappeared, proliferated and vanished again, and presidents governed with their support. However, there may be said to have been four fairly constant parties at this time – Conservatives, Liberals, Nationalists and Radicals. This number was then augmented by the appearance of the Democrats; and then, after the civil war and President Balmaceda's suicide, seven further parties. The period of parliamentary rule, from 1891 to 1920, was an era of ministerial instability and near-abrogation of the President's powers by the oligarchical parties. From 1920 up to the present day the electorate has managed to assert its independence through the disorganization of the old oligarchical system and the appearance of new types of party corresponding more closely to existing social classes – notably the proletariat and the middle classes, the development of which has kept pace with the modernization and urbanization of Chile.

The contemporary period may be further divided into several phases:
– The Popular Front from 1938 to 1941, under Pedro Aguirre Cerda's presidency.
– A modified Popular Front, from 1946 to 1948, under the presidency of Gabriel González Videla; however, in 1947 the latter dismissed his communist ministers, then banned the Communist Party and kept himself in power until 1952.

3. This division into periods is the one proposed by Gil, Federico, *Genesis and modernization of political parties in Chile*, Gainesville (Flo.), University of Florida Press, 1962. (Latin American Monographs 18.)

– 1952–8 was the period of *ibañismo*, i.e. the 'populist' nationalism of the old right-wing dictator General Carlos Ibáñez del Campo, elected to the presidency quite legally in 1952, who once again recognized the Communist Party towards the end of his term of office.

– In 1958–64 the liberal-conservative alliance took power once more with the election of the liberal Jorge Alessandri Rodríguez, son of president Arturo Alessandri of the 20s. This period was also marked by the reorganization and increasing importance of the Frente de Acción Popular on the one hand, and the Christian Democratic Party on the other.

– 1964 saw, for the first time in Chile and in Latin America, the rise to power of the Christian Democratic Party on its own.

– 1970 saw, for the first time anywhere in the world, the democratic election of a Marxist (though not Communist) President.

On the political plane, the dual evolution that has been sketched above – disintegration of the old oligarchic system, followed by the creation, growth to maturity and consolidation of new kinds of party – explains the internal divisions and eventual disappearance of the old party groupings, and the emergence of the current parties. In about 1949, parties and electoral organizations of all kinds began to proliferate in Chile.[4] After the election of General Carlos Ibáñez del Campo to the presidency in 1952, the Chilean electorate 'rebelled' against the traditional parties once again, and the Congressional elections of 1953 bore witness to the diversity of political allegiance : besides the twelve groups already represented in Congress, twenty-four new groupings took part in the campaign, eight of which managed to have representatives

4. Gil, Federico, op. cit. However, in the opinion of the author this was not entirely attributable to the system of proportional representation, which merely gave a more faithful reflection of the existing state of political forces.

returned to Congress. In the congressional elections of 1957, eighteen organizations put up candidates.

However, after the formation of the FRAP (Frente de Acción Popular) in 1957 largely by the Socialist and Communist parties, and the reorganization of the Christian Democratic Party in the same year, and partly because of the repercussions of the Cuban revolution of 1959, the presidential elections of 1958, 1964 and 1970 and the congressional elections of 1961, 1965 and 1969 witnessed a regrouping of Chilean political forces around the following factions and parties composing the Chamber of Deputies and the Senate : for the right, the Conservative Party and the Liberal Party which in 1965 fused to form the National Party; for the left, the Socialist Party, the Communist Party and the minor National Democratic Party; for the centre, the Radical Party, an anti-clerical middle-class party, and the Christian Democratic Party.

Parties of the Right

Partido Conservador Unido (PCU) and Partido Liberal (PL)

The Conservative Party and the Liberal Party were the only two historic parties to take part in elections in 1964 and 1965. Their history is inseparable; while they may have opposed one another violently in the beginning – more as conflicting oligarchical groupings than as parties in the modern sense of the word – since the 1930s a *de facto* alliance has grown up between them, to consolidate itself gradually until their final amalgamation in 1965 into a single National Party.

These two parties were formed in the course of the political struggles that followed the resignation of O'Higgins, the independence hero, in 1823. The Conservative Party (*pelucones*) was the party of the landed oligarchy, a combination of the old colonial families and the big estate owners. The appearance and rapid growth of a middle class produced the Liberal Party (*pipiolos*) that violently opposed the clerical Conservative Party. The opposition of the two in fact centred on the 'theological question' (1864): the Liberal Party demanded secular education, the suppression of ecclesiastical privileges, civil marriage, and the separation of Church and State.[5]

These disputes are now outdated. The Liberal Party underwent numerous internal divisions until the 1930s. The Conservative Party, which until the beginning of the 1940s was the Catholic Party *par excellence*, recognized that the separation of Church from State (in 1925) had not brought about the 'social chaos' predicted, and that an alliance with the Liberty Party would have considerable advantages. This alliance was cemented, especially after 1930, by the consequences of the world economic crisis, and in particular by the serious social conflicts that resulted; it rested on the defence and preservation of the economic and social *status quo*.[6] This is the proper interpretation of Arturo Alessandri's second election to the presidency in 1932 (he had already been President from 1920–25), the control that the two parties exercised over Congress (even under the presidencies of the Radicals Aguirre Cerda, 1938–41, Antonio Ríos, 1942–6, and Gonzáles Videla, 1946–52), the accession to the presidency of Jorge Alessandri in 1958, and the success of the two parties in the local elections of 1960, in which they won 363,000 votes, almost a third of the total number of votes cast. However, a decline in the electoral strength of the two parties has been noted in

5. Cf. Pike, Frederick B., *Chile and the United States 1880–1962*, Notre Dame (Ind.), University of Notre Dame Press, 1963, pp. 1–46; cf. also Edwards Vives, Alberto, and Frei Montalva, Eduardo, *Historia de los partidos políticos chilenos*, Santiago de Chile, Editorial del Pacífico, 1949, pp. 20–37.

6. Pike, op. cit., pp. 208–13 & 243–50.

recent Congressional elections. In 1957, six Conservative senators and twenty-two deputies were elected, while the Liberals returned nine senators and thirty-two deputies; in 1961, the Conservatives sent four senators and seventeen deputies and the Liberals nine senators and twenty-six deputies to Congress.

In 1964, the Conservatives and Liberals were forced to seek an electoral alliance with a centre party that was once their mutual enemy – the Radical Party. At the beginning of the campaign for the presidential elections of 1964, the Conservatives, Liberals and Radicals combined to form a Democratic Front supporting the candidature of Julio Durán. However, the coalition collapsed before the campaign ended, and the Conservatives and Liberals supported the Christian Democrat candidate, Eduardo Frei. In the 1965 congressional elections, the Conservatives only returned two senators and three deputies, and the Liberals five senators and six deputies. They then decided to amalgamate and set up the Partido Nacional. The interests represented and defended by the Conservatives have always been those of the large landed proprietors, and the industrial and commercial elites. The party's firm electoral base for many years (until 1964) was provided by the small tenant farmers who depended on the big landowners, and by a quite considerable sector of the Catholic middle class. The Conservatives' electoral support was eroded from two directions in the 1964 and 1965 elections: by the Communist Party, which for the first time and to everyone's surprise won a number of rural votes, and the Christian Democratic Party, which attracted votes from the urban middle class.

The Liberal Party represented the interests of the mining companies, industrialists and bankers. In the long run, these interests ran parallel to those of the landowning aristocracy – the defence of economic liberalism, and social and political conservatism. In 1969, in a climate of mounting disillusionment with the Christian Democratic government, the National Party climbed to 20 per cent of the vote (compared with 14 per cent in 1967). The strongest challenge from the right however came with the candidature of former President Jorge Alessandri in the election of 1970. Alessandri's personal popularity, and the fear of many middle sectors at the increasingly radical campaign of Christian Democratic candidate Radomiro Tomic, led to a very close result with Alessandri's 34·9 per cent of the poll only 1·4 per cent behind Allende. In the municipal elections of 1971 the National Party gained just over 18 per cent of the poll. Conservatism is still an important political force in Chile.

Other Right-wing Parties

Other right-wing parties, such as the old Partido Nacional – closely connected with the higher civil service – have long since disappeared.

Between 1932 and the beginning of the War, Chile had a Partido Nacional Socialista which was the most ideological of Latin America's Nazi parties.[7] It was led by a writer and demagogue, Jorge González von Marées, and drew its support mainly from the bourgeoisie and from some immigrant German farmers in the south of Chile. Its candidate in the 1938 presidential elections, standing against Arturo Alessandri, was General Carlos Ibáñez, the ex-dictator. Following an attempted coup d'etat and some bloody incidents, for which the Alessandri government was held responsible, Ibáñez was obliged to withdraw his candidature and the National Socialist Party decided to vote for the Popular Front.

The extreme right is still present in Chilean political life, and manifests itself either sporadically as an independent political formation or, more frequently, as a faction within the conservative or Christian groupings. Recent neo-fascist

7. ibid., pp. 204–8.

movements include the Movimiento Revolucionario Nacional Sindicalista (MRNS).[8] A corporatist Catholic movement ran a daily newspaper between 1950 and 1957 called *El Debate*. Between 1949 and 1954 the ex-Nazi Jorge Prat published a weekly paper, *Estanquero*; this man became a very influential minister during Carlos Ibáñez's second presidency (1952–8), and stood for the presidency himself in 1964.

The Partido Agrario Laborista (PAL) was a right-wing nationalist movement founded in 1945. In 1952 it supported the candidature of Ibáñez – as also did the Partido Socialista Popular, representing the non-Communist far left – and in the Congressional elections of 1953 was the party that won the largest number of votes. With Ibáñez's decline, the PAL disappeared as an independent organization, in 1958. The extreme right was discredited by its complicity in the assassination of the Commander-in-Chief of the Army, General René Schneider, shortly after the election of Allende.

Parties of the Left

Social conflicts became more acute during the period of so-called parliamentary rule. The first strikes in Chile took place in the 1880s, but the first really major strike was in 1901, in Iquique; it lasted sixty days, and was eventually suppressed by force; another similar one occurred in Valparaíso in 1903. The labour movement started to organize in the first decade of this century, and in 1909 the Gran Federación Obrera de Chile (Chilean Confederation of Labour) was set up; this trade-union confederation was popularly known as the FOCH, and was at first led by a conservative lawyer. After 1917–19 it became a revolutionary organization. The labour movement's chief centres of support at that time were the port of Valparaíso, the coal mines of Lota, the nitrate mines in

8. ibid., pp. 414–15.

the north, and finally Santiago; the political currents then dominant in the labour movement were anarchism and socialism.[9]

Soon after, the leadership of FOCH was taken over by Luis Emilio Recabarren (who had accomplished the feat of being elected to the Chamber of Deputies in 1906, only to be barred from it at once). In 1912 he founded the Workers' Socialist Party, which in 1922 became the Chilean Communist Party, still under his leadership. In 1921 the FOCH, which now had about a hundred thousand members, decided to join the red Trade Union International.

Under the dictatorship of Ibáñez (1927–31) the labour movement suffered repression, but the Communist Party managed to strengthen its organization and its influence in the labour and trade-union world. After the fall of Ibáñez a few trade-union leaders set up a minority organization, the Chilean CGT, with ten thousand members, in competition with the FOCH; however, this smaller federation did not last very long.

Partido Socialista (P S)

The decision by the Workers' Socialist Party to join the Third International in 1922 was opposed by Manuel Hidalgo, who subsequently rebelled against the Stalinist leadership to form a Trotskyist-influenced Communist Party. By the end of 1931 there were many socialist and revolutionary parties, tendencies and movements, amongst them the Partido Socialista Marxista, Partido Socialista Unificado, Orden Socialista and Nueva Acción Pública – the latter founded by Alberto Martínez, a friend of Recabarren's, and Eugenio Matte Hurtado.

The division of Chilean socialism did the movement a great deal of harm, and after the failure of Carlos Davila's

9. cf. Edwards Vives, and Frei Montalva, op. cit., pp. 145–63 & 230–34.

hundred-day 'Socialist Republic' – the result of a coup d'etat – on 19 April 1933, the socialist forces regrouped themselves into a single party, the Socialist Party, which the Trotskyists later joined. The Socialist Party, which gained a large number of new members, subsequently played a very major role in Chilean political life, and even became for a time the most powerful of the mass parties.

In its inaugural manifesto, the Socialist Party declared itself Marxist, in favour of the collectivization of the means of production and the temporary dictatorship of the proletariat, a form of workers' councils, the abolition of the state, political and economic union of the Latin American countries and the establishment of an anti-imperialist continental bloc of Socialist republics. It rejected the Third International and the USSR's predominance over the international labour movement, and thereby assumed a fairly anti-Communist position, matched by bitter opposition to it from the Communist Party.

The Chilean Socialist Party is today still the only Latin American Socialist Party to possess a solid base of working-class support. As early as 1937, in the time of the Popular Front, it had three senators and nineteen deputies returned to Parliament. In 1938 the Popular Front, of which it was a part, brought to power a right-wing Radical, President Pedro Aguirre Cerda, and three ministries in the government were given to Socialists. In 1940, the Socialist Party left the Front, which disbanded itself shortly afterwards.

By leaving the Popular Front and engaging in polemics with the Communist Party over the origins of the Second World War and other questions affecting the working class, the Socialist Party isolated itself and was soon riven with dissension. In 1946 another coalition of the Popular Front type had the Radical Gabriel González Videla elected to the presidency. On this occasion, however, the Front included Liberals, Radicals and Communists (each of which had three ministers in the government until 1948), but no Socialists. Personal rivalries and internal disputes then grew and multiplied in the party, with the result that it broke up into several different organized groups or factions: Marxists, social democrats, anarcho-syndicalists, etc. By 1950 one of the breakaway groups, the Partido Socialista Popular, was stronger than the other main Socialist Party: the PSP won sixteen thousand votes in the 1950 municipal elections, whereas the PS only got just over ten thousand. The leaders of the Popular Socialist Party were Eugenio González Rojas and Raúl Ampuero; in 1952 the party collaborated with the right-wing nationalist party PAL (Partido Agrario Laborista) to get Carlos Ibáñez elected to the presidency. This temporary alliance with the nationalist right caused some dispute in the ranks of the Socialists when Ibáñez's influence began to decline, and ended up with the PSP's withdrawing its support from Ibáñez.

After 1956, the two socialist parties re-established contact as a result of the creation of a new Popular Front (Frente de Acción Popular, or FRAP), which brought together the two main Socialist organizations of the time, the Partido del Trabajo (Labour Party) and the Partido Democrático del Pueblo (People's Democratic Party), and the Communists (still under proscription). At a big Congress held in July 1957 the Marxist Socialists managed to overcome their differences and united to form the Partido Socialista under the leadership of Raúl Ampuero Díaz. The next year one of the party's best-known members, Salvador Allende, stood for the presidency as the FRAP candidate, and lost the election by about thirty-five thousand votes. (He was again the FRAP's candidate in 1964, and the victorious candidate in 1970.)

However, the earlier splits had weakened the Socialist Party; after 1960 it lost the majority it had enjoyed on the executive committee of the United Trade Union Federation, the CUTCH (Central Unica de Trabajadores de Chile), which included Socialists, Communists and Christian Democrats.

In the 1957 elections to Congress the Socialist Party obtained 11·9 per cent of the vote, returning sixteen deputies; in the 1961 elections, it won 11·2 per cent of the vote (149,122) and only managed to get twelve deputies and seven senators elected; in the 1965 elections seven senators and fifteen deputies were returned, with 10·2 per cent of the votes cast (237,081).

The party is strong in the Chilean mining centres, in certain rural areas and it also has the support of students and intellectuals. In the elections of 1971, following Allende's victory, the party rose to 23 per cent of the poll (compared with 14 per cent in 1969).

The party's leading figures include Salvador Allende; the former Rector of the University of Chile, Eugenio González Rojas; Senators Carlos Altamirano, the present General Secretary, and Aniceto Rodríguez, a former General Secretary. Raúl Ampuero, a dominant figure for many years, split from the party in 1967 and now leads an insignificant Marxist group.

From the ideological point of view, the differences and points of dispute with the Communists are numerous and weighty, both on international issues – the Socialist Party advocates a neutralist position, independent of the socialist camp and close to that of Cuba – and on national questions, where the Socialist Party has at different periods in its history swung between a moderate or right-wing position and a radical leftist attitude approaching Castroism.

After Allende's defeat in the 1964 presidential elections, the Christian Democrats hoped to make capital out of the disagreements between the Communists and Socialists – who claimed to be more left in their opposition to the Frei government – and hoped that the FRAP and CUTCH would break up. Their hopes seem to have been disappointed; FRAP overcame its internal dissenions and took part in the congressional elections of 7 March 1965, and united in alliance with other parties (the Radicals being the next largest) in the electoral campaign of 1970.

Partido Comunista de Chile

Three years after the death of its founder Luis Emilio Recabarren, the Communist Party was forced underground in 1927 for the duration of Ibáñez's dictatorship (1927–31), but emerged with its organization relatively intact.

The great economic crisis of 1930, which was one of the causes of Ibáñez's fall, also enabled the left to increase its support among the masses, especially the Communist Party, which became legal once more and subsequently concentrated on trade-union work, enabling it to become Chile's leading working-class party.

From 1931 to 1947, the Party's General Secretary was Carlos Contreras Labarca, who had been the leader of the Federation of Chilean Students (FECH) from 1920 to 1922. In 1932 the Communist Party was represented by two deputies in the lower house. Towards the end of the 1930s, thanks to its sustained efforts in this field, it won a majority in the new United Trade Union Federation, the Confederación de Trabajadores de Chile (CTCH), founded in 1936 and embracing the majority of the country's industrial and craft unions. During the period of the Popular Front (1938–41) the Communist Party, in contrast to the Socialists, continued to support the Front throughout while criticizing the weaknesses of the government, and managed to increase its influence among workers, trade unionists and intellectuals still further. In 1937 it got one senator and seven deputies elected. In the congressional elections of March 1941 it obtained 55,000 votes. During the war it rapidly increased its influence among the working class. In the 1946 elections, its support was decisive in the election of the Radical Gabriel González Videla to the presidency. The Communists thus became members of the government coalition until 1948, with three ministers – together with three Liberal and three Radical ministers. The young economist José Cademartori, a one-time deputy, became director of CORFO (Corporación de Fomento), a development council set up by the first Popular Front government.

In the 1947 municipal elections, the Communist Party made considerable progress, as it did also in the trade unions. But this consolidation of its position coincided with the intensification of the Cold War. Chile was at that time the only Latin American country with Communists in the government. President González Videla, on the pretext of a wave of social unrest, strikes and claims for the improvement of living standards, abandoned his erstwhile allies and in 1948 Congress passed a law, 'for the permanent defence of democracy', banning the Communist Party.

Although persecuted, the Communists remained active under a variety of labels – Proletarian Party, for instance – and after 1952 (with the return of Ibáñez) they were allowed to engage in political activity relatively unmolested, both in the trade-union and the electoral field. They began to win some support among agricultural workers.

Before the congressional elections of 1957, the Communist Party, as we have seen, set up a new electoral coalition, the Frente de Acción Popular (FRAP), including the Partido del Trabajo, the Partido Democrático and the Partido Democrático del Pueblo (a breakaway group from the Democratic Party), and excluding the Radicals. The Communist Party was still banned at the time of the congressional elections of 1957, but was legalized again in 1958. In the elections of 1958 the FRAP candidate came within an ace of victory; in the 1961 congressional elections, the now legal Communist Party obtained 154,130 votes (11·5 per cent of the total) and had sixteen deputies and five senators returned to Parliament, overtaking the Socialists. By 1964 its membership was estimated at more than thirty thousand.

In the congressional elections of 7 March 1965, despite the FRAP's electoral defeat the year before, the Communist Party recorded a modest improvement, with 286,157 votes (11·97 per cent), eighteen deputies and three senators, which made it the biggest left-wing party, although it still trailed far behind the Christian Democrats. During the same period it increased its influence in the trade unions: in 1962 eleven members of the council of the CUTCH were Communists, and at the 1965 Congress not one Christian Democrat was elected to the council, though they returned in 1968 and in 1971 the party rose to 17 per cent of the poll.

A number of Chilean intellectuals, economists, historians, the poet Pablo Neruda, and some leaders of the Chilean Writers' Association either joined the Communist Party or were influenced by Marxism. The leaders of the party who have attracted most public attention during its history include Luis Emilio Recabarren, Elías Lafertte, who has been party chairman, Carlos Contreras Labarca, who was General Secretary, Luis Corvalán, the present General Secretary, Volodia Teitelboim, a politician and novelist, the economist José Cademartori and René Frías Ojeda.

The party publishes a daily paper called *El Siglo* in Santiago that is also distributed to other countries in which the Communist Party is banned. Since 1941 the party has also published a monthly theoretical journal, *Principios*.

The party's minimum programme was partly identical with that of the FRAP, outlined below. It laid particular emphasis on the struggle against imperialism and against the landed and financial oligarchies, and for a 'popular government', for the nationalization of the banks, insurance companies and mines (copper, nitrates, etc.), for eradication of the mammoth estates and for social reform.

The party argued, correctly, that peaceful conquest of power through the FRAP was possible. The other Latin American communist parties are following this development with interest – the only successful example in the whole continent. The Chilean Communist Party also has long-standing links with the Italian, French and Soviet Communist Parties.

The FRAP's defeat in the 1964 presidential elections aroused considerable discussion within the Communist Party. However, the Party's basic line did not change: unity of action with the Socialists, the extension of the FRAP to include independent left-wing groups and dissident left-wing Radicals, and 'unity of action of all workers, whether they vote for Allende or for Frei'. The Communist Party in fact considers a joint Communist and Socialist policy to be the cornerstone of any useful political structure, and thinks that 'nothing that effects the democratic movement should be done without reference to that unity'. As a more distant objective, the Communist Party sees a possibility that the two working-class parties will eventually unite into a single Marxist-Leninist party. Its policy towards the Frei government was of 'firm and active opposition' to the Christian Democrats' pretensions to exercise a political monopoly, but with support for certain reforms, while at the same time proposing amendments to make them more far-reaching. The party has been the firmest and most consistent supporter of President Allende.

Frente de Acción Popular (FRAP) and the Unidad Popular

The Popular Action Front did not only contain working-class parties – the Communists and Socialists – but also a number of smaller parties of the centre-left and left such as the National Democratic Party (PADENA) and the Vanguardia Nacional Popular (VNP); it also concluded alliances with other left-wing political groupings and parties.

The Popular Front tradition in Chile is unique in Latin America. The years of Popular Front government from 1939 to 1941 and the years from 1946 to 1948 when the Communists participated in the government were both periods of major social and economic reform.

The FRAP programme included agrarian reform by expropriation (with compensation in some cases), nationalization of the banks and insurance companies and of the petroleum and sugar industries, the creation of state-run enterprises and mixed public-private companies in heavy industry, higher taxation of high incomes, a change of direction in foreign trade, particularly with the socialist countries and the other Latin American countries. After its defeat in the 1964 elections, the FRAP persevered in its efforts and managed to increase its number of deputies by four in the parliamentary elections of 7 March 1965, though still falling far behind the Christian Democrats (who returned more than fifty-four deputies).

Gaining support as the Christian Democrats declined in popular standing, the various parties of the FRAP joined with the Radicals, the MAPU (a breakaway party from the Christian Democrats) and the Acción Popular Independiente (a personalist party organized around Senator Rafael Tarud) to form the Unidad Popular (Popular Unity). Though the process of formulation saw several crises and frequent disagreements, Popular Unity nevertheless adopted an electoral programme similar to that of the FRAP. Choosing Allende as their candidate the coalition gained a very narrow lead over Alessandri in the 1970 elections. The choice of the electorate was subsequently ratified in Congress, with nearly all the Christian Democrats throwing their votes to Allende.

The Centre Parties

Partido Radical (PR)

The Radical Party was founded in 1861, during the last period of the 'Autocratic' or 'Aristocratic Republic', by Pedro León Gallo, a wealthy mine-owner in the north and leader of an abortive coup, and the brothers Manuel Antonio and Guillermo Matta. At first the Radical Party was no more than a small group of liberals demanding political reforms and ready to launch a vigorous opposition campaign. It was the expression of the rise of the new bourgeoisie enriched by the development of the mining industry in the north on the one hand, and of the resistance of the agricultural provinces in the south – the 'land of the pioneers' – to the concentration of power in Santiago. However, its cause was soon espoused by intellectuals and merchants from the petty bourgeoisie, members of Reform Clubs, and Freemasons, and as a result the Radical Party became a political force to be reckoned with; by 1932, and until 1964, it was Chile's biggest and most important political party.

In the early days, the Party's programme comprised four principal points: constitutional reform, state control of education, administrative decentralization, and universal suffrage. The militant anti-clericalism characteristic of European radicalism did not appear until later.

Towards the end of the parliamentary period, the Radical Party was the one with the broadest base of all the parties;[10] other parties that attempted to rally the middle and lower classes – such as the Democratic Party and the Liberal Democratic Party – were confined to a secondary role. However, at its congress in 1888, the Radical Party had still not formulated any precise doctrine or made any concrete claims in the economic or social spheres. Nevertheless, its influence con-

10. cf. Gil, op. cit.

tinued to grow.[11] Side by side in its ranks could be found big
landed proprietors from Concepción, wealthy mine-owners
from Copiapó, merchants from Santiago, teachers, civil servants, artisans, and other sectors of the middle classes. The
party was divided into two principal factions: on the one
hand was the wing led by Enrique MacIver, which was opposed to any popular or working-class participation in political life; on the other, the wing led by Valentin Letelier,
which favoured certain moderate reforms; this group included Pedro Aguirre Cerda, Alfredo Frigoletti, Luis Salas
Rimo and Eugenio Frías Collao. After 1906 the so-called
socialist Letelier faction triumphed over that of Enrique Mac-
Iver, and the party soon began to express the desire for reform felt in the middle class. In 1920, under Pedro Bannen,
the Radicals passed though Congress a law providing for obligatory primary education.

The economic crisis of 1929, and the resultant intensification of social struggle, brought about major changes in the
Radical Party because it was after all a mass party with a very
large and diverse support. After 1931 the reforming spirit of
the lower middle classes gained the upper hand in the party,
which henceforth accepted, in theory, the existence of the
class struggle. The alliance between the liberals and conservatives in the same period made the Radicals draw closer
together, improving the party's cohesion and also pushing it
to develop towards a moderate leftist position.[12]

Radical Party policy has always been typified by constant
hesitation and opportunism. Middle and lower middle class
elements dominated party assemblies and political debates,
while conservative interests controlled its day-to-day policy.
The party would conduct its electoral campaigns on a left-
wing platform, with left-wing slogans, and in alliance with
the Socialists or Communists – but once in power it slid in-

11. Pike, op. cit., pp. 83–93 & 117–18.
12. Edwards Vives and Frei Montalva, op. cit., pp. 227–9.

exorably to the right and ended up in an alliance with the Conservatives and Liberals.

The Radical Party was the dominant party in the Popular Front government of 1939–41, and also the one that won the most immediate profit from that alliance. The President at that time was the moderate Radical Aguirre Cerda. After his death, the party retained the presidency from 1942 until 1952, first through the right-wing Radical Juan Antonio Ríos, then, from 1946 to 1952, through Gabriel González Videla, who first governed in alliance with the Communists, only to expel them from the government and ban the party altogether during his rapid swing to the right.

During this period, the Radical Party became the centre of gravity of Chilean political life, dominating any left-wing coalition. But apart from a few reforms introduced by the 1939–41 Popular Front government and by the 1946–8 government, the coalitions led by the Radical Party did not bring about any major changes in the social sphere. However, during the years of Radical predominance, efforts were made to strengthen social security and extend education; trade unions flourished, and the Constitution was more or less respected.

However, all the Radical Presidents proved helpless to halt the rise of inflation, and a disillusioned electorate brought the old dictator, Carlos Ibáñez, the 'man with the new broom', back to the presidency in 1952. The failure of this change to bring about the hoped for results enabled the Radical Party to recover its position as the country's biggest party in the parliamentary elections of 1957, when it obtained 21·2 per cent of the vote and had thirty-six deputies elected. However, in the 1958 presidential elections, the Radical Party candidate, Bossay, only won 192,110 votes, as against 356,499 for the FRAP's candidate, Allende, and 389,948 for the victorious candidate, the liberal-conservative Alessandri.

Wild swings in success at the polls are typical of the Radical Party: thirty-four deputies in 1949, eighteen in 1953, thirty-six in 1957, thirty-nine in 1961, twenty in 1965.

The party's programme is neither very detailed nor very precise. In point of fact, it bore a considerable share of the blame for the failures in economic policy on the part of the governments from 1938 to 1952. During the 1957 election campaign, the Radicals confined themselves to attacking Ibáñez without proposing any practical alternative. During the 1958 presidential campaign, they recommended agrarian reform, without touching the estates of the *latifundia* but rather by the settlement of deserted and uncultivated land, for they considered the inadequate production of foodstuffs as one of the causes of the inflation process. The party asserted that capital development could continue to grow if excess consumption on the part of the higher income groups were restrained. It also favoured state intervention to 'safe-guard the interests of the underprivileged classes in the face of industrialization'.

The Radical Party cooperated with President Alessandri in his programme of expansion and 'stabilization', which resulted in an annual rate of inflation of around 40 per cent, a rise in food prices, the stagnation of industrial production and a rash of wage claims. Julio Durán Neumann, who stood for the presidency of the republic in 1964 on the Radical Party ticket, only obtain 125,112 votes – 4·9 per cent.

The Radical Party recovered its electoral standing after the defeat of its candidate in 1964. In the 1965 congressional elections it gained 13 per cent of the vote; in the 1967 municipal elections 16 per cent; and 13 per cent in the congressional elections of 1969. Its support was crucial for Allende's victory in 1970 and it was rewarded with three posts in his Cabinet (Education, Defence and Mining). But the party was not united in the decision to join the Popular Unity. A small but important parliamentary group left the party to join Alessandri's campaign; and since the election of 1970 another group has left the party in opposition to its increasingly Marxist pronouncements. Divisions were reflected in the party's poor showing in the 1971 elections when it gained only 8 per cent of the poll.

Partido Democrático Nacional (PADENA)

This is a centre-left nationalist party, born of a split in the old Democratic Party. PADENA was founded in 1960 by left-wing supporters of the old President Carlos Ibáñez del Campo. Its principal leader was Carlos Montero. One of the reasons for its importance is that it was able to provide an electoral ticket for a number of left-wing independents. In 1961 PADENA lost its six senators, but was able to return twelve deputies.

At the time of the 1964 presidential campaign, a small section of PADENA broke away to support Eduardo Frei's candidature. The majority of *padenistas* stayed in the party, though it has since then divided yet again and is now of very minor importance.

Partido Demócrata Christiano (PDC)

This party is the last-born of Chile's political parties, but currently the strongest in terms of the number of its voters, for it managed to win an absolute majority both in the presidential elections of 1964 and the congressional elections of 1965, and was still the largest single party in the municipal elections of 1971.

The distant origins of the PDC go back to the 1930s, to the period of the great world economic crisis and the Ibáñez dictatorship.[13] In the wake of the encyclical *Rerum Novarum*,

13. Cf. Pike, op. cit., pp. 201–2, 259–61, 423–4.

new ideas regarding Catholic social action began to take root among young people in the universities – somewhat confused ideas, it may be said, mingling paternalism, Christian socialism, corporatism and charity. In general, however, these students considered that the traditional conservative ideology was out of date. The crisis itself led a number of conservatives to take the view that concessions to the working class were necessary if the 'social order' was to survive.

The younger generation conservatives therefore tried to introduce into the Conservative Party – the traditional, semi-official Catholic party – an element of the reformism of Christian social movements in Europe. From this arose the conflict between the party leadership and Juventud Conservadora, later the Falange Conservadora, which broke away from the parent party in 1938. After the break, the Falange Conservadora became the Falange Nacional. At this early stage, the leaders of the National Falange already included Eduardo Frei, Manuel Garreton Walker, Bernardo Leighton, and Radimiro Tomic, all of whom were influenced by the contemporary influential Catholic theorists. One of the most illustrious figures among the conservatives, Rafael L. Gumucio, father of one of the present-day leaders of the Christian Left, joined the new party for a time, a gesture which made a big splash at the time. In its early days the National Falange, led by Garreton Walker who was influenced by fascism, had corporatist ideas and its electoral support was very limited. For the Chilean clergy, the faithful, and the ruling oligarchy, the official party of the Catholic Church was still the Conservative Party.

In 1945 Eduardo Frei, a law graduate of the Catholic University of Santiago who had travelled in Europe in 1933–4, became Minister of Communications in the government of Juan Antonio Ríos, a right-wing Radical elected with the support of the National Falange. In 1949 he was elected Senator for Atacama and Coquimbo (Norte Chico). Nevertheless, the National Falange was still a very weak group electorally, a state of affairs that was not helped by the creation in 1941, by a reformist conservative, Eduardo Cruz-Coke, of an identical rival party called the Partido Conservador Social Christiano, which relied heavily on votes that would normally have gone to the Falange. As a result, the Falange only won 6,860 votes in the 1950 local elections in Santiago, while the Social Christian Conservatives won 25,602. Fortunately for the Falange, Cruz-Coke's Social Christian Conservative Party was dissolved, most of its members joining the Falange in 1957. From that time on, the Falange became less conservative in its attitudes and its influence increased rapidly. Eduardo Frei, who had meanwhile published a number of political works (*The Shape and Direction of Policy, Truth's Hour Will Come*) was elected senator for the province of Santiago in 1957.

The same year, the National Falange changed its name to the Christian Democratic Party (PDC), 'the political instrument for the application of Christian social principles, that reject both the Marxist and the fascist solution'. In the 1957 congressional elections, the party already won a significant number of votes (9·2 per cent returning fourteen deputies). In 1958 Eduardo Frei stood in the presidential elections, but only managed to come third, with 255,777 votes. However, in the congressional elections of March 1961, the Christian Democratic Party obtained 212,604 votes, overtaking the Conservatives (who had 196,965 votes) for the first time, and thus acquired a leading position in Chile and in the whole Latin American Christian Democratic Movement.

The programme drawn up by the Party provided for a 'communitarian society'. Christian Democratic leaders and intellectuals asserted that unregulated monopoly capitalism was contrary to Christian morality. In his writings, Eduardo Frei emphasized the need to 'replace the profit motive by that of Christian fraternity'. Christian Democratic doctrine appears to accept the need for a 'limited class struggle' in order to force the privileged sectors of society to accept a 'new order' based upon 'distributive justice', under the pressure of the masses and with a Christian Democratic government. In these circumstances, cooperation between classes would become possible.

The party's programme paid a certain amount of attention to economic problems. Chiefly for social reasons, it did not entirely accept the kind of solution proposed by the right (fighting inflation by extremely austere monetary and fiscal measures), since this could provoke a dangerous fall in the country's growth rate, and aggravate poverty and unemployment. The solution proposed and tried by the Radicals (giving free rein to consumption, profits, wages and prices in the hope of stimulating production) also seemed to the Christian Democrats dangerous from the social point of view. Their proposal for a solution was a 'policy of restriction, with control of investment, wages and credit, but in an evolutionary rather than a strict way'; the long-term policy was one of priority investment in basic capital sectors, monetary stabilization closely linked with industrialization, agrarian reform by immigration and settlement of non-cultivated land and by a few expropriations with full compensation, 'levelling-up' of incomes by increasing productivity and cooperation between private and state-owned industry. The Christian Democratic Party also set itself the task of raising the Chilean national income by 70 per cent in ten years; the standard of living of the working class was to be doubled and the incomes of other social groups would rise by 30 per cent; the annual rate of inflation would be progressively reduced from 40 to 10 per cent. This was in effect a 'national offensive against the poverty of three million Chileans'.

An analysis of the progress of the 1964 election campaign, which resulted in placing a Christian Democratic Party alone in the seat of power, for the first time in the history of Latin America, gives an insight into the Chilean public's reaction to this programme. Four candidates stood for the presidency : the FRAP put up Salvador Allende, the Christian Democrats Eduardo Frei, the Liberals, Conservatives and Radicals, representing the coalition then in power, campaigned for the Radical Julio Durán, and finally on the extreme right stood an 'independent' candidate, the ex-Nazi Jorge Prat, with little chance of success.

The progress made by the FRAP and the Christian Democrats first in congressional and then in local elections gave grounds for thinking that the first three candidates would all come very close to one another. Then, in the spring of 1964, a partial election was held in the rural province of Curicó. The three main political groups each presented a candidate, and, to general stupefaction, the FRAP's Socialist candidate easily defeated the Liberal-Radical-Conservative candidates; the Christian Democrats' candidate, who achieved a remarkable increase in his party's vote, could only manage third place. In the days following this sensation, the right-wing coalition broke up; Durán withdrew his candidature and then, after considerable hesitation, the Liberal and Conservative parties called on their supporters to vote for Frei. Then Durán again put forward his candidature, this time in the name of the Radical Party alone. The Centrists and Conservatives knew that a single united candidature could collect a majority of votes and defeat the Socialists and Communists; however, Durán's candidature was maintained as a diversionary tactic designed to prevent the Radical Party's anti-clerical vote from going to the FRAP. The campaign immediately came alive as the stakes became clear : would a Marxist coalition take power, legally and peacefully, in a Latin American country? The issue was clearer in 1964 than in 1970 when three strong candidates were standing.

The Liberal and Conservative parties stood for social conservatism, particularly in the sphere of agriculture. The Radical Party was torn between conflicting factions, and contented itself with a campaign that was vaguely anti-Communist in tone. The FRAP's election programme called for the nationalization of the copper, nitrate and iron mines, and agrarian reform by expropriation of the *latifundia*. The Christian Democrats, finally, campaigned on the slogan of 'revolution with freedom' and the defence of representative democracy; it came out in favour of some degree of agrarian reform, and of the 'Chileanization' of the copper industry (the Chilean state was to take a large part in investment, extraction, and above all overseas sales of ore).

The Liberal and Conservative Parties endeavoured to modify this programme, while still supporting Eduardo Frei's candidature. The FRAP's efforts to woo the Radical Party only managed to win over its left-wing fringe. The electoral campaign lasted almost six months. It was conducted with powerful weapons: the candidates made systematic use of the railways and the radio (Frei had the voice of thirty-nine transmitting stations); special vehicles with loud-speaker systems were used by the Christian Democrats, rallies and cavalcades were held, all organized by electoral 'task forces' independent of their party leaderships. The Trade Union Confederation (CUT), although it took no official position, indicated its preference for Allende. The Catholic hierarchy, through the mouth of the Cardinal Archbishop of Santiago, called on the electorate to vote 'Christian' to ward off the Communist menace. The government adviser at the American Embassy, Joseph Jova, was suspected of exerting pressure to get various socialist civil servants dismissed. It seems that the Christian Democrats did not go short of funds, especially after the right-wing parties came over to support Frei's candidature. From that moment on, the style of the campaign changed; Christian Democratic election organizers began to employ American electoral campaign techniques such as broadcasting brief slogans in the middle of a football match or a play, special party-political broadcasts and 'slanted' songs. Nine dailies in Santiago and forty-five others in the rest of the country campaigned for Eduardo Frei with full page illustrated advertisements and display placards.

At the same time, it seems there was a campaign of systematic intimidation carried out in Chile, with the object of exaggerating the strength – which certainly existed – of the extreme left-wing parties and the FRAP. The latter were so sure of victory that they devoted considerable trouble to thinking up and finding counter-measures to the kinds of reaction that their victory might provoke – a coup d'etat, armed intervention – so as to force the parties of the centre and right to re-group around the Christian Democrats.

The elections proceeded without incident, and the results were as follows: Frei: 1,418,101; Allende: 982,122; Durán: 125,112; blank votes: 7,417; spoiled ballot papers: 15,266. With an absolute majority of the votes cast, Eduardo Frei therefore became, on 3 November 1964, Chile's first Christian Democratic President. If the votes cast by men and women are considered separately, Frei received 744,423 women's votes and 675,678 from men, and Allende 375,766 women's votes and 606,000 from men. The feminine vote, largely under the influence of the Catholic Church, was decisive in the poll, as also was the big-city vote: in Santiago, Frei obtained 621,466 votes and Allende 365,502 (FRAP's forecast had been Frei 446,000 and Allende 475,000); Valparaíso: Frei 160,313, Allende (a native of the city) 95,686 (FRAP's forecast: Frei 104,000, Allende 137,000). Only Concepción gave Allende a 7,000-vote majority.

In contrast, therefore, to the FRAP leadership's fears, it was not the countryside, in which they were not strongly entrenched, that came out against them, but above all the middle class in the big cities, some sectors of the non-union working class, and part of the sub-proletariat of the shanty towns.

Some Christian Democrats had hoped for the sudden dis-integration of the FRAP after the elections, through the de-fection of the National Democratic Party and the Socialist Party. Nothing of the sort occurred, however, and these parties renewed their alliance for the congressional elections of 7 March 1965.

It may well be asked how the small group that the Christian Democrats were until 1957 managed to become the biggest party in Chile. There are a number of different factors and levels to be distinguished in this transformation. The first is a historical factor: the importance of the Catholic political tradition in Chile, especially among the ruling classes. Then there were objective conditions that played a part: according to Eduardo Frei, Chile was passing through a 'revolutionary' or 'pre-revolutionary situation' as a result of galloping inflation, the constant decline in the economic indices, and increasingly numerous and prolonged social conflicts. Subjective conditions: the divided Chilean oligarchy could never agree on the best formula for govern-ment, and feared another three-cornered contest such as that of 1958, when the FRAP almost came to power thanks to the divisions in the ruling class. As for the political situation, the strength of the FRAP, popular pressure and so on had forced the oligarchy to join forces with the reformist middle class in an effort to find a new political instrument able to face up to the country's dramatic social problems. This new political instrument – Christian Democracy – already existed and was busily organizing, had long sought a broad popular base, and was making gradual progress; after 1957, its open-ings for recruitment and organization suddenly multiplied. What had happened in these few short years? First of all the two Christian Democratic parties had reunited; secondly, the Chilean Church, or at least some sectors of it, had changed its attitude towards Christian Democracy; and finally, the party had received considerable assistance from the international Christian Democratic movement.[14]

In the trade-union field, too, the Chilean Christian Democrats have made a sustained effort to train union officials, thanks to the assistance of CLASC (Latin American Conference of Christian Trade Unions), which came into conflict with the American unions of the AF of L–CIO and the Inter-American Trade Union Organization, ORIT. Immediately after the Christian Democrats' electoral victory, they made an attempt – unsuccessfully – to set up a parallel trade-union machine, or even to split the United Trade Union Federation, CUTCH. Meanwhile, the Christian Democrats trained one thousand peasants for party political work.

Christian Democracy in power. Composed largely of young men, President Frei's governing team included a large number of lawyers, together with industrialists and technologists. The principal points on the government's programme were as follows :

– In domestic policy : constitutional reform; the strengthening of the executive at the expense of the legislature by recourse to referenda; the right to vote to be extended to il-

14. For example the influence and the role played by the Belgian Jesuit Father Vekemans, who arrived in Chile in 1957, has been considerable in the field of Christian social action, as has the role of his collaborator, the American Jesuit Fr Joseph H. Fichter. Some importance has been attributed to the aid given by German Christian Democracy both in Chile and in the German Federal Republic, for there are long-standing traditional ties between Chile and Germany. In 1959 in the Federal German Republic, the bishops launched a campaign, 'Misereor', which collected millions of dollars for underdeveloped countries. In 1960 the Centro para el Desarrollo Económico y Social de América Latina (DESAL) was founded in Chile, which received contributions from Germany and trained Christian Democratic party workers, who were sometimes sent to the Institute of Social Solidarity in Bonn to complete their training.

literates. In social affairs : agrarian colonization and reform including expropriation, with compensation paid in government bonds appreciating in value to take account of inflation; reform of the labour laws, pay increases and 'workers' participation in company management', etc. In economic affairs : the fight against inflation, redressing the balance of payments by increasing exports, restriction of purchase of foodstuffs, accelerated industrialization; the 'Chileanization' – although not by nationalization – of mineral wealth, and fiscal reform to tax higher incomes more heavily.

– In foreign policy : while reaffirming Chile's membership of the western bloc, and his own ties with fraternal parties in Europe, President Frei decided to maintain diplomatic and trading relations with every country in the world, including the socialist countries (but excluding Cuba), notably the Soviet Union, which seemed ready to grant Chile substantial economic aid. President Frei hoped to maintain excellent relations with the United States, on condition that Chile be treated 'on an equal footing', as a true ally. In actual fact, American hegemony was not threatened.

In an interview with the Spanish newspaper *ABC*, Frei explained that the differences between Christian democracy in Chile and in Europe were due to the facts of Chilean life which 'demand of the Christian Democrat Party revolutionary structural changes and the progressive recovery of the country's natural riches, exploited by foreigners', and 'in the field of foreign affairs ... a policy of non-alignment and the establishment of trading relations with all countries ...' The object of Christian democracy was to put into effect the 'revolution in freedom' by outflanking the FRAP, and to 'move over into the popular camp and fight Communism at the level of the people'.

However, there was a problem facing President Frei. How was he going to put his programme into operation? In the Chamber of Deputies, the Christian Democrats only had twenty-three deputies out of one hundred and forty-seven, and in the Senate fourteen out of forty-five senators. Right-wing congressmen would boycott his agrarian reform bills, the extension of the franchise and such like. Extreme left-wing congressmen were not likely to give him any support, and in any case he did not ask for it. The Socialists proved extremely intransigent. So were the Communists, but in a more subtle fashion : they were willing to vote for some reforms, but would oppose others that they considered favourable to foreign interests or likely to favour the political monopoly of Christian Democracy through integration with the state machine. They therefore opposed the government's request for special powers, the reinforcement of the executive, and agreements with American mining companies which would exclude nationalization. On the other hand, they supported the introduction of a tax on capital and the 'Chileanization' of the electricity and telephone companies.

President Frei skilfully exploited these numerous conflicts with Congress to prepare public opinion for the congressional elections of 7 March 1965, which resulted in a political landslide. The Christian Democrats won an absolute majority in the Lower House, with 989,629 votes (41·06 per cent), eighty-two elected deputies and thirteen senators.

It seemed that there would now be no obstacle to the application of the reform programme put forward by President Frei. Even the United States supported him, even though they had to accept certain sacrifices resulting from the increased participation of the Chilean state in mining profits, and though they had to agree to allow the Chilean government a degree of independence in its foreign policy. However, Chilean political life in the coming years was to be determined partly in relation to the agrarian question, but above all by problems of economic independence and industrialization.

An analysis of the poll of March 1965 shows, finally, that

Socialist and Radical votes held steady, while the Communists increased their vote slightly. Eduardo Frei's victory was therefore due to the massive shift in Conservative and Liberal votes to the Christian Democrats. This right-wing support did not remain loyal to the party. From its high vote of 42 per cent in 1965 the party's share declined to 31 per cent in 1969. In the presidential election of 1970 their candidate, former Senator and ex-Ambassador to Washington Radimiro Tomic, came third with 28 per cent of the poll. Yet the defeat of the party did not, as frequently happens in Chile, result in an abrupt drop in support. In the 1971 municipal elections the party remained the largest single party with 26 per cent of the poll.

Why did the Christian Democrats fail? Their promises were not fulfilled. Inflation was not controlled – instead of the promised price stability for 1969, the rate of inflation was over 30 per cent. *Per capita* incomes rose on average only 2 per cent per annum over their period of government – hardly the promised 'revolution in liberty'. The achievements of agrarian reform fell far short of the promises. The record in education and housing – though creditable – was far from meeting demand or expectation. Though the Christian Democrats did achieve notable successes in redistribution of income, in a favourable balance of payments situation, in effecting social change in the countryside, too many of their achievements were attained in the first three years of the government. The last three years disappointed the party's own supporters and led to the formation by a breakaway 'rebel' group of the Movement of Popular United Action (MAPU) which supported Allende. The attack on trade unions and the attempts to impose strict wage controls alienated much popular support. And, finally, the left-wing campaign of Tomic frightened many middle-class and Catholic supporters into supporting Alessandri.

The Marxist dominated Popular Unity government took

office in November 1970. The cabinet posts were distributed amongst all the members of the coalition, the Communists took Labour, Public Works and Finance, the Socialists Foreign Affairs, Housing and Interior, the Radicals Defence, Education and Mining, MAPU Agriculture, the Social Democrats Health and Land, API Justice, and the key Economics post went to an independent though left-wing economist, Sergio Vuskovic.

The first year of the Allende government saw dramatic change. The copper mines were nationalized; the banking system was taken over; nitrates, coal, steel, many key industrial concerns joined the state sector. Agrarian reform rapidly accelerated. Unemployment fell and income was redistributed in favour of the poor. Even inflation was reduced to 18 per cent. Economic growth reached a high level of a 7–8 per cent increase in the GNP.

This economic change was achieved without massive social dislocation or resort to authoritarian measures. The Constitution is respected, the army still neutral, the press still free and Congress is still powerful – and with the opposition in the majority. Fidel Castro's visit to Chile was a great success, but Allende shows no signs yet of imitating Cuban methods.

The new regime faces many and severe problems – can it sustain economic growth? Can it deal with an increasingly unfavourable balance of payments situation? Can it cope with opposition from the extreme right and the extreme left? Nevertheless, its progress in its first year has brought about irreversible changes in Chilean politics, society and the economy.

Conclusion

Chilean political life is in strong contrast to what goes on elsewhere in Latin America, not only because democratic freedoms are rather more deeply rooted there than in other countries but above all, in the author's opinion, because of the decisive role played by the political parties.

In contrast to other countries on the continent, Chilean politics are conducted through the medium of the political parties – the parties are not incidental or in opposition to the general political trend. As we have seen, this has not always been so. This result of a lengthy process depends on the one hand on the objective conditions of Chilean socio-economic development and on the other hand on the feats of organization carried out by politicians and social classes. The existence of two powerful working-class parties of a developed and modern type that are moreover united in a single anti-imperialist front has made a major contribution to the strengthening of political organization and participation by polarizing Chilean politics. Chile is a good example of the fact that in Latin America one of the ways of clarifying the political situation and developing the democratic process is through political parties that correspond to social classes, and through an alliance between those forces that desire national economic independence.

September 1966: revised February 1972

Notes on the Regions of Chile [15] (See Figures 9 and 10, pp. 275–6.)

Norte Grande
24 per cent of the total surface area of the country and 5 per cent of the population: mining area (copper, nitrates), 75 per cent of the population live in towns.

Norte Chico
16 per cent of the surface area of the country and 5·7 per cent

15. From Gil, Federico, *The Political System of Chile*, Allen & Unwin, 1966.

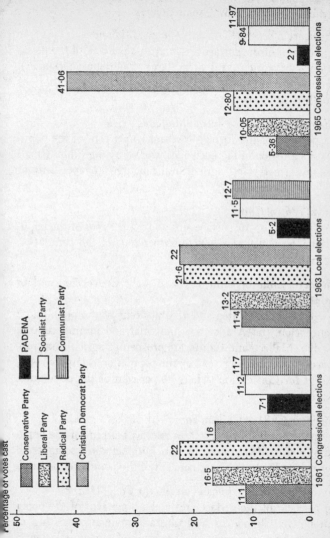

Figure 8. Votes Cast for the Main Parties in Various Elections 1961–5

of the population : mining and agricultural area, 55 per cent of the population is rural (small-holders).

The heart of central Chile (the Chilean Midlands)
4·4 per cent of the surface area and 43·4 per cent of the population : an agricultural area (large traditional *haciendas*), combined with industry (with a heavy concentration of middle-class people).

The rural part of the Chilean Midlands
4·2 per cent of the surface area and 10 per cent of the population : a region of big *haciendas* worked by *inquilinos* (small tenant farmers) and agricultural labourers (67 per cent of the population is rural).

End of central Chile
39·9 per cent of the surface area and 7·3 per cent of the population : agricultural region – 66 per cent of the population is rural.

Southern Chile or Chilean Forest – the Concepción and La Frontera region
7·4 of the surface area and 18·6 per cent of the population; Concepción and Arauco are industrial and mining centres; Bío-Bío, Malleco and Cautín are prosperous agricultural provinces (cattle farming, maize); the population is largely rural, except for Concepción (where 76 per cent of the population is urban).

Southern Chile or Chilean Forest – the Lakes
6·2 per cent of the surface area and 7·7 per cent of the population : a cattle-farming district, but including some small agricultural properties; 65 per cent of the population is rural.

Southern Chile or Chilean Forest – the Canal District
33 per cent of the surface area and 2·8 per cent of the population : in Chiloé, an agricultural province consisting of medium-sized properties, 82 per cent of the population is

rural; Aysen, a sheep-farming province (three million sheep), has a population that is 56 per cent rural; in Magallanes (coal, oil), 81 per cent of the population is urban.

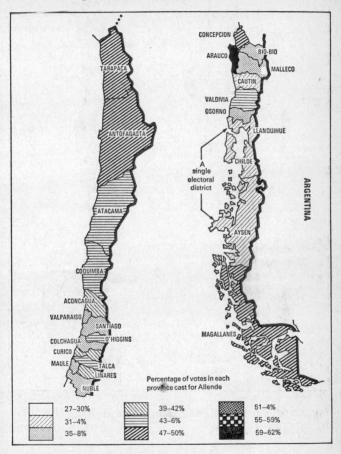

Figure 9. Votes Cast for Salvador Allende in the 1964 Presidential Elections

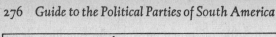

Figure 10. Votes Cast for Eduardo Frei in the 1964
Presidential Elections

PIERRE GILHODÈS

Colombia

Introduction

The most remarkable characteristic of this country is the durability of two parties, the Liberals and the Conservatives, throughout the history of Colombia since independence. It is customary to trace this division back to the rivalry between the military dictator Bolivar and the civilian Santander in the early independence period, the former being cast as the father of conservatism and the latter as the founder of liberalism. These attributions of paternity are highly dubious, to say the least, as Santander could only remotely be considered a liberal up to the time of the overthrow of Urdaneta's Bolivarian dictatorship, and during his period in opposition the undisputed leader of nineteenth-century conservatism, Mariano Ospina, was his ally.[1] The historian Lievano traces the division even further back, to the eve of independence, contrasting the Creole oligarchs (Camilo Torres, Jorge Tadeo Lozano) with the more popular federalist *caudillos* such as Antonio Nariño.

It was not until 1849 that the two political currents made their appearance in a more or less clearly defined form, each with its own programme. That of the Conservative Party was the work of Caro and Ospina. The same year, the con-

1. Lievano Aguirre, Indalecio, *Los grandes conflictos socio-económicos de nuestra historia*, Bogotá, Tercer Mundo, pp. 557 ff.

servatives were to lose power under the pressure of the democratic artisans' guilds, which carried José Hilario López to the presidency, supported by the young middle-class intellectuals who were to leave their mark on liberal thought for the next half-century – the Sampers, Camachos, and others.

What were the reasons for the antagonism between these two groups at that time? (They could hardly yet be called parties.) On the philosophical level, the Liberals drew their inspiration from Bentham,[2] and on the economic plane from the Manchester school. However, in the wake of the European movements of 1848 a vague form of socialism, derived chiefly from Louis Blanc and Eugène Sue, found its way into the liberal ideology.

Politically, the Liberals favoured federalism, the abolition of slavery and the restriction of the prerogatives of the Church; they also believed in free trade. Colombian liberalism is essentially the product of an alliance between the urban artisan class and the merchant middle class connected with the import-export trade. It enjoyed the support of the black population, which provided the backbone of its revolutionary armies.

The Conservative programme was diametrically opposed to these points of view. The Conservatives of 1849 were clericalist, pro-slavery (the abolition of slavery was to provoke the Conservative insurrection of 1851), and centralist. This party's economic doctrine is more difficult to define; it could be described as the economic viewpoint of the Spaniards in the colonial era, advocating in particular state intervention (although the abolition of the state tobacco monopoly that was to bring about Colombia's first economic boom was begun by the then Conservative President Mosquera). It should also be pointed out that between 1853 and 1861 the Conservative Presidents Mallarino and Ospina took full advantage of

2. Jaramillo Uribe, Jaime, *El pensamiento colombiano en el siglo XIX*, Bogotá, Temis, 1964, pp. 149 ff.

federalism to strengthen their hegemony over the province of Antioquia, their bastion.

The democratic guilds, which were particularly active in Bogotá and Cali, were defeated after they encouraged General Melo to take power by a coup d'etat in 1854. They were opposed by the first National Front in Colombia's history, composed of moderate Liberals and Conservatives.

In 1861 President Ospina was overthrown after a bloody civil war begun by the invading ex-conservative General Mosquera, who seized power in protest against unwarrantable interference by the federal government in the state of Cauca, of which he was President. This was to be the only instance of a successful political insurrection in Colombia. Mosquera's second presidency is notable for the confiscation of Church property, and for the approval of the federal Constitution of 1863 (the Constitution of Rionegro), which was to ensure Liberal preponderance until 1886. Several Conservative insurrections were crushed, and then, after a split in the Liberal Party caused by a breakaway faction under Rafael Núñez, the Conservatives returned to power. This process has been analysed as follows: 'This demonstrated the application of the electoral strategy of the third force – the force regularly created with elements of both parties (i.e. the opposition and the government party); it is the traditional mechanism for the conquest of power, as instanced by the Independent Party of Núñez, the Republican Party of Restrepo, the National Concentration of Olaya Herrera, or Mariano Ospina's National Coexistence group.'[3] This was, in fact, the only way in which power could have passed from one party to the other in 1886, 1930 and 1946. There is no instance of an opposition party taking power after an election without such a split in the governing party.

Núñez's presidency, and then that of Caro, mark the period

3. Garcia, Antonio, *La democracia en la teoría y en la práctica*, Bogotá, Cooperativa Colombiana de Editores, 1957, p. 63.

of 'Regeneration' modelled on the Spanish 'Restoration' of Cánovas del Castillo, ushered in by the introduction of the centralist, presidential Constitution of 1886 (which has been described as a 'monarchy without a king') and by the establishment of a Concordat which granted to the Church a position that is almost unique in the world. Both Constitution and Concordat are still in force today.

The reaction against the political anarchy brought about by the Rionegro Constitution was manifested not only in official statutes, but also in deeds. The Liberals were persecuted throughout the country and forced to renounce all hope of parliamentary representation, and were banned from public service. The emigration of persecuted Liberals was one of the factors influencing the colonization of the west of Colombia by the Antioqueños.[4] Twice (in 1895 and 1899) they attempted a comeback by means of civil war, and twice they were crushed. The representation of minorities was not permitted until the authoritarian government of Rafael Reyes (1904–9); it is remarkable to note that the major legislative reforms have been the fruit of regimes that came into power by force of arms. This is in fact a historical phenomenon that a civilian tradition has tended to ignore. It may well be more fruitful to look beyond the struggle between Liberals and Conservatives and consider a process of alternation – popular *caudillos* supported in power by force, followed by civilians who get the country to assimilate the changes introduced by the former; a period of stagnation then follows, which finally results in another violent coup, and so on.

During the period of Conservative hegemony, the country was gradually becoming modernized. Although it lost Panamá in 1903, the compensation later paid by the United States was one of the chief factors in the economic expansion of the

4. See the thesis, still relevant today, of Parsons, James J., *Antioqueño Colonization in Western Colombia*, California University Press, 1969.

country, enabling a public works programme to be carried out. The prosperity brought to the country by the development of commercial coffee-growing was manifested by the first signs of industrialization in Medellín. The communications necessary to establish national unity were developed: railways, roads and even air routes. Up till then the country had been sharply divided, under the imperatives of geography and colonial tradition, into east and west. This problem of national unity still exists today, moreover. Particularist tendencies exist in several provinces; the recent move towards integration has been less the result of deliberate policy emanating from the capital than of the colonization of the rest of the country by the province of Antioquia, itself the consequence of industrial, financial and demographic growth.

Meanwhile, the Liberal Party was revising its ideology, and under the influence of Rafael Uribe Uribe became markedly impregnated with socialist ideas.[5]

It needed inflation and the fall of the standard of living in the years leading up to the 1929 crisis to bring about a division of the Conservatives into two camps, exhausted as they were by the exercise of power and impotent in the face of a social movement that took shape in a strike of the employees of the United Fruit Company. The Colombian Ambassador in Washington, a moderate liberal, was then elected to the presidency, and first formed a bipartite government. The Liberal Party, in a minority in the country, did not shrink from using violence to maintain its position in the provinces, notably in Santander and Boyacá.

In 1934, the President was succeeded by another Liberal, Alfonso López Pumarejo, who in the atmosphere created by

5. At this time, as Eduardo Santa has pointed out in his *Sociología política de Colombia*, Bogotá, Tercer Mundo, 1964, p. 86, both parties were re-examining their doctrinal positions: 'While Liberalism was drinking at the fount of the French socialist leader Jaurès and, later, of Harold Laski, Conservatism turned its face towards Leo XIII.'

the New Deal and the European Popular Fronts announced that the Revolution was under way. The government programme, which strove to eliminate the legacy of the past as expressed in the economic structure of the country, met with powerful opposition within the Liberal Party itself. The 'Revolución en Marcha' manifested itself in a limited number of changes, despite a real legislative effort; however, popular pressure, especially in agriculture, fired by Jorge Eliécer Gaitán and the young Communist Party, was no longer repressed, and trade unionism began to develop rapidly. A halt to the programme was called in 1938, when the proprietor of the daily *El Tiempo*, Eduardo Santos, emerged at the head of a moderate Liberal government. However, he proved unable to prevent the re-election of López, whose second term witnessed a succession of spectacular upheavals which dramatically sounded the death-knell of Colombian reformism: a military rising in 1944 and the President's removal in 1945 by the Liberal Party itself. Gaitán's vigorous denunciation of 'Lopism' and 'Santism' provoked positive convulsions in the Liberal Party. In 1946, Gaitán refused to bow to the instructions of the Party leadership (with the surreptitious support of the Conservative Party, which saw in the disunity of the Liberals an unhoped-for opportunity of returning to power), and two Liberal candidates stood for the presidency, with the result that the Conservative Mariano Ospina was elected by a simple majority.

After the election, Gaitán won over a large number of Liberal supporters, and his dynamism and popularity eventually brought him the party leadership. 'Gaitanism' was the only serious movement to shake the hegemony of the two parties and enable very wide sectors of the population to take part in political life. This movement was carried entirely on the shoulders of its leader, a Bogotá barrister influenced to some extent by Marxism who had fought in the defence of peasants and trade unionists, and it was beginning to seem irresistible when its chief was suddenly assassinated. Its importance lay less in its programme than in the messianic appeal of its leader – 'I am not just one man, I am the people' – and the new forces whose appearance on the political scene he precipitated – the poor quarters of the towns, which were expanding rapidly, and the small peasantry hitherto subjected to caciquism. A speech by Gaitán, capable on its own of inflaming a crowd or halting it in its tracks, and all the more powerful for being expressed in the language of the people, was in striking contrast to the turgid rhetoric and atmosphere of refinement characteristic of the traditional ruling circles in this 'Athens of South America'.

Gaitán's position as sole leader of Colombian Liberalism, which he assumed in 1948, was a two-edged sword, since the traditional Liberal party workers' conversion to Gaitanism enabled the establishment around him of a party general staff that was able, when the time arrived, to neutralize him and isolate him from his old supporters.

This problem is closely bound up with the complex nature of Liberalism; like Janus, the Liberal Party has two faces, one for when it is in power and one for when it is in opposition. In opposition, Liberalism in fact represents a coalition of all anti-Conservative forces. It appears as a leftist party with popular leaders of advanced views, who then give way to much more reassuring faces when the party is returned to power (witness the example of Olaya Herrera in 1930, the Conservative government's ambassador to Washington). This is a reflection of the dual nature of Liberalism, enshrined in a party with close links with the commercial and financial oligarchy, and frequently connected much more closely to foreign interests (English in the nineteenth century, North American at the present time) than the type of Conservatism represented by Laureano Gómez, for example, who relied more on a sort of national and even nationalist demagogy. It is also a party, on the Caribbean coast at least, of big land-owners, although these do not represent the dominant inter-ests in Liberalism. Finally, it is also a popular party, in which the politically conscious elements of the urban masses, white-collar workers and minor civil servants, place their hopes for change, for a transformation of society. This authentically popular aspect of Liberalism should never be forgotten if the contradictions of Liberal policy are to be understood.

To maintain itself in power when faced with the Liberals under Gaitán, who had a majority in Parliament, the Conser-vative Party did not hesitate to resort to repressive and vio-lent measures in its turn. This violence culminated, on 9 April 1948, in Gaitán's assassination, which provoked a savage insurrection in Bogotá and several other towns that was only put down with difficulty.

After 1949 the repression conducted by the police and, to a lesser extent, by the army was countered by a more or less spontaneous peasant war that flared up in several parts of the country, lasting until 1953, when a military coup brought General Rojas Pinilla to power with the support of the Liberal Party and a moderate wing of the Conservatives. His appeals for peace were by and large heeded, and both parties cooperated with him until they discovered that the General was trying to exercise power over their heads and attempting, on the lines of Argentine Peronism, to create a third party based on a nationalist doctrine. He was finally overthrown in 1957 following a general strike provoked by the National Association of Industrialists, with students pro-viding the hard core of the strikers. At this the two parties, who were also in danger, became reconciled and decided to share power for sixteen years, giving the presidency first to the Liberal Alberto Lleras (1958–62), then the Conservative Guillermo Valencia (1962–6), then the Liberal Carlos Lleras (1966–70), and finally to the Conservative Misael Pastrana in 1970.

The National Front

ACCORDING TO STATUTE

The Front is the result of a series of agreements, subsequently regularized in the form of Statutes approved by referendum in 1957, and finally of appendices to these agreements reached between the majority factions of the two parties.[6]

The Benidorm Declaration (24 July 1956) signed by Alberto Lleras and Laureano Gómez 'recommends the two parties to join forces to achieve a rapid return of political life to proper institutional forms ... considers necessary and fully possible the creation of a government or succession of governments based on a broad coalition between the two parties'.

On 20 March 1957 the two parties published a joint declaration (while General Rojas Pinilla was still in power) in which 'they faithfully and solemnly engage to set up a civilian government exercised in the name of both parties, which would represent both of them equally and in which both would collaborate, which would be supported by a firm alliance ...'

Finally, after Rojas Pinilla's overthrow, the Sitges Declaration was signed, which affirmed among other things the need to consult the people by means of elections, proposed integration of Liberals and Conservatives in Parliament on a parity basis, with similar provisions for the administration, and finally emphasized the need to restrict the powers of the presidency.

The referendum was held on 1 December 1957. It ratified the Constitution of 1886 and all subsequent amendments, and proposed further amendments, viz. parliamentary statutes to be approved by two-thirds majority and party

6. See Hernández Rodríguez, Guillermo, *La alternación ante el pueblo como constituyente primario*, Bogotá, Ed. América libre, 1962, pp. 91–9.

representation in the Cabinet to reflect that in Parliament; similarly, the Supreme Court of Justice and the Council of State were to be composed of jurists from the two majority parties, on a parity basis, and magistrates were to be appointed for life.

These amendments, which were to be permanent, were accompanied by one other that was only transitory, laying down that Liberal-Conservative integration on a parity basis in deliberative assemblies should last until 1974 (four presidential terms of office). After this period, proportional representation was to be restored.

An Act of Parliament of 15 September 1959 laid down that 'between the 7 August 1962 and the 7 August 1974, the function of President of the Republic will be fulfilled alternately by citizens belonging to one of the two traditional parties, the Conservative Party and the Liberal Party, such that the elected President shall belong to a different party from his immediate predecessor'.

IN PRACTICE

The origins of the Front lie chiefly in Colombia's domestic history. For many years, and perhaps even from the very beginning, the sources of conflicts between the Conservatives and Liberals lay less in their different programmes, which seemed mere pretexts for dispute, than in the clash of powerful personalities, particularly those of the Generals in the wars of independence: Obando (Liberal), Herrán (Conservative) and Mosquera (first Conservative, then Liberal).

Each period of party hegemony played its part in shaping present-day Colombia, and both parties were responsible for the country's slow rate of economic development. For instance, without the Liberal reform of the period of the United States of Colombia, the progress recorded under the subsequent Conservative governments would not have been possible. The parties only broke up and political crises only occurred during difficult times: for instance when tobacco or quinine exports dropped, or later when coffee prices fell.

Political differences tended to become blurred after 1901 when the Liberals accepted the centralist Constitution and the Concordat. Moreover from the second half of the nineteenth century on there came to be a confusion between the political and business personae of political leaders: men like Ospina and Samper are the best examples; their economic collaboration was entirely without any political colouring, it did not even interfere with their party conflicts. In this light, it is perhaps less astonishing to learn that there have been precedents for the Front. For example in 1869, the Conservative Party united with a large sector of the Liberal Party by a pact which laid down (articles 3 and 4) 'that the two entities shall be represented equally, as far as is possible, both in Congress and in other public bodies ... Public offices of equal importance shall be held by Conservatives and Liberals in equal numbers.' Similar pacts were signed in 1885 and in 1909, when General Rafael Reyes was toppled from power. In 1924, the Liberal leader Alfonso López was chairman of a bank of which one Conservative leader, Laureano Gómez, was secretary. More recently, Carlos Lleras was nominated to stand for the presidency of the Republic by the Conservative Misael Pastrana. The former was ex-chairman of the big Colombia-based American company Celanese, of which the latter was the chairman.

This coexistence between the two parties, on a parity basis or else alternating the holding of important offices, has been practised more or less continuously since 1906 in the Society of Agriculturalists of Colombia, the Federation of Coffee Planters, and later in the National Association of Industrialists (ANDI).

WHAT DOES THE NATIONAL FRONT MEAN TO THE COUNTRY?

At first the Front was greeted with a great sigh of relief by the population, who saw in it a means of restoring peace and putting an end to the violence which had claimed hundreds of thousands of victims in ten years.[7] Violence in Colombia was often supposed to be the result of the two parties' struggle for power. As time passed, however, and as the troubles in the countryside persisted, it began to be apparent that the violence could have other causes – economic, social, religious, even racial – that it was in fact the expression of a general crisis affecting national structures and that the Front was merely the establishment of a hegemony that refused to allow new political formations to take their rightful place in the country's political life.

It is interesting to note that only in 1962, and under the pressure of growing popular unrest, was any economic and social plan formulated. Up till then, neither party had envisaged any far-reaching reforms, at any rate outside the strictly political sphere. Moreover the plans, which were purely a pre-election device, were never put into practice. Even with the presidency held by Carlos Lleras Restrepo, Alberto Lleras's cousin, under the slogan of 'Front for National Renewal', the reforms projected to put the Front on a better course were, with the exception of some moves towards agrarian reform, mainly politico-administrative in nature: the abandonment of the two-thirds majority and return to the simple majority principle, reform of Parliamentary procedure and of the electoral calendar.

Parallel to these developments, outside the framework of the two parties' regular official structure, national, regional

7. Guzmán, Monseñor Germán, Fals Borda, Orlando & Umaña Luna, Eduardo, *La violencia en Colombia*, 2 vols., Bogotá, Tercer Mundo, 1963 and 1964.

and local committees are being set up on a bipartite basis, sometimes with the direct participation of leading industrialists (e.g. in Medellín).

CONSEQUENCES OF THE NATIONAL FRONT

After these years of government by the Front, a number of conclusions may be drawn concerning its operation.

The Conservative Party, in a minority in the country since 1930 (if we except the 1949 presidential elections which the Liberals boycotted), seems to have made progress, and since 1964 has found itself in a majority again (taking all factions together). At the same time, the Liberal Party machine and its elected representatives have increasingly become dominated by the party's moderate wing. This seems largely the result of the parity arrangement, which has enabled Conservatives to make their appearance for the first time in areas where their influence was previously very small (in particular on the Caribbean coast).

This steady Conservative success has however been marred by an increase in the number of abstentions, a highly significant phenomenon since in present circumstances it illustrates popular disenchantment with the regime and also a weakening of the traditional method of controlling the population – caciquism. Practically all political groupings appear to be affected by the abstentions, and to a similar extent; they seem more prevalent in the towns than in the country. Moreover, the effect should be qualified by reference to structural abstention, which has been very carefully investigated by Mario Latorre.[8]

In Colombia, as in many Latin American countries, the

8. Latorre Rueda, Mario, 'Como ha evolucionado en quince años la votación del Partido Liberal y del Partido Conservador', *Acción liberal* 2, Oct.–Nov. 1965, pp. 84–115.

decisive electoral power is the *cacique* of the village, the man who knows the electors and can get them to vote the right way because they are afraid of him or else obliged to him for favours or services. In some regions of the big agricultural estates, it will be the big landowner or his bailiff; a 'doctor' (i.e. a lawyer or notary), so important in areas of small properties where litigation is rife; or finally he may simply be a one-time 'strong-arm man'. At election time, efforts are made to remove the lukewarm or opposition official who may occupy a position regarded as strategically important; this will range from the village doctor or the local police inspector, down to the bank-clerk in the Agricultural Bank, or the official responsible for artificial insemination.

When election day arrives, the elector finds a lorry to take him to the polling station (which will be in the biggest village of the rural district, or in the centre in the case of towns). The lorry may belong to his employer, or the local land-owner, or to the local public works department. A ballot paper is handed to the elector near to the ballot box, and a party activist detailed to look after him leads him to the ballot box. It should not be forgotten that 30 to 40 per cent of the population is illiterate, and that ballot papers are supplied by the parties, not distributed to electors by impartial officials at the polling station; as a result, in such and such a village it is impossible to obtain the ballot papers for such and such a list. Not long ago – although such practices are now tending to disappear – if the elector could show his finger dipped in ink (a sign that he had fulfilled his electoral duty), the local party officer (or the local landowner) would give him a free meal, a drink, five pesos, or some other re-ward. If he refused to vote, or voted the wrong way, he would be bombarded with threats and difficulties – he would be un-able to obtain credit, or any official papers. Obviously, such practices are by no means the exclusive prerogative of one party; the gradual awakening of the population to political consciousness is, however, limiting their effectiveness, and acquired habit also makes them less necessary.

Election results by electoral district show a considerable political polarization (with the exception of the big towns).

Districts	Liberals	Conservatives
Chiscas (Boyaca)	2,134	3
Cabrera (Santander)	0	1,074
Alpujarra (Tolima)	22	1,320

It should be emphasized moreover that within the districts in which the vote seems to be more evenly divided, the situation is in fact often identical. The hamlets of these electoral districts (often very large in area) are politically homogeneous. The parish of Fresno (Tolima) is divided into 1,360 Liberal votes (most of which are revolutionary Liberals) and 3,609 Conservative votes (from an extremist sector of that party). The parish is situated on the Magdalenan slopes of the central Cordillera, and the settlement which serves as the polling centre is just about in the middle. The Conservative vote is concentrated above the settlement (to the west), where the population is of Antioqueñan origin, occupied chiefly in coffee planting and stock-farming. The Liberal vote is concentrated below the settlement (to the east), cast by a population of mixed blood occupied in polyculture and providing seasonal labourers to the big *haciendas*. The phenomenon is easily observable on the Bogotá–Manizales road which crosses the district, where red posters at election time are suddenly supplanted by blue ones. The border between the two areas is, needless to say, a zone in which violent armed clashes frequently occur. This more or less clear-cut situation applies all over Colombia, but local government statistics tend to blur the outlines of the problem.

In the 1966 parliamentary elections, contrary to all expectations, the number of abstentions did not diminish; this phenomenon expresses a clear disaffection, if not hostility, on the part of the population.

The development of electoral participation under the National Front [9]

	Referendum	Presidential Elections	Parliamentary Elections
1957	73%	—	—
1958		58%	68%
1960		—	58%
1962		40%	58%
1964		—	37%
1966		35%	39%
1968		—	33%

A second consequence of the National Front has been that the party political struggle has been replaced by a political struggle (often no less violent) to win a majority within the parties. These are fragmented into rival factions. What Eduardo Santa has called the 'polyclassism' of the parties [10] is changing gradually into a horizontal structure, but from within. The parties are broadly divided into two sectors, the supporters and opponents of the National Front, which appear to cancel each other out, two for two, in each party, which seems very reasonable to the supporters of the system but much less so to its opponents.

Finally, the political monopoly held by the two parties and the growing unwillingness of the people to conform have brought about the appearance of a number of new trends or party groupings which find it difficult to gain a voice within

9. According to figures published in 1964 by the Registraduría nacional del Estado civil.

10. Santa, Eduardo, *Sociología política de Colombia*, p. 73. 'Both traditional parties have members from every socio-economic stratum in the nation.'

the present legal framework, and all of which aim to alter or abolish it.

Apart from restoring a measure of peace to the country, and regaining some precarious control over the armed forces, what is the Front's credit balance? Some reforms have certainly been passed by Parliament: agrarian reform (1961), and judicial reform (1965), but these were not particularly indebted to the National Front and the first, at least, was passed under pressure from the Alliance for Progress, and quickly turned into a simple agricultural development plan, providing for irrigation, credit, etc. The need for bipartite agreement within the Front has meant that the wording of Bills presented to Parliament has often had to be watered down. The Front has not been able to set up a proper public administration; on the contrary, party patronage and prebends have never been so common. Planning, which was improvised during Alberto Lleras' term, has remained without impetus, and the objectives of the ten-year development plan have not been achieved. The fiscal reform that was thought necessary has not been carried out and the provincial governments still depend for funds primarily on their monopoly of sales of spirits and on lotteries. There has also been some resurgence of violence, on the part of the government in the first instance, to suppress opposition groupings, especially in the countryside. The financial and stock market crisis is worsening, and in 1965 the regime had recourse to devaluation for the third time. The cost of living (especially food and housing) is rising at an alarming rate.[11] This deterioration in the social climate under the Front helps to explain both the

11. The statistics which show an increase in *per capita* income (which is in any case a questionable indicator) do not take account of the true increase in the population, underestimated by two million inhabitants. (At the end of 1966 Colombia had 18,500,000 inhabitants, and 20,000,000 at the end of 1968; the annual growth rate of the population is 3·2 per cent.)

increasingly heavy rate of electoral abstention, and the threat of a general strike in January 1965, accompanied by a serious crisis in the upper ranks of the Army (resulting in dismissal of the Minister of War, General Ruiz Novoa, of the Chief of Police, of the Air Chief Marshal, and others).

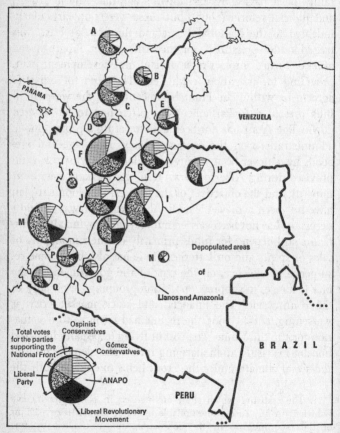

Source: *Espectador*, (Bogotá), 25 March 1966.

Figure 11. *Results of the March 1966 Elections*

The leaders of the Front are aware of the problem, but it is not easy to see how they will reverse the trend in a country whose future is already mortgaged by a very heavy burden of foreign debt; politically, their problem was to win a majority (of two thirds, it will be remembered) in the parliamentary

Results of the March 1966 Elections
(% for the various parties)

	Provinces	Liberal	Ospinist Conservatives	Gómez Conservatives	ANAPO	MRL
A	Atlántico	48	15	19	13	5
B	Magdalena	36	17	17	9	21
C	Bolívar	47	14	20	9	10
D	Córdoba	44	22	11	11	12
E	North Santander	27	27	6	28	12
F	Antioquia	30	34	4	19	13
G	Santander	32	20	16	18	14
H	Boyaca	35	11	12	36	6
I	Cundinamarca	45	8	9	29	9
J	Caldas	43	23	13	11	10
K	Chocó	79	12	8	1	0
L	Tolima	44	11	11	10	24
M	Valle	42	12	10	23	13
N	Meta	26	6	14	32	22
O	Huila	27	13	23	15	22
P	Cauca	45	24	8	9	14
Q	Nariño	35	24	24	10	7

elections of 1966 in order to get a certain number of reforms accepted. Since they did not obtain this majority in March 1966, the Front will have to exercise sufficient seductive charm (i.e. hand out enough cash by way of inducement) to win over opposition votes on a number of important issues. In this respect, the decision of the great majority of the MRL to support the Liberal Party was of some significance. This paralysis of Parliament is aggravated by the fact that in time of crisis some sectors of the economy, the Bank of the Republic (privately owned but granted a monopoly in issuing banknotes) and the National Association of Industrialists have taken over the management of the country's affairs directly, going over the heads of constitutionally established bodies and forming a commission at a so-called 'higher level'. Similarly, when it became clear that something would have to be done in the face of the steady fall in the value of money, the financial houses, during one dramatic night, forced President Valencia to accept one of their nominees as Minister of Finance. More recently, the International Monetary Fund practically faced President Lleras with an ultimatum, forcing him to devalue and draw up an austerity plan; despite his words of defiance and hostility towards international bodies, Carlos Lleras was in the end forced to accept these measures.

THE PARTIES OF THE NATIONAL FRONT

Which parties currently support the Front for National Renewal?

The Liberal Party

This party is also sometimes called 'officialist' (to distinguish it from the Liberal Revolutionary Movement). Traditionally, this is the 'Red' party (Colorado), as opposed to the Conservative 'Blues' (Azules). Although it has been in the majority in the country since 1930, its voting figures have declined over the eight years since the Front was set up. In elections to the Chamber of Deputies it has won :

in 1960 : 1,185,684 votes (46 per cent of the total vote),

in 1962 : 1,081,103 votes (35 per cent),

in 1964 :   738,437 votes (32·6 per cent),

in 1966 : 1,117,000 votes (38 per cent).

The resurgence in Liberal votes in 1966 was due to the fact that the real question behind the elections was clearing the way for the presidential candidature of the Liberal Carlos Lleras. In a regime centred very much on the presidential system of government, the Liberal Party will normally win its full complement of votes in elections like this one, which was not the case in the presidential elections of 1962 when the candidate was affiliated to the Conservatives. In the Conservative Party, the opposite may be observed as regards the 1966 elections. It should be added that part of the Liberal Revolutionary Movement's voters in 1962 were not an expression of the Liberal left, but rather of Liberal sectarianism, that preferred not to vote for a Conservative. In 1966, these votes returned to the Liberal mainstream. The percentage obtained in 1968 is explained by the unification of the official Liberal Party and the MRL, coupled with the rise in the number of abstentions.

It is as well to note at the same time that the parliamentary elections held in the middle of a presidential term of office (1968, for example) arouse much less interest than those held two months before the presidential elections under the old system, and now with the presidential election.

The Liberal Party's strongholds have in the past been the departments on the Caribbean coast, with the towns of Barranquilla, Cartagena and Santa Marta, the department of Cauca (Popayán) and above all Cundinamarca, the chief town of which is Bogotá. The department of Chocó, where the Liberal Party gains 78 per cent of the vote, is very underpopulated, and there are grounds for suspecting some irregularities in polling. In 1964, the Liberal Party obtained an absolute majority in the towns of Bogotá, Barranquilla, Cartagena and Pereira. When it is not divided, Liberalism has also been dominant in Medellín, Cali and Manizales.

The Liberal Party leadership. The Liberal Party is sometimes led by one man, and sometimes by a directorate elected by party convention. The latter form of leadership is favoured at the present time. The party convention, the members of which are in theory appointed in accordance with statutory procedure, in fact represent two or three factions that dispute the party leadership between themselves, the strongest of these being an electoral pressure-group dominating the town of Bogotá. The Party's candidate for the presidency is also chosen by the convention. In 1962, the Liberal Party convention had to choose a Conservative candidate out of a list of five submitted to it by the Conservative Party. In a pre-election period (the Party hardly exists outside election time) the Directorate nominates the leadership in the various departments, and the latter the leadership in the electoral districts, ignoring the Statutes which technically grant the rank and file a greater voice in the choice of leadership; on the other hand, the Directorate takes account of the statutory representation of various influential groups: students, women's section, officials; it also takes care not to omit representatives of the regions supplying the most Party votes, for fear of provoking them to submit a separate list (elections in the most densely populated departments are by proportional representation).

The Party leadership is consulted by the President when he is choosing his Cabinet, and on all major questions of policy; but it has trouble in imposing its will on the party's deputies, who always have their own patrons and clients.

Liberalism is supported above all by the predominance of the Liberal press: the two biggest Colombian newspapers, *El Espectador* (which has the largest circulation in the country and has a faint left-wing bias) and *El Tiempo* (whose circulation is currently falling) are both Liberal papers.

The influence of Liberal officials is also very great. In every province either the governor (appointed by the central government) or the secretary (who has the right to appoint mayors, the most effective election agents) will be a Liberal Party nominee. The provincial Public Works offices, the Alcoholic Beverages board, and the councils controlling the public lottery and welfare departments are also excellent electoral springboards, because of the subsidies and jobs that they control.

Another far from negligible means of controlling the masses is the trade-union confederation, the CTC, especially since it got rid of its Communist minority. It is largely run by civil servants and seems to be losing ground at the moment.

The Party's finances, which only acquire importance during presidential elections, are dependent on voluntary contributions, usually supplied by economically powerful party supporters (large landowners, banks, factories run by Liberals) at the request of the Party treasurer. In other elections the candidates finance their own campaigns. Within the framework of the National Front, the presidential elections of 1966 were financed jointly by the Liberal and Conservative Parties. Heavy calls are made upon local officials who are of necessity either Liberals or Conservatives. Departmental sources of income e.g. from lotteries and sales of spirits also go to help finance campaigns.

Whatever its present difficulties, and they are considerable, the Liberal Party is still considered to be the party of the people. The example of Gaitán is revealing in this respect : in 1934 he failed in his attempt to create a new socialistic party, the UNIR, and had to reintegrate with the old Liberal Party to win back popular support. The Liberal Party further considers itself close to the Venezuelan Democratic Action party (whose chairman Leoni was active in the Colombian Liberal Party during his exile) and to the Peruvian APRA.

The mechanism of party splits and reunifications provides one possible explanation for the continued survival of the two-party system in Colombia, and in particular for the survival of Liberalism. Whenever the party has seemed to fall into somnolence, and adopted conformist and conservative attitudes, non-conformist, often youthful sectors of the party (Rafael Uribe at the beginning of the century, Gaitán in the years from 1934–44, Alfonso Lopez Michelsen, 1960–7) have broken away or amassed support on the left wing of the party and produced an incisive list of demands. After a more or less extended period of bitter conflicts, giving the impression to the casual observer that liberalism was at its last gasp, the Liberal Party has always managed to come up with a two-pronged strategy of political horse-trading (offering inducements to individual dissidents, combined with attempts to arrive at a compromise programme) that succeeds in containing the radical element and reabsorbing it, preserving the integrity of 'the old firm'. However, this process does not usually entail absorption pure and simple. The ex-dissidents, all aggressive militants, are quickly granted high positions in the party and may even be led to believe that they have taken over its leadership. The essential element of the new ideas that they represent is incorporated in party doctrine, which is to that extent transformed.

The Liberal programme. For the immediate future, the party projects a policy of cautious birth control (cautious because account still has to be taken of the Church, and the time when the Liberal Party was entirely secularist and its militants were nearly all freemasons is long past), acceleration of agrarian reform, tighter price control, an urban housing programme, and the pursuit of integration within the Latin American free trade area. It should be added that this programme is only a broad indication of Liberal policy, since actual policies and especially economic policy are in fact dictated by pressure groups.

From the point of view of economic policy, it is customary to distinguish between two big rival schools of thought in Colombia, even though the adherents of one more often than not have interests in the other. The Manizales school represents the viewpoint of the merchant classes and the coffee exporters who dominate the powerful Federation of Coffee Planters (coffee accounts for about 70 per cent of the total value of the country's exports); it is interested in questions relating to foreign trade; it is accused of being devaluationist and of generating inflation (for feeding the National Coffee Fund which regulates the internal price of this product). The other school represents more the industrial interests centred on Medellín, which until recently controlled the National Association of Industrialists. It is in some respects nationalist, protectionist, and unenthusiastic about the introduction of foreign capital and the edicts of international financial institutions. Its influence has been threatened by the heavy influx of foreign capital that now dominates the industrial sectors of Bogotá and Cali and recently won control of the ANDI; these foreign capitalists are busily engaged in making alliances with native Colombian capital in joint investment companies and financial corporations. Both policies have supporters and opponents in both Colombian parties.

Under constant attack from the opposition and the anti-Llerist faction among the Conservatives, the Liberal Party has continued to resort to sectarian appeals to jolt the Liberal elector out of his apathy. The Liberal press promises a hail of calamities and the return of anti-Liberal violence if the opposition emerges victorious from the parliamentary elections. Appeals for support are made to the Liberals in the civil service, who constitute 50 per cent of the total – going so far as to threaten dismissal to those who fail to heed them. As the ex-Minister of War, General Ruiz Novoa, has shown, the party is prepared to call on the armed forces to intervene in politically dissident areas, on the pretext of warding off the communist menace.

The Unionist Conservative Party

This party is also called 'Ospinist' after its leader, the ex-President Mariano Ospina (1946–50). It is a member of the government and wholeheartedly supports the National Front. Its bastions of support are Antioquia and Caldas, Nariño, part of Cundinamarca and Boyacá, regions which it controls thanks to its preponderance in the Federation of Coffee Planters and the Agricultural Bank, and thanks too to the support of part of the clergy. Its union with the doctrinaire conservatism represented by Laureano Gómez (now dead – his son Alvaro Gómez has taken his place) lasted less than two years. However, it was originally the doctrinaire faction that signed the agreements with the Liberal Party to form the National Front, while Mariano Ospina and his minority faction were opposed to it. However, once the Ospinists became a majority in the Conservative Party, the Liberals thought it more expedient to establish friendly relations with them. The Unionist Conservative Party is also run by a directorate, which is likewise appointed by the party convention. However, Mariano Ospina is the true leader of the party, and his wishes are unconditionally respected by the executive, of which he is not even a member. The party convention is not a gathering of the rank and file, but is constituted by party dignitaries (ministers, ex-ministers and provincial governors are members by right), and to make up the numbers, Parliament employees who are members of the party are invited to attend (on a parity basis).

The Unionist Conservative Party represents the interests of the big industrialists of Medellín and the leading lights of the Coffee Corporation. Property interests in the big towns also hold an extremely powerful position in the party. It enjoys the support of a number of state employees, and of small peasants of Antioqueño origin, in whom it arouses a kind of nationalism, tinged with racism, and who are dominated by a patriarchal and paternalistic Christianity. The range of its social work (e.g. clerically-run centres for women workers in the textile industry), and slogans such as 'one cow for every poor peasant's home' give some idea of the nature of the Unionists' appeal. Their most important press mouthpiece is the big daily *El Colombiano* published in Medellín; the Bogotá daily *La República* should also be mentioned.

The Unionist leaders were not wholehearted in their enthusiasm for Guillermo Valencia when he was President of the Republic, despite the fact that he had been elected from amongst themselves. They resented his failure to offer them a fat enough slice of the cake when he came to share out jobs; as part of his policy of what he termed 'millimetrism', he offered them one third of the posts in his Cabinet, or two ministries, while the rival sector composed of the ex-Laureanist and Alzatist faction was given four ministries. Although they were not provoked into abandoning the government altogether, this was only because the provincial ministries and governments in the gift of the central government provided an electoral base from which no one cut himself off without risking political suicide. Moreover their Liberal allies were not in the least bit eager to find themselves sharing ministries only with doctrinaire anti-Llerist Conservatives.

The Unionists sometimes associate themselves with Christian Democracy (as indeed does the Liberal Party, which has taken over the slogan of 'Revolution in Freedom' coined by the Chilean president Frei). Their political programme is drawn up jointly with the Liberals, from whom they are perhaps only distinguished by a somewhat more paternalistic attitude and a greater emphasis on Christian values and peasant virtues. Some of their leaders, such as Hernán Jaramillo, a very powerful member of the coffee planters' lobby, wear the badge of Christian Democracy quite openly.

This party has always had a very closed political leadership dominated by powerful dynasties, of which the Ospinas (three Presidents of Colombia in the last hundred years) are the best example; however there has been a tendency in recent years to promote politicians who have risen from the middle class : not, indeed, from the largely parasitic semi-feudal middle stratum attached to the big landowning and planting interests, but representatives of a new class, especially from Antioquia, such as J. Emilio Valderrama and Octavio Arismendi, so-called 'young wolves' who have succeeded in breaking the monopoly of the party aristocrats. (Incidentally, the same phenomenon is observable in the Liberal Party, in such men as Hernán Agudelo, Hernán Toro and others.) It is revealing to note that this phenomenon has made its appearance in Antioquia, where the level of development has enabled the appearance of an authentic middle class, neither parasitic nor bureaucratic. However, the dead weight of the country's social structure is such that in the end the 'young wolves' will probably be devoured by the party machines, instead of being the means of destroying those machines.

In 1964, the two main Conservative factions went to the polls more or less united; in 1960 and 1962 the right-wing extremist group known as the Alzatists, after their leader Gilberto Alzate (now dead), allied themselves with the Unionists, while in 1966 they were split between Unionists and Doctrinaires. Analysis of the votes in 1966 shows that the Unionists won a clear advantage, benefiting from the open support of the ecclesiastical hierarchy and of their Liberal allies. It is however sometimes difficult to attribute votes correctly to one sector or the other, because of local peculiarities or 'unnatural' alliances such as that between Mariano Ospina and the National Popular Alliance (ANAPO) in Córdoba. It is interesting to note that the noisiest accusations of electoral fraud in 1966 and 1968 were exchanged by the two main Conservative factions, in those departments where the result was in doubt and also in the smallest departments, termed *de arrastre*, where elections are held on a simple majority ballot.

	Doctrinaires (or independents)	Unionists	% of the vote (for both factions taken together)
1960	438,153	621,217	42
1962	487,733	794,688	41·5
1964	794,00		35·1
1966	330,000	450,000	31
1968	186,000	475,000	28

Independent Conservatism

This group is now under the leadership of Alvaro Gómez, son of the ex-President Laureano Gómez (1950–53), from whom derives the name 'Laureanist' sometimes given to it. The faction has been reinforced by supporters of another Conservative *caudillo*, now deceased, and like Gómez strongly influenced by the ideology of modern Spain, Gilberto Alzate. Alvaro Gómez was previously chairman of the party executive calling itself Independent Conservative, but which its opponents called 'Alvarist' or 'Alvaro-Alzatist'.

Doctrinaire Conservatism draws its main electoral support from the votes of the minor peasantry of Huila, Tolima, and the north of the province of Valle, and from the province of Santander. It can also count on the support of a large number of civil servants. But the interests it represents are chiefly those of the big landowners, stock-farmers and sugar-cane planters, as could be inferred from the parliamentary debates on agrarian reform.

Alvaro Gómez's faction supported the Valencia government, of which it was part. On the other hand it opposed the government of Carlos Lleras. It is possibly more hostile to the latter's person than to Liberalism as such. The logic of the National Front dictates that the presidential candidate of one party should in the last analysis be chosen by the other party, which to protect itself against possible treachery always picks out the most inoffensive personality. These considerations led the Liberals in 1962 to pick Guillermo Valencia out of five names put forward by the Conservatives. The Liberals thought that the latter, a man of integrity and courage, with some popularity in the country but almost entirely ignorant of administrative and economic affairs, would prove amenable to their demands. Against all expectation President Valencia ignored their appeals and took decisions entirely on his own initiative.

The opposition of the Alvaro Gómez group, discreetly supported by Valencia who ended his term of office with some popularity – again unexpectedly – can be explained in two ways: firstly it firmly supports the social *status quo*, especially in the countryside, which Carlos Lleras, who represents urban and to some extent progressive elements, threatens to transform; secondly it hopes, out of purely tactical considerations, to recover through its opposition to the government some of the votes of those malcontents who currently vote for General Rojas Pinilla or abstain. The electoral defeat of Alvaro Gómez's supporters in 1966 placed the latter in a difficult situation personally. Gómez has long-standing ties of personal friendship with the ex-MRL leader Alfonso López Michelsen, a friendship that is very characteristic of Colombian politics. Such family and friendship ties are very close, and often help to explain incongruous alliances. To give only two of many possible examples, Carlos Lleras's sister, now dead, was married to an Ospina; and the Conservative leader Misael Pastrana married the daughter of the ex-Liberal presidential candidate, Carlos Arango.

It should be emphasized that Doctrinaire Conservatism claims to support the National Front; it is sometimes strongly nationalist in tone, and is violently anti-Communist but has formulated no alternative programme. It can count on the support of old-time 'rabid' Conservatives and of a substantial section of the lower clergy which is in a position to dictate election results in areas containing many independent small-holdings. Such village priests are very strongly committed politically and still see in the Liberals the incarnation of the Devil.

The Legal Opposition Since 1958

This was practically non-existent in the early days of the Front, and has gradually built itself up since then. A distinction must be drawn between those opposition parties who have the right to sit in Parliament (the Liberal Revolutionary Movement and the National Popular Alliance, ANAPO) and those who although not systematically persecuted have no direct legal means of expression (the Social Christian-Democratic Party and the Communist Party) under their own banners.

The Liberal Revolutionary Movement

This Movement was born of a breakaway by the Liberal left wing in 1958–9. Being a liberal party led by the son of ex-President López, the MRL had no difficulty in gaining permission to present candidates at elections. The MRL rejected the policies of the National Front, and in particular the statutory alternation of Presidents, the principle of parity and the restriction of other parties' political rights.

The MRL preached a policy of agrarian and urban reform, and greater political and economic independence. It openly acknowledges its debt to socialism; Alfonso López Michelsen, its undisputed leader, was for a short time a pupil of Harold Laski.

At its most successful, this party had the allegiance of the majority of the country's students and younger officials. But López Michelsen was not strongly provided with one vital component of any political machine that is to function successfully in this country – the village *cacique*. The latter is the expression of the dominant social forces in the rural world of South America, and obviously cannot support – except out of tactical or purely local considerations – forces seeking to overthrow the existing structures, the ultimate effect of which would be his own destruction. The institution of caciquism provides a regime desiring 'political centralization and administrative decentralization' with a hierarchic organization in which 'mayors owe their jobs to provincial governors, who in turn owe theirs to parliamentary deputies or to the President; the President relies on the machine run by his subordinates to maintain the flow of employees of his party. A fierce and irresponsible party solidarity is set up from Bogotá down to the smallest hamlet in the Republic, a partisanship that is the automatic condition for keeping your job.'[12]

The MRL, most of whose electors are country-dwellers, counted on the support of areas where agricultural labourers work (or commonly find no work) on the big *haciendas* of Córdoba, Magdalena, North Tolima, and Valle, or in areas once controlled by Liberal guerrillas whose leaders, often one-time militant supporters of the movement set up by Gaitán, have gone over to the MRL (Santander, Llanos, South Tolima), and finally on the pioneer inhabitants of the jungle-clearance areas, who live in the most appalling conditions (and many of whom, incidentally, are political refugees): Central Magdalena, Caqueta. It should not be forgotten that Gaitán's movement was extremely powerful. It did, of course, disintegrate on the disappearance of its leader – one-time

12. Guillen Martinez, Fernando, *Raiz y futuro de la revolución*, Bogotá, Tercer Mundo, 1963, p. 143.

Gaitanist militants were the first to suffer official persecution. As a result of this persecution, the only organization which offered them ideals similar to their own was the MRL, even though the personalities of López *père et fils* (Gaitán used to refer to López Michelsen as *el hijo del ejecutivo*, 'the executive's son') were strongly criticized by Gaitán himself. Movements which aspired to be purely Gaitanist, like the United Front for Revolutionary Action set up by his daughter Gloria Gaitán, failed for one reason or another. Moreover Gaitán's relations with the Communist Party (which regarded him as a fascist, and in 1946 for example called on its supporters to vote against him and in favour of the official Liberal candidate) were sufficiently bad to ensure that most ex-Gaitanists did not join the party, despite its later volte-face. There are, however, notable exceptions to this rule in the important province of Sumapaz and in South Tolima, where there has been a general tendency to move away from liberalism towards communism.

The MRL electorate was also swollen by supporters from the Communist Party itself. The Colombian CP cannot take part in elections in its own name, and so makes electoral pacts with local or regional MRL candidates favourable to its legalization, and who sometimes reserve a place for it on their own electoral lists.

The MRL had no regular press outlet; however, it did make use of the free platform granted it by the daily *El Siglo* to enable some of its militants to express themselves in print; also, *El Espectador* published the major speeches of Alfonso López in the form of paid political advertising. At election time, the MRL resurrected a number of periodicals: *La Calle*, *Izquierda*, MRL, among others. The party leader also owned a number of radio stations. (Most of these stations are privately owned, and are run on commercial lines, allowing free expression to political movements that have the necessary funds. In 1966 a number of commercial firms hired broadcasting time which was then put at the disposal of the National Front.)

The MRL obtained its biggest ever number of votes in 1962 (more than 600,000), winning 20 per cent of the votes cast. It was then supported by Liberal voters unwilling to vote for a Conservative presidential candidate. In 1964, it was affected by the growing number of abstentions just as much as the other parties, and perhaps more: this was the direct result of a split that divided it into two factions – an orthodox or 'Lopist' line, moderate in outlook; and a much more radical hard-line group. The electorate was thoroughly disconcerted by this split, which was the result of personal differences rather than real political disagreements, and proved unable or unwilling to choose sides. The hesitations of its leader (a better political theorist than politician) and the constant defections of the party's upper ranks caused disillusionment among the electors, many of whom joined the much more dynamic National Popular Alliance. In March 1966, the MRL only won 350,00 votes, or 12 per cent of the total.

The Liberal Revolutionary Movement was the only party that made any formal concessions to the wishes of its electors. Its local or regional committees are elected, not appointed from above; its candidates are also chosen by general assemblies. However, not too much faith should be placed in these democratic procedures. Factional or personal disputes are always decided by the party's sole arbitrator and leader, Alfonso López Michelsen (although with the assistance of an executive committee), who will in the last resort always make his own decision if any of his personal friends are involved, but also occasionally allows the 'rank and file' (in practice the local election agent) to settle its own differences. This resulted in practice in an over-judicious share-out of favours to the two wings of the movement: that which looked towards the Liberal Party, in the hope of eventual reunification with the parent party (a tendency which in fact represented López's own aspirations), and that which looked to a revolutionary alliance with the Communists, or even with ANAPO. This kind of balancing act is in fact imposed on all political forces in Colombia; it is facilitated by the system of substitutes, allowed to take office for a limited time, which enables a party that only wins one seat in an election still to conciliate two conflicting tendencies.

In 1967, the majority of the Liberal Revolutionary Movement, led by Alfonso López, finally returned to the official party, which made the Liberal Party machine available to it once more. A small left-wing minority (three deputies) preserved its autonomy. This faction went to the polls under the label People's MRL, in alliance with the PCC, and obtained two seats in Bogotá and Cali.

The National Popular Alliance

Also called ANAPO or Rojismo. It was founded and is still led by the ex-President of the 1953–7 military government, Gustavo Rojas Pinilla, and his daughter María Eugenia Rojas de Moreno.

Like the MRL, with which it has sought an alliance, the ANAPO is opposed to the National Front. The party is avowedly nationalist, broadly reformist, and bears strong similarities to Argentine Peronism.

Rojismo proposes to return General Rojas to power, 'by election or other means', despite the handicap of his age. The revolution this movement hopes for would usher in a policy of neutralism in international affairs, nationalization of the big banks, and in particular the Bank of the Republic.

ANAPO won considerable successes in the 1964 and 1966 elections, especially the latter, mainly in the poor areas of the big towns (such as Ciudad Kennedy in Bogotá, built by the Alliance for Progress): Bogotá, Medellín, Cali, Pereira,

Cúcuta; and among the small peasantry in some rural areas, especially in Boyaca, General Rojas' native province. This is the only party which seems to have maintained real loyalty and support in the population, or which at any rate is capable of arousing genuine mass demonstrations. It owes this to its implacable hostility to the regime, its refusal to enter into any pacts with the forces of the system, the persecution to which it is subjected, and the nostalgia of some of the under-privileged for the period when it was in power (when a number of major public works projects were completed, helped by the high price of coffee on the international market in 1954–5 : 1 dollar per pound, today only 42 cents). It also owes some of its popularity to the dynamism and organizational ability of the general and his daughter, who tour the country untiringly, visiting the smallest villages and the poorest areas, something which other politicians, apart from President Carlos Lleras and Alfonso López, would not dream of doing, contenting themselves with elite meetings in aristocratic circles or addressing groups of businessmen.

ANAPO is hampered by its lack of political officers. Its attempts to launch a daily newspaper have long been thwarted by the discreet measures on the part of the government to block imports of paper. It does control a number of low-circulation weeklies.

ANAPO was further limited by the fact that it at first drew electors solely from the Conservative sector, to which the General himself belonged. This very fact, however, was of enormous significance. Up till now, the revolutionary parties (with the partial exception of Gaitanism) only managed to win votes at the expense of the Liberal Party, the only one remotely receptive to their ideas. A compact Conservative bloc always remained, solid and inviolate, guaranteeing the maintenance of the existing system. But it is precisely in the Conservative camp that ANAPO has been most active, where it has successfully spread the doctrine of violent revolution. It can therefore be considered as one of the factors in the emergence of a popular class consciousness.

The Alliance causes the business community in the country a great deal of anxiety, and arouses undisguised fear in some North American observers. Influential opinion in the United States on Colombia's parties and political future seems divided into two schools of thought: the International Development Agency and sectors such as the banks (the 'Grace Line') seemed impressed by the technocratic flair of the Lleras government, while remaining highly sceptical of the chances of survival of the paralysing and inefficient system of the National Front. The United States embassy, on the other hand, while maintaining excellent relations with the parties in power, also attempts to establish equally cordial relations with some opposition groups, notably the MRL and the trade unions of the UTC. But both groups fear ANAPO, seeing in it the harbinger of Communism in Colombia.

Although the lack of international confidence is a drawback, ANAPO can nevertheless count on the support of part of the lower clergy (somewhat on the Carlist, Navarrese pattern, to draw a Spanish analogy) and on the somewhat tortuous and equivocal policy of the country's chief trade union federation, the UTC. This federation was originally founded by the Conservative Party, with the object of providing a counterweight to the influence of the left-wing unions. As it grew more powerful, the UTC severed its links with conservatism (the leading posts in the federation are held by MRL and ANAPO militants) but still has close ties with the Society of Jesus, which provides it with moral counsellors at every level of its hierarchy. The Jesuits are a considerable power in Colombia – not to be confused with the upper echelons of the Church, which Colombians call the Curia. They enter politics not so much on behalf of one party rather than another (Jesuit candidates – Javerianos, ex-pupils of their two universities – stand for election under the label of every political grouping) as to represent and safeguard the privileges of the Society itself. The latter has been somewhat disturbed in recent years by the progress made by Opus Dei, the most notable member of which is the Conservative governor of Antioquia, Octavio Arismendi.

The Alliance presents candidates on two lists in each department, one Liberal and one Conservative. Out of the twenty-seven Rojista deputies in the Chamber consisting of representatives elected in 1964, one was a Liberal. In March 1966 ANAPO had eighteen senators and thirty-six deputies returned, obtaining about 550,000 votes (out of a total of 2,843,450 votes cast). This vote was however heavily dependent on the urban electorate, except in the department of Boyaca and one or two other areas, and the fastest growth is recorded on the liberal wing of the movement; its candidate for the Presidency of the Republic obtained more than 700,000 votes in May 1966. In 1968 ANAPO won about 522,000 votes (out of a total vote of about 2,340,000) which gave it a total of forty parliamentary seats (including six liberals). By far its most dramatic advance came in the presidential elections of 1970, when its near-success seemed to transform the political atmosphere of the country at a stroke.

The Unrecognized Opposition

The party groupings considered under this heading cannot be classed as Liberal or Conservative, and because of this cannot or do not wish to participate in official political life. It should be noted that if the Communist Party were to take the absurd step of calling itself 'Liberal Communist', no existing law could prevent it from putting up candidates for election. In fact something similar has happened in various parts of the country where lists under the label 'People's Liberal' have included known Communist candidates.

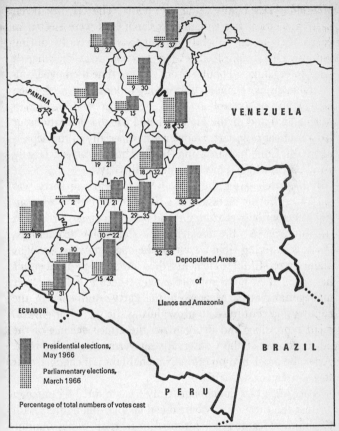

Sources: 'Senatorial elections, March 1966', *Espectador*, 25 March 1966 (97 per cent of the results);
'Presidential elections, May 1966', *Tiempo*, 3 May 1966 (final results).

Figure 12. Votes Cast for ANAPO in 1966

The Communist Party of Colombia

This is the biggest of the illegal parties. It was founded in 1930, the successor to a rather sketchy Revolutionary Socialist Party. Its general secretary is Gilberto Vieira, a man of middle-class family from Antioquia. The CP has taken part in politics, and Communist candidates were elected to parliament under Liberal governments, especially during Alfonso López's presidencies (1934–8 and 1942–5), when it tried to organize a Popular Front. At the time it enjoyed considerable support among the labour unions that were then being built up (petroleum workers, seamen and dockers in Magdalena) and in the big coffee and banana plantations. It led a number of squatter movements, especially in the departments of Cundinamarca and Tolima, and became a largely rural party, which it has remained to this day.

Immediately after the Second World War the Party was weakened by the secession of a 'Browderist' faction advocating a merger between the CP and other progressive forces in the country. At the moment, the Colombian Communist Party is suffering from a split on the opposite wing, brought about by pro-Chinese elements; these are small in number but have won their main support among students and the lower managerial classes. Meanwhile the Party's influence in the countryside continued to grow during the period of government repression, and it organized the armed defence of the peasants against the Conservative governments of the time. After the proclamation of the National Front, it changed over to a strategy of self-defence.

Since 1964 the Colombian Army has mounted a campaign against the rural areas where one-time guerrilla fighters with Communist leanings have retired to regroup, zones improperly dubbed independent republics. Guerrilla fighting has broken out again in these regions – South Tolima, Huila, Caqueta – under the leadership of Communist groups that go by the name of Armed Forces of the Colombian Revolution (FARC). In fact, these guerrilla formations are the only means of expression for peasant claims to the land in many areas, and have a specially strong appeal for native minorities. Since this is primarily a peasant movement, it is very different from the Castroist guerrilla groups found elsewhere in Latin America.

In other areas the Communist Party enjoys some support among the peasantry, although in the absence of elections it is difficult to measure. Moreover there seems to be a tendency among the population to draw a clear distinction between e.g. the Liberal Party, for which one votes out of habit or tradition, and the Communist Party, which has had little electoral experience in the course of its history, and consequently seems an entirely different kind of animal, a phenomenon completely non-electoral and therefore able to win the support of those same Liberal voters.

The CP and its youth organization have sympathizers among students, and the party is represented on the leadership of the National University Students' Federation. It also plays a major role in the trade-union movement. The CSTC Federation which it controls represents primarily the petroleum workers, building workers, and labourers on the sugar plantations. By means of various legalistic subterfuges, the government has so far managed to avoid granting legal status to the CSTC. Communist militants are also represented in other trade-union federations, in which they sometimes play a leading role. Finally, the party directs housing committees in the poor areas of the big cities – e.g. Bogotá, Cali, Montería.

The CP can call meetings more or less as it pleases (its last congress, the tenth, was held at the beginning of 1966). A certain number of peasants and workers are represented on its Central Committee as also are representatives of the guerrillas, but its Executive Committee is still dominated by intellectuals. The Party controls a weekly paper, *Voz proletaria*, with a circulation of over 25,000, and a monthly review, *Documentos políticos*. It publishes local newspapers and the FARC issue a duplicated bulletin. The circulation of the Communist press is restricted in the provinces by the police

Figure 13. Areas of Communist Party Influence

and the military authorities. However, Soviet and Chinese journals are fairly readily obtainable in the big cities. There is no doubt that Colombia's bipartisan tradition and the prestige still enjoyed by the two traditional parties, in spite of everything, are a hindrance to Communism. Nor is it certain that its strategy of all-out struggle is fully understood; in practice it will vary from time to time and place to place, taking legalist or right-wing forms at one moment, and underground or left-wing forms at another.

In its minimum programme, the Communist Party opposes the National Front, demands full and complete legal recognition, supports an alliance of all opposition forces, with the emphasis on condemnation of the United States' Latin American policy. It vigorously proclaims its solidarity with the Cuban revolution, despite some differences on the tactics to be adopted in the struggle. In fact the Colombian Communist Party consider that every form of struggle should be employed in present circumstances: political, economic and military struggle, with the object of achieving the Colombian revolution, which it regards as basically anti-imperialist. It also supports a policy of agrarian reform and nationalization of the banks and of the oil industry.

Up till now, it has concluded electoral pacts with the MRL, enabling it to win minimum representation in elected assemblies, especially local councils. In view of the aggressively nationalist and popular nature of ANAPO, the CP makes frequent attempts to win support among the rank-and-file of this movement.

Since 1963 the Colombian CP has adopted a position hostile to the Chinese in the Sino-Soviet dispute; it enjoys good relations with other Communist Parties, especially its nearest neighbours in Ecuador and Venezuela, and used to have a permanent representative in Cuba. Its weekly paper is held in high esteem by other Latin American Communist Parties, and a translated Latin American edition of the International Communist journal, *Problemas de la paz*, is published in Bogotá.

In 1964, a number of young Communists, one member of the party leadership and several militants from the Bogotá region and the Caribbean coastal provinces were expelled or broke away from the party, and together with other organizations (MRL Youth; Workers, Students and Peasants Movement) formed a clandestine Marxist-Leninist Communist Party in July 1965, dedicated to the violent overthrow of the National Front by force of arms. Most of its members seem to be students and intellectuals. Its leadership includes a number of jurists.

The Workers, Students and Peasants Movement (MOEC) was until the merger with the pro-Chinese Communists a secret organization of young university students who supported armed insurrection and urban terrorism. This movement was greatly weakened by the assassination of its leader, Antonio Larrota. The Popular Liberation Army (EPL) which operates in southern Córdoba is apparently an offshoot of the CP and the MOEC.

The Social Christian Democratic Party

With the exception of Medellín, where the PSDC enjoys the discreet support of the Catholic hierarchy and of one trade union, the ASA, affiliated to the Latin American Confederation of Christian Trade Unions, its influence hardly extends beyond a small group of intellectuals. However, it is making progress among the student population. Its best-known leader is the Professor of Canon Law at the Jesuit University, Alvaro Rivera Concha.

Some Conservative personages, such as the ex-minister Belisario Betancur, seem to be moving closer to Christian Democracy, but this development is hindered by the attitude of the majority of the Catholic hierarchy.

The PSDC's policy is somewhat hesitant. It recommended abstention at the 1964 elections, but decided to canvas for votes in 1966; since it only obtained a few thousand votes, it supported General Ruiz Novoa for a time, then turned towards Camilo Torres' United Front.

The Social Christian Democratic Party owns one weekly,

and gets indirect support from European ecclesiastics – Belgian, Dutch and German. It is strongly critical of the Christian Democratic government in Chile, which it considers to have broken its promise of reform.

The United Front

More than a party, this organization was initially a front of all left-wing opposition parties – Communists, Christian Democrats, MRL and other very small organizations such as the Popular Nationalist and Socialist Avant-Garde. It also canvassed support from the non-aligned, that is to say malcontents and oppositionists unable to find a comfortable resting-place in any of the existing opposition movements. At the beginning of January 1966, the United Front decided to embark on a policy of clandestine armed struggle. Its undisputed leader was the ex-priest Camilo Torres, sociologist, university chaplain, a man to whom the Cardinal of Bogotá had at one time given important responsibilities (he represented the Church on the Board of the Institute of Agrarian Reform, which enabled him to travel all over the country and establish contacts with the peasants). Camilo Torres was killed in February 1966 among the resistance fighters of the National Liberation Army (ELN), a pro-Castro organization based primarily on disaffected student support, and operating in the province of Santander on the fringes of a number of political parties and movements. The United Front then broke up and some student leaders from the Front also joined the resistance in the mountains. However, some Camilist groups still survive in the universities, and the name of Camilo Torres still evokes hopes of some kind of messianic salvation in the Colombian countryside where he was best known. The death of Camilo Torres was the signal for a crisis in the ranks of the younger Colombian clergy that no longer wished to be associated with the preservation of the political and social *status quo*.

Conclusion

The two big traditional parties are currently in crisis : firstly an ideological crisis, although their history shows that it is not the worst; they are short of voters, which is more distressing; and the divisions afflicting them will not be easily overcome. However, Colombian history teaches us not to underestimate their capacity for survival. They have experienced serious crises in the past (Gaitanism is the most recent example). Nevertheless, the internal structures of the country, the social mechanisms of domination, only change very slowly in Colombia; they are very well run in. It is true that the parties are finding it increasingly difficult to exist. It seems almost as if they were content simply to hang on, without a programme, mere conglomerations of men and groupings who only unite under the cloak of a purely formal democracy in order to share out the benefits of political power. Still, they are enabled to survive because little has changed in the social structure of the country. The gradual urbanization of the population does little, and that very slowly, to extend class relationships developed in a semi-feudal rural setting, for it is rarely accompanied by industrialization, and long after he has settled in the town the migrant remains a peasant in his behaviour and attitudes. Revolts often appear nothing more than a conflict of generations; they merely indicate some minor difficulties accompanying the transference of power within the ruling class. The young radicals of 1849 turned into the wealthy bankers of 1880, the rebellious student of 1956, after doing his time in the MRL, became the party official or deputy hardly troubled by a single impulse to non-conformity.

In this light, the development of the Front towards a permanent alliance between the two formations of which it is composed was a kind of solution. It was a dangerous solution, because it destroyed the central anchor of Colombian politics, the traditional two-party system, to replace it with a system that is much more modern in trend, where progressive elements no longer need subject themselves to the yoke of the two traditional parties. Things have not come to this pass yet, however.

Developments have taken place within each of the parties. They have been carried through only after a grim struggle, and have produced identical results in both cases, i.e. the elimination of those interest groups most closely connected to the *latifundia* agrarian system, to the benefit of those sectors interested in the industrialization of the country: the industrialists of Medellín and Cali (or those active in the state capitalist sector – oil and the merchant marine) and the emergent agricultural capitalists producing cotton and rice, sugar and vegetable oils. These changes are a reflection of those that have taken place within the trade confederations representing the various sectors, notably the Society of Agricultural Landowners and the ANDI. They came about at the cost of alternate struggle and compromise, just as the relations between Colombian capitalism and the economically dominant foreign power that is the main importer of Colombian products and the main supplier of capital are composed of struggles and compromises. This process of substitution and transference of power is complicated by the existence of social forces that do not consider this change to be fast or far-reaching enough, and might easily rush into the breach that a declared conflict would open up. This is true in particular of the radical peasantry, who pose a problem for the Colombian government by their very existence; it is also true of the working-class suburbs of the big towns, which have been politicized by Communist and ANAPO propaganda.

The distance separating the real Colombia from its political reflection, to borrow a formula first developed by Gaitán, cannot be over-emphasized. Any description attempting to synthesize Colombian politics according to European or North American patterns would undoubtedly leave out a number of important factors. To say that Colombia's illiteracy rate is only 35 per cent, or that it is a Catholic country, is simply to play with worthless statistics. What is the degree of literacy of the other 65 per cent of Colombians? What is the significance of the 60 per cent of illegitimate births recorded in the country every year? In its worst moments, the widespread violence in the country has given a hint of the series of phenomena that go to make up the hidden substratum of national political reality, a sub-stratum that is almost totally unknown and unexplored (except by the political *cacique*). The people still exhibit some admiration for the *doctores* educated in French, British or American schools, who buy their clothes in London and discuss French and English politics, the representatives of the traditional political class. But a better reflection of the difficult, disillusioning but still hopeful quest for a Colombian national identity may be found in the popularity of ex-President Valencia, who wore a woollen *ruana*, sat proudly on his horse, talked loudly and interlarded his speech with plenty of popular expressions, an enthusiastic huntsman and convivial drinker; or again the even greater impact of a similar type, Rojas Pinilla; or of the 'Indian' Gaitán.

Yet the National Front stumbles on from crisis to crisis, and has managed to surmount such difficult hurdles as the 1966 elections. It should be said that these elections witnessed a regrouping and better definition of the opposition, the same disaffection on the part of the electorate, and finally did not enable the Front to win the necessary two-thirds majority in the two Houses, thus forcing it to govern by martial law for several years, in violation of the liberal tradition. Draft reforms of the land laws have met with the hostility or passivity of Parliament. Agrarian interests are still very powerfully represented in elected assemblies, on both the Conservative and Liberal sides, especially among members from Caribbean coastal constituencies – Magdalena, Atlántico, Bolivar and Córdoba.

Party Representation in Parliament
Senate

National Front		Opposition	
Liberals	46	MRL	7
Unionist Conservatives	21	Conservatives	14
		ANAPO	18

House of Representatives

National Front		Opposition	
Liberals	70	MRL	21
Unionist Conservatives	38	Conservatives	24
		ANAPO	36

Since the elections, all the senators and eighteen deputies have joined the Liberal Party. Some ANAPO members have joined the Unionist Conservatives. A two-thirds majority is required.

Party Representation in Parliament in 1968
Senate

National Front		Opposition	
Liberals	53	Conservatives	14
Unionist Conservatives	22	ANAPO	17

House of Representatives

National Front		Opposition	
Liberals	95	Conservatives	21
Unionist Conservatives	48	ANAPO	40
		People's MRL	2

The financial and monetary crisis has not yet been resolved, and foreign debts are increasing; coffee prices are falling, despite the 1962 world coffee agreement, which was in any case disastrous for Colombia; for the first time, the purchase price paid to the coffee planters has had to be lowered.

Is there no question of overthrowing the regime by electoral means? Can it then be overthrown at all? ANAPO favours its overthrow, but while the party is able to achieve considerable electoral success, it is not very likely to be able to carry off a coup d'etat, in view of the hostility of the senior echelons of the Army. The latter are still recruited from the traditional oligarchy, and generals with middle-class origins do not normally accede to the supreme command. (Whenever they do there is a crisis: Rojas in 1953, Ruiz in 1965.) However, ANAPO is popular among non-commissioned officers and in the police.

Younger officers of ranks sometimes as high as colonel are hostile to the National Front because of its reactionary, do-nothing policy, and exhibit a concern for the future of the country and the fate of its population, considering the fact that its standard of living is hardly rising. Is there any possibility that the regime might be threatened by the military at a time of fortuitous civil crisis, a threat which would not necessarily imply a dictatorship of socially conservative forces? A development in this direction would perhaps not be unpleasing to the United States military mission.

The chances of the regime's being overthrown by a movement like the present-day guerrillas seem slim in the short term. There are currently two guerrilla groups, one of which (the FARC) is much more the expression of the peasants' struggle for the land than of a revolutionary desire to seize power – although there is always the possibility that these two objectives might intersect at some point. These guerrillas have much more of a catalytic effect at the moment, bringing political consciousness to the countryside. Their presence and the air of permanence and invincibility they have managed to acquire have caused townsmen to doubt whether the government of the Front is going to provide the most effective solution to the problem.

It is not possible to make a choice between these two hypotheses – the survival or violent overthrow of the Front. There seem to be too many elements of chance and other imponderables entering into the question. However, the survival of the Front is by no means the least likely possibility, given help to overcome its periodic crises in the form of repeated injections of foreign capital, while it pursues its erratic course in an atmosphere of suppressed violence. If this does happen, the situation can only deteriorate gradually, and a general decay of standards and of the political parties themselves will be the result.

March 1968

Developments since 1968

For a time prospects appeared to be dramatically changed by ANAPO's success in the presidential elections of April 1970. Misael Pastrana Borrero, who had emerged as the Front's candidate, was eventually declared victorious, but only after a long recount carried out under state of siege. The last two years of President Lleras Restrepo's government saw the coalition labouring under increasing strain. The vigorous, not always politically tactful reformist policies of the President caused undercurrents of opposition in the coalition itself, and his administration's reputation for honesty was severely damaged by its mishandling of a dispute between the Minister of Agriculture and Senator Ignacio Vives: all Colombian Presidencies must bear some scandalous revelation in pre-election year; this one was allowed to achieve phenomenal publicity and impact. Meanwhile the Conservative party also ran into trouble: its convention was unable to decide on a candidate, and its leader Mariano Ospina failed to get a majority for his nominee Pastrana. In the event there were four presidential candidates – Pastrana, the coastal dissident Evaristo Sourdis, the progressive Belisario Betancur, and the ANAPO leader General Gustavo Rojas Pinilla. Liberal support for a Conservative is never as strong as for a Liberal, and Lleras's influence was weakened not only by his being at the end of his term, but also by the scandal above-mentioned. Pastrana scraped in amid loud cries of fraud with 40 per cent of the vote, Rojas Pinilla followed with 38 per cent, Betancour and Sourdis securing 11 per cent and 8 per cent respectively.[13] It was widely argued that without the last candidature, which may have taken more Rojista votes than it did from Pastrana, General Rojas would have won. It is more certain that the three-fold Conservative split gave ANAPO what it had not previously had – a fighting chance – and that this galvanized its supporters into an unprecedented effort: figures for abstention were lower than for some years.

President Lleras handled this difficult situation with great aplomb: few acts of his government showed such political skill as the way he managed the hand-over of power to his successor. But Pastrana entered office without a clear Congressional majority, without coherent plans either political or economic to face not only the country's endemic problems but the additional political problem of a return to free political competition.

His position has proved somewhat less weak than expected: with all major political groups looking forward to the elections of 1972 and 1974, none has wanted to make his position so difficult that the regime itself should be threatened by military coup, in which case elections would not occur. And his own Conservative party has persuaded itself

13. The figures were approximately: Pastrana, 1,612,000; Rojas, 1,546,000; Betancur, 465,000; Sourdis, 322,000.

that its decline has been less, and that its prospects are brighter, than is the case with the traditional Liberal opponent. A 'time-bomb' legacy of President Lleras's energetic policy of peasant organization has been a marked increase in pressure for land distribution from the Asociación de Usuarios which at present disavows party ties. The government has as yet shown no sign of a consistent policy in this field, and its urban policies too have been rather confused and contradictory.

This has not been very damaging. The political scene has become increasingly atomized, coalitions forming and reforming in an experimental way. ANAPO has survived its opponent's continual predictions that it will disintegrate, and the entry into and departure from the movement of the flamboyant Senator Vives. It manages to combine the appearance of exclusion from office with the fact of enjoying much local and congressional power and patronage. The movement is populist in most of the senses that that word has carried: it does not preach the Class War nor attack the Church, nor take a clear line on agrarian reform. It knows who it is against better than what it is against, and what it is against better than what it is for. In this fluid situation no obvious bets can be made, and no politician dismissed confidently as finished. The Liberals are weak, and have decided not to participate in the municipal elections of 1972, but ex-President Lleras still enjoys more prestige among peasants than any other figure, and both he and Alfonso Lopez Michelsen have never figured among the arch-enemies of ANAPO. The increasing respectability of ANAPO, the growing open contracts between members of that group and those of the two traditional parties, is another factor. From it a new coalition system may emerge.

February 1972

HUGO NEIRA
Ecuador

THE COUNTRY

Ecuador has a population of more than 5½ million, over an area of 106,178 square miles. Of the three regions that make up the country's territory (the coast, the sierra and Amazonia), the sierra is both the smallest (23 per cent of the territory) and the most densely populated (56 per cent of the total population). About 38 per cent of the population live on the coast, while Amazonia and the Galapagos archipelago (twelve islands 250 miles from the coast) are very sparsely populated regions. Racially, the population consists of about 10 per cent whites, 39 per cent Indians, 41 per cent half-castes (white and Indian), 5 per cent Negroes and mulattos, and 5 per cent other coloured peoples.[1]

On the political plane, the low level of education (42 per cent of the population over 15 is illiterate) and the very uneven geographical distribution of the working population (66 per cent of the labour force lives outside the towns) considerably restricts popular participation in public affairs. In fact the parties represent minority groups. Their ruling elites generally belong to the white and creole sectors of the population; the Indians and half-castes (1,250,000 in the sierra, with a smaller, unknown number on the coast, where they

1. 'Ecuador en cifras', in El desarrollo económico del Ecuador. Santiago de Chile, CEPAL, 1964.

are called *montuvios*) only provide, at best, their electoral clientele.

Urban and Electoral Centres

The two biggest towns in Ecuador are Guayaquil and Quito. Guayaquil (population: 700,000) is a port on the Pacific coast, and is the country's most important commercial centre; Quito (population 500,000) is the political and administrative capital.

Political and Administrative Organizations

The country is divided into twenty provinces and one 'national territory', the Galapagos archipelago, administered by the National Defence Ministry. Each province is divided into cantons, and the cantons into parishes (there are 169 urban and 626 rural parishes); the provinces are governed by a provincial council and the cantons by a municipal council.

In 'normal' times, direct universal elections are held to renew the mandates of the executive and the two houses of parliament (in the Chamber of Deputies there is one deputy for every fifty thousand inhabitants, or seventy-three deputies in 1963; in the Senate, there are two senators for each province). The 1946 Constitution (in force until 1963) laid down that the Senate should also include five senators to represent the various economic interest groups in the country, without being affiliated to any particular party.

The regime is unitary in form. The latest Constitution only permits three parties: the Conservatives, the Liberals and the Socialists; no President of the Republic is eligible for re-election; a Supreme Court is established under the Constitution; every citizen aged twenty years who has completed his primary education is entitled to vote. The military junta which took power in July 1963 suspended the Constitution.

HISTORY

So far as concerns the emergence and establishment of the national state, Ecuador has followed the same course of development as the other countries born of the old Spanish American Empire. After the wars of independence, the country found itself part of 'Greater Colombia' (as Bolivar had wished). In 1830, however, the southern region of this Colombian federation embarked on a secessionist movement, and at Riobamba drew up a Constitution and appointed a President, the Venezuelan Juan José Flores, then commander-in-chief of the armed forces in the southern region. This man remained in power until 1845 (with a short interruption from 1839 to 1844). In the ensuing period, there was a nationalist reaction against 'foreign militarism' (as in Peru and Bolivia), and Flores was removed from power. From 1845 to 1859, liberal and progressive governments introduced a number of reforms, such as the emancipation of the slaves in 1861, and the abolition of the death penalty for political offences in 1859. Between 1861 and 1875 a Conservative reaction directed against the Liberals and their reforms, and also against the Army which supported them, brought Gabriel García Moreno to power.

This third period in the history of Ecuador witnessed the beginnings of the alliance between the ruling power and the Church, despite Liberal and anti-clerical opposition, and it laid the foundations for a future Conservative and clericalist party. García Moreno established a dictatorship based on theocratic principles. The government's frontier disputes with Peru, and the major public works projects embarked upon (for instance the Guayaquil–Quito railway) were to give this government a remarkable cohesion and dynamism. From 1875 to 1895 neither the Conservatives nor the Liberals managed to win a majority.

The fourth period in Ecuador's history began in 1895,

when Eloy Alfaro installed a Liberal and secularist regime, following a popular revolution. Between 1895 and 1933 the country was affected by a number of changes. Under Eloy Alfaro's inspiration, a divorce law was adopted in 1902, and in 1908 a law was passed expropriating ecclesiastical property (the law of *manos muertas*); in 1906, General Plaza's government drew up a Constitution that was to serve as the model for all the others subsequently adopted in Ecuador. (There were to be twenty-two.)

Economically, Ecuador has increasingly concentrated on the export of a single product – cocoa – and falling prices of this product, coupled with a drop in exports (in 1929), go far to explain the repercussions on this country of the 1930s economic crisis. This was the period during which Ecuador signed frontier treaties with Brazil (1904) and Colombia (1916) through which she lost about 300,000 km² in the Amazonian region, or almost half her entire territory.

From 1924, the political system, based on the opposition between Liberals and Conservatives, was shaken by the appearance of new forces on the political scene. By 1922, the Confederación Obrera del Guayas (the province to which the town of Guayaquil belongs) dominated economic life on the coast and was in a position to paralyse the country's principal port at will. In 1925, again in Guayaquil, a military coup d'etat took place, led by Ildefonso Mendoza with the support of the younger officers; the uprising provided the spark to inflame the whole country, and the revolt quickly spread. This was not a coup d'etat of the traditional type. A (civilian) ruling junta was set up, but it was based on military juntas in the provinces. These military rulers (nicknamed 'the ideologues') shortly handed over power to civilians (demonstrating that they had not intended to seize it for themselves) and undertook a substantial revision of the structures of the state. With their support, the provisional President Isidro Ayora carried out a number of important measures,[2] such as the creation of the Ecuador Central Bank, the Mortgage Credit Bank, and of a development bank, the establishment of a Ministry of Social Welfare and Labour, and a General Inspectorate of Labour. New parties made their appearance in Ecuador at this time: the Social Democratic Party was born in Quito in July 1925, and in December of the same year the Ecuadorian Socialist Party held its inaugural assembly. In 1932 the final conflict between Conservatives and Liberals on the question of the election of Neptali Bonifaz (Bonifaz, the candidate of the right, won the election thanks to the Liberals' internal divisions) paved the way for the appearance of a new political force connected neither to the Liberals nor the Conservatives: this force was what we shall here term Velasquism.

Partido Conservador (PC)

The Conservative Party came into being during the theocratic dictatorship of García Moreno (1859–71). When the

2. These measures were inspired by the North American Kemmerer trade mission. Between 1920 and 1931, a group of American financial consultants, led by Edwin W. Kemmerer, visited a number of Latin American countries, notably Colombia, Ecuador and Peru. The Kemmerer mission recommended to the various governments that had invited and financed it a number of measures based on the strictest financial orthodoxy – the establishment of a modern banking network, the improvement of public services, etc. But the mission's chief aim was to stabilize the currencies of these countries within a monetary zone that remained loyal to the Gold Exchange Standard, i.e. to ensure the convertibility of these currencies into gold, dollars or sterling. The key currencies thus became the dollar and the pound sterling. This was, in fact, an episode in 'dollar diplomacy' in Latin America. As a result, through their attachment to British and American monetary circuits, these countries were profoundly affected by the 1929 crisis, and after 1932 by the fall in the prices of raw materials.

latter disappeared from the scene, the Conservatives and Liberals took turns in power until 1895. In that year a revolution, possibly the only popular revolution in Ecuador's history, brought to power Eloy Alfaro and the Liberals. The Liberal hegemony was further reinforced in 1925 by a military coup carried out by progressively-minded army officers. Since then, the Conservatives have only won elections twice: in 1931 Neptali Bonifaz won the election with the support of a number of dissident Liberal groups; in 1956 Camilo Ponce won the election with only 29 per cent of the votes, and the elections were denounced by the opposition as rigged. Finally, Arosemena Gómez, a Deputy belonging to the Constitutional Democratic Concentration, was elected President by the Constituent Assembly in November 1966 (with the support of the Social Christians).

In defining Conservatism in Ecuador it is important to examine the role within the Conservative Party itself played by a number of different forces, especially the Church and the Army; the latter acts as a regulator when the balance between the parties is disturbed either by excessively autocratic presidential rule or by mass movements operating outside the framework of the traditional parties. It is unusual for the Army to act on its own initiative without reference to the wishes of the Conservative Party. It has happened twice, however, in 1925 and in 1947. For this reason the Army will be considered under a separate heading.

As for the Church, while it plays no direct role, it is nearer to the Conservative Party than to any other. Following the publication of papal encyclicals such as *Rerum novarum* and *Quadragesimo Anno*, the Church has become the prime source of Conservative ideology, as the latter recognizes in its programme and manifestoes. No study of Conservatism in Ecuador can therefore ignore this bond between the Church and the Party. The intellectual bond that unites the party's leaders to the clergy is nourished within the party itself by an internal pressure-group that acts as a kind of 'think-tank', whose effectiveness is proportional to the clergy's influence over political decisions. Moreover the Conservative Party, as an avowedly Catholic party, declares its submission to an international authority – the authority of the Pope. The 1952 split, which gave birth to the Social Christians, can therefore be explained as a conflict within the Conservative Party between the 'old guard' concerned with the preservation of the *status quo* and younger elements in the party who pressed for the application of the Church's social policy. The Conservatives claim to represent 'order', but then so do the Liberals. The only question on which they are really divided is therefore the religious question, the Liberals being traditionally 'rabid anti-clericalists'. On other questions – e.g. the nature of the ruling oligarchy, conditions of party membership, the relations between the various social classes – they hold similar attitudes. Both Liberals and Conservatives in fact support the maintenance of the *status quo*, a representative republic and the legitimacy of the presidential power. On the economic plane, they are in favour of free trade and the defence of private property, and both are equally opposed to state intervention in the economy. Socially, the Liberals and Conservatives spring from the same social class, that is to say the upper middle class with its urban and rural dependants.

There is in reality only one Conservative Party, but various forces and pressure-groups are clustered around this party. Two similar but for the most part mutually hostile types of conservative faction can be distinguished, differing in the criterion which came uppermost in their decision to support the Conservatives: the Conservatives with Christian leanings, and the Conservatives with fascist leanings.

The Christian tendency is represented by:
 – The Movimiento Social Cristiano, a wing of the Conservative Party led by Camilo Ponce Enríquez. In its electoral

alliances, and in its opposition to the military junta after 1963, this movement has proved independent of the Conservatives. This opposition is chiefly one of personalities within the Conservative Party itself. The Social Christians and the Conservatives presented joint lists at the elections of 1967 (for the Constituent Assembly) after the fall of the military junta.

– The Frente Anti-Comunista de Defensa Nacional (FADN); this movement was very active under the presidencies of Velasco and Carlos Julio Arosemena, and organized Christian militias to fight the 'communist menace'.

The fascist tendency is expressed by:
– The Alianza Revolucionaria Nacionalista Equatoriana (ARNE). The Alliance made its appearance in 1948, during Galo Plaza's government, under the influence of the Partido Sinarquista Mexicano and the Spanish Falange. It recruited most of its sympathizers from among the younger members of the upper middle class. It is avowedly nationalist and Christian. Small in number, but militantly anti-Communist, its supporters attend workers' meetings to provoke direct confrontation with active members of the Socialist and Communist Parties. They are highly disciplined and readily engage in street battles. The main leader of the group in 1965 was Jorge Luna. Together with the rest of the Conservative Party, the ARNE gave its support to Velasco.

Extent of Conservative Party Support

The Conservative Party is very influential in the provinces of the sierra where 60 per cent of the population live (Azuay, Canar, Loja and Pichincha). The Party is led by a small number of aristocratic land-owning families and middle-class merchants, recruiting most of its support among the half-castes of the sierra, in Quito and in the smaller towns, and in that sector of the middle class associated with the civil service and therefore sensitive to changes of President.

Social Structure of the Conservative Electorate

Peasants and tenant farmers dependent on the big land-owners are only enabled to work on the land by means of temporary contracts of employment. Although they do not vote, these sectors do constitute potential manpower for the 'right-wing *jacqueries*' that have frequently broken out in Ecuador since 1923. By their participation in Conservative meetings in the towns, the peasants also exercise some influence on the coastal region (which has many migrants) and on the so-called *montuvios* (more independent half-castes of the coastal region).

Small artisans, especially in the provinces of Azuay and Canar. The *toquila* straw weavers (the only exported Ecuadorian manufacture) are also a Conservative group.

The urban middle class, state employees, connected to a Conservative *cacique* by bonds of personal loyalty. This group also includes the half-caste and white middle class, which is devoutly Catholic and votes Conservative to preserve its social status.

The aristocratic families that are traditionally Conservative.

Structure of the Party

The Conservative Party does not have a strongly-articulated chain of command, but it does organize national conventions to choose its candidate. In the Constituent Assemblies of 1938 and 1947, the Conservatives succeeded in having the number of legally permitted parties reduced to three: the Liberal Party, the Socialist Party, and the Conservative Party – a state of affairs that obviously favoured them. In the pattern of elections and electoral alliances, the Conservatives have emerged as the most stable force in Ecuador's political system.

Election Results

In 1933 the Conservative Party won the elections in alliance with Velasco, whom they had backed for the presidency. However, it is difficult to say exactly what share of the vote cast for Velasco (60 per cent) is attributable to Conservatives and how much to Velasquists.

In 1948 the Frente Democrático Nacional, which supported Galo Plaza against the Conservatives, inflicted a severe defeat on them. In 1952, the Conservative candidate Ruperto Alarcón was again defeated, this time by Velasco; however, the party obtained 105,000 out of 340,000 votes, or 31·1 per cent of the total cast, thus representing the country's second most powerful electoral force, after Velasquism. It actually obtained a majority in the Senate (sixteen seats out of thirty-four) and twenty seats in the Chamber of Deputies, only one fewer than the Velasquists.

In 1965 the Conservatives won the elections under the leadership of Camilo Ponce Enríquez, but this victory was disputed by its opponents, who denounced various electoral malpractices. The Conservative Party had allied itself with the Christian Democrats on this occasion, and had only won 27·9 per cent of the vote (or 178,421 votes out of some 600,000) : President Ponce was therefore forced to bring four Liberals and two Christian Democrats into his Cabinet, accompanied by one solitary Conservative.

In 1960, the Conservatives came second, with their leader, Gonzalo Cordero Crespo, only obtaining 150,254 out of 800,000 votes in the presidential elections. The Conservative Party nevertheless remained the second largest political force in the country, after the Velasquists. It held seventeen seats in the Chamber of Deputies, and eight in the Senate. However, the number of votes cast for it had proportionately diminished by comparison with previous years. On the other hand, the Conservative Party was victorious in the local elections both in 1957 and 1961 over the whole of the country except for Guayaquil and Portoviejo.

Party Alliances

In 1944 the Conservative Party joined with the Liberals, Socialists, Velasquists and Communists in a Democratic Alliance to oust President Arroyo del Río, following the war with Peru and the subsequent treaties.

In 1956, the party joined the centre-right Popular Alliance to promote the candidature of Camilo Ponce Enríquez, with the support of Francisco Illienworth Icaza of the Social Christian Party. In 1964 it joined with the Social Christians in the Constitutionalist Front led by Camilo Ponce and opposed to the military junta in power.

Main Leaders

Gonzalo Cordero Crespo, the chairman of the party, Camilo Ponce Enríquez, and Enrique Arroyo Delgado, who all belong to the 'Christian' faction.

Press Outlets

El Mercurio (circulation: 8,000), a Social Christian daily published in Cuenca; *El Heraldo* (circulation 3,000), a Conservative paper published in Ambato.

Partido Liberal Radical

Historical Outline

The Traditional Liberal Party. The Liberal Party was founded in 1878, and was the ideological expression of the groups opposed to the personal exercise of power and to Church participation in national politics. To some extent, this Liberal tradition has continued into modern times, taking the form of opposition to the authoritarian caudillism of a Velasco, or of alliance with the Socialist left through opposition to Conservatism or through anti-clericalism.

Despite this, the period of Liberal Party hegemony (1895–1925) is directly associated with the actions of two (Liberal) caudillos: Eloy Alfaro and Leonidas Plaza. Once in power, the forces of Liberalism initially embarked upon a series of reforms on two levels, administrative and economic. On the administrative plane, the Church was separated from the State, education was secularized and greatly expanded in a crash programme against illiteracy; new penal and commercial codes were promulgated, and a new law governing the police was introduced; a law of 1908 made inroads on the property of the Church, the country's biggest landed proprietor. On the economic plane, the railway and road networks were extended, and agriculture, which was too heavily concentrated on cocoa production, was diversified. Finally, from the social angle, Liberalism represented the interests of the new middle class on the coast (commerce and finance) as against those of the upper classes in the Andean region (landowners).

The Liberal Party from 1925 to the Present Day. Neither the application of the early Liberal programmes nor the coastal bourgeoisie's rise to power and influence were enough to transform Ecuador and prepare it for the changes of the period from 1920–30, which brought about profound changes in the face of the country and of the Liberal Party itself. The cocoa crisis and the emergence of new social forces both had their effect on the party. Between 1922 and 1933 the first labour unions were founded (in Guayaquil) and the Socialist Party also made its appearance. This period is characterized by the first sortie into politics by the military, in the July revolution of 1925, with the object of increasing the role of the state. Moreover, the revolutions in the Soviet Union and in Mexico influenced intellectuals and some sectors of the coastal middle class opposed to the traditionalism of the Andean oligarchy. While continuing the old polemic struggle with the Conservative Party on the role of the Church in the political life of the country, Liberalism itself began to change (witness the 1923 Liberal programme), and adopt some Marxist ideas, finding in the Socialist Party its most determined ally in opposing the new authoritarianism that had emerged in Ecuador.

As its power and influence began to wane, the Liberal Party found itself in a paradoxical situation. In practice, almost all the Presidents of the country claimed allegiance to the Liberals, but without actually belonging to the party. (Velasco is the most notable example.) New leaders such as Galo Plaza, who started out as the United Fruit Company's lawyer, were ideologically very close to the Liberal Party but regarded themselves as 'independents'. The Liberal Party's prestige was therefore greater than its electoral strength, and extended beyond the framework of the party proper. The reasons for this prestige reside primarily in the Liberal ideology (the party's 1952 programme based itself on the Rights of Man). Its second source of prestige was the social origins of the Liberal Party workers, who wished for the modernization of Ecuador and were therefore ready to make alliances which would accelerate some of the structural changes they wanted, although without going so far as to support the claims of the far left.

Ideology and Programme

In Ecuador, Liberalism is distinguished from the forces of Conservatism primarily by its intransigent anti-clericalism (the legacy of the nineteenth century and of European influence). This is its basic characteristic, for as far as economic and social policy is concerned, the Liberals, like the Conservatives, are champions of private property and in favour of a representative and Republican political system. The alliances made by the Liberal Party with the Socialists and Independents (who are Liberals not officially connected with the Liberal Party itself) were dictated more by political than economic considerations.

In the Liberal Party programme and ideology, a distinction should be drawn between the ideas inherited from the nineteenth century and the newer elements, i.e. the content of the 1923 programme. Anti-clericalism is the traditional element in the Party's programme. After 1923, Liberalism placed greater emphasis on economic and social questions than on its older demands, which were for the most part based on questions of high principle: respect for the individual, the right to vote, separation of Church and State and so on. In particular it demanded the protection of the rights of the Indians, subjected to three-fold exploitation by the Church, white man's alcohol, and the *huasipungo* system.[3] For this reason the Liberal Party was the first to call for land reform. The Liberals are moreover opposed to the personal exercise of power, and the Ecuadorian people's economic and political dependence on the upper class and on foreign interests. In other words, they are opposed to the practices of the *caudillo*, the oligarchy, and imperialism.

3. In Latin America, the *huasipunguero*, like the *inquilino*, the *finquero*, etc., is a peasant. He is a small farmer who in exchange for his labour owns a life interest in the land which he cultivates. Although he is dependent on the *hacienda* system to which he is attached, he is protected to some extent by the network of conventions between his *status* (in the American sense) and the *hacienda*. Hence the Liberals' opposition to this system, which resulted in the maintenance of traditional ties between the boss (the *hacendado*) and his personal clientele of native *huasipungueros*.

The Liberals have also proposed a number of measures designed to set up new production areas in the Amazonian region, and to increase the role of the state as the protector of the family and its standard of living. In the agricultural sphere, they demand the conversion of private property in accordance with the needs of technology and of social welfare.

This programme, which is based on technical progress, on safeguarding the national interest, and the integration of new categories of consumer and producer into the national market, bears certain similarities to that of the Social Democrats; its chief defect is perhaps that it is over-optimistic for a country whose main natural resources are based on the production of one single crop – also a major factor in creating social instability.

The Party's Social Composition

For historical reasons that go back to the foundation of the Liberal Party, some of Ecuador's oldest aristocratic families can be found among its leaders. However, the party recruits its support chiefly among the social classes of more recent appearance in the towns of the interior, following the economic development of the littoral and the expansion of trade. The Liberal Party electorate may be broken down as follows:

The Upper Middle Class of Guayaquil (bankers and exporters). The expansion of this class between 1910 and 1920 coincides with the heyday of Liberalism. This class was concerned primarily with the exploitation of exportable agricultural products of the big plantations (at that time cocoa, bananas, coffee, coconuts, sugar cane and cotton), and benefited from a number of Liberal measures such as the law of *manos muertas* (expropriating Church property) of 1908. Moreover because of the constant migrations from the sierra (in 1946 only 61 per cent of the population of Guayaquil originated in that province; 25 per cent came from other provinces and 11 per cent from the sierra), this middle class was faced with social problems very different from those typical of the plateau. Some indication of this is given by the dynamism exhibited by the Guayaquil authorities in the social field. A major portion of local revenue from the harbour was used for social purposes. (For instance a welfare committee was set up, a central Public Assistance Board for the province of the littoral was created, an anti-malaria campaign was instituted, a League of Education to combat illiteracy was founded, a child welfare society was established.)

The middle class. The educational profession, including both primary and secondary school teachers, constitutes a traditionally liberal sector, first of all because educational reform was born of Eloy Alfaro's secularist policy and finally became a reality in 1925, and secondly because a liberal law (*ley de escalafón y salarios*) gave them stability of status and protected them from arbitrary dismissal.

The middle classes of Guayaquil: this town far outdistances the rest of the country in the level of trade and public services (the average utilization of libraries and the cinema is far above that of the capital, Quito, and other towns), and artisans (6,422 in the town itself), merchants and white-collar workers vote both for the Liberals and for other parties opposed to the Conservatives (in particular the Concentración de Fuerzas Populares, or CFP, which in Guayaquil rivals the electoral strength of the Liberals and the Velasquists). These same sectors tend to vote Liberal in the rest of the country.

The low density of Liberal votes is accounted for by the numerical weakness of these sectors of the middle class.

Chief Areas of Support

The party is strongest in the port of Guayaquil and in the urban areas in the Andes; it also enjoys some support in the coastal provinces of Esmeralda, Manabi, Los Ríos, Guayas and El Oro.

Structure of the Party

The Liberal Party has the same type of structure as the Conservative Party : candidates for parliamentary and presidential elections are chosen by national convention. In each province the Liberal clientele is grouped around a few notables; the Liberal leaders belong to families that are traditionally connected with the party, or are members of the Liberal professions from the urban middle class (generally known as *liberales populares*).

Election Results

From 1925 to 1940, the Liberal Party did not win a single election. In 1940 it brought Carlos Arroyo del Río to the presidency, but the results of these elections gave no clear indication of the party's strength since electoral malpractices played a very important part in the victory. In 1948 the Liberals and Socialists together were unable to prevent the election of Galo Plaza (a non-party Liberal) who won the election with the support of independent centrists who themselves did not constitute a party.

After the split in the party in 1950, the Radical Liberal Party supported José Ricardo Chiriboga Villagómez; it won a majority in Guayaquil and Quito, but was beaten over the rest of the country. The presidential candidate only obtained 65,000 votes, against 150,000 for Velasco and 105,000 for the Conservative candidate Ruperto Alarcón. The votes cast for the Radical Liberal Party in this election were augmented by those cast for the Democratic Alliance (17,000) which under Modesto Larrea Jijón represented the dissident faction in the Liberals. Two dissident Liberals were brought into Velasco's Cabinet. The Liberals were very poorly represented in Parliament: they obtained nine seats in the Senate (as against sixteen for the Conservatives, seven for the Velasquists and one to the Independents), and thirteen in the Chamber of Deputies (as against twenty-one to the Velasquists, twenty to the Conservatives and five to the Independents). After these elections, the Liberals were therefore only the third strongest political force in the country.

In 1956, after Velasco's exclusion from the elections, the central struggle was that between the Liberals and the Conservatives. The latter, under Camilo Ponce, won, but only just. The difference was only 6,000 votes (Ponce: 178,421 and Raúl Clemente Huerta: 172,979). It should be mentioned that the Liberals were allied with the Socialists and Independents in the Frente Democrático Nacional (FDN) for these elections. In 1960 Galo Plaza, this time the official candidate of the FDN, came third (146,867 votes), beaten by Velasco (323,348 votes) and by the Conservative Gonzalo Cordero Crespo (150,254 votes). The Liberals won about the same proportion of seats in the two Houses as in the previous elections (seventeen deputies and four senators). However, the percentage of votes obtained by the Liberal Party had risen slightly: in 1952, it represented 19·29 per cent of the electorate, and in 1956 27·90 per cent (although it fell back to 23 per cent in 1960). In October 1966, it opposed the election of Otto Arosemena Gómez, putting forward its own candidate Raúl Clemente Huerta, who obtained 35 out of 78 votes in Parliament in the election for President of the Republic. After his election, he proposed a coalition Cabinet.

Alliances and Schisms

Electoral Alliances. In 1944 the party joined the Democratic Alliance, with the Velasquists, the Conservatives and the left (Socialist and Communist) against the regime of Carlos Arroyo del Río. These disparate groups were united in this incongruous alliance by nationalist sentiment and the fear of fraudulent elections.

In 1960, the party joined with the Socialist Party and some other groups of the centre-left in the Frente Democrático Nacional. The Front was defeated, obtaining only 23 per cent of the votes, as has already been mentioned. The FDN resulted from an electoral agreement at national level between the Socialists and the Liberals. In local elections, this alliance was sometimes maintained and sometimes the two parties presented separate candidates. In 1957, for example, the Liberals and Socialists stood separately in the Quito council elections; in Guayaquil, on the other hand, they united under the FDN label to fight the candidature of Luis Robles Plaza, the candidate of the CFP (Concentración de Fuerzas Populares). Every time the FDN presented joint lists, it found itself faced by adversaries who were also in alliance. In 1960 the Archbishop of Cuenca branded the Liberals, Socialists and Independents supporting Galo Plaza as 'atheists' and 'Marxists'.

Schisms. Some sectors broke away from the Liberal Party in 1948 to form the Movimiento Cívico Independiente, which supported Galo Plaza and carried him to victory. In 1952, some Liberals grouped in the Partido Liberal Auténtico swelled the ranks of the Democratic Alliance; their candidate, Modesto Larrea Jijón, obtained 17,000 votes out of the total 340,000 cast. In 1960 'authentic Liberalism' supported Velasco Ibarra against the Radical Liberals' candidate.

Main Leaders

Pedro José Arteta and Alfonso Mora Veintimilla.

Press

Dailies: El *Telégrafo* (circulation: 12,000) and El *Universo* (50,000), published in Guayaquil; El *Comercio* (45,000) in Quito. One monthly journal, *Vistazo* (40,000), Radical Liberal in tendency, published in Guayaquil; finally La *Calle* (2,000), an independent Socialist periodical, published in Quito.

Velasquism (1933–61)

The great tradition of caudillism lives on in Ecuador in the form of Velasquism. Before it became a party, as late as 1952, Velasquism was a movement the principles, aims and ideology of which were embodied by one man: José María Velasco Ibarra. However, both in the composition of its political following and the means it employs to gain power, Velasquism goes well beyond the normal bounds of personalism; nor is it precisely identical to the type of caudillism represented by José María Urbina or by Eloy Afroy in the nineteenth century. On the political level it is an expression of the appearance in Ecuadorian society of new political forces resistant to integration in the traditional parties, and on a sociological level Velasquism bears witness to the impact which a charismatic leader can make on a country where there has always been a strong tendency for power to become personalized. As in the case of Vargas's Brazil or Perón's Argentina, the programme and organization of the new mass party ('Getulismo', 'Peronismo', 'Velasquismo') should be considered rather as a function of the series of alliances entered into by the party leader in order to gain power than from the point of view of the actual aims of the party or its frequently ambiguous and contradictory electoral platform.

Tendencies and Methods

Velasquism first appeared as a political movement in 1933. Between 1933 and 1960 it brought José María Velasco Ibarra to power four times. Velasquism has oscillated between the right and left: it started off as a Conservative movement in 1933, but in 1944 called itself Liberal Socialist. In 1952 and 1960, however, it presented itself in its true colours, simply calling itself Movimiento Nacional Velasquista. But in any case Velasquism always enjoyed a current of popularity quite independent of allegiances to other groups, regardless of the vagaries of its own political line. When the Velasquist movement did not support the candidature of Velasco himself (in 1952 it supported Camilo Ponce) it seemed to lose strength and even tended to melt into the other parties. The first condition for the existence of Velasquism is therefore the candidature of Velasco in person.

The methods which he used to obtain power also varied; in 1933, 1952 and 1960 he got in after free elections. (It should be noted that with the exception of the 1948 elections, which brought to power the independent liberal candidate Galo Plaza, the election of Velasco Ibarra has coincided with the only periods of democracy in the political life of the country.) Although Velasco won power three times by election, this was not the only means employed by Velasquism to get itself in : it also exerted pressure on the two Houses to declare the presidency vacant (the method used in 1933 against Juan de Dios Martínez Mera), or obtained a posteriori recognition of a coup d'etat by a constituent assembly (1944). Velasco for his part, was unable to complete his term of office during any of his periods in power except one (1952–6); he was overthrown by the Army on three occasions, in 1935, 1947 and 1961, although that same Army once brought him to power, in 1944.

Ideology

Opposition to the Parties. By rejecting other political parties as valueless and unworthy of consideration, Velasco Ibarra endeavoured to create a mass movement on the margin of the traditional parties. How is his own popularity to be accounted for? It is in no small part due to the reaction of the 'people' to the obsolescence of the other parties' programmes:

> On 1 June (1952), the people of Ecuador voted against those organizations that call themselves political parties. In recent years, there have unfortunately been no political parties in Ecuador. When national morale weakens, political parties disappear. There can be no political party without a doctrine and without mass support to back it up.[4]
>
> ... Ideally, political parties like to be small committees of individuals calling themselves socialists, liberals or conservatives, with no contact with the people, no contact with the nation, having absolutely no communion with the collective consciousness. All this calls itself 'avante-garde political ideas' and in the name of all this I am forbidden to return to my country and govern with the help of the people.[5]

Nationalism. First of all, Velasco's intransigent position on the problem of Ecuador's frontier with Peru should be emphasized. In 1933, he accused Martínez Mera of weakness in foreign policy, which provoked the latter's fall. In 1944 President del Río was brought down by exploitation of the defeats suffered in the war against Peru (the province of del Oro was occupied by Peruvian troops in 1941) and of the

4. Velasco's speech on assuming the presidency, 1 September 1952.
5. A speech made on 2 March 1952 to a welcoming demonstration in Guayaquil.

general discontent aroused by the Treaty of Rio de Janeiro (a treaty 'de paz, amistad y límites') between Peru and Ecuador. On this nationalist platform Velasco constructed the Democratic Alliance, which included Liberals, Conservatives, Communists and Socialists.

Liberalism. Although he opposed the Liberal Party and actually banned it, Velasco always laid claim to some degree of liberalism, in which he included a number of very general notions, mainly spirituality and respect for the individual. The notions of morality and democracy were often added.

Velasco's programme also contained other points, such as decentralization, greater autonomy for the provinces, free and secular education, and included periodic attacks against the 'liberal and conservative oligarchy' and against imperialism. Velasquism constantly professed its anti-Communism in the name of Christianity and individualism; it defended private property and was favourable to foreign investment.

Velasquism and the Other Parties

In 1933 Velasco won the support of the Conservatives, since he first appeared on the scene as one of the disciples of Neptali Bonifaz, a Conservative *caudillo*. In 1944 the Conservatives joined the Democratic Alliance, which in the course of that year organized an uprising to counter the possibility of electoral fraud, and a constituent assembly set up in 1946 was dominated by that party. A new Constitution was adopted (the sixteenth), and Velasco was elected President of the Republic. In 1952 and 1960 the Conservatives presented their own candidate in competition with the Velasquists (who by then campaigned under their own party label).

The Liberals, who allied themselves with the Velasquists in 1944 to overthrow Carlos Arroyo del Río, joined forces with the Socialists and Independents in 1956 and 1960 (Frente Democrático Nacional) to oppose them.

The Communists joined forces with the Velasquists in 1940, 1944, 1948, 1952 and 1960. They opposed them whenever Velasquism in power moved towards authoritarianism with no other object than to preserve its power. As a result, the anti-Velasquist opposition in 1961 included socialist and communist elements, in particular the *Central de Trabajadores del Guayas*, the *Federacíon de Estudiantes Universitarios del Ecuador*, intellectuals and part of the press.

Electoral Support

Velasquism, which is able to call upon a mass electoral support outside the framework of the traditional parties and their electoral clientele, is perhaps partly the product of the growth in the country's population, illustrated by the increase in the Ecuadorian electorate between 1875 and 1960. In 1875 the electorate totalled about 45,000; by 1933 (when Velasco Ibarra won his first victory at the polls) it had risen to 62,000, and in 1960 the total number of votes cast amounted to 800,000. In 1968, the number of registered electors was 1,178,613. Voting is compulsory for those over 18 and literate.

The social composition of Velasquism is varied and heterogeneous. The first to support Velasco Ibarra's candidature and programme were the so-called *compactados* (a kind of mercenary in the pay of local *caudillos*) from the Andean region (Quito), half-castes and Indians who supported the Conservative leader Bonifaz. The Liberals, for their part, called this social group the *chusma* (the rabble), an expression which indicates both the humble origins of Velasco's first supporters, and the prejudices or lack of understanding on the part of the Liberal elite in the face of new social phenomena in the Ecuador of that time. Velasquism also seems to have won the support of the middle class, seduced either by the nationalism or the liberalism professed by the Leader. The third group of supporters consisted basically of the population of the town of Guayaquil, the country's commercial centre; this fact is of some importance, since of the 249,000 electors registered in the province of Guayaquil in 1962, 222,000 were on the urban electoral list. The concentration of unskilled labourers and dockers, a middle class formed primarily of merchants and members of the liberal professions, and a rural proletariat organized in trade unions (especially on the banana plantations) made Guayaquil an electoral region highly receptive to the Velasquist ideology. It should be emphasized, however, that these same sectors may contribute to the success of other political currents such as the Unión Popular Republicana (UPR) of Carlos Guevara Moreno that are just as far removed from the Liberal-Conservative axis as Velasquism. In general terms, the UPR and Velasquist electorate of the town of Guayaquil stands confronting the much more conservative electorate of the sierra.

Electoral Results

In 1933, the Velasquists won 60 per cent of the total vote. In 1952, Velasco Ibarra won 153,934 votes (out of a total of 352,000 electors), or almost 45 per cent of the votes, seven seats in the Senate and twenty-one in the Chamber of Deputies. In 1960, the number of votes had risen again: 323,348 votes out of almost 800,000 registered electors, or more than 41 per cent of the total vote. After these elections, the composition of the two Houses was as follows: in the Senate, eighteen Velasquists as against seventeen members of opposition parties (Conservatives, Democratic Front, Independents), and in the lower house thirty-two Velasquists out of a total of seventy-three deputies.

Velasquism in 1960–61

Whereas the movement had both a conservative and a liberal tendency during the 1935–45 period, between 1950 and 1956 it was heavily influenced by Argentine 'justicialism' (although Velasco publicly rejected any identification between his own ideas and those of Perón). What is certain is that in May 1952 Galo Plaza's government expelled the Argentine Ambassador, César Salvador Mazzetti, who made no secret of his sympathies and activities on behalf of Velasco.

However, by 1960, when Velasco returned to power, the focal point in foreign affairs was the Cuban question, not the Peronist question. Various domestic problems had arisen, moreover. There was agitation among the students, the Popular Republican Union was enjoying increasing popularity with the poorer sections of the electorate (at the expense of Velasquism), a number of militant anti-Communist groups had appeared, the working class was hostile, and finally the Army used its power to act as ultimate arbiter. Velasco's fall was due to this combination of international and national pressures.

In foreign affairs, Velasco supported his Foreign Secretary, Chiriboga Villagómez, in 1960 in the adoption of a kind of neutralist position, the famous 'Third Course'. When the leaders of a new movement called the Anti-Communist Front for National Defence accused him of cowardice and compromise with the extreme left and the USSR, Velasco replied, 'Bananas have no ideology.' In his opinion, Ecuador needed to find new markets, and with this in mind Carlos Julio Arosemena, Vice-President of the Republic, paid a visit to the Soviet Union. There was an instant reaction: a Christian militia announced its readiness to 'die sword in hand', the Radical Liberal Party went over to the opposition, and a number of terrorist outrages were carried out against Velasco in November 1961. The left wing, on the other hand, was not satisfied with the government's neutralist policy; on his return to Ecuador, Carlos Julio Arosemena seemed to have decided on a more left-wing policy, but still did not manage to win the confidence of the Confederation of Ecuadorian Workers and the Ecuadorian University Student Federation, both of which departed to swell the ranks of the opposition. Finally, the Army intervened, on 7 November 1961, to halt the regime's growing tendency to authoritarianism (a major scandal was caused by an attempt on the life of a strongly anti-Velasquist journalist). Following this coup d'etat, Arosemena automatically succeeded to the presidency.[6]

Velasquismo has proved a political force capable of bringing its leader to power on several occasions, but incapable of keeping him there. The variety of its social composition, and the absence of any definite programme, have enabled it to assume a variety of political attitudes: Liberal, Conservative, Social-Christian, justicialist, and finally moderate left. It remains to be seen which way the mass Velasquist electorate will jump when its leader disappears. Because of its nationalist sympathies, and its founder and guide's penchant for audacious and combative oratory, it seems likely that if Velasquism does not disintegrate of its own accord its supporters will join a group with authoritarian tendencies, whether of the left or of the right.

Biographical Note

José María Velasco Ibarra was born in Quito on 19 November 1893. He studied law and philosophy in Paris, at the Sorbonne. He started his political career as a member of the Quito council, and then of the Consultative Council of the

6. He should not be confused with a subsequent President, Otto Arosemena Gómez. The Arosemena family has provided three Presidents of Ecuador, not one of whom was elected by the people.

Ministry for Foreign Affairs. He was elected deputy for the province of Pichincha in 1932, taking his seat as an independent of Catholic and conservative views. He was elected Speaker of the Chamber of Deputies in 1933. He became President of the Republic in 1934, from which post he was deposed in 1935. After a period in exile in Colombia, he travelled around Latin America and returned to Ecuador in 1944 when the Democratic Alliance, which he had founded from exile, came to power. In 1946 he was elected President by a Constituent Assembly, and overthrown shortly afterwards by a military coup, inspired on this occasion by the left. Velasco returned to power in 1952, this time following a General Election, and again in 1961. He was elected again in 1968, and deposed in 1972.

Concentración de Fuerzas Populares (CFP)

The Concentration of Popular Forces resembles Velasquism in several respects: most of its votes are concentrated in the coastal region, and it is led by a charismatic leader; it is able to make alliances with either the right or the left, either with the object of plotting insurrection or for electoral ends. It is a kind of Ecuadorian version of the APRA.

In 1944, the founder and leader of this party, Carlos Guevara Moreno, nicknamed 'the people's captain', was secretary to the central administration and then Minister of Home Affairs in Velasco Ibarra's Cabinet. Although he called himself a Marxist and probably fought in the International Brigade in the Spanish Civil War, he banned the Ecuadorian Socialist and Communist parties. In 1946 he founded the Unión Popular Republicana, which in 1948 became the Concentración de Fuerzas Populares. He vilified the leaders of Ecuadorian Marxist Socialism, calling them 'old dodderers'.

Party Following

The CFP is strongly represented in Guayaquil : the *montuvios* and the mass of the dock workers provide its most loyal support.

Areas of Support

Like the Velasquists, the CFP is strongly entrenched in the working-class areas of the coast (especially in the Confederacíon de Trabajadores del Guayas). Its influence even extends to some of the coastal military garrisons.

Leaders

These include Carlos Guevara Moreno, the party's founder; Germán Alarcón, José Hanna-Musse, Assad Bucaram (mayor of Guayaquil in 1967) and Rafael Coello Serrano, a dissident from the PCE. Intellectuals and artists who support the CFP, especially in the coastal region, should also be included in this group : Agustín Vera Loor, Jorge Icaza, Hugo Maldonado Dueñas, Alfonso Zambrano Orejuela, Elías Gallegos, and others.

Electoral Results

In 1960, the CFP candidate for the presidency of the Republic, Antonio Parra, won 150,000 votes, and the CFP won two seats in Parliament. At this time, the movement was also called Movimiento de la Segunda Independencia and included the Communists and some Socialist groups; Antonio Parra was at that time rector of the University of Guayaquil, Minister of Education and Ecuadorian delegate to the General Assembly of the United Nations.

Ideology

The party tends towards authoritarianism; it opposes the oligarchy and imperialism, i.e. excessive power for the ruling class in the political and economic fields. It is also opposed to foreign investment, especially from North America. In 1950–54, the CFP proclaimed its sympathy for Perón. It has also been attracted to Castroism, which it regarded as a form of 'Creole Socialism'.

Partido Socialista

Although it represents the left in the spectrum of Ecuadorian political parties, the Socialist Party has always had close connections with the Liberal Party. A number of factors exist which help to explain both this bond and the birth of the party.

The Socialist Party was set up in 1925, just at the time when the Liberal Party was adopting a programme based on neo-Marxist principles. The working-class nucleus of the province of Guayas (the first in Ecuador to found a trade union), and intellectuals and university students provided the Socialist Party's early support, and these same sectors were the ones on which the new liberalism also relied. This was the first reason for this centre-left alliance; moreover, after 1931, both the Liberals and the Socialists were opposed to Velasquism (having in 1925 already united to support a left-wing military coup).

The first groups to call themselves Socialist appeared in Pichincha, Loja (where they soon went over to the Communists), Azuay and Manabi. In 1924, a Social Democratic Party with no very clearly defined programme was created in Riobamba, and this party was to provide leading personalities of both the Socialist and the Communist parties. The working class in the province of Guayas provided the toughest and most militant Socialist leaders.

Both the Soviet and the Mexican revolutions had a marked impact on Socialism: in 1925, a Society of the Friends of Lenin was founded, and the Mexican ambassador, Rafael Ramos Pedraza, exercised considerable influence over the party's intellectuals.

The Ecuadorian Socialist Party's affiliation to the Third International coincided with a period of internal crisis between the leaders and the rank and file, and also with the appearance of Velasquism. As in most Latin American countries, a minority faction in the party broke away to form the Communist Party. Despite its hopes of representing the whole of the new working class and the emergent middle class, the Socialist Party's influence was soon limited to intellectuals, because of the rigidity of its party programme, which was almost entirely borrowed from European Socialist Parties. To combat the resurgence of conservative caudillism between 1931 and 1961, the Socialists united with the progressive Liberals, and acted in alliance with them in Parliament.

The Socialist Party never managed to become a mass party. It was limited to a few sectors of the working class, to intellectuals and to students; it borrowed slogans from the Communists with the object of attracting the masses; nevertheless, it remained impotent in the face of Velasquist demagogy. Moreover the Socialists had little understanding for the new needs of the social groups that had recently emerged in Ecuador, who oscillated between political inertia and bloody insurrection, those of the new sectors of the middle class associated with petty commerce, or those of the marginal sectors of the population (the unemployed, casual labourers, etc.). Nor did the party's ruling elite have any contacts with these new groups. The Socialist Party therefore became a party of the intellectual sector of the Ecuadorian middle class. As a result, following the crisis in the traditional parties in 1964 and the overthrow of Velasquism by a military coup, the Socialists suffered an internal crisis of their own which resulted in a split. Two distinct wings emerged within the party, with different nomenclatures: The Ecuadorian Socialist Party (the moderate wing) and the Revolutionary Socialist Party (hard-line); one further group may be mentioned in this context, the Unified Socialist Party.

The Moderate 'Democratic' Line of the Ecuadorian Socialist Party

This group includes the older party officials and keeps to the traditional line of collaboration with the Liberals. The object of this collaboration was to secure for the party its legal reintegration in the democratic, parliamentary and party system from the military junta, or any other authoritarian regime.

This attitude reflects the Socialist Party's traditional line. In 1933, in conjunction with the Liberals, the Socialists put up against Velasco a candidate who was soundly beaten, winning only 11,500 votes out of 62,000. In 1948, again supported by the Liberals, they opposed Galo Plaza and suffered another defeat. In 1952, this time in alliance with the Communists and other groups in the Democratic Alliance, they supported Larrea Jijón: they only won 17,000 out of 340,000 votes and had five deputies returned to Parliament. In 1956, again in alliance with the Liberals in the Frente Democrático Nacional (FDN), the Socialists put forward their own presidential candidate, Raúl Clemente Huerta, who won only 172,974 out of 600,000 votes. In 1960 the Front supported Galo Plaza's candidature, and he only managed to come third, after Velasco and Gonzalo Cordero Crespo (Conservative), with 146,000 votes as against 323,000 and 150,000 respectively.

The internal crisis in the party was unavoidable, although the party obtained a few seats in Parliament in 1960, thanks to the FDN, was fairly strongly represented in the Workers' Federation in the province of Guayas, and supported by a large number of intellectuals. In 1954 Guillermo Jaramillo Larrea was elected General Secretary at the 26th Party Congress. In order to avoid a schism, the party then defined itself as the centre of an anti-Conservative group, since the disagreements in the party were over the continuance of the alliance with the Liberals. However, after 1960 the university agitation against Velasco, in the first instance, and subsequently in favour of Arosemena Monroy (1961) and the military junta, brought out the divisions between the two wings of the Socialist Party even more clearly. The hostility between these two groups came out into the open in September 1964, at the time of the party's twentieth congress.

The main leaders of the moderate line are Francisco Leoro and Clímaco Bastidas.

The Pro-Castro Hard Line in the Ecuadorian Socialist Party

In the 1960 elections part of the Socialist Party, led by Antonio Parra and Benjamín Carrión, decided to ally itself with the CFP and the Communists to put forward Antonio Parra's candidature for the presidency, forming the self-styled Second Independence Movement; this movement was largely controlled and influenced by the CFP and the dissident socialists.

However, this dissident group still only indicated its split from the parent party on the electoral level. After the 1961 military coup, carried out against Carlos Julio Arosemena, and also as a consequence of the agitation against the junta led by the Federación Estudiantil Universitaria Equatoriana and the growing influence of Castroism among intellectuals, the left-wing socialists proposed an action programme which was rejected by the Party's 30th Congress. From that moment, the minority hard-line socialists came into existence as a separate entity.

The main leaders of the hard-line are Telmo Hidalgo, Rafael Villalva and Neptali Zuñiga.

The main Socialist newspaper is *La Tierra*, a left-wing Socialist weekly.

Partido Comunista

This party has the same origins as the Socialist Party: it was also born out of the crisis of the Liberal Party in its early days, plus various other influences, such as the progressive military coup of 1925, the Russian revolution of 1917, and the Mexican revolution. It also finds its support among the same sectors of the population: part of the working class, intellectuals, and students.

The internal struggle between moderates and extremists resulted in the formation, in 1925, of a Socialist Party and a Communist Party. As in other Latin American countries, the existence of the Socialist Party prevented the Communist faction, affiliated to the Third International, from setting up popular fronts. The CP's internationalism and its extremism (because the Socialists were allied with the Liberals, the Party represented the extreme left) resulted in continual persecution and repeated bans.

In contrast to the Socialist Party, the Ecuadorian Communist Party did not always oppose military coups or the rise of Velasquism. They even found themselves occasionally in alliance with the Conservatives against centrist coalitions, for example in the Democratic Alliance, which triumphed over President Arroyo del Río in 1944, in the leftist coup of 1947, and in the 1952 and 1960 elections.

Like all the Latin American Communist Parties, the Ecuadorian Party proved highly sensitive to the effects of the Cuban revolution and to the Sino-Soviet dispute. After 1952 it joined forces with the CFP, an authoritarian grouping with a political following used to Velasquism and with a broader electoral base than the CP itself. At the moment the (now legal) CP is endeavouring to join up with the various Socialist Parties and the National Arosemenista Movement (led by C. Arosemena Monroy) in the Front of the Popular Left (FRIP).

Party Organization and Programme

Although the Ecuadorian CP's programme contains the basic traditional principles of all Communist parties (dictatorship of the proletariat, national liberation from imperialism), it is still fairly sensitive to national problems. For example, it demands land reform, the diversification of agriculture and the re-establishment of Ecuador's natural frontiers in Amazonia. On this latter point, the Ecuadorian CP supports the traditional claims put forward by the country against the injustice of the Treaty of Rio (1941) between Ecuador and Peru, laying down the frontiers. Since the United States happens to be one of the three guarantors of this treaty, the Communist Party has taken the opportunity to associate its nationalist demands with those of anti-imperialism. It is therefore violently 'irredentist'.

Because of its well-known links with Velasquism, the CP has played the role of something of an *éminence grise* in Ecuadorian politics. Some of its leaders have held major posts in the administration, and from this position of strength have attempted to put into practice an agricultural, financial or foreign policy in keeping with their political principles (these indirect links with the ruling power have rarely lasted for any length of time, because such Communist ministers were soon denounced by anti-Communist elements, who succeeded in getting them removed).

Areas of Support

On the coast : workers affiliated to the Northern Federation of Agricultural Workers, and to the Guayas Confederation of Labour.

In the sierra : urban areas, and in particular the students and intellectuals in the Ecuadorian Federation of University Students. In the countryside, the Communists are supported by the Ecuadorian Indian Federation.

Main Leaders

The CP has been led since its foundation by Pedro A. Saad, who is still its leading personality. His leading colleagues include Enrique Gil, Luis Castro Villamar (workers' leader on the coast), Oswaldo Esteves, Gustavo Estrella, S. Manuel Agustín Aguirre.

1967

Subsequent Developments

A four-man military junta had ruled from 1963 to 1966, and in that year the junta asked the Congress to elect an interim civilian President to prepare for elections to be held in June 1968. The choice of the Congress fell on Dr Otto Arosemena Gómez, who was supported by the Conservative Party.

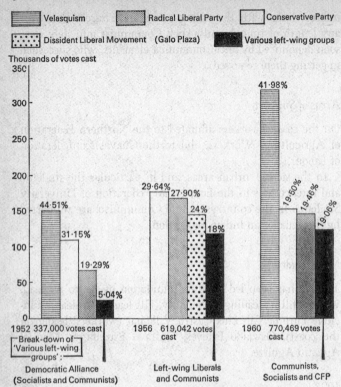

Figure 14. Votes Cast for the Various Parties in the Presidential Elections of 1952, 1956 and 1960

The results of the elections held on 2 June 1968 were as follows:

1 José María Velasco Ibarra (aged 75)   274,782
2 Andres Fernandez Cordova Nieto (aged 76)
   supported by the Liberal Party and the CFP   259,508
3 Camilo Ponce Enríquez (aged 56) supported by
   the Social Christians and the Conservative Party,
   business circles and most of the army   251,628

4 Jorge Crespo Toral, supported by ARNE   28,000
5 Elias Gallegos Anda, supported by the Communist Party and other leftist groups   13,000

In his inaugural address in 1968, Velasco called for support for the Pope's views on birth control, banned the use of miniskirts and make-up by female employees of the government, and forbade all government employees to smoke while at work.

Velasco had no majority in Congress and was forced to rule through a coalition. The large conservative element in Congress was hostile to Velasco's taxation measures, and when he tried to force them through by decree, the Supreme Court declared this to be illegal. In June 1970, Velasco wanted to resign, but after being urged by the army not to do so, he seized supreme power, closed the Congress and sent troops into the university.

Elections were scheduled for June 1972, but on 16 February 1972 Velasco was once more deposed by the army, the new President being General Guillermo Rodriguez Lara. It appears that sections of the army were concerned about the possible victory in June of Asaad Bucaram and the CFP, and had urged Velasco to remain in power for another two years. Velasco refused, and was overthrown.

February 1972

HÉLÈNE GRAILLOT

Paraguay

THE POLITICAL CONTEXT

The study of Paraguayan politics and political parties is greatly hampered by the sparseness of news from this state. Paraguay is a land-locked country, relatively small by Latin American standards (with a land area of about 157,000 square miles and 1,949,000 inhabitants), which has long kept itself secluded from the outside world. However, after 1935 its leaders were obliged to abandon their isolationist policy in order to face up to the imperatives of economic development. The Second World War, in the course of which the United States began to take a closer interest in Paraguay, gave a further impetus to this development towards a greater intercourse with the outside world. Nevertheless, despite the progress made since 1957 with the help of foreign countries and international financial bodies, the social and economic situation remains precarious.

The present Constitution dates from 1940. As has often been said, it is the 'shortest Constitution in the world'. It provides for a presidential regime so omnipotent that all powers are concentrated in the hands of the President,[1] who is elected by universal suffrage for a term of five years. Parliament consists of one House only, with very limited powers,

1. The President appoints ministers, officials in the administration, members of the diplomatic corps and the judges of the Supreme Court.

also elected by universal suffrage for a period of five years. Women have been granted the vote, and took part in elections for the first time in 1963.

The President of the Republic since 1954 has been General Stroessner, who was brought to power by a military coup against President F. Cháves. General Stroessner, who is leader of the Partido Colorado (or National Republican Party), has set up a thoroughgoing dictatorship, despite his continual protestations of democratic government. The opposition is in practice confined to a few political parties. The President is assured of the support of the armed forces, who receive many favours from the regime, and more than 30 per cent of the national budget is spent on them (sometimes as much as 50 per cent). Moreover any will to opposition on the part of the trade unions (who are at the moment very small) is doomed to failure, since the Confederation of Paraguayan Workers has been under government control since 1945, following a series of strikes.

This dictatorship, supported by a single ruling party, weighs heavily on the political life of the country. Political parties do exist, certainly, and periodic elections are held, but they do not have any great significance.[2] Restricted to an opposition role, the parties have no means of influencing the executive or controlling its actions in any way. Moreover the fact that most of them have two rival leaderships, one in exile and one inside the country, effectively paralyses any action they might consider taking, and increases their weakness. Recent struggles between supporters and opponents of active participation in politics have further aggravated the situation by provoking numerous splits, from which even the official (Colorado) party has not been free. Despite similarities in

2. Information on the results of elections has deliberately been omitted from this chapter; government pressure and malpractice have taken away from them any value they might have had in illustrating the relative strength of the various political currents.

their attitude towards the regime and the claims they put forward, these parties have never succeeded in setting up a durable common front, because they are unable to overcome the rivalries between their respective leaders.

Is any study of Paraguayan political groupings justified in these circumstances? It would seem that it is, to the extent that they represent specific political trends which have survived or developed despite the series of dictatorships which the country has had to suffer, and may therefore come to play an effective role if the political situation were one day to change.

Asociación Nacional Republicana (Colorado Party)

Before 1887, there were no political parties properly speaking in Paraguay. An uninterrupted succession of dictatorships clearly prevented the development of normal political life. This situation changed after Paraguay's defeat in the War of the Triple Alliance (1865–70), which brought about the fall of the dictator F. Solano López.

The first political organizations then to emerge bore more resemblance to clubs than to parties in the modern sense. This period was one of great instability, accentuated by the rival interventions in Paraguayan affairs by the Argentine and by Brazil, who alternately supported one faction or the other. The situation clarified gradually, and two groups emerged, both undermined by internal dissensions, but with one in power and the other in opposition. The organization of these two groups into political parties dates from 1887, the year in which the opposition sector acquired its own structure and took the name of Liberal Party; in response, the faction which had held power since the end of the war founded the Asociación Nacional Republicana (popularly known as the Colorados) under the leadership of General Bernardino

Caballero; the chief ideologist of this group was José Segundo Decoud.

The Colorado Party held power until the 1904 revolution, which marked the beginning of the Liberal era. The unity established between its ruling groups remained more apparent than real, however, and internal rivalries between opposing factions led to considerable political instability. The Colorados remained excluded from power, and refused to take part in official public life until the end of the Second World War. The leadership of the party at that time was disputed between two groups: one, so-called democratic, group was led by Federico Cháves, and the other, authoritarian faction (called the Guión Rojo) was led by Natalicio González. The latter won the support of the dictator H. Morínigo, and thanks to him the Colorados once again came to play a major part in the conduct of the country's affairs.

After Morínigo's fall, Cháves' 'democratic' sector finally won the upper hand. The *junta de gobierno* of the Colorado Party became the principal organ of the state. In 1954, however, a military coup led by General Stroessner re-established the Army's dominance, after a period of complete dependence on the Colorado Party. However, the latter did not disappear from the political scene – on the contrary, it became the official party of the regime. Until recently, it remained the only party to be represented in Parliament. General Stroessner is its honorary President.

Party Support and Organization

From its creation in 1887, the party enjoyed the support of the majority of the richest and most important families in Paraguay, the wealthy merchants and big landowners, together with their followers and dependents. At the moment, the Colorado Party recruits its support in two ways. First of all, through family tradition: support for the Colorados is generally passed on from father to son; the second source of support is the obligation on certain classes of citizens to belong to it – notably members of the armed forces and a large number of civil servants. In a number of private spheres, and in business, the chances of getting or keeping a job are frequently dependent on membership. Party funds are replenished largely from obligatory political levies of 2 to 5 per cent on salaries.

Until 1960 the political centre of the Colorados was the 'Blas Garay' group, now dissolved following some slightly too cutting criticisms of government policy made by certain of its members. Its role has now been taken over by the *junta de gobierno*.

The leading figures in the party are its president, Juan R. Cháves, and the vice-presidents Fabio da Silva, Edgar L. Ynsfrán and Ezequiel González Alsina.

The Party's Programme

Strictly speaking, the Colorado Party has no particular programme or electoral platform. Where a political group has enjoyed a monopoly of power for so long, it would be more to the point to speak of achievements rather than policies; and it is achievements that provide the material for official propaganda at election time. However, the biased information provided by supporters or opponents of the regime, in Paraguay or elsewhere, makes it very difficult to arrive at an objective assessment of these achievements.

Like many other Latin American parties, the Colorado Party thinks in exclusivist terms. According to General Stroessner, it was 'born to be the social, political, economic and historical expression of the entire nation'.

The keynotes of Colorado policy are nationalism and anticommunism. The party openly supports the United States, favours the Alliance for Progress and collaboration with international organizations. In the economic sphere, the Colorado Party exhibits fairly orthodox conservatism; it favours free trade and is opposed to any form of central planning. It is perhaps in this sphere that it has been the least successful, since Paraguay has inherited from its series of dictators a long tradition of state control.

In point of fact, despite its privileged position, the Colorado Party does not govern. It is more controlled by than controlling the Army, 1954 having marked a significant milestone in the development towards this state of affairs.

It should also be pointed out that the Colorado Party is itself divided. The Movimiento Popular Colorado (MOPOCO), set up in 1958, is the result of a split in the party. This new movement does not operate inside the country. Its leaders, Osvaldo Cháves and José Zacarías Arza, once important members of the party's ruling clique, are now in exile. Another Colorado politician, Epifanio Méndez Fleitas, has joined them, after holding office for a while in Stroessner's government.

This movement is one of the weakest of the opposition groups, and it has not as yet succeeded in weakening the Colorado Party. Its fiery revolutionary declarations do little to disguise the fact that the divisions of which it is a symptom are due more to a conflict of personalities than to a true difference of principle.

The Liberals

The Club Democrático, subsequently to take the name of Liberal Party, was founded in 1887 chiefly by Antonio Taboada and José Luis de la Cruz Ayala, and by Cecilio Báez, who provided its ideological foundations.

The organization of the opposition into a political party

374 Guide to the Political Parties of South America

was precipitated by the Treaty of Aceval-Tamayo of 1887, which conceded a sizeable lump of Paraguayan territory to Bolivia. The founders of this party collected around them a considerable proportion of the student population, hostile to the old political *caudillos* in power. The new party also won the support of peasants dispossessed by the sale of common land after the War of the Triple Alliance to big Paraguayan and in some cases even Argentinian landowners.

In 1904 the Liberals supported a revolution and a considerable sector of the population and even some sectors of the Colorado Party put an end to Colorado preponderance and brought the Liberals to power. They were to retain it until 1936, when they were overthrown by a military coup. This period witnessed a number of important progressive changes, in both the political and the economic spheres; it was also punctuated by a series of disturbances which actually led to civil war. The Liberal Party suffered a number of schisms, but succeeded in spite of everything in lining up into two main groups on the eve of the Chaco War (1932–5). During General Estigarribia's presidency (1939–40) the Liberals once again enjoyed a brief period with a hand in the running of political affairs, but they were emphatically removed from all positions of power with the advent of the dictator H. Morínigo (1940–8). All their attempts at a coup to re-establish themselves in power failed, in particular that carried out in 1947 with the help of the Partido Febrerista and the Communists.

As in the case of the Colorado Party, family tradition plays the biggest part in the recruitment of the Liberal Party's support. The circumstances surrounding the birth of the party nevertheless had an appreciable influence on its composition and its electoral support. It is certainly true that it includes wealthy landed families and merchants, especially since 1904, but to a lesser extent than the Colorado Party. Its main support comes from intellectuals (Freemasons played a large part in the foundation of the party) and the middle class. This may help to explain the constant threat of strain between a radical-minded elite and other groups more sympathetic to the philosophy of the nineteenth-century liberal parties.

The Liberal Party has undergone a long period of political decay, largely due to the succession of dictatorships. Once the sole great rival of the Colorado Party, it has been greatly weakened by internal divisions and rivalries, which have sometimes become so severe as to lead to splits. At the moment, the Liberals are divided into two parties: the old Liberal Party (which for the sake of convenience we shall call the traditional Liberal Party) and the breakaway Movimiento Renovación del Partido Liberal. These two groups themselves are further fragmented. The two groups do not differ appreciably in electoral following, internal organization, or even political policy; their mutual hostility results chiefly from the difference in attitude towards the present regime.

The Traditional Liberal Party

This party campaigns for the re-establishment of liberty and democracy: it demands the convocation of a constituent assembly and the drafting of a new electoral law, an end to the state of emergency and the return of political exiles. Like those of the Colorado Party, its economic ideas tend towards conservatism and against state interference. It proposes a policy of austerity to improve the state of public finances, and is hostile to any increase in direct taxation. The traditional Liberals are irreconcilably hostile to General Stroessner and refuse to take part in political life as long as he remains in power. Nevertheless, it is interesting to note that they have asked for official recognition of their party, and the right to participate in elections; these requests have been refused.

The basic unit of the party's structure is the committee. Its members are in principle elected, but in practice they are more often appointed by the party's political leadership, because of the various difficulties affecting the organization of such elections. The party is financed from individual subscriptions, which still only provide a small fraction of its actual resources, the major part of which is supplied by the gifts of a few wealthy sympathizers.

The party's chief leaders are Gustavo González (Chairman), Justo P. Prieto, Aniano D. Estigarribia, and Ranulfo Gill (Secretary); another important figure is Justo Pastor Benítez.

As has already been hinted, the traditional Liberals are themselves divided. Some of them carry on their political activities in exile; this group, led by Carlos Pastore, includes the most revolutionary elements in the party, influenced by Marxist and especially Castroist ideology, and advocating violence and guerrilla warfare. Some of them, under the leadership of Walterio Mercado Alder, have finally broken with the party leadership inside the country, which they accuse of temporization, and in 1966 founded the Comité Liberal de la Frontera. This, again, reflects a tactical rather than ideological disagreement. A third group, called Unionists, under the leadership of A. Vargas Peña, Rafael Ferreira and Juan B. Wasmosy, is concerned to re-establish the unity of the Liberal Party, although to the exclusion of the Renovación faction.

Movimiento Renovación del Partido Liberal[3]

This organization was founded by a small group of liberals expelled from the party for having attempted to take part in

3. Also known as the Revolutionary Leadership of the Liberal Party, or Levirales, after the name of its leader.

national politics, in defiance of the directives of the party's executive committee. It seems likely that the appearance of this new group, under the leadership of Carlos Alberto Levi Rufinelli, was the result of a skilful manoeuvre on the part of the government, designed to weaken the largest opposition party. This interpretation seems to have been justified by the fact that the government has managed to get the Electoral Council to recognize the Renovación movement as the only legal representative of the Liberal Party.

This party's programme is largely identical with that of the traditional Liberal Party; it demands that civil rights and liberties be respected, the independence of the judiciary, the elimination of state intervention in industry, and social reforms to improve the condition of the peasants and working class. It is in some ways conservative in outlook, and plays the government's game in that it denounces every other opposition group, especially the Febrerist Party, for being allegedly communist-infiltrated.

The Renovación movement took part in the elections of February 1963, when it presented its own presidential candidate, Ernesto Gavilán; the provisions of the law meant that merely by presenting itself at the polls the party was enabled to win one third of the seats in the Chamber of Deputies (twenty seats). Thus for the first time, a fraction at least of the opposition was represented in Parliament. There is no doubt that initially Renovación raised the hopes of quite a large number of opponents to the regime, weary of inaction and the incessant squabbles between the traditional parties; however, the timidity it exhibited in making any stand at all against the government and the fact that it turned a blind eye to many government excesses soon brought accusations of collusion with the ruling power. Its support in the country is very limited.

Generally speaking the Liberals, although still the Colorados' major political rivals, are currently very weak, both because of the very existence of the dictatorship and because of their internal dissensions.

Partido Febrerista Revolucionario

The Febrerist Party owes its origins and its name to the military coup d'etat which put an end to the then Liberal government on 17 February 1936. It was carried out primarily by a group of Chaco War veterans led by Colonel Rafael Franco, who subsequently became President of the Republic.

This revolution was encouraged partly by the social agitation going on throughout the 1930s and by the renascent nationalism aroused by the Chaco War: the Liberals were accused of having introduced no social or economic reforms and of having sold out the national economy to foreign interests. Some foreign influence may however be detected in the motives of the Febrerists themselves, notably the example set by contemporary European totalitarian movements. The men of February allied their revolution to those carried out in Europe, and wanted to create 'a new Paraguay'. Their group includes a number of highly diverse currents; it included Liberals and Colorados, left-wingers and men with fascist leanings, as well as a group of national intellectuals, the Liga Nacional Independiente.

The coup was carried out practically without any programme of action and without any party, and it was only after the insurgents had taken power that these two shortcomings were repaired. A movement was founded, the Unión Nacional Revolucionaria, with the specific object of supporting General Franco. Since it had no real power-base in the country, this sketchy prototype of the Febrerist Party disappeared with the fall of the regime. The movement's left-wing minority set to work to draw up a programme of government, providing for a number of major social changes, notably the expropriation and redistribution of land. A start was made on putting these reforms into effect: a Ministry of Labour was established, social legislation to protect the worker was introduced. However, this work could not be completed, on the one hand because of the opposition of right-wing groups within the movement, and on the other because of the rapid fall of the new regime. (Franco was deposed by another military coup in August 1937.)

Loss of power did not mean the end of the movement. On the contrary, despite the persecution to which it was subjected, it organized itself much more efficiently in opposition than it had done when in power. The first move was the establishment of Febrerist Clubs by students. After 1944, communication was established between these groups in the interior and organizations in exile, through the medium of a Revolutionary Organization Committee; this was replaced one year later by the Concentración Revolucionaria Febrerista, an organization with a more highly developed internal structure but which allowed considerable autonomy to its various constituent groups. The Partido Febrerista Revolucionario was not formally created until 1951, at a national convention held in Buenos Aires.

The Febrerist Party has gradually moved further to the left, to a position entirely analogous with that of the Peruvian APRA, from which it openly draws its inspiration. In 1960 it was joint signatory to a manifesto of the Democratic Left put out together with the Peruvian Aprist Party, the Venezuelan Acción Democrática and the Argentine Social Democratic Party. It represents the moderate, nationalist left. However, the Febrerists are far from presenting a united front to their foes; conflicts between factions, and even individuals, have multiplied since the party's foundation, and a national convention has rarely been concluded without further splits or expulsions. At the moment, side by side with the left-wing 'reformist' or Aprist faction, led inside the country by Carlos Caballero Gatti and in exile by Elpidio Yegros, there is a much more extremist faction which models itself on the example of Castro; this group, which advocates violent revolution, took part in the Havana tricontinental conference. As in the case of the Liberal Party, the rivalry between these two tendencies finally led to a split, and in 1964 the revolutionary group broke away from the party leadership.

This leadership is organized on similar lines to that of the Liberal Party. It is based on local committees whose members are in principle elected, but in practice often appointed by the national executive committee. The national executive itself is elected by the party delegates attending the national convention, which is held every four years. The main source of party funds is from gifts and covenants rather than individual contributions; the Febrerists also receive aid from the Socialist International, of which they are members.

The Febrerist Party's following is primarily urban and consists chiefly of intellectuals, professional people, businessmen and artisans. The Febrerist vote is based on rational rather than emotive or traditional considerations, in contrast to the Colorado and Liberal Parties. The Febrerists enjoyed a period of fairly high popularity, coinciding with the arrival in power of the APRA in Peru (1945–8). The party then seemed to the younger generation to offer a real alternative to the traditional parties. The partial recovery of the latter has harmed it to some extent, inside the country at least. Abroad, on the other hand, the Febrerists enjoy considerable prestige, no doubt largely due to their excellent propaganda machine.

In August 1964 the Febrerist Party won legal recognition from the Electoral Council, provided it fulfilled certain conditions, and in particular renounced the pact of Paraguayan National Unity signed with the Liberal Party in 1959 with the object of overthrowing the Stroessner government.

It is hard to see what the Febrerist Party hopes to gain

from legal recognition. Does it hope to take over the leadership of the opposition by profiting from the prohibition of the traditional Liberal Party and the discredit into which the members of the Renovación movement have fallen? As it is primarily a party of intellectuals, it seems unlikely that it will succeed in this, especially since the Liberal Party has a decisive advantage over it, namely that it is one of the two big parties controlling the votes of a majority of the electorate through ties of family tradition.

Movimiento 14 de Mayo

The Movement of 14 May [4] was set up in 1949 by two groups of younger dissidents who had broken away from the Liberals and the Febrerists. Above all, however, it was directly inspired by the example of the Cuban Revolution, and indeed the movement is an exact replica of that founded by Fidel Castro. It proposes to liberate Paraguay from Stroessner's dictatorship by every available means, and principally by recourse to direct action. It advocates the establishment of guerrilla movements inside the country: in 1959 its supporters even undertook an armed invasion from Argentine territory, which was brutally crushed.

Naturally enough, this party operates in exile; it is very difficult for it to maintain any real contact with the Paraguayan population, so that it is forced to recruit almost all its support from émigré circles. Its principal leaders are Vargas Peña and Valdovinos.

Apart from a few subversive actions led from outside the country, the movement cannot do anything that would represent a real danger to the present government. Already weak

4. The movement's name refers to the date on which Paraguay was liberated from Spanish rule.

in numbers, it is also a prey to internal disputes between an extreme left-wing faction and a more moderate group.

Partido Social Demócrata Cristiana (PSDC)

The appearance of a social Christian political movement in Paraguay is of relatively recent date. It goes back to 1959, when the Movimiento Social Demócrata Cristiano was set up under the leadership of Jorge H. Escobar; in 1964 the movement was transformed into a party by a decision of the national convention, and Jerónimo Irala Burgos was elected party leader.

The structure and organization of the PSDC are identical to those of the major parties studied above. Its programme closely resembles those of other Latin American Christian Democrat parties in that it is more concerned with social reform than with ideology. It also has close ties with the Venezuelan COPEI and the Chilean Christian Democratic Party, from which it receives substantial aid.

It is a declared aim of the Paraguayan Social Christian Democrats to win over from the Communist Party its student and working-class following. In the early days, they seemed to be succeeding in this. The campaigns undertaken by the Christian Democratic Workers' Youth won them the support of certain sectors of the working class and enabled them to penetrate the trade-union organizations. The foundation of a Catholic university at Asunción also enabled the PSDC to make a more direct appeal to the student population. It has also tried to establish itself in the countryside, but apparently with less success.

Despite the fact that it is an opposition party, the PSDC has so far been treated with considerable tolerance by the ruling power, which is reluctant to attack it so as not to attract the hostility of the Church, which currently supports the Christian Democrats. This somewhat ambiguous situation has both advantages and drawbacks for the PSDC; on the one hand it is allowed to expand and develop more or less at will, on the other it risks being accused of collusion with the regime. Such an accusation is all the more damaging because the party's early success was due primarily to the fact that for many Paraguayans it brought hope of a change, a break in the unending pattern provided by the two big traditional parties.

Two factors threaten to limit the Social Christian Democratic Party's expansion. The first of these is the narrowness of the sector of the population to which it has chosen to make its appeal: industrial workers and students are in a minority in the country. The second is its ties with the Church, which have aroused some doubt as to the sincerity and strength of its reforming zeal: for even the critical attitude towards the Stroessner government recently adopted by part of the clergy is not enough to counterbalance in the public mind the ultra conservatism of the Archbishop of Asunción, Mgr Aníbal Menaporta.

Partido Comunista

The Communist Party has existed in Paraguay since 1928, but has never managed to win legal recognition except for brief periods. Despite its very small membership, it has always proved very active; in 1947, for example, it took part in the rebellion against the Morínigo government, together with the Liberal Party and the Febrerists.

The aims and methods of the Paraguayan Communist Party are identical to those of other communist parties all over the world. After a period of voluntary isolation, the party went over to a policy of joining fronts, as laid down by Moscow. It has tried, and is still trying without success, to conclude an alliance with all the organizations and parties opposed to the dictatorship.

The Communist Party's position with regard to the government is often equivocal: sometimes the latter uses it as a threat to secure the protection and favour of the United States, sometimes it uses it against the other parties. (In 1959 the Communist Party contributed to the failure of the abortive revolution mounted by the Movimiento 14 de Mayo.)

Communist Party activity is carried out largely through the intermediary of an organization which it dominates entirely, the Frente de Liberación Nacional or FULNA. Although its strength inside the country is small (it only has eight hundred members), FULNA has proved very active abroad since 1957, having recruited the support of about two thousand five hundred exiles (especially in Argentina). This organization also advocates a union between all the opposition parties. Its political and economic programme is fairly moderate, to make it acceptable to all the various factions; in the political and social sphere, it demands the restoration of all civil liberties, the convocation of a constituent assembly, the formation of a coalition government and the adoption of specific social legislation; in the economic sphere, it preaches full land reform, price control, stabilization of the currency and of public finances, and a plan to revitalize the economy and foreign trade.

In effect the Communist Party, whose resources inside the country are somewhat limited, concentrates mainly on trying to influence the left wings of the Liberal and Febrerist parties.

The Communist Party's opportunities for expansion are very limited, for various reasons. First of all, the party is itself far from united. In fact it is riddled with violent internal disputes. In particular, it has suffered greatly from the Sino-Soviet dispute, and is now split into two groups, both with their headquarters in Buenos Aires: a pro-Soviet wing, led by Oscar Creydt (until he was expelled in May 1968) and Obdulio Barthe, founders of the party, and A. Soler, and a pro-Chinese faction led by Alfonso Guerra and Alfonso Acorta. The Communist Party is further hampered by the numerical and political weakness of the urban proletariat, on which it concentrates its activity and its propaganda. Moreover its efforts to woo this limited electorate are being successfully rivalled by the Febrerist Party and even more by the young Social Christian Democrat Party.

Conclusion

As will be seen from the foregoing, the presence of a dictatorship upheld by an official party and, more important, by the Army, introduces a considerable element of distortion into Paraguayan political life. In this situation the existence of several different political parties can only be explained by the fact that they give a semblance of democracy to the regime, which they have no possibility of challenging. Faced with a power whose workings they are not even permitted to inspect, let alone criticize, they find themselves in a position of subservience which effectively condemns them to impotence.

It is frequently asserted that political parties wear themselves out in power. In Paraguay, because of the peculiar conditions created by the dictatorship, the reverse is happening. Every day the gulf widens between the party bosses inside the country, forced into a certain degree of moderation, whose chief concern is to ensure their party's survival, and the leaders in exile, who are more extremist and reject all temporizations. While the radicalism of this latter group is partly the result of the distance separating it from domestic political realities, it is further fed by the political illusions aroused by the very large numbers of Paraguayan émigrés[5] – and they

5. It is generally estimated that more than 600,000 Paraguayans have sought refuge in Argentina, Brazil and Uruguay. This figure represents almost one third of Paraguay's present population.

are certainly illusions, for the vast majority of emigrants leave the country for economic rather than political reasons.

The personalization of politics, which helps to explain the lack of internal cohesion within the parties, is also one of the main factors affecting their failure to establish a united front, which the similarity of their objectives ought to have facilitated. Also any explanation of this situation would be incomplete without some tribute to General Stroessner's tactical skill. His adroit political manoeuvring has actually contributed to the divisions and weakening of the parties; for example, by recognizing the Liberal Party's Revolutionary Directorate as the only legal representative of that party he certainly struck a heavy blow at the Colorado Party's closest rival. In dealings with the outside world, General Stroessner has taken pains to present a reassuring picture of his regime, and has won the support of a number of countries; he has also played skilfully on the rivalry between his two powerful neighbours, Brazil and Argentina, and by turning alternately to each for help has managed to insure himself against the risk of armed invasion from the territory of either of these states, and has got them to compete with one another in carrying out major projects that will enhance his own prestige.

However, to regard the Paraguayan political parties as no more than a democratic veil drawn over the face of a dictatorship would be to do them less than justice. The fact that small groups (the Communist Party, the PSDC) have managed to survive or establish themselves in the face of extremely difficult circumstances is not without significance: the ideological currents which they represent correspond to the aspirations of part of the population. As for the two big parties, Colorado and Liberal, although they are hardly in a position to make or approve political decisions at national level, their influence still predominates at local level: the vast majority of Paraguayans, especially in the rural areas, continue to belong to one of the big traditional party groups.

Combined with the survival of the system of patronage, the tradition of family (and even ancestral) loyalty to one of the two parties has enabled each to collect around itself a clientele (in the true sense of the word) which regards them as inter-mediaries able and likely to grant them personal favours. It would seem, therefore, that as long as the political parties continue to perform certain functions traditionally expected of them, despite their present weakness, and in view of the fact that successive regimes have always relied on the support of one or other of them, they are assured of retaining the majority of their clientele even in the most adverse circum-stances.

The dominant position enjoyed by these patron parties may further be considered the main reason for Paraguay's difficulties in establishing a truly democratic form of political organization. The system calls of necessity for the institution of an authoritarian regime (whether Colorado, Liberal, or supported by one or other of these) because the patronage system continues to operate in a society that is still dualistic and has little industry, where there is no counterweight able to balance or limit the strength of the ruling power.

Summer 1966

*

Since these lines were written, a number of changes have come about in Paraguay that are worthy of mention, although their effect on the functioning of the political system seems likely to be negligible, at least in the immediate future.

First of all, with regard to institutions, mention should be made of the new Constitution adopted in August 1967. This does not include any major basic changes to the previous text, except to reinforce still further the executive's powers (wider emergency powers and less precise guarantees of the rights of the individual). Its chief purpose seems to be to enable General Stroessner to seek election for a further term of office as President, which he could not legally have done under the 1940 Constitution. This interpretation seems to be confirmed by the fact that, while the new text also prohibits presidents from standing for a second term, it provides expressly for a procedure of total or partial revision of the Constitution five years after its promulgation. It is difficult to see what purpose this provision could serve unless it were as a precaution for the future, in case General Stroessner should decide to stand again in 1973.

At party political level, the changes have also been minor. A number of leaders have been replaced or eliminated, especially in the Colorado Party (notably E. Ynsfrán), but these expulsions have not affected the organization, aims or strength of the parties. Nevertheless, there has been one event which might have repercussions in the future: the legal recognition of the traditional Liberal Party. This legal recognition was won at the beginning of March 1967, and the party was able to take part in the elections on 7 April the same year, under the new designation of Radical Liberal Party (to distinguish itself from the Levirales, formerly the only legal representatives of the Liberal Party proper). The party's President is Gustavo Riart.

In spite of this late recognition, the PLR managed to prove at the ballot box that it was still the main rival to the official party, despite its long spell underground; it is even fairly significant that it managed to win about 100,000 votes against 300,000 cast for the Colorado Party, in a country where elections have always had a strictly symbolic significance. There will thus be four candidates in the 1968 presidential elections: General Stroessner, Gustavo González (PLR), Carlos A. Levi Rufinelli (Liberal Party) and Carlos Caballero Gatti (Febrerist Party).

It is worth noting that the American embassy seems to have played an important part in initiating the reconciliation between Stroessner and the Liberals. The United States seems to want to exert pressure on the government, in order to give at least the semblance of democracy to the regime, even if Paraguay is not converted into a shining example of a military regime's transformation into a benevolent democracy, which some people think is what the US really wants. For the moment, given the opposition's present state of impotence, legalizing it is not likely to create any illusions unless there is a radical change in political practices.

Politics since 1968

The liberalization which preceded the 1968 elections was in fact short-lived. Stroessner was re-elected, as expected, with an overwhelming majority. Early in 1969 the four opposition parties attempted to discredit the government over the 'Farias affair': a political detainee named Farias had died under interrogation. Stroessner banned all opposition radio broadcasts in retaliation and soon restored full authoritarian rule. The regime's subsequent conduct in its relations with the Church serve to confirm that the period of liberalization had been a hollow façade designed to please the United States.

Until 1968 the Church hierarchy either took no active part in politics or cooperated with the government. Admittedly, the Church had inspired the formation of the Ligas Agrarias – a grass-roots cooperative movement among farmers which tried to instil political consciousness in the peasants – but these groups had become increasingly independent of the Church leadership. Nevertheless, relations between the Church and the government were harmonious until 1968. In August that year a group of young priests and bishops at a Latin American Episcopal Conference in Colombia severely criticized the living conditions of the majority of Paraguayans. The result of this appears to have been to encourage the Paraguayan clergy to support the current opposition campaign on behalf of certain political prisoners who had been incarcerated for several years. At the time the government was attacked in *Comunidad*, the weekly Church publication.

In July 1969 *Comunidad* expressed the views of the opposition when Nelson Rockefeller came to Asunción as President Nixon's special envoy. Demonstrations were also organized to which Stroessner reacted by killing, imprisoning, or exiling many of his opponents within the Church.

The hostility between the Church and the government was intensified when in the following month Stroessner submitted to Congress a law 'For the Defence of Democracy'. This bill provided severe penalties for those suspected of the intention to commit political crimes. Twelve bishops immediately protested that the new law embodied a form of total absolutism.

In October 1969 a Jesuit priest, Francisco de Paulo Oliva, was exiled for his critical broadcasts on university radio. Demonstrations by students and priests were strongly repressed by the police. The Archbishop of Asunción, Aníbal Menaporta, then excommunicated all those responsible, including the Chief of Police and the Minister of the Interior, and placed Asunción under interdict. Stroessner warned the clergy that they could not hide behind their cassocks, but in spite of these threats the Church continued its activities throughout 1970 by distributing its publications at services, as *Comunidad* had been banned.

Church–State relations reached their lowest ebb in February 1970 when the new Archbishop of Asunción, Ismael Rolón, refused to take his seat on the Council of State until civil liberties had been fully restored. The Stroessner government replied that the Archbishop had a duty to serve on the Council and accused him of offering encouragement to terrorist groups. A week later, the government refused to release a Uruguayan priest, named Monzón, on the grounds that he had allegedly confessed to being a Tupamaro guerrilla. Church leaders protested that the confession had been extracted under torture.

The Christian Democratic Party. The government's hostility towards the Church has had repercussions for the PSDC, which has still not been allowed to register as a party authorized to contest elections. It has also been refused permission to publish a newspaper and broadcast on the radio. In December 1969, five leading members of the party including its ex-President, Geronimo Irala Burgos, were expelled from the country and only two have since been permitted to return. In July 1971 the party's biannual conference was stopped by the police because it had not obtained permission from the police to hold a meeting. But the party could not apply for permission because it was not registered and therefore did not exist officially.

Paraguayan–American relations. An important development for the Stroessner regime has been the deterioration in its relations with the United States as a result of drug smuggling into that country from Paraguay. For years the US government has ignored the smuggling activities of Stroessner and the military which have made them multi-millionaires. Most of the contraband has been in whisky and cigarettes bound for Argentina and Brazil. But the discovery of heroin- smuggling from Paraguay has resulted in American pressure on Stroessner to stop the trade in hard drugs. The dilemma for Stroessner is that he must take into consideration the vested interests of the generals, whose support he needs, and the fact (according to one source) that the revenue from the heroin traffic is used to finance the intelligence organization, RI-14. He has to balance the interests and strength of the military with the possible loss of substantial aid from the

United States if he fails to fulfil its requests. It appears that the US government has already retaliated by reversing a previous decision to give Paraguay a sugar quota. The resentment which this broken promise has caused may also be a problem for Stroessner at home.

At the moment the attacks of the Church on the one hand, and the worsening of United States relations with Paraguay on the other, appear to be major irritations for the Stroessner regime but do not seem to present any real danger. Whether these irritations develop into something more significant remains to be seen.

Alfredo Stroessner has already been proposed as the Colorado Party's candidate for the 1973 elections. It is likely that he will win, although, in view of the events outlined above, one is perhaps a little less confident in this prediction than one might have been three years ago. In passing, one must mention the formation in September 1971 of a Socialist Party composed of splinter groups from the Febrerista Party, the Liberal Party and the Christian Democratic Party. It is, of course, too early to say anything about this new party. If it proves to be as weak in its opposition as the other parties it will present no threat to Stroessner.

February 1972

HUGO NEIRA

Peru

Introduction

Peru's emancipation from Spain left an emergent Creole bourgeoisie at the summit of the social hierarchy. Although this
new dominant class chose representative democracy as the
form of government (a mixture in equal parts of the French
and the eighteenth-century American models), it was not
able to reconcile this utopia of an egalitarian republic with
the reality of *caudillos*, other colonial vestiges, and a complex system of social castes and interest groups. Either because it was obliged to preserve the existing structures inherited from the liberators after the wars of independence,
or because it lacked experience in the government of men and
things, the Creole middle class did not succeed in establishing itself firmly at the centre of political power until the
end of the nineteenth century.

From 1827 to 1866, the period of the awakening of
national consciousness (during which frontier problems arose
and various attempts were made at a confederation with
Bolivia), power remained in the hands of military leaders.

The subsequent brief period of economic prosperity arising
from the production of guano and saltpetre was interrupted
by a serious financial crisis (1868–79) and then by the Pacific
War (1879–83), the result of makeshift and wasteful policies
during the preceding period. Thus the signs of an energetic

effort to pacify and develop the country on the part of a coherent ruling class did not appear until after 1885, or more specifically from 1895 to 1919.

The economic and social climate in Peru suddenly brightened at the beginning of the twentieth century. There was a fantastic growth in exports that continued until 1920: the level of foreign trade rose from £6,000,000 in 1909 to £17,000,000 in 1915 and £32,000,000 in 1917. Politically this wave of prosperity corresponded with the rise to power of a new 'all-conquering bourgeoisie'[1] which managed to establish its hegemony until 1919. During this period, the new bourgeoisie controlled the Army and established the rules governing political activity, which was limited to clubs: the Civil Club, founded in 1876, and the Democratic Club, founded in 1888. The system worked, and legal governments succeeded one another almost without a break. Creole capitalism developed coastal agriculture for export, and stock farming and mining in the cordillera. The relative economic expansion which took place in these years was expressed

1. This expression 'all-conquering bourgeoisie' is taken from Charles Marazé's work *Les Bourgeois conquérants*, Paris, A. Colin, 1957. The reasons for applying this concept to Peru relate to the nature of this dominant class in Peru at the beginning of the century, and the control which it exercised over the centres of economic, social and political power. Indeed neither the English import-export companies nor the first American companies to penetrate the Peruvian economy were at first able to gain the upper hand over this national bourgeoisie. Moreover, the latter enjoyed considerable social prestige; it also controlled political power through a combination of a political club system and property-owner suffrage. In the 'Aristocratic republic' the same people had both the wealth and the power. On top of this, the material power was augmented by a 'spiritual' power – all the most important writers, thinkers and teachers of the period came from this class, notably the positivist philosophers Javier Prado and García Calderón. This national bourgeoisie merited the epithet of 'all-conquering' in that it put forward the first plans for developing the territory, and the effects of these were to be deep and lasting, especially in the Andean region of the interior.

ideologically by the appearance of an intellectual elite which was scientistic, Comtian and pragmatist.

The Great War and the appearance of new forces on the Peruvian political scene brought about major changes in this situation, and in this respect 1919 is a crucial date.[2] The growing part played by American capital in the life of the country was the most direct consequence of the Great War and the opening of the Panama Canal: the United States replaced Britain in the role of chief customer for Peruvian exports. Not only did this fact transform the country's

2. After 1919 the power of the bourgeoisie was eclipsed. Although it continued to enjoy a monopoly of social prestige and economic power, it relinquished its political hold to other forces, to Leguía, then to the Army, to the Alianza Popular Revolucionaria Americana (APRA) and the political parties. This theme lies at the heart of any discussion of contemporary Peruvian society. François Bourricaud bases his study of contemporary Peru on the idea of an 'oligarchy faced with the problems of mobilization'. (See the Introduction to *Pouvoir et société dans le Pérou contemporain*, Paris, A. Colin, 1967.) Why did this dominant class withdraw after 1919 to become an invisible force, or, to those who prefer the term, an 'oligarchic' force?

It may be useful to draw attention to the following facts. After 1931, the ruling classes' criteria of legitimacy were called in question. Secondly, from that date a distinction began to emerge in Peru between the *dominant social class* and the new *ruling political elites*. The latter include the officer corps of the Army, trade-union leaders, the Aprista elite (at any rate until 1948), the leaders of the populist parties which have sprung up since 1956, and the intellectuals, who no longer belong to the dominant social groups.

The rules of the game and the political style adopted were thus worked out between the political parties (whose strength may be measured by elections) and the invisible oligarchic groups. This guide to political parties is therefore not competent to give a full picture of political activity. It ought to be supplemented by an analysis of the functions of this oligarchy and of the other semi-visible political forces: the Army, the Church, the freemasons, rural *caciques* and *caudillos* and so on. The importance of these considerations and the difficulty of dealing with them in the circumstances of modern Latin American society should not be underestimated.

economy, but it also brought a change in the behaviour of the local bourgeoisie: during the period of its alliance with American capital, it seems to have lost between 1919 and 1930 the 'historic dynamism' it possessed at the beginning of the century. A further significant factor, this time social in origin, should be added to this: the appearance during the post-war period of new social groups representing a new political clientele with new claims that found no echo in the preoccupations of the enlightened middle class's political clubs. These were groups which had until then been excluded from or kept on the fringe of active politics: the educated middle class emerging from the universities, the industrial workers of Lima and Callao, and the agricultural workers from the north. Great masses of people who had not until then been organized in parties suddenly erupted into the political arena. (There were labour disputes and strikes in 1918–19 for an eight-hour working day and demonstrations for university reform in 1923.)

Peruvian political life was profoundly influenced by these new facts. The political clubs disappeared (this is one of the reasons why, in contrast to the parties of Chile, Argentina or Colombia, none of Peru's present-day parties goes back to the nineteenth century). The members of these clubs and the holders of economic power nevertheless violently opposed the mass parties which now came into being and which attracted the intellectuals and the new, discontented client groups. Their opposition was expressed in a veiled, indirect fashion. The Apristas, who were to dominate the Peruvian political scene after the First World War, spoke of an 'oligarchy'; this should be understood to mean a regime in which the major decisions are taken by a privileged minority, without the people's consent. Between 1931 and 1956, the life of the country turned on the conflict between the Aprista Party and the 'oligarchic' power. The former attempted to win recognition and a full part in politics, and the latter to regain the control it had lost as a result of the 1930 crisis.

This political impasse came to an end in 1956: the 'oligarchic' pressure groups were finally forced to accept a 'political staff' of Apristas, and the chief leaders of the party, many of whom had spent ten years or more in prison, became higher civil servants, deputies, senators, ambassadors, mayors and ministers. The Partido Aprista Peruano (PAP) was allowed to operate in the open, together with its trade unions, its press, its radio stations, etc. This state of affairs was not even altered by the military coup of June 1962. Relations between the holders of economic and social power and the leaders of the Aprista masses were governed by a tacit agreement.

The most notable result of this agreement lay in the political continuity of the twelve years 1956–68. A further factor, reinforcing the illusion of balance and 'development', entered the picture, namely the favourable effects of foreign demand on the Peruvian economy. Since 1950 the country had enjoyed the benefits of an export boom, and the economic situation once more came to favour the agriculturalists of the coast, whose cotton and sugar products were in an advantageous position on the international market, the foreign mining companies producing and exporting ore (zinc and lead by the Cerro de Pasco company, copper from Toquepala) and the magnates of the fishing industry, which after 1959 became the largest in the world. Finally around Lima and Callao on the coast and in some towns in the interior the boom also affected light and consumer goods industries (textiles, construction, leisure services, etc.) through the stupendous urban growth of the past few years.

Peru thus gives an impression of some prosperity; its rate of development has been one of the highest and most regular in Latin America: between 1960 and 1965 the annual growth rate of the Gross National Product was 6·3 per cent, and the growth of income per head was 4·3 per cent. Again in overall figures, the illiteracy rate seems to have dropped between 1940 and 1961 from 61 per cent to 37 per cent, and over the same period *per capita* income rose from $120 to $250 *per annum*. Finally, the population rose by 67 per cent over the same twenty-year period, from 6,900,000 in 1944 to 11,000,000 in 1961. The visible signs of this new expansion and general prosperity are the growth in the national budget, the stability of the currency and its rate of exchange with the dollar, and the major public works projects undertaken. Nevertheless, it is worth pointing out that these benefits have only affected participants in the boom sectors, and the abrupt modernization of the country accelerated the crisis in the traditional sector. A few of the main consequences of this disparity will be mentioned here, just to give an indication.

The first major consequence has been the migration of rural workers to the towns and the ballooning growth of shanty towns as a result: according to the 1961 census, 500,000 persons have thus swollen the population of Lima, and there are some 2,000,000 'displaced persons' in the whole of the country. Lima today is a city of 8,000,000 inhabitants, and is growing by about 250,000 a year. Peru's infant industry, the mines, the large agricultural cooperatives on the coast and the demand for domestic services in Lima are hardly able to cope with this massive influx. According to O. Dollfuss,[3] 'urbanization far outruns industrialization'. Secondly, the urban middle class has been affected by the rise in the cost of living and troubled by new aspirations to progress. Finally, the percentage of people affected by promises of imminent change over the whole country is continually growing, thanks to the process of homogenization engendered by the expansion in communications and information outlets. The emergence of this new public, awakened to the

3. *Le Pérou, Introduction géographique à l'étude du développement*, Strasburg, 1965.

idea of a radical (but for the moment peaceful) change, resulted in the first instance in the birth in 1956 of new political followings, political parties, and professional politicians. Since 1958 other groups, lower down the social ladder than those who made their appearance on the scene in 1956, have succeeded in acquiring recognition in political life. Consequently the stability reached through the agreement between the PAP and the oligarchic pressure groups has been consolidated in recent years, thanks to the participation of new parties: Acción Popular, Democracia Cristiana, Unión Nacional Odrista, for instance. Nevertheless the party political system was still too narrow to accommodate the mass of the population affected by modernization who, because they were illiterate, were excluded from the suffrage.[4]

Peruvian Political Parties

This survey of parties begins with APRA, partly because it is the first in chronological order, but above all because a study of antecedents and origins of the PAP is at the same time a study of the antecedents of contemporary political life, since the PAP made its appearance at the same moment as the modern political forces it was to represent for thirty years. For this reason, we shall examine first the Aprista hegemony (1931) and then the multi-party system (after 1956).

There are other reasons why the PAP deserves particularly close attention. In the course of the long conflict between the PAP and the system, the rules of the game, the style in which it was to be played, the whole conduct of Peruvian politics were laid down – a combination of compromises, realistic agreements and rapid expedients reached in the face of urgent necessity. The characteristic features

4. However, the overall increase in the electorate should not pass without mention. In 1931, there were 350,000 electors, 597,000 in 1939, 1,575,741 in 1956, 1,692,744 in 1962, 2 million in 1963.

of Peruvian politics have been determined by the cynicism and experience of the 'oligarchy' and the realism and prudence of the Apristas, and these features reappear in the organization, aims and political style of other non-Aprista groups. The PAP, as Bourricaud has suggested, is not the highest factor but the common denominator of Peruvian politics.[5] Finally, Aprismo is a doctrine that is continental in its appeal and relevance, and has had its effect on other reformist movements in Latin America: the Bolivian Movimiento Nacionalista Revolucionario, Acción Democrática in Venezuela, the Colorado Party in Uruguay and the Paraguayan Febreristas. An analysis of the PAP is central to the study of the anti-imperialist movements of the 1930s that still play an important part in the politics of the continent.

Even if APRA had not had such far-reaching effects on the South American continent, the mere fact that it tried to develop an original doctrine specifically designed for Latin America, together with its tendency to reject European models, means that its point of view demands consideration.

Finally, the 'populist' parties that grew up between 1956 and 1961 are shown in the table, after the PAP. Logical convenience is given precedence over chronological order, and the Communist Party is therefore studied together with the other left-wing parties, some of which have grown out of it.

---

5. 'If we seek the great divide in Peruvian politics, the point from which problems of political mobilization begin to arise – mobilization achieved through a two-pronged attack, firstly a radical critique of neo-colonial society and secondly through a passionate statement of belief in national integration – there can be no doubt that Victor Raúl deserves very considerable credit for having blazed the trail. I shall therefore attempt to analyse the main themes of the Aprista ideology, and to see how the same problems are attacked and what solutions are proposed by the conservatives – whom I shall place to the right of the APRA – and the advocates of revolutionary violence – whom I shall place to the left of the APRA.' See Bourricaud, *Pouvoir et société dans le Pérou contemporain*.

Partido Aprista Peruano (PAP)

Founded in 1924 in Mexico, the Alianza Popular Revolucionaria Americana (APRA) first appeared on the Peruvian political scene in 1931, in which year it supported the candidature of its founder Victor Raúl Haya de la Torre. The APRA in Peru took the name Partido Aprista Peruana (PAP), and it is this organization that we shall consider here, not the continental movement.

Regimes, Political Followings and Parties

Years and regimes	Following	Parties
1860–95 1860 Constitution: property-holding suffrage, restricted popular participation in politics.	Traditional clienteles: urban bourgeoisie, workers on large estates loyal to their *caudillos*, merchants and artisans in the towns.	Clubs: Democrats, Liberal, Civil, Constitutional.
1895–1931 'Pure oligarchy' from 1895–1919. Constitutions of 1919 and 1933: direct ballot, increase in popular participation. Illiterates not permitted to vote.	Appearance of new clienteles: Industrial workers in Lima, sugar workers in the north, miners; students, intellectuals, urban petty bourgeoisie, merchants, school-teachers and so on. Political agitation in the native communities.	Parties: Peruvian Aprista Party (1924–31). Communist Party from 1928.
1931–56 Period of hegemony of Peruvian Aprista Party (civil war and political deadlock between the PAP and the hostile forces of the right: Army, surviving political clubs, etc.).		

Regimes, Political Followings and Parties (contd)

Years and regimes	Following	Parties
1956–67 Multi-party system.	Appearance of new urban classes, entrepreneurs primarily concerned with technical development, migrants, shanty-town dwellers, industrial proletariat (mines, fishing, and the Lima and Callao industrial complexes). Organization of the peasantry into trade unions (tenant small-holders, péons, etc.) and their rise to political consciousness.	Parties: Popular Action, Christian Democrats, Odrist National Union. Movements: Social progressives of the revolutionary left (MIR), National Liberation Front.
1968 Peruvian 'Revolution'.	Military government takes power with support of Christian Democrats, Communists, a sector of Acción Popular, Social Progressives, and elements of the revolutionary left.	Parties: as above but without access to institutional power, parties tend to fade rapidly in importance.

THE ANTECEDENTS OF APRISMO

From 1895 to 1919, that is to say during the period immediately preceding the birth of Aprismo, Peruvian society and the country's economy underwent a number of profound transformations. Heavy doses of American capital were invested in agriculture and mining; the war and the opening of the Panama Canal altered the rhythm of traditional export activity and suddenly increased the wealth of the Peruvian ruling class, bringing about a dizzy rate of development of the coast (and some areas of the *cordillera*), an imbalance between the various regions, and the first appearance of a rural working class (Chicama, in the Trujillo valley) and an urban proletariat (Lima and Callao). A middle class was just springing up at the moment that the old parties and clubs of the nineteenth century were disappearing (e.g. the Piérolist party, the Liberal Club, the Civil Club). These social changes were not accompanied by any political change. The 1860 Constitution, under which only property-owners were able to vote, remained in force until 1933. The masses were therefore excluded from participation in politics.

APRA first made its appearance as a protest movement, as a campaign to win integration into political life for the new classes which had emerged since 1919 (industrial workers, white-collar workers, students), whose aspirations exceeded the programmes of the old nineteenth-century parties. The APRA ideology was profoundly influenced by the Russian and Mexican revolutions, which enjoyed considerable prestige. The Peruvian intelligentsia thus became land-reformist and Marxist. This ideology was moreover to be influenced by anti-American lines of thought as expressed by the Uruguayan José Enrique Rodó (in *Ariel*), the Argentinian José Ingenieros (in *Las fuerzas morales*) and the Argentine Socialist leader Alfredo Palacios. This anti-Americanism gradually became more sophisticated in the hands of APRA, to develop into anti-imperialism. Finally, Aprismo was to become impregnated with two attitudes very fashionable at the time: the notion of the decline and decadence of the west (Spengler's book had an impressive response in Latin America), and a contempt for democracy, borrowed from fascism and bolshevism. The former of these notions had a decisive effect on Aprista ideology, which was concerned to dissociate itself from European models (Haya for example would refer to Indo-America, and never to Latin America or Spanish America); the second affected the very structure of APRA and its attitude. Finally, the effect of strictly Peruvian influences should be emphasized. APRA took over the spiritual heritage of one particular thinker, Manuel Gonzales Prada (*Páginas libres*, 1888; *Horas de lucha*, 1909). Prada's teachings gave birth to the anarcho-syndicalism professed by the workers' leaders in the northern plantations, the Indian nationalism taken up with enthusiasm by the APRA and the intellectuals of Cuzco (Luis Valcarcel, Uriel García and others), the anti-clericalism active since the liberals of the nineteenth century (Laso, Vigil) and now revived by the democrats and subsequently by the Apristas, in a post-war period when organizations such as the YMCA, Protestant evangelical societies and the Freemasons were vigorously active.

FORMATION AND DEVELOPMENT FROM 1919 TO 1931

From Worker–Student Unity to the United Front of Manual Workers and Intellectuals

This notion of unity between students and workers lies at the root of the origins and formation of the APRA. It is the result of the parallel development of the two groups, and the phenomenon of 'communicating vessels' created between them in the course of their political rise. A Students' Federation has existed in Peru since 1916, and since 1919 it has taken a lively interest both in the activities of industrial workers in the country itself and in the student rebellion movement originating from the University of Córdoba in Argentina. (The movement for university reform to change outdated methods of education was the expression of a socialist tendency in the new generation.)

In 1919 textile workers, on strike to obtain an eight-hour working day, called on the Peruvian Students' Federation for assistance. The students' delegate to the workers' strike committee was Victor Raúl Haya de la Torre, then a student of literature. Closer ties between students and workers were established as a result. The Federation of Textile Workers, which was to provide a number of leading figures in Peruvian Aprismo, was set up under the auspices of the Peruvian Students' Federation (FEP) and of Haya. In 1920, the Students' Congress of Cuzco called for the establishment of popular universities in which students connected to the reform movement would give classes for workers. These popular universities, which were a direct offshoot of the FEP, called themselves, significantly, 'Manuel Gonzales Prada Popular Universities'. They operated in Lima and Vitarte, both working-class centres. The courses included an energetic campaign against alcoholism among the working class. These courses were given the seal of official approval by President Leguía. The relationship established between Leguismo, the university movement and the infant workers' committees was to last until May 1923.

On that date, with the official consecration of the Republic to the Heart of Jesus (Leguía had sought the support of the Church to obtain re-election), the university students, student workers from the Popular Universities, anti-clericalists, freemasons and Protestants, anarcho-syndicalists and members of the YMCA congregated for a demonstration organized by the FEP, with Haya de la Torre at its head. The union of workers and students received a baptism of fire – one student and one worker (Ponce and Alarcón) were killed. A United Front of manual workers and intellectuals was set up and called for worker and artisan solidarity with the students. But Haya was deported to Mexico, and other leaders of the FEP and students at the Popular Universities followed him into exile.

Birth of the Anti-Imperialist APRA in Mexico

On 7 May 1924, in Mexico, Victor Raúl Haya de la Torre presented to the Federation of Mexican Students a flag bearing a map of Latin America, with the letters APRA embroidered on it in gold. The programme of this new organization contained five fundamental objectives:

– action against Yankee imperialism;
– for the political unity of Latin America;
– for the progressive nationalization of land and industries;
– for the international control of the Panama Canal;
– for solidarity with all oppressed classes and peoples.

The organization's aspirations extended over the whole of the continent. Cells were set up in Buenos Aires, Chile, in Cuba, in Puerto Rica, in Santo Domingo; in Europe, Aprista branches were opened in Paris and London. Progress was achieved in Peru, thanks to the trade-union nucleus in Trujillo (led by Alcides Spelucín and Antenor Orrego) and to the then cordial relations established with José Carlos Mariátegui and his journal *Amauta* published in Lima.

APRA – United Front or Party? 1928–31

Once the APRA had been created, its founder – and henceforth undisputed leader – had to decide between two possible strategies: should he launch the infant organization on the grandiose enterprise of creating an Aprista International, covering the whole of the continent, or concentrate all his efforts on Peru? Imperceptibly, force of circumstances pushed him towards the second option. But there was an even more pressing problem. Should the APRA be a movement of the oppressed classes, a united front, with no specifically party organization, or should it become a full-blown political party?

This dilemma was otherwise expressed in a personality conflict between Haya and José Carlos Mariátegui, founder of the Socialist Party (later the Communist Party), one of the most lucid intellects of the Latin American left. Mariátegui wanted the APRA to retain the characteristics of a univer-

sal movement, and set up a separate 'class party' in Peru
as well. Haya refused to compromise with the Communists.
This conflict, which was to determine the APRA's future,
is reflected in Haya's own writings: reference may be made
to his article 'What is APRA?' published in 1926 in *Labour
Monthly*, and, for his polemic with Julio Antonio Mella
(founder of the Cuban Communist Party) and with Mariátegui in Lima, to his two books, *Apra's Anti-Imperialism*
(1928) and *For the Emancipation of Latin America* (1928)
and his speech to the anti-imperialist Congress in Brussels,
where he defined the APRA's position as hostile to the Third
International. In 1929, the first steps were taken to set up
a Peruvian party on the basis of the APRA. In 1931, Haya's
candidature was put forward from New York. The dilemma
was resolved thus: the APRA was to remain a movement
for the continent, and become a party in Peru.

The most important political feature of APRA's incuba-
tion period is the appearance of new unattached political
clienteles independent of the old political clubs – the northern rural working class and the university students, which
after 1931 were to be given a programme and organization
of their own by the APRA. Hence the leaders who were to
direct the Aprista party machine received their initiation
either in the struggles for university reform or in the
workers' committees which operated hand in glove with the
students and received instruction from them in the Manuel
Gonzales Prada Popular Universities. The former group included the Aprista leaders Manuel Seoane, Carlos Manuel
Cox, Serafín Delmar and Luis A. Sánchez, while the second
group produced Arturo Sabroso (textile workers' leader and
for thirty years boss of the Confederation of Foreign
Workers), Fausto Posada (carpenter), Miguel Garate (a tram-
way clerk), Samuel Vásquez (a driver), Samuel Ríos, Fausto
Nalvarte, Guillermo Conde, and others.

DEVELOPMENT SINCE 1931

Two clear periods may be distinguished in this development: the first is marked by the conflict between the PAP and the traditional forces of the system (the last political clubs surviving from the nineteenth century, the Army, financial groups, fascist sympathizers, etc.); the second period opened in 1956, and is characterized by mutual concessions between the party and the system, a relative loss of popularity by the PAP and its assimilation into the established political order: this is still the situation today.

1931–56: 'From the Catacombs to Legality'

From the moment of its birth, the APRA exhibited considerable political maturity; this fact is illustrated by the 1931 election campaign. A small group of exiles from the Aprista cells in Buenos Aires, Paris and Santiago returned to Peru and organized a party with 50,000 members. The PAP's national congress took place in Lima in May 1931, and the party's leaders, Manuel Seoane, Heysen, Luis A. Sánchez, toured the country drumming up support. When Haya de la Torre returned to Peru, he found a fully organized party waiting for him. The events which followed set the pattern for a political drama that was to continue until 1945: Haya made a speech in the public arena, in August 1931, before 100,000 persons; a group of Black Shirts supporting General Sánchez Cerro (who had overthrown President Leguía) made its appearance and formed a rival body to the APRA. Then followed the 1931 elections, in which Haya was just beaten; Aprista uprisings and demonstrations in Trujillo, Huancavelica and the south; police persecution and the closure of Aprista offices and newspapers, Haya's imprisonment, a popular uprising in Trujillo on 7 July 1932 (a number of army officers were killed, an event which irretrievably poisoned relations between the Army and the Apristas). In 1933 Sánchez Cerro was assassinated, probably by an APRA supporter. General Oscar R. Benavides then established his dictatorship and accorded a truce to the PAP. However, this only lasted a few months, and the party went back underground for a further eight years. In 1945, the PAP organized a National Democratic Front together with one-time supporters of Leguía and the Social Christians (both of which then constituted opinion groups only, and were not organized as political parties). In the subsequent elections the Apristas received 45 per cent of the vote, and a Social Christian lawyer, José Luis Bustamante y Rivero, was elected. The APRA was immediately legalized, under the name of the Partido del Pueblo. The honeymoon between the new government and the Apristas was brief; after 1947 the situation began to deteriorate. On 3 October 1948 an attempted revolution by the Aprista rank and file failed, and instead a successful military coup installed a dictatorship that was to last until 1956. The PAP once again began to campaign for legal recognition. By giving their support to Manuel Prado, a member of the old oligarchy connected to a powerful banking family, who had fought pitilessly against them from 1939 to 1945, the Apristas finally succeeded in regaining legal recognition in 1956.

Programme and ideology. The programme of the PAP was finally defined during this latter period. The 1931 Aprista programme for Peru will be considered here, called the 'minimum plan for immediate action', to distinguish it from the 1924 'maximum plan' containing the five general principles mentioned above and on which the APRA was founded. This 'minimum programme' has not been appreciably modified since that time, and in its election programmes for 1956, 1962 and 1963 the PAP has been content to add or enlarge upon one or two points, particularly with regard to economic development and planning. The 'maximum plan' on the other hand has undergone a profound transformation as a result of the ideological development of the APRA, under the impact of the Second World War, the failure of the PAP's experiment in sharing power between 1945 and 1948, Haya de la Torre's five-year confinement in the Colombian embassy in Lima, and finally the concessions made in 1955 to the liberal right (Peruvian Democratic Movement) in order to obtain the party's release from proscription.

The 1931 programme. The PAP programme contained a number of concrete proposals. With regard to the State, it recommended the introduction of a corporate system for Parliament, i.e. the inclusion of trade-union representatives; re-drafting of electoral boundaries on the basis of economic criteria (to do away with domination by parliamentary *caciques*); decentralization; and a new census (the last had been in 1876). The programme proposed the creation of new ministries : Labour and Industry, Agriculture, Mines, Public Works, Education, Health and Social Assistance. (Such ministries were in fact set up between 1936 and 1945 by governments hostile to the PAP.) The programme also demanded votes for women, reduction of the age of majority to eighteen, and separation of Church from State.

On the economic level, the two dominant features of the PAP programme were protectionism and statism. The Apristas demanded the introduction of anti-trust legislation, control and restriction of capital exports, and introduction of special legislation for foreign investments and the creation of a National Bank. With regard to the nationalization of foreign private industries, the PAP opted for a cautious line and recommended 'progressive' nationalization.

Finally, on the agrarian question, the programme exhibited some weaknesses : it did include the expropriation of the big estates (*fundos*) but only after compensation, to be settled through a lengthy and complex procedure. It stated as a moral principle that the country must repair the wrongs done to the Indians, but hardly gave any indication of how this was to be achieved in practice. In fact, it was content to insist on the defence of small properties, and of the native communities (something already enshrined in the 1919 constitution), and on state supervision of legal disputes between big landed proprietors and their native tenants (*yanaconas*).

In spite of everything, this programme did seem very left-wing at the time; it contains all the essentials of the Peruvian reformist philosophy.

1956–67: From Coexistence to the Multi-party System

From 1956 to 1962, the Aprista Party went through a phase of *entente cordiale* with the political forces traditionally opposed to it. This was the period of coexistence (the *convivencia*). Was this a strategic move with the object of winning power (under Haya de la Torre of course) in 1962? Was it a symptom of the party leaders' weariness of so many years in hiding? Did it indicate a development in the ruling class's thinking, so that it came to accept the 'impossibility of governing against the APRA'? Whatever the underlying reasons, this period of coexistence marks the end of the PAP's hegemony. The party lost prestige with the university students and some sectors of the middle class, with the result that new left-wing political movements and parties appeared. In the 1962 elections, when he was opposed by six other candidates, Haya de la Torre only managed to win 32·98 per cent of the vote – just under the 33 per cent required by the Constitution for election to the presidency. The subsequent coup d'etat is explained by the favourable impression made on the military by Belaunde Terry, and their longstanding bitterness against the Apristas. The PAP responded with a general strike (in conjunction with the Confederation of Peruvian Workers) which failed. Resigning itself to the situation, it took part in the 1963 elections, in which the alliance between Popular Action and the Christian Democrats was victorious. This was the PAP's first electoral defeat.

Subsequently, however, a coalition between the PAP and the Odristas in Parliament managed to win control of the executive between 1963 and 1967, and to strengthen Aprismo. On the one hand, the two Houses exercised their veto against the adoption of certain bills (land reform, among others), while at the same time they dictated the distribution of public funds intended for the various provinces. Thanks to these funds, and to the provincial juntas administering them, the influence of Parliament and of the parties controlling it grew, at the expense of the prestige of the paralysed executive. As Haya de la Torre himself has emphasized, this was the period of parliamentary preponderance. The 1967 local elections, from which the coalition emerged greatly strengthened, demonstrated the provincial electorate's gratitude for the sums voted by parliament in the state budget to finance public works in the villages.

ORGANIZATION

At first sight, the PAP seems to have adopted a horizontal structure, largely for electoral reasons. The party's basic unit, the 'sector' (analagous to the 'branch' in the European Socialist parties), is the starting point from which a chain of representatives to higher bodies springs: district committees, provincial committees, departmental committees. The latter send four delegates (one for each region) to the national executive committee, the party's ruling body. However, the relative autonomy thus given to the departmental committees is only apparent. In fact this form of organization disguises the true structure of the party, which is really vertical, and through which the control of the party machine is actually exercised. This vertical structure, a hangover from the period of proscription and a proof of the corporatist tendencies of the leadership and of their taste for hierarchical structures, is retained partly because of the need to control the Aprista trade unions, and partly because it ensures greater efficiency and guarantees survival in times of persecution.

The leaders of the party are appointed democratically, and must have made their career in the party. Sometimes Apristas become 'professional politicians'. The national executive committee, which is re-elected at each party Congress, elects a General Secretary. But the whole of this hierarchy is dominated by the personality and influence of Haya de la Torre, the party's 'supreme head' and 'guide'.

Vertical and Horizontal Chains of Command

All the Aprista militants (who call each other 'companion' to distinguish themselves from the Communist 'comrades') belong to two basic units at once: the 'branch' of their own locality, and the 'cell' at their place of work. The cells are in turn grouped into 'commands' – thus there is a workers' command, a students' command, and commands of teachers, bankers, doctors and so on. These receive their instructions from the national executive committee, directly supervised by Haya. The mystery in which the work of these groups is shrouded, and their great efficiency, have produced excellent results, but at the same time have given the PAP a somewhat sinister reputation as a fascist party.

Because of this organizational structure, the structure of the national executive committee itself is extremely complex. On the one hand, its twenty bureaux or political secretariats coordinate the activities of other bodies throughout the country through the medium of the departmental committees. On the other hand, it has ties with entities such as the Aprista Parliamentary Group (which consists of the party's deputies and senators), the various commands and the Peruvian Aprista Youth.

The party's line is laid down by party conventions and plenary assemblies on which the leaders of professional and trade-union branches and local branch delegates are all represented. The Apristas have held seven National Congresses (the most important of which took place in 1931, 1948, 1959 and 1962), and a much greater number of conventions. In recent years the post of PAP General Secretary has been bitterly contested; it has grown in importance recently because of Haya's frequent trips abroad, and if Haya should disappear from the scene altogether the General Secretary would take over as leader of the party.

The Leader's Role

The above account gives the impression that the PAP is a modern party, firmly entrenched with a strong chain of command. Yet the overriding influence exerted by Haya within the organization demonstrates that caudillism has not been eliminated from it, but has rather taken a new form : it is exercised in the framework of a well-oiled political machine. The leader's personal charisma places him above the internal discussions between the different wings of the party. It enables him to get rid of party leaders that he does not want (on three occasions, in 1932, 1934 and 1942, he has dissolved the national executive committee on his own authority) and get the plenary assemblies to elect the leaders of his choice by persuasion (as in the case of elections to the post of General Secretary). There is no indication that Haya's influence on the party machine has in any way diminished.

APRISMO IN THE LIFE OF A NATION

Areas of Support

Although the PAP is organized on a national scale, since it has a political office (or 'house of the people') in every departmental capital, its electoral support is very unevenly distributed. It is strongly entrenched in the north, is losing ground in the centre of the country (although towns like Huancayo are still Aprista strongholds), and is weak in the south, a backward region with a Quechua majority; in Lima its power is also small. The PAP's prime characteristic from the electoral point of view, therefore, is its great strength in the northern departments, that is to say in the most highly developed and literate region of the country (with the exception of Lima). Election results in the departments of La Libertad, Cajamarca, Ancash, Lambayeque, Huanuco and San Martín have always been so favourable to the PAP that the Apristas have called these departments 'the loyal north'. In fact ever since 1931 and in the elections of 1945, 1962 and 1963 the north's loyalty to the PAP has been one of the few constant factors in the development of the Peruvian electorate.

Within the framework of the present electoral system, which favours the areas of high literacy, this situation gives the PAP considerable advantages. Electorally the votes the Apristas win in the north compensate for the deficiencies in their vote in other regions (witness the 1962 elections). In trade-union affairs, the high level of agricultural and industrial development in the north (especially on the coast, where there are large sugar plantations, oil in Piura, fish-meal and iron at Chimbote) has meant a high level of trade-union organization, both in the country and the towns, and these unions are guided and led by the Aprista leadership. The PAP's political hegemony in both the electoral and trade-union sphere is thus the direct result of the party's good fortune in having established a firm base of popular support in a region which has only become developed within the last thirty years.

Following

One major question arises: why is the north so attached to the PAP? The fact that Haya de la Torre was born in Trujillo, capital of the department of La Libertad, is not enough to explain this phenomenon. At the time of the APRA's revolutionary baptism, the north already provided its toughest activists and was the scene of the most dramatic episodes in its early existence (when 6,000 Apristas were killed around the ancient pre-Colombian fortress of Chan-Chan in the revolutions of 1932–3), but this again only begs the question. Why was it this particular region that proved so receptive to the APRA's message? The answer may be found by an examination of the party's following and its ideology. Its following consisted of agricultural workers on the big sugar plantations (Grace and Gildemeister) who were receptive to the PAP's early anti-imperialist propaganda; petroleum workers; the small rice-growers of Lambayeque; the peasant communities like those of Chepen and Moche; merchants and new middle-class people in the prosperous coastal towns; migratory workers who would come down to the coast from Cajamarca; intellectuals and 'decent folk' (*gente decente*) whose standard of living had been affected by the unfavourable economic climate of the 1930–5 period. All these groups together constituted a social amalgam whose aspirations the PAP had been able to exploit. These aspirations were expressed in cooperativism, a desire for national and local development, a desire to see foreign investments controlled, and supplemented by a heavy dose of regionalism and class feeling.

A mutual aid system has subsequently been established between the party and its following; some groups of workers, the petroleum workers and some agricultural labourers for example, have been able to improve their standard of living thanks to Aprista trade-union action. In return, the PAP's popular following votes faithfully for the party and substantially augments its funds with party subscriptions.

Party Following in the Centre and South. Despite the large population in the centre and south of the country, its electoral weight is small: 300,000 votes out of a total of 2,000,000 in 1963. (The two regions with the largest number of electors are the north, with 683,000 voters, and Lima with 900,000.)

The PAP's following in the centre and south, in contrast to the north, is not recruited from among the agricultural and industrial workers, but from the lower middle class in the urban and tertiary sectors (especially school teachers and white-collar workers) and even the big landowning class. Whereas the great majority of the native peasantry (tenants on the big estates or peasant smallholders) are indifferent and sometimes even hostile to the PAP, as is the case in the Cuzco region, some more prosperous and sophisticated native communities in the region of Junín and Pasco are sympathetic to the Apristas.

The variegation of its following from region to region and even within departments presents the PAP with considerable problems of coordination which other political groups do not have to face. The party consequently attaches great importance to its regional and departmental branches, since its political strategy, based on the aspirations of different if not mutually antagonistic kinds of followers, is utterly dependent on their flexibility of approach.

Lima – a Special Case. The capital, which accounts for 42 per cent of the national electorate, has for some years been hostile to the PAP. In 1962, Haya de la Torre only managed to come third in Lima, with 164,000 votes, preceded by Fernando Belaunde Terry (207,000 votes) and General Odría (234,000 votes); the respective positions of the three candidates in Lima was precisely the reverse of that which they occupied over the country as a whole. In 1963, Belaunde took first place frm General Odría, while Haya came second, thus losing in the capital the advantage he was assured of by the 'loyal north'.

These electoral reverses date from fairly recent times: in 1945 and 1956, Lima had in fact supported candidates put up by the PAP. Lima's anti-Aprismo is probably due to the hostility of the mass of communications media (newspapers and television) to the PAP; the present composition of the city's population, with its 45 per cent of uprooted provincials sympathetic to an authoritarian line as represented by General Odría; the appearance of a new proletariat opposed to the reformism of the CTP's Aprista leadership, and of a middle class of similarly recent origin (consisting for the most part of professional people) which, in contrast, rejects the PAP's violent past; and finally by the political weight of the traditional sector of the population which still regards this party as the incarnation of provincial hostility to the capital and the cause of the people's irruption into its politics.

Electoral Strength

The Problem of the Aprista Vote. While they were excluded from legal political activity, the Apristas on several occasions supported independent candidates, both for parliament and the presidency, thus becoming for many years the arbiters of electoral life. This makes the study of the Aprista electorate no easier, since it thus becomes confused with that of other, smaller organizations. This happened most notably in the

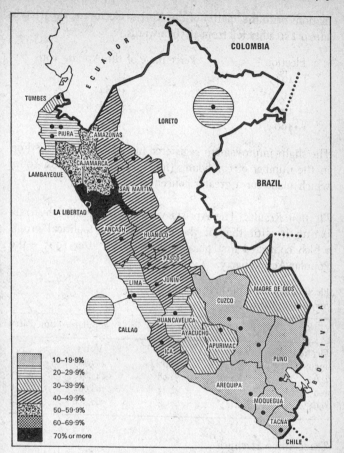

Figure 15. Votes Cast for the PAP in July 1963

elections of 1945 and 1956, when the then banned PAP supported the candidature of José Luis Bustamante and Manuel Prado, respectively, carrying both of them to the presidency.

Whether it be due to the appearance of new political formations or to the apathy of the Aprista electorate, the party's support steadily fell from 1956 onwards.

Election	Percentage of the Aprista vote
1945	45
1956	42·87
1962	32·98
1963	34·35

The slight improvement registered in 1963 is due to the drop in the number of candidates (four instead of seven in 1962) which made for a greater concentration of votes.

Election Results. The Aprista vote may be studied by comparing it with that of the most powerful political group which contested first place with the PAP after 1965 – the Popular Action party.

Election Results of the PAP and the AP for 1956–63 Compared

	Peruvian Aprista Party		Popular Action Party	
Election	Votes	%	Votes	%
1956	567,713	42·87	457,966	34·58
1962	558,276	32·98	543,828	32·12
1963	623,501	34·35	708,662	36·26
1963[6]	712,122	33·98	747,750	35·68

Trade-union Strength

With two hundred and forty thousand members, the Confederation of Peruvian Workers (CTP), controlled by the PAP, is the country's biggest trade-union organization. For many years, the Aprista unions were both the instrument through which the new working class made its social claims, and the PAP's best pressure group, mobilized by the party

6. Local elections.

with the object of achieving its return to legality or to impose its demands on the political scene. However, this very fact, that the CTP was being used for political ends, was the organization's great weakness. After 1958, the Aprista trade-union leadership was faced with serious internal disputes which lessened its power on both the trade-union and the political level.

The CTP was born in 1939 out of the old General Confederation of Peruvian Workers, founded by the Socialist José C. Mariátegui. A ruling nucleus consisting of anarchosyndicalist workers quickly emerged, and this group affiliated to the PAP after 1931 (they included Arturo Sabroso, who was General Secretary of the CTP for twenty-five years). In 1945 the CTP became the Apristas' trade-union arm. The life of the organization ran parallel to that of the party: banned from 1948 to 1952, it gradually built itself up from that time on and won back recognition in 1956. At that time, however, the tacit agreement made between the PAP and the Manuel Prado regime ('coexistence', which went further than a simple electoral pact) forced the CTP to support a working-class policy that was against its own interests. This could not have happened at a worse time, for a number of industrial strikes declared 'illegal' by the regime broke out just at this moment, and the CTP found itself in a position where it was unable to support them; the peasants invaded the big estates, and government repression of these outbreaks was exceptionally severe (a record number of workers and peasants were killed in clashes with the police). The CTP was completely stymied; on the one hand, it could not express approval of the regime's reactionary policies, since this would produce strong protests from its members; on the other hand, it could not disavow the government's actions either, for fear of providing a new pretext for preventing the PAP from coming to power. As a result, a number of regional trade-union organizations broke with the CTP in

1958: the Arequipa regional federation, the regional federations of Puno and Cuzco, the Building Union and Federation in Lima, and the very large Peruvian Peasants' Confederation. This regionalist movement was led by the Communist Party. All subsequent attempts by the CTP Apristas or by the various local union headquarters and the unions which left the movement at the time of Prado to reunite the trade-union movement to their own advantage have failed.

As a result, the most moderate and best-organized unions belonging to the biggest production sectors are the ones which have remained in the CTP. These unions are affiliated to the CTP through their trade federations, under the control of the PAP: the Federation of Sugar Workers (35,000 members), the Federation of Petroleum Workers (10,000 members), the federations of textile workers, school-teachers, transport workers, bank employees and so on. However, strike calls put out by the Confederation are not always respected. Hence the call for a general strike put out by the CTP in July 1962 in response to the military coup was fully obeyed in the north, only partly in Lima and Callao, and ignored by the regional headquarters in the rest of the country. This resulted in the failure of the strike.

The Populist Parties

The parties which came into being between 1956 and 1961 may be included in this category. They have been given this label and grouped together here for several reasons. First of all because these are parties with a highly variegated following, born out of the prestige won by a powerful personality, and whose electoral support is principally urban. Secondly, because they represent the new social forces which have appeared in Peru during the years of economic expansion

following 1956, years characterized by accelerated urbanization and the growth of the tertiary and industrial sectors.
Lastly, because these parties are in reality nothing but electoral machines; they frequently give the impression that
they define themselves principally in terms of a team able
to carry through any given programme, the programme
and ideology themselves being merely secondary considerations.

The parties here included in the category of populist parties
are the Popular Action Party, the Odrista National Union,
Christian Democracy, and the Social Progressive Party. The
first two have managed to become big national parties, while
the two latter have remained satellite parties, consisting
largely of party officers and with little mass support. All
these groups may be clearly distinguished from the APRA
on the one hand (which since the Second World War has
come rather to resemble European social democracy, because
of its long-standing working class support), and, on the other
hand, from the extreme left-wing groups and parties.

The appearance of populism after the Second World War
really marks a turning-point in the history of Peruvian
politics. First of all, the appearance of a new group of parties
implies a profound change in forms of political activity : the
choice between the APRA and the oligarchy, which was
the only possibility between 1930 and 1956, now became a
proper party system; in other words, the PAP, till then the
only dominant and organized party, began to weaken and
became more tolerant after 1956, giving way to a multi-
party system. Given the very wide dispersion of votes, the
system which was then established was based on a series of
shifting alliances and compromises.

On the other hand, the appearance of the populist parties
did not bring about any modification of the system of electoral
representation, merely a slight expansion in participation,
since the illiterate were still excluded from voting. Whereas

the population of the country increased by 63 per cent between 1940 and 1961 (growing from seven to eleven million inhabitants), the electorate grew from less than one million in 1945 to 1,575,741 in 1956, and then to 2,222,926 in 1962. The major part of this increase consisted of a floating electorate which neither the PAP nor the Communist Party, i.e. none of the parties in existence before 1956, had managed to assimilate. The populists did not attempt to win over the PAP's following, however, preferring to address themselves to the new middle strata (which after 1958 began to include some sectors of the peasantry). A map of electoral support thus emerged showing clear differentiations both according to region and to social following. The populists abandoned the north to the PAP; their aim was to capture Lima, the country's great electoral and economic centre, and also the centre and south.

Finally, to complete this brief sketch of the populist parties, some of their characteristic features should be underlined: caudillism; the important part played by the new middle class; a concentration on 'technical' solutions to social and economic problems; and the similarity in social composition between their electorates.

PARTIDO ACCIÓN POPULAR (AP)

Origins and Formation

The birth of Popular Action coincided with the sudden change in the political situation in 1956. Since General Odría's dictatorship was going through a period of crisis, the latter decided to relinquish power and organize elections. Eight years of political reaction (1948–56) thus came to an end in an unlooked-for fashion, with a lively election campaign, in which the PAP was not permitted to take part. At this very moment the political forces described above made their appearance on the political scene. Some of these, including a number of 'dignitaries' just as violently opposed to the military dictatorship as to the Apristas' reintegration into politics, groups of professional people hoping for social change, and the middle classes sprung from the economic revival of recent years found a leader in the person of Fernando Belaunde Terry, principal of the Faculty of Architecture.[7] This nucleus of supporters put forward his candidature for the presidency as the best bet against Manuel Prado, secretly supported by the PAP, and General Odría's crown prince, Hernando de Lavalle. As will be seen, Belaunde adapted himself better to the main themes of the election campaign than his rivals.

Although the Popular Action party did not yet exist as such, a Belaundist electoral machine had already moved into action. In this embryonic phase of the party, still tainted with caudillism, the activity of the leaders of the bourgeoisie, the upper middle classes, and certain other groups such as the National Front of Democratic Youth and Left Social Action, who were to form the nucleus of the future party, could already be discerned. The Belaundist popular following was attracted largely by the dynamic campaign conducted by the young academic, who spoke all over the country, got the national electoral court to accept his registration, and in his speeches emphasized certain points of an ambitious programme of social renewal (land reform, oil nationalization), to sum up, demanded 'profound and immediate social change'. The multi-coloured alliance of this charismatic leader – top professional men and the other new electoral groups – ultimately accounts for the electoral success that marked the beginnings of Belaundism: 34·58 per cent of the votes, or 457,966, as against 567,713 (42·87 per cent) for Manuel

7. Perhaps Belaunde's youth (he was 44 years old in 1956) by comparison with his rivals attracted votes from the new electors and women voting for the first time. At the time of writing (1972) Belaunde is 60, Haya de la Torre 76 and Odría 74 years old.

Prado, supported by the PAP and his small personal following.

Electoral success, however, is not everything; the movement had to progress beyond this stage. In 1956, Belaunde himself founded the Popular Action party. This party remained in opposition between 1956 and 1962. In 1962, it made an attempt to win power. Finally, in 1963, its alliance with Christian Democracy enabled it to gain the votes it needed to beat the Apristas and Haya de la Torre; Popular Action won the elections, bringing its leader to the presidency.

From 1963 to 1967, the AP underwent all the hardships endemic to a party in power: the appearance within it of disparate elements which developed into special interest groups as a result of their administrative or financial connections; loss of popularity; and, in the background, the crushing weight of its leader, President of the Republic, in the party's internal counsels. The internal elections of the party, held in 1967 after the catastrophic results of that year's local elections, demonstrate that a powerful sector of the party machine is endeavouring to carve out an independent path for the party, which would mean that its fate is no longer irrevocably bound up with that of the present regime.

In order to complete this analysis, three significant episodes in the development of the Popular Action party should be considered: the nature of the 1956 electoral campaign and its main issues; the struggle for power between 1962 and 1963; finally the AP's attitude after 1963.

The Electoral Campaign of 1956 and its Issues. This campaign represented a clear break with any that went before it. The striking feature was that the initiative for it was taken by non-party groupings. Thus in 1955, a national coalition led by the industrialist Pedro Rosello (supported by

Pedro Beltrán's daily newspaper *La Prensa*) launched a 'pilgrimage of liberty', attacking General Odría and his associates in their own strongholds, Ica, Piura, Tacna, etc. In response to the activity of the plutocrats and the oligarchs of the coalition, the Apristas reacted: their General Secretary, Ramiro Prialé, returned secretly to the country. However, other groups were mobilizing: the friends of Manuel Prado (who was then living in Paris), under the leadership of Manuel Cisneros Sánchez, editor in chief of the daily *La Crónica*, set up a Pradista electoral machine that worked very efficiently throughout the country. Subsequently Hernando de Lavalle, a lawyer representing a number of big foreign companies, and a director of the North American company Cerro de Pasco, who hoped to continue the General's work, launched an extremely expensive campaign on North American lines (with slogans like 'Lavalle's the one'). Finally Belaunde, whose family, if not one of the richest, was at least sufficiently old-established, made his appearance on the scene, thus giving the final touches to this election. An electorate with visible progressive tendencies was now obliged to choose a President and parliamentary deputies from among three 'dignitaries' (Prado, Lavalle and Belaunde).

The campaign thus acquired a new style, less dramatic than that of 1945, where meetings and public speeches (Haya is a consummate orator) played a decisive role. This time the campaign was very much an American-style affair: a profusion of posters, marches, the use of cars and loud-speakers, in short full exploitation of mass communications media. These features were further accentuated in the subsequent elections (where television had an important effect on the results in Lima and the coastal towns).

Some of the main battle-cries of the campaign were remarkable for their consistency, general interest and novelty: the rejection of dictatorship, return to legality, land reform, and economic and social development. The rejection of dictatorship arose not only from a general disquiet at the 'fiddles' worked by the dictator and his associates, but also from a deep-rooted anti-militarism. As for the return to the rule of law, it showed the desire of these enlightened political followings, paradoxically enough created during the dictatorship, to return to a formal democracy; the weight of this electorate was to increase in the years to follow and helps to explain the stable and moderate tone of Peruvian politics over the last dozen years. Finally, it was now possible to speak openly of land reform, oil nationalization, etc.

Of all the candidates, Belaunde was the most at home with these themes. Lavalle in fact could guarantee neither the return to the rule of law nor rejection of dictatorship, since he claimed to be the representative of 'continuity'. Prado guaranteed the rejection of the military regime but not the return to legality, since he was supported by Aprismo, the eternal factor making for discord and violence; and in any case his programme did not contain any proposals likely to satisfy the social aspirations of the new electors. The desire for change did, however, help Belaunde. Although the subject of land reform had already been taken up by the APRA, the founder of Popular Action considered it from the practical – or according to his supporters, 'technical' – point of view. The new professional classes surrounding him regarded this pragmatism and absence of ideological preoccupations as a remedy and a response to Aprista messianic belief. Popular Action, therefore, by using the same rallying-calls as the APRA, appeared in 1956 in the shape of a kind of Aprista heresy – a heresy of the upper middle classes, the technocrats, the planners. A heresy which, unlike the APRA in 1931, avoided a frontal attack on the Church and on imperialism.

The Struggle for Power: 1956–62, 1963. Between 1956 and 1962, the opposition in the two Houses (Christian Democrats and Social Progressives) included a small but active group of populist representatives. During the same period, Popular Action was beginning to establish itself, and its leaders met at a number of Congresses in the north, centre and south of the country. The architect Belaunde, leader of the party and its chief candidate in elections, covered the country with a team of technical aides, mostly recruited from among his sometime pupils. Belaunde and his advisers (*asesores*) developed a mystique constructed around the history of Peru and its glorious past, expressing confidence in the ability of the population to solve its own problems at local level (this was the origin of the programme of 'popular cooperation') and founding a cult based on the geography and landscape of the country ('Peru is its own doctrine'), for which he was bitterly attacked by doctrinaire Christian Democrats.

There is no doubt that Prado's mistakes and the difficulties experienced by the Apristas in adapting themselves to the unpredictability and complexity of the system of 'coexistence' for which they had opted improved the chances of the AP and its leader. In 1962, after Haya's hairbreadth victory (32·98 per cent of the vote as against 32·12 per cent for Popular Action), Belaunde revealed his connections with the military establishment, and especially with the violently anti-Aprista inter-services command. He called for intervention by the armed forces to counter the alleged 'electoral malpractice' of the Apristas. In reality, the Apristas had won the election perfectly fairly, thanks to their electoral strength in the north, where they obtained most of their votes. In July 1962 the country was taken over by a military junta. After some ups and downs (an internal coup in September 1962, withdrawals of General Bossio, and of General Pérez Godoy), the junta organized fresh elections. To win power, the AP used both its good relations with the military and with the other populist parties. While it consolidated its alliance with Christian Democracy, the junta undertook to clamp down on the left-wing parties (many leaders were rounded up in a big sweep in May 1963). The dispersal of votes was thus avoided, and in 1963 Belaunde gained the victory over Haya de la Torre.

After 1963: from Nasserite Experiment to Super-coexistence. Belaunde's enormous popularity among the regular army officers can be measured by the 1962 military coup and the junta's subsequent activity. His most radical supporters were keenly aware of this, and dreamed of setting up a Nasser-style government, i.e. a government that would enjoy the support of the Army in its clashes with a parliament dominated by the PAP and the UNO. What could be simpler than to abolish the Houses, govern by decree, carry out the promised changes, including oil nationalization and the reform of agricultural land laws, and so forth? But the AP's leader, made wiser by his tenure of the presidency, gave his party 'hot-heads' (*termocéfalos*) to understand that he was 'President of all the Peruvians'. Gradually the regime moved towards a system of cooperation between the various powers and the parties (while Haya maintained that the supreme power in the state was the power of Parliament). The President's enemies were to call this system 'super-coexistence'.

However, Popular Action was to emerge the loser from this process. In the 1967 local elections, when the 'hot-heads' were expecting the party to win 70 per cent of the vote (as predicted by the journal *Oíga*, by Eduardo Orrego and others), it in fact lost some of its strongholds, including Arequipa, Tacna and Cuzco. Over the whole country, the electorate swung away from the regime and its party.

Party Programme

In the national interest, the party initially adopted a position near the centre of the political spectrum. 'The dilemma between capitalism and communism, between right and left, between Washington and Moscow, is frequently presented to our political organizations as an invitation to take a decisive step and opt once for all for one extreme or the other; we consider such a choice impoverishing.'

During the 1962 and 1963 election campaigns, Popular Action seemed to be moving towards left of centre. Apart from some general observations on imperialism (expressed in the party's Declaration of Principles), the AP gives the impression in its campaigns of a nationalist and democratic party that favours the application of immediate solutions to the land problem, the mining problem and the problem of the banks. At the same time, its programme emphasizes a point which may be considered the dominant feature of its ideology : the possibility of achieving social, democratic and peaceful development through the application of technology. After 1963, when the AP found itself in the seat of power, its nationalist slogans were somewhat played down in favour of the technocratic solution.

The AP's economic programme was constructed around three points : pragmatism, reformism and a measure of state intervention. Thus the AP came out in favour of land reform to eliminate the *latifundia*, but preserving the productive sugar and cotton plantations of the coast. Belaunde was opposed to a credit monopoly, and during his 'hundred days' (a term coined by his supporters to draw a deliberate parallel with Roosevelt) he set up a National Bank, and increased the reserves and the efficiency of the State banks. Finally, the party supported flexible planning, gradual decentralization (the 'emancipation of the villages') including a programme of 'popular cooperation', i.e. public works of local importance carried out jointly by the population and teams of students.

In foreign policy, its position was contradictory : it was faithful to the Organization of American States, favoured the revival of the Alliance for Progress, and toyed with the idea of joining a Latin American Common Market. After the appearance of the guerrillas in July 1965, the party's anti-Cuban policy hardened.

Organization of the Party

The party is organized on a national scale. Its highest governing body is constituted by a plenum elected at the party congress; this plenum consists of twenty secretariats and as many under-secretariats (political bureaux, domestic affairs, relations with the government, etc.). The party also has other bodies: an executive committee, a political committee and control committees for various special fields. The organization is divided into geographical units and also by sectors of industry. The most responsible post is that of General Secretary which comes up for election at every congress. Apart from these congresses, the AP organizes conventions, assemblies and more widely based meetings.

However, this democratic form of organization disguises a structure that is in reality autocratic. The problem may be summarized as follows: from the start, Belaunde surrounded himself, within the AP, with a group of people bound to him by ties of kinship, friendship or class.[8] Moreover this ruling clique belonged to the middle bourgeoisie which regarded Belaunde as its figurehead. While Belaunde's influence as party leader made itself felt from the first, after 1963 his power increased even more: for many party leaders with positions in the state machine, the leader of the party was at the same time the Head of State. Only when prodded by various threats (the electoral crisis resulting from the 1967 local elections and the proximity of the 1969 general elec-

8. Resignations tendered to the AP in recent years contain revealing details about the true chain of command in the party. See R. Letts Colmenares in the journals *Gestos*, February 1965, and *Figuras*, March 1965.

tion) did the party begin to react. The plenum elected at Cajamarca in 1967 was contrary to the tastes and interests of Belaunde himself; the General Secretary elected at that time was the 'land-reformer' Edgardo Seoane, ex-ambassador to Mexico.[9] Other leading personalities in the party include Eduardo Orrego, Juan José Vega, Raúl Pena Cabrera, all of whom were elected at the same congress; Oscar Trelles and Gastón Acurio.

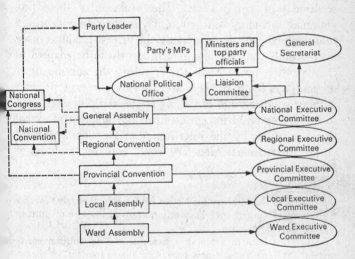

Figure 16. Organigram of the AP in 1967

9. Edgardo Seoane was the author of the draft land-reform bill submitted to Parliament by the executive in 1963. Seoane also held the posts of Vice-President of the Republic and director of the National Office for Land Reform (ONRA). Both the draft bill and ONRA itself were severely criticized by opposition members of parliament and by the National Agrarian Society (a powerful farmers' and land-owners' association) and a war of words broke out between ONRA and its critics in the press. The bill that finally became law in 1964 was very heavily watered-down by comparison with Seoane's original draft, which was regarded as radical. Further, ONRA passed into

The Problem of Power

Belaunde's professional training, his long stay in the United States, the absence of ideological preoccupations in the AP's highly pragmatic programme all contributed to creating Belaunde's private dream of getting the country 'on the move', and undertaking an ambitious public works programme (roads, factories, coastal or Amazonian highways, settlement of virgin lands). The weakness of these programmes, including land reform, lay in their dependence on international capital. As a result, the firmest promises made by Belaunde the candidate had prudently to be adapted to circumstances by Belaunde the President; the annulment of oil contracts (with the IPC at Talara) or the expropriation without compensation of the big estates could in effect lead to the drying-up of foreign credit or the adoption of exceptional measures by the Inter-American Development Bank or the International Monetary Fund, both big creditors of Peru.

---

the control of the Ministry for Native Affairs, which ensured greater parliamentary control over the institution given the task of putting land reform into practice.

Seoane was born in 1903; an agronomist and agricultural entrepreneur, he represented a new type of farming promoter. In charge of the big Mamape estates belonging to the Pucala Agricultural Association on the north coast, he revolutionized agricultural techniques. A Catholic, he first entered politics in 1956, standing as candidate for the post of Senator for Lambayeque, on the Popular Action ticket. In 1958 he visited Europe as a delegate of Peruvian Catholic Action. In 1960 he visited the north of Mexico to inspect the irrigation works there. In 1961 he was elected party candidate for the vice-presidency of the Republic at the AP's Congress at Iquitos. In 1962 he published a book on the agrarian question, *Surcos de paz.* In 1963 he became Vice-President of the Republic. When his land-reform schemes were blocked, he left as ambassador to Mexico, where he stayed until 1967. On his return to Peru, he was elected General Secretary of Popular Action.

Electoral Strength

From the beginning, the AP's electorate proved remarkably stable; between 1956 and 1963 the AP remained the largest opposition party. None of the three major national elections brought any significant change (see table, p. 420).

The figures have to be treated with a certain degree of caution, however, as they do not represent Popular Action's net electorate. The Party's development and the skill with which Belaunde has placed it at the cross-roads of a number of different trends make analysis difficult. In 1956, for example, the Belaundist following was very fluid, and even included some Apristas; in 1962, part of the communist vote went to Belaunde; and in 1963 the Christian Democrats supported him.

Areas of Support

The regions where the party was very strongly entrenched were primarily the industrial zone of Lima, Junín, a stock-farming area with a large native community, and the departments in the south where the Quechua-speaking population is in an overwhelming majority: Cuzco, Puno, Apurimac and Ayacucho. A third area should be added to these, that of Arequipa and Tacna, also in the south, but which has achieved a certain level of industrial and commercial development. The areas where the party was weakest were the northern departments, Huanuco and Pasco in the central *cordillera* and Ica on the coast.

The contradictions implicit in this distribution (with Lima on the one hand, the country's commercial and industrial centre, and the south, the most backward region, on the other) may be explained by the following hypothesis: the AP's programme attracted the urban classes by its insistence on economic and social development, and the Quechua areas by its promise to reform agricultural property laws, a slogan which earned a particularly sympathetic response from the native communities in the centre of the country, the valleys of the Apurimac and the Cuzco and in the thickly populated border areas of Lake Titicaca.

The case of Lima and its relations with Acción Popular deserve a closer look. In 1956, Belaunde beat Prado in the urban zone of the capital by 161,778 votes against 159,163; but in the rural zone (Cajatambo, Canta, Cañete, etc.) where the APRA is strongly entrenched, Prado outdistanced Belaunde. However, the AP's electorate grew in subsequent years as the urban sector expanded, while the rural sector remained stationary. In 1962, Belaunde won 32·3 per cent of the vote in the capital, and Haya only 25·51 per cent (which was why he lost the general election, through Lima's very great electoral weight in the country), but in fact it was Odría who came first in the capital, with 36·54 per cent of the votes, or 234,242 votes out of 642,667; the shanty-town dwellers and some rich areas voted for the General. In 1963 Belaunde won back first place (38·03 per cent) and his electoral following remained faithful in the 1963 and 1967 local elections.

Belaundist Following or Party Following?

Being an electoral machine designed simply to attract votes for Belaunde's candidature (1956, 1962, 1963) the AP was much less fortunate in parliamentary elections, e.g. in 1962:

Representation of the Various Parties in Parliament in 1962

Parties	Deputies	Senators	Total
Alianza Democratica[10]	88	26	114
Acción Popular	62	16	78
Unión Nacional Odrista	31	11	42
Others	5	2	7

10. The joint Aprista and Pradista ticket in these elections was suppressed by the military junta.

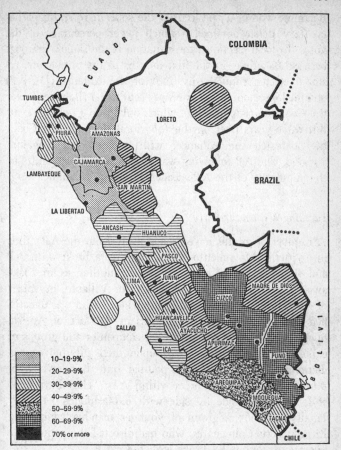

Figure 17. Votes Cast for the AP in July 1963

In 1963, Belaunde was faced with the same problem: a Parliament in which the Apristas and Odristas were in the majority. Some elections, like those in Cuzco, give a good illustration of this duality in voting patterns: whereas

Belaunde won 61·27 per cent of the votes in 1963, his parliamentary ticket obtained a much lower percentage of the votes. In local elections, the situation is the same: in 1963, because Belaunde, in the first months of his presidency, restored elected councils, list four of the Alliance (DC-AP) obtained 747,000 votes (35·68 per cent), or a slight lead over the Coalition (PAP-UNO), which only won 33·98 per cent. But three years later, in the 1967 local elections, the Coalition defeated the Alliance, with 960,000 votes against 797,000. The AP following was highly sensitive to shifts in the popularity of the AP's leader, President Belaunde.

Factions Within the Party

A number of groups have broken away from the AP: thus in 1956 the Movimiento Social Progresista broke with AP and founded a new party. In 1964, another sector broke away from the party to follow Senator Villarán, organizer of the 1962 and 1963 election campaigns, who was dissatisfied with the President's weakness in the face of Aprista opposition, the pressure of the oil companies and groups of exporters. The Apristas seized upon these internal contradictions with delight; they pointed out the presence of mutually antagonistic forces within AP: 'They have new-style plutocrats side by side with old-fashioned leftists.'[11] Finally, in 1965 a group of younger members, including Ricardo Letts Colmenares, who had directed the popular co-operation programme, broke with the party.

None of these splits endangered the party's existence. However, as Letts himself pointed out after his resignation, many party members were dominated by their fear of losing a secure public appointment, stifled by the muzzle which helped to isolate the leader from his base, and paralysed by the 'presidential taboo'.

11. Speech made in the House by Andrés Townsend.

Alliances

The party is formally allied to the Christian Democrats. In accordance with this alliance, the AP and the DC put forward the same candidate for the vice-presidency, a Christian Democrat, Mario Polar, who during Belaunde's presidency was the second Vice-President. The two parties also presented joint lists for parliamentary elections. On the other hand things did not always run so smoothly in local elections: in Callao, for example, a conflict arose between a mayor affiliated to Popular Action and a group of Christian Democrat local councillors. The agreement also included a joint plan for social reform.

Other, non-official alliances also existed. In 1956, 1962 and 1963 between Belaunde and the pro-Soviet leadership of the Communist Party, and with groups of Social Progressive advisers and technicians. Acción Popular was in fact the common meeting-point of all the various populisms except for Odrismo.

*

Whereas politics were dominated by the APRA before 1956, this role was then taken over by Acción Popular. While the APRA represented the middle and working classes that grew out of the First World War, the AP embodied newer social groupings. The nature of the party was obvious, but its true function was less so. For some of its members, the party was primarily an electoral machine to bring their leader to the presidency and to give him constant support once he had acquired that position. Others claimed that the AP had a mission of redemption: like elections, the party ought to be the instrument of a profound transformation. The advocates of this revolutionary vocation did not shrink from demanding the introduction of emergency measures, including military intervention, to counter the malpractices and obstructionism of the two Houses of Parliament. Belaunde attempted to maintain a balance between his 'palace counsellors' who preached collaboration with the parliamentary opposition and the 'hot-heads' who called for intransigence. AP's political stance oscillated between extreme intransigence at election times and an equally extreme flexibility when the party was in power.

PARTIDO DEMOCRATA CRISTIANO (PDC)

Origins and Development

After 1945 a very active Social Christian nucleus appeared in the entourage of President José Luis Bustamante y Rivero. But the political flowering of Christian Democracy, like that of the other forms of populism, only dates from 1955. Bustamante returned to Peru (he had been overthrown by the military coup organized by General Odría) and, in the 1956 elections, the department of Arequipa returned some Christian Democratic senators and deputies. These were to provide the party's ruling group and original inspiration. They included Mario Polar and Hector Cornejo Chávez, while the ageing Bustamante became the party's *éminence grise*.

Between 1956 and 1962, Christian Democracy concentrated its activity on the parliamentary level. Its representatives' opposition to President Prado was skilful and dashing, but to the country it was an utterly unknown quantity. When the Christian Democrats put forward Hector Cornejo as a candidate for the presidency in 1962, he only won 2·88 per cent of the vote. Worse still, not one of its parliamentary candidates was elected: The military coup and the prospect of fresh elections gave it time to introduce a number of prudent changes, however. The trend in the party that favoured collaboration with the AP eventually triumphed, although not without meeting resistance and hostility from the 'orthodox' group that tried to uphold the party's independence. At all events, it was partly due to Christian Democratic votes that Belaunde finally managed to break the electoral balance between the AP and the PAP and tip the scales in his own favour. Within the framework of the alliance, a number of Christian Democrats were elected to Parliament.

The Christian Democrat programme is nationalist, in favour of state intervention and community-minded. Without abandoning the moralizing tone which seems to be endemic in this particular political attitude, one group of intransigents advocated oil nationalization, a stricter fiscal policy, control of foreign capital, etc., in spite of the alliance with the AP.

The Party's Role in National Life: Electoral Weakness?

The party's chief problems seemed to stem from its electoral weakness. The mere 48,828 votes obtained by Cornejo Chávez in 1962 forced the party to make an alliance. But the local elections and the struggle for the mayoralty of Lima opened up new avenues of approach to them. One of the Christian Democrat leaders, Luis Bedoya Reyes, succeeded in 1963 in defeating both the PAP and the UNO in Lima, at a time when the latter had put up María Delgado de Odría, the General's wife who was very popular in the slum areas of the capital, for election as mayor. They repeated this success in 1967, when Bedoya defeated a serious contender for the mayor's office, the engineer Jorge Grieve, candidate of the PAP. Does this mean that there is a big Christian Democratic following in the city, or a personal following loyal to Bedoya, a very active mayor who has embarked on major projects of urban redevelopment, a great orator, a man of humble origins, enjoying great prestige among the population of the capital? It is still too early to say. In any case, what should be emphasized is the crisis brought about by this electoral explosion achieved by the PDC.

In the end, the centre-right tendency grouped around Bedoya came into conflict with the hard-line sector led by Cornejo, and, when it proved unable to carry the day, broke away to create a new party, the Popular Christian Party (PPC). Orthodox Christian Democracy seems to have retained most of the party workers and the younger supporters, while the PPC devoted itself to winning a new Bedoyist following, but failed to make very impressive inroads on the old party. The most right-wing factions of the Christian Democrats were the ones that went over to the PPC.

Areas of Support; Following

The Christian Democrats do not possess a true faithful following, as does the Aprista Party or Popular Action. It attracts a certain number of women voters, usually from the urban middle classes, more susceptible to the personality of the party's leaders than to political argument. A long-standing anti-clerical tradition which has not entirely disappeared tended to operate against the Christian Democrats when they tried to canvass Catholic votes. Its areas of support are the same as, though weaker than, those of AP: Lima, the towns in the south and so on.

Organization

Small in number but well-organized, the Christian Democrats are directed by a national executive committee, regional committees, and bodies representing special sections (teachers, workers, youth, women). The supreme body of the party is the plenum. There was also a parliamentary group consisting of senators and deputies. Its principal leaders included Senator Hector Cornejo Chávez and Alfredo García Llosa,

Emilio Llosa Ricketts, Javier Silva Ruete, and Rafael Cubas.

MOVIMIENTO SOCIAL PROGRESISTA (MSP)

Origins and Development

This movement was born during 1956, like the other populist movements, but never managed to expand and gather strength like the AP, or even Christian Democracy. The importance of this party lay in its ideological role rather than in its chances of winning elections. In 1956 the Social Progresistas provided the basic framework of the Belaundist programme. Recruited largely from the professional class, their confidence in the power of technology, the social sciences and planning to solve Peru's problems brings them very close to the pragmatism of the AP.

The MSP soon found itself faced with a dilemma: should it become entirely integrated in the AP, or try to make its own way? In the end it chose the latter course. However, since they were unable to address the people in tones that were likely to be understood and had no leader with the range of a Belaunde, the Social Progresistas' election results (they presented a candidate for President in the 1962 elections, Alberto Ruiz Eldridge) have been catastrophic: 9,076 votes for the whole country, or 0.53 per cent of the electorate. They made no further appearance on the electoral scene, neither in the presidential and parliamentary elections of 1963, nor in the local elections of 1963 and 1967.

Disappearance?

Other factors played as great or greater a part in the eclipse of *social progresismo* as their election fiasco. First of all, its sympathies oscillated between two opposite poles: solidarity with the Cuban revolution on the one hand, and eagerness to put technocratic skills to immediate use on the other. In the former case, the radicalization of the Cuban revolution has made the principles of *social progresismo* (social humanism, planning) incompatible with the revolutionary Marxism of the Cuban revolution. Furthermore, Belaunde's accession to power appeared to a number of MSP militants as an opportunity to apply their scientific and technical talents at once to the solution of the nation's problems. In the end, whereas some moved leftward and joined a Peruvian branch of the Castroist movement (including Sebastián Salazar Bondy), others opted for technical cooperation with the ruling power. This cooperation indicated the gradual disappearance of the movement, which became a party of *éminences grises*. Its best-known leaders are Alfredo Ruiz Eldredge, Jorge Bravo Bressani, José Matos Mar, Augusto Salazar Bondy, Francisco Moncloa. The importance of these men was greatly increased following the military coup of October 1968.

UNION NACIONAL ODRISTA (UNO)

Origins and Development

Set up in 1961 by General Manuel Odría, the UNO occupies the far right of the Peruvian party spectrum. Its origins go back to the regime set up by General Odría after the coup d'etat of 27 October 1948 (the *revolución restauradora*), which put a sudden and violent end to the democratic experiment undertaken by President José Luis Bustamante y Rivero with the support of the APRA and the Social Christians. A military junta held power until 1950, when elections were held, with a single candidate, Manuel Odría, who continued in office until July 1956. Before leaving the country, he gave his support to the candidature of Hernando de Lavalle in the elections held that same year; the latter only obtained 222,916 votes against 567,713 for Manuel Prado (secretly supported by the APRA) and 457,966 for Fernando Belaunde.

However, far from falling, General Odría's popularity steadily rose between 1956 and 1962. In 1961, he was even able to return to Peru and organize the UNO, which became indisputably Peru's third biggest political force after the Aprista Party and Acción Popular.

This popularity may be explained first by the effect on the country of the great number of public works projects undertaken by the government between 1948 and 1956. Because of these, unemployment was greatly reduced and a number of new administrative posts were created at the same time. However, the international market situation (high demand for raw materials, especially minerals, as a result of the Korean War), which enabled a certain degree of wastefulness at government level, also encouraged increased speculation and the misappropriation of public funds, and produced a class of new rich, especially amongst civil servants, parliamentary deputies and local authorities. Manuel Prado's government therefore inherited a large domestic debt at a time when the foreign economic situation was becoming much less favourable. This only reinforced the myth of abundance associated in the public mind with the government of the strong man of the period, General Odría. The UNO was therefore able to find a double base – one popular, the other consisting of the financial and commercial bourgeoisie.

Areas of Support; Following

The popular base included the new social groups which had arisen largely as a result of population expansion, economic and social changes, and migrations from the sierra to the coast, or from the coast to the capital. These were all groups which had not been assimilated by the so-called doctrinaire parties. The following chief categories may be distinguished:

Inhabitants of the Shanty-towns (barriadas). In 1962, General Odría won a plurality of the votes in Lima, while he only came third over the country as a whole. In Lima, he won 234,242 **votes** (or 36·54 per cent), thus beating Belaunde (32·34 per cent of the vote) and Haya de la Torre, third with only 25·51 per cent of the vote. Lima's most underprivileged areas (the *barriadas* of San Martín de Porres and Rimac) voted for him, as did the working-class area of Victoria, despite its traditional left-wing bias. In 1963, Lima remained the political centre in which the UNO obtained the greatest number of votes proportionately to the rest of the country.

The Conservative Vote in the Provinces. In the last two elections (1962 and 1963) the APRA and the AP contended for first place in every department in the country, with the UNO usually only managing third place, except in three departments: Piura (on the north coast) and Tacna (on the south coast), both classic illustrations of the nature of the Odrista vote, and Callao.

In Piura, the UNO obtained 36,000 votes, as against 19,043 for the AP-DC Alliance and 19,545 for the APRA. The dam and irrigation works undertaken on the Quiroz River during the years of Odría's dictatorship played an important part in the election: the small farmers and day-labourers of the upper and lower Piura thus rallied to the support of the General. Moreover the authoritarian aspects of the UNO programme did not provoke the same hostile reaction in this area as in most other departments. In Piura (one of the richest departments in the country, with cotton plantations and oil wells) the relations between rural workers and the big landowners are tinged with paternalism, with a system of rewards and sanctions quite outside the framework of the law, and thus bear a resemblance to the kind of relationship established between General Odría and the rest of the country when he was in power. Under this system, leaving political parties out of account, the judiciary, Parliament and so on were all left to the good will of 'paternalism'.

The UNO's most striking characteristic in Tacna is its practically 'irredentist' nationalism. Tacna is the frontier department between Peru and Chile; during the dictatorship a number of major public works projects were carried out there, with the specific object of demonstrating to neighbouring Chile the wealth and power of Peru. Tacna thus remained faithful to the ex-dictator's work in the elections.

Odría's Restauradora' (Restorationist) following. Like a number of his predecessors, General Odría found it necessary, once in power, to create an official party. This was called the Peruvian Restoration Party (Partido Restaurador del Perú), an allusion to the restorationist revolution of 1948. The creation of this party enabled General Odría to place a number of leaders loyal to the government in key posts in the trade unions (from which Aprists and Communists were excluded) and to control middle-class organizations; the chief object of this party was to serve as intermediary with the ruling power. Its following (the restorationist following) consisted in part of state employees, and partly of families of humble origin to whom the regime had accorded – as a special favour – a job, free medical treatment or other similar services. Since public services and the national income increased considerably at this time, it must be admitted that quite a large number of people were affected by the 'generosity' of the restorationist regime.

Other groups still belonged to the Restoration Party's following: first of all the new middle class which had appeared between 1951 and 1956 and made its pile in speculation in property and exchange, or through extortion; secondly, the traditional exporting oligarchy, which could hardly help associating itself with a regime which attacked the Aprists, then in revolt, coincided with a period of increased demand for exported goods, and instituted complete freedom of exchange within the country.

The restorationist following with its dual origins, popular and bourgeois, was therefore to integrate perfectly with the Unión Naçional Odrista which took over from the old party in 1961.

Party Programme

Apart from a few basically conservative principles like 'the defence of the Catholic faith' and guarantees to investment capital, the UNO's programme hardly differs from that of the other parties, in that it aims for 'social justice' and 'the struggle against underdevelopment'. In actual fact, the party's programme is indissolubly bound up in the public mind with the prestige attaching to General Odría's achievements in power. Besides the rather pragmatic approach indicated by the party programme, some mention should be made of the disdain felt by UNO and its followers for democratic procedures; the idea that the party system is synonymous with inefficiency lies at the root of this feeling. Authoritarianism therefore rejects the Liberal system and its institutions in the name of efficiency. The UNO's rallying-calls are of the type, 'You can't eat democracy', and 'Deeds not words'. Ideology is therefore despised, to the advantage of an authoritarian minority composed of ex-army officers and Creole executives and managers, that takes advantage of a political following recruited from the most under-privileged and unstable strata of Peruvian society; an extremely simplistic programme is perfectly adapted to the wishes of both the elite and the following surrounding General Odría.

Party Organization

As has already been indicated, authoritarianism and the cult of personality are the dominant features of the UNO. The party does possess an organizational structure nevertheless, despite the preponderant role played in it by General Odría. The UNO is in principle directed at the top by a national executive and a consultative committee; the leadership is kept in touch with the base through shop and area committees. Apart from General Odría himself, the chief personalities in the UNO are Julio de la Piedra, leader of the parliamentary party and also party chairman; María Delgado de Odría, the General's wife; Victor F. Rosell, Eduardo Villarán and David Aguilar Cornejo.

A 'Renovation Front for National Action' has recently been set up in Lima. This group has gathered under its banner a number of one-time restorationists resentful of the UNO's playing second fiddle to the PAP, including some ex-ministers in General Odría's government, G. Augusto Villacorta and Juan Mendoza Rodríguez, and also some ex-deputies from the period of the Odrista dictatorship. An organizing committee has apparently already been set up.

Electoral Strength

The 222,619 votes collected by Hernando de Lavalle in 1956, before the UNO was set up, provide the first indication by which to judge the group's electoral strength. In 1962 General Odría, the UNO candidate, obtained 28·44 per cent of the vote, or 481,404 votes, of which 234,000 were won in the capital. In 1963 this percentage dropped to 23·69 (463,085 votes).

The peculiar position of the Odrista movement, entrenched in the capital and its surrounding shanty-towns and in the departments where the dictatorship had carried out major public works projects (Piura and Tacna) provided the UNO with a following recruited both from the most dynamic industrial sectors and the most conservative agricultural regions (Valle de Piura, Ica, etc.). Thus the underprivileged from Lima's shanty-towns, and some categories of minor officials as well, united by a common nostalgia for the old system of caciquism, joined the Odristas.

The party has been relatively successful in elections. The UNO is the third most powerful electoral force in the country, and in the last elections managed to increase its representation in Parliament; in 1962 it held a total of forty-two seats (thirty-one deputies and eleven senators). In 1963, in alliance with the PAP under the badge of the People's Coalition, it won a clear majority in the two Houses. In 1967 the Coalition reaped benefits from the growing unpopularity of the Belaundist regime, and won 967,000 votes in local elections, compared with the 797,000 obtained by the alliance between Popular Action and Christian Democracy.

The Extreme Left-Wing Parties

From 1928 to 1956, the only extreme left-wing organization that was well entrenched in Peru was the Communist Party (if we except the revolutionary phases of the PAP). However, there has been a proliferation of left-wing formations in recent years. An analysis of the causes of this phenomenon is outside the frame of reference of this work. It will suffice to indicate briefly some of the external causes, such as the de-Stalinization process and its major ideological repercussions, the influence of the Chinese and Cuban revolutions, and some of the internal causes, such as the appearance of middle-class and progressive bourgeois parties (the AP and Christian Democracy) concerned to achieve immediate social

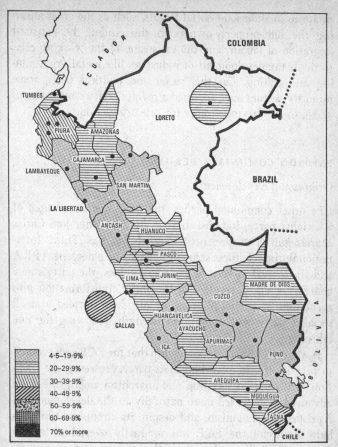

Legend:
- 4·5–19·9%
- 20–29·9%
- 30–39·9%
- 40–49·9%
- 50–59·9%
- 60–69·9%
- 70% or more

Figure 18. Votes Cast for the UNO in July 1963

improvement, the appearance of a mass peasant and worker movement, the radicalization of the petty bourgeoisie (university students and intellectuals), and the appearance of a small but devoted extreme left-wing following. It is appropriate to include some social factors, such as the crisis affecting the big property-owners in the Andes, the constant migration of labour, and the expansion of the working class through the development of industries like metallurgy, mining and fishing. On this social and political basis, some minority sectors have acquired a revolutionary consciousness and provide varying recipes for practical action.

PARTIDO COMUNISTA PERUANO (PCP)

Origins and Development

Like other communist parties, the PCP was an offshoot of a socialist party, founded in 1928 by the writer José Carlos Mariátegui. The pressures exerted by the Third International, the relentless struggle against the emergent APRA and the arrival in Peru of Eudocio Ravines, the party's new general secretary, resulted in its official transformation into a communist party. A group of dissidents formed a small socialist party with some local strength, following the line taken by L. Castillo.

It was under Ravines's leadership that the PCP endeavoured to turn itself into a working-class party. However, the tradition of libertarian socialism and anarchism among the more advanced workers led more naturally to the development of Aprista trade unionism, and despite its strenuous efforts to halt the trend the PCP was gradually overtaken by the Aprista CTP. Banned on several occasions, it took part in the 1954 elections in a Democratic Front, together with the PAP, supporting Bustamante's candidature. In 1948 it was again declared illegal. Although article fifty-three of the Constitution, which prohibits international parties, in principle prevents the party from participating in public life, it was in practice tolerated in the 1956 and 1962 elections, and also took part in the local elections of 1963 and 1967.

The same tolerance enables it to publish a periodical, *Unidad*, and to have communist representatives at trade-union meetings and conferences; its members are permitted to travel freely inside the country and abroad. This ambiguous situation means that its leaders, in the absence of any legal status or recognition, may be arrested at any time, and its offices sacked; but at the same time it is enabled to maintain a precarious existence.

Party Programme

While the PCP's ultimate objective is the dictatorship of the proletariat, the Communist Party leadership is currently preoccupied by other more immediate problems. Some of the more important tasks set down by the third and fourth national congresses of the party are: to gain control of the trade unions, still for the most part in the hands of the 'yellow' CTP; to take part in trade-union activities (especially though the medium of the National Liberation Front); and to create alliances with non-communist anti-imperialist and anti-oligarchical forces of democratic and nationalist leanings. The PCP supports the Cuban revolution and fights for the cause of world peace and peaceful coexistence. The core of the party's founders which has opposed the PAP over the years today forms the pro-Soviet faction in the party.

The existence of a national bourgeoisie opposed to imperialism and amenable to negotiation represents a key factor in Peruvian politics where the Communist Party is concerned. It should be emphasized that this is one of the points of major disagreement with the pro-Chinese faction, the various Castroist movements and the Trotskyists. Belaunde's identification with the national bourgeoisie enabled the communists to enter into the elections of 1956 to 1963 with a good conscience.

Organization

The party is organized on the same lines as other communist parties, and conforms to the principle of democratic centralism: local cells, regional committees (of which Lima has the largest), and a central committee; there is a number of allied organizations – youth sections, women's sections and so on. Intellectuals, artisans and a few workers predominate among the party's leaders. The party's publications appear fairly regularly, and it puts out numerous pamphlets.

Role in National Life; Electoral Strength and Areas of Support

Despite its 'illegality' and the absence of any leader of national standing, the PCP has always had a part to play in the life of the nation, either by supporting the claims of the workers or by intervening in one way or another in elections. It was represented at the CTP's reinauguration in 1956, in particular through the regional federations in Arequipa and Cuzco, which it controls. Belaunde was supported by the communists in 1956, and received especially strong electoral support from them in the south. In 1962 the PCP put forward L. Castillo as its own candidate, a move which ended in complete fiasco: 16,766 votes were obtained, or 0·99 per cent of the total. At the same time, however, a proportion of communist voters supported the FLN candidate, who obtained 34,595 (2·04 per cent), while others supported Belaunde. In 1963, when the party was not able to stand at the elections, its voters certainly gave their support to Belaunde. Finally, in 1963 the party obtained 40,123 votes in local elections.

The PCP is supposed to have about 10,000 members. This figure is difficult to check, and it is likewise difficult to measure the degree of prejudice aroused by its disputes with the FLN, the pro-Chinese faction, and other left-wing groups.

The influence of groups of intellectuals (especially in Cuzco and Arequipa), the fact that the PAP has been unable to win political supremacy in the region, the existence of groups of workers and artisans influenced by the anarcho-syndicalism of the 1930s all help to explain the communists' strength in the south. In recent years, the PCP's influence has extended to the peasants of the south, to Lima and Callao, and the industrial areas of the centre and south (Croya, Toquepala, Tacna), and it is now just beginning to acquire the dimensions and breadth of support of a national party.

The party's chief leaders are Raúl Acosta, a printing worker and the party's general secretary; Jorge del Prado, an intellectual; César Lévano, a journalist; and Gustavo Valcarcel, a writer.

FRENTE DE LIBERACIÓN NACIONAL (FLN)

Origins and Programme

Set up in December 1961 with the immediate concrete objective of 'intervening in the national elections', the National Liberation Front first appeared as a simple front organization of the Communist Party. However, in 1962 the party was torn between supporting General Pando, the FLN candidate, Luciano Castillo, a socialist, and even Belaunde. Analysis of the ballot papers shows that the 34,599 votes then won by Pando and the FLN amounted to double the number obtained by the socialist Castillo, and that departments such as Ancash, Arequipa, Junín, Pasco and Callao were particularly strongly attracted by the Front. The latter organization then drew up a nationalist and progressivist programme, whose immediate minimum claims were the nationalization of oil, land reform and the restoration of full civil and political liberties; its long-term objective was to win the country's 'second independence', that is to say to put an end to dependence on the outside world and to imperialism. The two leading lights of the FLN, the priest Salomón Bolo Hidalgo and the journalist Genaro Carnero Checa, are fervent supporters of the Cuban revolution, a cause which they often preach at public meetings.

The FLN's Role in the Life of the Nation

The FLN is the result of a movement to organize and give precise (principally electoral) aims to a new left-wing following which, although not integrated in the PCP, adopts a distinctly anti-reformist line. The state of mind and general attitude of this 'non-partisan left' which flocks into the public squares to listen to the highly popular Father Bolo are the result of demographic, social and cultural changes which have taken place in modern Peru and of the influence of Castroism. However, this potential following, consisting of students, the unemployed, migrants, and the lower classes generally (or provincial exiles living in Lima) prefers on the whole to give its votes to other candidates, seeing in this their only hope of achieving concrete results. It is therefore probable that the FLN supporters voted for Belaunde in 1962 instead of for Pando, who had no chance, in order to avoid a split vote which would inevitably have carried Haya to the presidency. This explains the apparent paradox that FLN candidates for parliamentary seats won more votes than its presidential candidate. In the 1967 local elections, the Front won 40,000 votes in the capital. This means that about 7 per cent of the Peruvian electorate may be classed as left wing, so that despite its disagreements with the PCP (especially violent in 1964) the FLN has managed to retain a role, consisting in expanding and making the most of the left-wing vote.[12]

THE PRO-CHINESE FACTION: PARTIDO COMUNISTA MARXISTA-LENINISTA (PCML)

The principal leaders of this group, Saturnino Paredes and F. Sotomayor, are still continuing the struggle to win over the party apparatus. Although they have had some success with a few groups (the Young Communists, some committees and cells in Lima, and the native communities of central Peru because of their close ties with the barrister Paredes), the pro-Chinese communists have not succeeded in supplanting the 'old guard' of pro-Soviet leaders in the party apparatus. They publish their own daily, *Bandero roja*, and are trying to branch out into areas neglected by the traditional communists, notably the trade unions and the Indian peasant organizations. However, the principal working-class areas such as Arequipa, Oroya, Callao and Lima, which by their nature provide the chief bases of the party's support, are still controlled by those leaders who are faithful to the Moscow line.

In 1965, when a number of guerrilla detachments were set up, a considerable proportion of the youthful members of the Chinese faction joined the National Liberation Army (ELN), a secret military organization which regards itself

12. The increase in the left-wing vote has upset the right, which hopes to make some changes in the electoral law to halt the gradual but steady advance. In 1962, Pando obtained 2·04 per cent of the vote; in 1963, the appeal to voters to abstain put out by left-wing parties, prevented from taking part in the elections by the repressive measures of the junta, was heeded by 4·79 per cent of the electorate. Finally, in the 1967 local elections the extreme left wing obtained more than 10 per cent of the vote (with the support of a number of independents).

as the 'mailed arm of the revolution'. The guerrilla group led by Héctor Béjar was for example part of the ELN.

MOVIMIENTO DE IZQUIERDA REVOLUCIONARIA (MIR)

Origins and Programme

The Movement of the Revolutionary Left (MIR) has very different origins from those of the other extreme left-wing groups. At first, the MIR called itself Apra Rebelde, and was in reality the old left wing of the PAP. The break occurred in 1959, at the third Aprista Congress, when Luis de la Puente Uceda, then a prominent member of the party leadership, put down a motion of censure which quite simply called in question the whole policy of 'coexistence'. This criticism of Haya's policy brought about the instant expulsion of Luis de la Puente and his friends, who set up an Aprista Committee for the Defence of Doctrinal Principles. Having broken away completely from PAP party tutelage, and with the idea of identifying itself with Castroism, in 1960 the APRA Rebelde became the Movement of the Revolutionary Left (MIR).

The MIR then published its minimum programme, which expressed a number of general claims (an amnesty, true land reform) and represented a thorough recasting of the Aprista programme of the 1930s: it aimed at the re-establishment of a united front against imperialism. However, Luis de la Puente and his friends subsequently declared themselves convinced of the impotence of electoral action to achieve these aims and the inevitability of armed conflict, and also of the impossibility of achieving development in Peru under the leadership of the national middle class. These ideas were proclaimed publicly by Luis de la Puente in a demonstration in San Martín Square in Lima, set down in the party's *Basic Principles* published in 1960, and reaffirmed in the articles and editorials in the movement's journal, Voz *Rebelde*. Curiously enough, however, neither the left nor the regime took its promise of 'setting the Andes on fire' very seriously.

Guerrilla Activity. Future of the Movement

In July 1965, the MIR put out a revolutionary proclamation which announced the creation of a number of guerrilla centres in the Andes. The manifesto bore the signatures of Luis de la Puente, General Secretary of the movement, Guillermo Lobatón, commander of the central area, Ricardo Gadea for the southern zone and Gonzalo Fernández Gasco for the north. The Army soon found Luis de la Puente near Cuzco, in the Mesa Pelada region, and Lobatón was seen in the central area in the course of various attacks on police detachments, big estates and bomb attacks on bridges. Once these two guerrilla command centres had been eliminated, that in the north broke up of its own accord, and the MIR seemed doomed to disappear. However, although the movement's best-known leaders fell in the struggle, not all of them disappeared.

THE TROTSKYIST PARTIES: PARTIDO OBRERO REVOLUCIONARIO (POR) AND THE FRENTE DE LA IZQUIERDA REVOLUCIONARIA (FIR)

The activities of the small group of Peruvian Trotskyists led by Ismaël Frías are almost completely confined to the most highly developed sectors of the working class (the metallurgy workers in La Oroya, for example). With its party cells, its very advanced level of trade-union organization, and the waves of strikes and claims which it instigates, the Peruvian POR's line does not differ appreciably from that of Trotskyist movements in other countries. The greater degree of success won by Peruvian Trotskyism is attributable to the

Hugo Blanco experiment in the valley of La Convención and to the fact that it is still affiliated to the Fourth International and has close ties with Argentine Trotskyism, despite the pressures imposed by other left-wing groups. Blanco first came into contact with Trotskyism while a student of agronomy at Buenos Aires. After 1962, Blanco set up the Frente de la Izquierda Revolucionaria (FIR); this movement rejects peaceful forms of struggle, follows the Cuban example and makes strenuous efforts to unite the forces of the left.

Blanco's achievements may be summarized as follows: in 1958 he discovered a spontaneous trade-union movement among the peasants in the valley of La Convención (Cuzco), and set about giving it a political aim and direction. This was so successful that by 1962 these unions (of which Blanco had by now become general secretary) dominated the valley, expelling the landowners and establishing their own political sway. The phenomenon bears some resemblance to that of the 'Self-Defence' areas in Colombia. Although the movement spread over the whole of the southern part of the country, it was brought to a halt by the capture of Blanco and the prosecution of the main peasant leaders who had supported him. Blanco's example, the manner in which he was able to control the peasant masses and the great admiration he commanded, provided a great boost to the Peruvian Trotskyists' trade-union activities. The latter are just as firmly opposed to the 'legalist' road chosen by the communists as were the guerrilla fighters of the MIR and the National Liberation Army.

The Military Coup of October 1968 and its Political Consequences

On 3 October 1968 the rules governing the political life of Peru changed yet again. The armed forces removed President

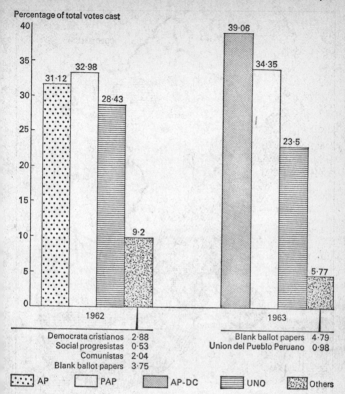

Percentage of total votes cast

1962

Democrata cristianos	2·88
Social progresistas	0·53
Comunistas	2·04
Blank ballot papers	3·75

1963

| Blank ballot papers | 4·79 |
| Union del Pueblo Peruano | 0·98 |

AP   PAP   AP-DC   UNO   Others

Figure 19. Changes in the Votes Cast for the Various Parties 1962–3

Belaunde from the Palacio de Gobierno and closed down Congress for an indefinite period. Political parties were permitted to exist but the purpose of their activity became somewhat uncertain. The chief of the Army's general staff, General Juan Velasco Alvarado, was successively proclaimed head of the ruling military junta and subsequently President of the Republic, a position he has retained ever since.

The coup was actually organized by a group of colonels.

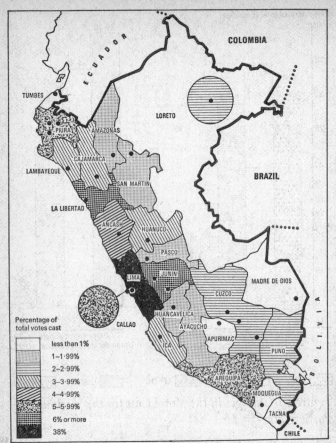

Figure 20. Results of the July 1963 Elections: Relative Weight of Each Department

NOTE: Two towns have been isolated. Callao, the port of Lima, is in an area of very high density in terms of registered electors, but must be shown separately because it has only 100,000 voters. (98·9 per cent of the population are illiterate.) Loreto, on the other hand, in the centre of an immense underpopulated region is the only place in the area of any electoral significance.

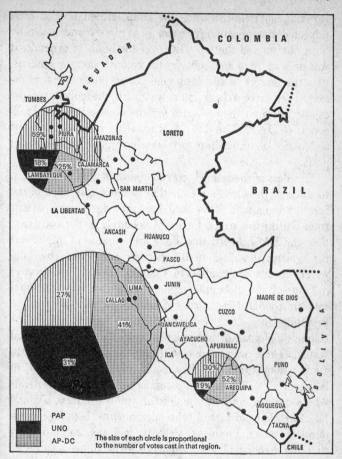

Figure 21. Votes Cast for the PAP, UNO and AP-DC in July 1963: Three Main Regions

Their intentions were highly political and went far beyond a mere response to an admittedly deteriorating institutional situation. The architects of 'Plan Inca', as their conspiracy was called, have largely controlled the policies of the

Peruvian government since the coup, although they have respected the prevailing system of seniority and generally have not entered the top posts over the heads of generals. It was only in 1970 and 1971, as the colonels became generals, that the leaders of the coup emerged to public view. However, they have kept a close watch on the policies of the cabinet through the powerful Comité de Asesores a la Presidencia (COAP). The COAP is made up of serving officers and many of its leading members have gone on to cabinet posts.

The ideas of the colonels corresponded, in very broad terms, to those of the orthodox Christian Democrats or even of the Social Progresistas. They had been among the supporters, from within the armed forces, of Belaunde in the 1963 election and had believed that he would be able to implement the reforms described in his election manifesto. The shipwreck of this programme in Congress and the progressive collapse of the Belaunde regime, highlighted by the final split in 1968 between sections of Acción Popular loyal to Belaunde and those led by Edgardo Seoane, drove the colonels to despair of any progress under the existing political system. There was no one with any prospect of victory in 1969 whom they felt they could support. This view of Belaunde's regime was quite common even among generals who were not actually involved in the conspiracy. General Edgardo Mercado Jarrin, who subsequently became foreign minister under President Velasco, said privately in 1967 that the Army had lost confidence in Belaunde because he was gutless and had not achieved the reforms the country had hoped for and needed.

Apart from the disappointment felt at the failure of the Belaunde administration to come to grips with the country's problems – problems which had hardly changed since APRA had first emerged as a reformist party more than forty years ago – there were a number of other factors, which helped the advocates of a coup d'etat to win acceptance for their plans, both within the armed forces and among civilian sectors.

(1) The years of Belaunde's presidency had been character-ized by a series of scandals, involving ministers and other public officials. Several of these cases, eagerly raked over by the press, had either involved or come close to involving members of the armed forces. Many senior officers felt that the spread of corruption could destroy the effectiveness of the armed forces. The example of Cuba under Batista was frequently cited and there was a strong feeling that the problem could not be tackled with Belaunde in power.

(2) The splits in Acción Popular and Democracia Cristiana made it almost certain that APRA would hold the key to the 1969 elections. Among older officers and in the more traditional sectors, APRA was still anathema on historical grounds dating back to the 1930s. To the young reformists, who were planning the coup, APRA was contemptible for having sold out to the oligarchy in 1956. Whatever the rea-son, a possible APRA victory in 1969 was viewed with suspicious gloom by the armed forces. Although it was probably true to say – as General Julio Doig said in March 1967 – that there was no longer a military veto against an APRA electoral victory, it was also true that the pros-pect was sufficiently unwelcome to contribute greatly to the acceptance of a coup in circles where it might otherwise have been opposed.

(3) The immediate excuse for the coup – to which rela-tively little importance need be assigned – was the govern-ment's bungling management of the settlement with the Standard Oil subsidiary, International Petroleum Company. Although the question is unlikely ever to be completely clear, it seems improbable that there was an eleventh secret page to the agreement signed between the government and the company. Nevertheless, the atmosphere of intrigue and collusion with foreign interests, which was indisputably gen-

erated by the affair, did contribute to popular acceptance of the coup.

(4) A growing number of young intellectuals, especially those grouped in the Instituto de Estudios Peruanos, believed that representative democracy was structurally incapable of coping with the problems of integrating the masses – both in the countryside and in the slums of the cities – into the economic, political and social life of the country.

Since coming to power, the military have not bothered to suppress the political parties, although with Congress closed and no prospect of national or municipal elections, the traditional politicians have little room for organizing a popular base. In some senses the political scene is freer than it was before. The Partido Comunista's Confederación General de Trabajadores Peruanos has achieved full recognition for the first time since 1948. Apart from the communists, APRA has probably survived the eclipse of parliamentary institutions better than the other non-revolutionary parties, which are really quite irrelevant today. If for some reason – at present unforeseeable – the military regime were to collapse in the way in which the Argentine military regime has done, it seems certain that APRA would be the party which would be able to dominate any subsequent elections.

The rump of the Christian Democrats, the wing of Acción Popular opposed to Belaunde, and the Social Progresistas, provide the backbone of civilian support for the regime – but as individuals rather than as political parties. The military has studiously ignored the old framework of political life and is attempting to build a new framework through the Sistema Nacional de Apoyo de la Movilización Social (SINAMOS). This was set up in June 1971 under the direction of General Leonidas Rodríguez, who was then commander of the key Lima armoured division. As head of SINAMOS, Rodríguez was given a seat in the Cabinet and was thus effectively the only minister with command of troops. He lost his division at the end of 1971, but remains an extremely important figure. SINAMOS has direct responsibility for seven other organizations which were previously answerable to either the President or the Prime Minister. These are:

The Oficina Nacional de Desarrollo de Pueblos Jovenes (ONDEPJOV) (Pueblo Jován is the official euphemism for the slums which ring Lima and other coastal cities.)

The Oficina Nacional de Desarrollo Cooperativo (ONDECOOP)

Oficina Nacional de Desarrollo Comunal (ONDECOM)

Fondo Nacional de Desarrollo Economico (FNDE)

Dirección General de Promoción Comunal

Dirección de Organizaciones Campesinas

Dirección de Promoción y Difusión de Reforma Agraria

These organizations, many of whose functions overlapped, will soon disappear in SINAMOS. However, there are few clues yet as to how SINAMOS will develop into the democratic instrument which its promoters have promised. Many of the most radical young Peruvians of the past decade – including the guerrilla leader Héctor Béjar and the writer of the historical portion of this chapter, Hugo Neira – are now working for SINAMOS, and there can be no doubt that they are seeking radical solutions to age-old problems. Whether participation without political parties is a realizable goal will not be known for many years. Even if the military government does not suffer from the kind of institutional erosion which has afflicted other military governments, both in Peru and elsewhere in Latin America, it could be twenty years before APRA effectively and finally withers away. Nevertheless, the functions of SINAMOS are likely to change the shape of Peruvian politics permanently. It will clearly be the instrument through which the present government will try to deal with the country's most pressing rural and urban problems. It is unlikely that the machinery will be dismantled easily if it has begun to operate in any meaningful sense.

Meanwhile, opposition to the government persists among many businessmen. This is not orchestrated through any organized political movement, and finds expression only in the pages of El Comercio and La Prensa, morning papers that are both querulous and rather frightened. APRA is behaving with a good deal of circumspection, but has remained strong throughout the north, fairly consistently defeating leftist candidates in union and university elections.

Among the revolutionary groups, Héctor Béjar and other former members of the ELN now back the government. The MIR has merged into the Vanguardia Revolucionaria and Ricardo Letts has assumed its leadership. It is by far the best organized and strongest leftist group opposing the government at the present time. Hugo Blanco, following his release from jail – together with all other political prisoners – in December 1970, began to organize peasants to demand their rights within the framework of the new agrarian reform laws. Early in 1972 he was expelled from the country.

February 1972

HÉLÈNE GRAILLOT

Uruguay

The Political Background

Despite its small size (about 72,172 square miles), Uruguay holds a strategic position on the banks of the River Plate and has long been the object of rivalry between contending foreign powers: first the Spanish and the Portuguese, then Argentina and Brazil (not to mention Great Britain) made successive attempts to annex her. Thanks to British intervention, based on that power's concern to protect its trading interests on the River Plate by creating a buffer state there, Brazil and Argentina finally signed a treaty in 1828 recognizing the independence of the eastern coastal province, thus marking the birth of the east-coast republic of Uruguay. The country's hard-won independence was followed by protracted civil wars; the longest of these, the Guerra Grande (1839–51), ended in the division of the country into two blocs, the ancestors of the two main political parties of today. The armed confrontation between the two camps (Colorados, or Reds, against the Blancos) lasted until the beginning of the twentieth century. As in Argentina, it was during this troubled period, despite everything, that the bases for Uruguay's future prosperity were laid down. Large-scale European immigration also contributed in no small measure to the population and development of the country.

Uruguay is a unitary state, indeed it is perhaps over-centralized; Montevideo, the political, economic and administrative capital, contains almost half the total population, which by 1963 exceeded two and a half million; moreover more than 80 per cent of the population live in towns of more than ten thousand inhabitants, despite the fact that the Uruguayan economy remains primarily based on the exploitation of agricultural and dairy products.

Uruguay's originality as a Latin American state has expressed itself primarily in the social and political fields. This country where socialist ideas were introduced at a very early date has long had a very advanced body of social legislation. For example, it is estimated that about 30 per cent of the population currently receives state aid in one form or another – retirement pensions, supplementary benefits, and the like.

Nevertheless, Uruguay's most remarkable characteristic is its exceptional political stability, partly due to the fact that it is one of the rare states in Latin America where neither the armed forces nor the Church have acted outside their proper sphere; the political parties have therefore held a monopoly of political activity. These function within the framework of a highly individual system, unique in Latin America, which permits free expression to various tendencies within any given political formation without compromising its unity. Thus under one and the same party label or *lema* (Lema Colorado, Lema Nacional) there exist a number of officially recognized factions or *sublemas* with their own organization, which present lists of candidates for elected offices independently of one another. The institution of the *lema*, which literally means 'label' or 'ticket', was principally designed to safeguard the cohesion of the Colorado Party and the National Party, both of which were seriously threatened with internal splits. Moreover these two political groups, which possess the most powerful factions (*sublemas*), have alone been able to enjoy the full benefits of this system, since the electoral law requires that the votes obtained by the various factions of one *lema* should be summated to the benefit of that main party. The combination of the 'law of the *lemas*' and the electoral system thus guarantees absolute political dominance to the Colorado and National parties.

Moreover, political stability, which might have been threatened by disputes between these two rival groups of practically equal strength, has in fact been preserved. This has been largely due to the regularity with which elections have been held, and above all to the progressive institutionalization of the political understanding arrived at between the two parties after 1917, which by granting the minority party a share in the exercise of power removes the temptation for it to resort to extreme measures in order to make its voice heard. The Constitution adopted in 1951 represents the most elaborate version of what has come to be called the system of 'co-participation', particularly with regard to the measures defining the organization of the plural executive. In this respect, Uruguay is one of the few countries in the world to have tried the collegial form. The history of its successive Constitutions is moreover one of a lengthy struggle between advocates of the presidential system and those of the collegial system.[1] In fact the persistent economic difficulties which Uruguay has experienced for the past decade have brought about political unrest, expressed in an almost universal questioning of the collegial system, which the political parties have made a scapegoat for the country's economic and social difficulties. For a year at least,[2] the election campaign has centred primarily on the question of the return to a presidential system of government.

Within the framework of the 1951 Constitution, which is currently still in force, the presidency of the republic has

1. Uruguayan Constitutions have followed the following progression: 1830, presidential; 1918, mixed; 1934, presidential; 1951, collegial. In the general election of November 1966, the electors were called upon both to appoint the holders of elected offices and to choose between four draft reforms to the Constitution. The result was a return to the presidential system.

2. This paper was written in 1966.

been replaced by a council of nine members, elected by universal suffrage for a period of four years and not immediately re-eligible; six seats are given to the victorious *lema* (four of these to the majority faction within that *lema*) and the other three go to the *lema* that comes second, the seats to be distributed proportionately between the various factions in the *lema*.[3] The elector therefore votes both for a party and for the candidates representing a particular faction within the party. The majority group on the Council may, however, have only a small majority in the Houses of Parliament, since although elections for all elected offices take place at the same time on a single-list system, the distribution of seats differs according to whether they are seats on the executive or in the legislature. Whereas the posts of national councillors are awarded according to a simple majority of the votes, the thirty-one seats in the Senate and the ninety-nine seats in the Chamber of Deputies are distributed on a strictly proportional basis between all the lists presented in the election.[4] The application of this type of ballot ensures that the smaller parties, excluded from any direct share in power, are at least represented in the two Chambers.[5]

To summarize, the Uruguayan party system to be con-

3. It is very important to emphasize that this collegial system, whereby the minority enjoys a share of power, is not limited to the strictly political sphere (elections of executive bodies at national, regional or local level); it has been extended to the civil service and to the management boards of the *Entes autónomos*, state-run enterprises with independent managements – a sector which is relatively highly developed in Uruguay.

4. Since many types of law require the approval of a special majority, the full importance of this measure may be readily appreciated.

5. The two most important draft reforms currently under consideration would not appreciably alter this system. The President of the Republic would be the candidate of the majority list in the victorious *lema*. He would however have greater powers than the nine councillors under the present system.

sidered in this chapter gives the impression of a dualist regime, certainly, but one in which, next to the two dominant parties, which themselves incorporate a multitude of different tendencies, various numerically small groups also exist, which generally have in common the fact that each owes allegiance to a specific ideology.

Partido Colorado

Historical Outline

The origins of the Colorado Party, and indeed of the Blanco Party, go back to the period of the civil wars which ravaged Uruguay during the period immediately after independence. These political formations derived their names from the colours that the two enemy camps adopted for purposes of recognition, and which appeared for the first time on the battlefield of Carpintería in 1836 : white for the supporters of General Oribe, allied to the Argentine federalists and to Rosas, and red (*colorado*) for General Rivera supported by the Argentine liberals (centralists and unitarians) and by Brazil.

The duration of the Guerra Grande (1839–51) contributed to the final crystallization of the division of the country into Whites and Reds; the armed confrontation between the two rival factions continued sporadically until the end of the nineteenth century. Nevertheless, during this troubled period the two parties gradually succeeded in defining their positions and in building up a systematic organization.

Initially the Colorado Party included a number of large landed proprietors. However, it soon began to recruit most of its following from the merchant families and the tertiary sector in Montevideo, and especially from new immigrants. It thus increasingly gave the impression, from the end of the nineteenth century, of being the party of the urban middle and working classes.

This development was precipitated and consolidated by the 'great man' of the Colorado Party, José Batlle y Ordóñez (1856–1929), whose programme and achievements today loom large in the ideology and phraseology of the Colorados. In fact, Batllist thought is neither a doctrine, properly speaking, nor an ideology, deriving rather from a kind of enlightened empiricism and a part-socialist, part-paternalist morality. Nevertheless, three dominant themes emerge from the policies carried out by José Batlle in the course of his two terms in office (1903–7 and 1911–15). In the political field, Batlle's chief preoccupation was to install a truly democratic system. He was a great admirer of the Swiss political system and advocated the substitution of the one-man presidential system by a collegial executive, the adoption of proportional representation and the development of civil liberties. He was also a strong supporter of the separation of Church from State.[6] In the economic field, his ambition was to free the country from the grip of foreign capital, as far as possible, by continuing the policy of nationalization that had already been begun and creating state enterprises able to compete with the remaining foreign concerns. Finally in the social field, Batlle's concern for justice brought him to push through legislation which at the time must have appeared positively revolutionary (labour legislation, paid holidays, pensions, and so on).

José Batlle's presidency gave a very encouraging uplift to his party, which from that time took on the mantle of the natural champion of the urban middle class (in commerce, industry, the liberal professions, civil service and trade). It also acquired a firm base of support in the working class, the principal beneficiary of the new social legislation, and among the small farmers and market gardeners on the banks of the River Plate and in the region around the capital, who had ex-

6. These ideas were partly incorporated in the 1918 Constitution.

perienced a considerable increase in demand for their products. The Colorado Party, which had held power from 1865, thus managed to install itself even more firmly and was not removed from its position until 1958, with the victory of the National Party.

The Colorado Party and its Sublemas

The Colorado Party has not escaped internal splits in the course of its history. The various tendencies which have appeared have sometimes provoked more or less long-lasting schisms. Apart from personal rivalries, the principal cause (or excuse) for disputes has been the question of the collegial executive; as early as 1913, during Batlle's presidency, it resulted in the Riverista group's departure from the party. Other groups subsequently broke away, and this centrifugal tendency was to remain fairly marked until 1940.

However, the seriousness of these splits was greatly reduced by the application of the *lemas* law, which meant that total rupture with the party ceased to be a sensible alternative, because the various factions could retain their independence while at the same time benefiting from the electoral advantages conferred by the ability to use one party label.

Moreover the strong personalities of some of the party's leaders had enabled it to keep together.

In recent years, however, the disappearance of these men has brought about a leadership crisis and an increase in internal divisions caused by the struggle for the succession. The leaders of some factions have on several occasions felt the need to improve party cohesion in terms both of organization and discipline. The fact that these attempts have not so far been very successful may be partly due to the existence of the law of the *lemas*. However that may be, the Colorado Party does not at the moment possess any undisputed authority, and is consequently divided into numerous factions (*sub-*

lemas), each of which has its own committee, its own leader and even its own newspaper. All the Colorado Party *sublemas* taken together may be broadly grouped into two major families: the Independents and the Batllists.

The Independent Colorados. This term covers all the non-Batllist factions in the Colorado Party. This sector, which is at the moment united, is the result of the gradual amalgamation of two groups, the Riveristas and the Independents. As has been mentioned the former, under the leadership of Pedro Manini Ríos, broke with José Batlle in 1913, on the pretext of opposition to his proposal to set up a collegial executive, but in reality through opposition to his social policy.

Until 1934 the Riveristas chose to enter elections either as an independent party or sometimes as a *sublema* of the Colorado Party. They represent a liberal tendency which is nonetheless noticeably more conservative than the other sectors of the party, and they are in fact closer to some groups in the National or Blanco Party. In the 1938 elections the Riveristas were overshadowed by the Independent Colorado faction born of the coup and founded by Gabriel Terra, who was succeeded by Eduardo Blanco Acevedo.

The electorate of this *sublema* is recruited largely in the towns of the provincial departments of the interior, where the Independent Colorados win about three times as many votes as in Montevideo. Between 1950 and 1958 it was greatly weakened as a result of a major internal split. The similarity of its political position to those of other Colorado or National *sublemas* has up till now operated in the same direction, since this group has been the chief victim of changes in voting patterns among floating voters. However, it is not beyond the bounds of possibility that this axial position will one day turn to its advantage.

In these circumstances, it is understandable that of all the Colorado *sublemas* this has been the one most eager to re-establish unity. Unity within the *sublemas*, on the one hand: in June 1961 the Unión Colorada Independiente was set up, uniting six political groups (including the Unión Democrática Reformista, representing a resurgence of Riverism, founded in 1958 by Alberto Manini Ríos), and supporting the candidature of General Gestido to the National Executive Council. On the other hand, it worked for unity within the *lema itself*: the Unión Colorada Independiente attempted to impose the principle of a single Colorado list for the 1962 elections, but without success except for a few Batllist groups, with which it combined to form the Unión Colorada Batllista. This group was reconstituted for the November 1966 elections, but this time instead of the agreement being with members of César Batlle's faction (List 14) it was concluded with the Frente Colorado de Unidad, uniting dissidents from the Batllist Lists 14 and 15. The Unión's candidate for the presidency and vice-presidency of the republic were General Oscar Gestido and Dr J. Pacheco Areco, respectively; the other leading figures of the *sublema* included C. Manini Ríos, J. L. Lezama and A. Legnani.

In the political field, the Unión, faithful to its traditional line, is firmly in favour of the re-establishment of a presidential regime and of the abolition of the system of political distribution of posts in the civil service and the nationalized industries. On the economic plane, it represents a moderately interventionist point of view, but firmly opposed to the 'false liberal trends' introduced into Latin America and Uruguay by the International Monetary Fund. In foreign policy, the Unión remains attached to the traditional Uruguayan principles of non-intervention and self-determination; it appears to be opposed to the creation of an inter-American peace force which has been mooted, but inclined to consider a revision of the structures and mode of operation of the OAS.

These political views find expression in two big daily newspapers closely connected to the independent Colorados, *El*

Diario, founded in 1917, and *La Mañana*, which is directed more particularly towards the business community.

The Batllists. This political current, representing the heirs to the doctrines and achievements of José Batlle y Ordónez, has been the majority faction in the Colorado *lema* since the departure of its illustrious leader. It constitutes the moderate leftist wing of the party. It bears close similarities to the old Radical Civic Union of Argentina. If we wish to fit it into the spectrum of European political parties, then it may be said to bear some resemblance to the French Radical Socialist Party. In contrast to the independent Colorados, the Batllists win more votes in Montevideo than in the interior, for their electorate is different: although they still retain definite ties with the upper class, in general their electoral following is recruited mainly from the middle and lower middle class and from the lower classes.

Despite their common loyalty to the memory of José Batlle, the Batllists no more form a homogeneous bloc than do the Independents. Although it ought to have been possible for them to agree to a single programme, any prospects of unity have been largely compromised by personal rivalries between leaders of the faction. As a result, the Batllist faction is subdivided into three *sublemas*, with fairly sharp differences of viewpoint.

– List 14 [7] led by César Batlle Pacheco [8] (son of José Batlle y Ordónez). This faction represents the most conservative line in the Batllist camp; it is in some respects the party of the *status quo*. It has taken no steps to adapt José Batlle's ideas to new developments in society; at practically every election, its programme has relied entirely on the slogan: 'For the

7. All *sublemas* have list-numbers for the elections. In distinguishing between the three Batllist *sublemas*, it has become common practice to refer to them by their list numbers.

8. Died in 1963.

ideals of José Batlle.' Under César Batlle's leadership, List 14 has emerged as resolutely anti-communist and anti-Castroist. On the Executive Council, C. Batlle, in alliance with the most conservative faction of the National Party, supported a hard line against Cuba in 1962. List 14's implacable hostility to the replacement of a collegial executive by a presidential system has caused it to break the electoral alliance it concluded in 1962 with the Unión Colorada Independiente and its candidate O. Gestido, and to conduct a violent press campaign against the Unión, Gestido and the projected reform in the columns of its daily *El Día*, a newspaper which enjoys great prestige thanks to the fact that it was founded by J. Batlle himself.

Like the Independent Colorados, List 14 is most strongly entrenched in the towns of the interior, where it has three times as many voters as in Montevideo, but it also picks up votes from a sector of the urban electorate put off by the somewhat too pro-labour policy of other Colorado groups. The average age of the officers and electors in this list is fairly high. For several years its vote has tended to remain static, if not actually decline.

– List 15, led till July 1964 by Luis Batlle Berres, José Batlle's nephew. This faction represents the centre-left of the Colorado Party. The formation of this List, in 1950, was the outcome of a long drawn out struggle for the domination of the party between a group led by César Batlle and his brothers, and a group led by Luis Batlle. In contrast to List 14, List 15 relies principally on the support of the organized working class in the industrial towns and on a substantial group of state employees, whom it has managed to convince that it is the true legatee of José Batlle's policy. Almost half of its votes come from Montevideo.

Vilified as a man of ambition and a demagogue because of his pro-working-class policy, Luis Batlle has often been the victim of parliamentary obstruction carried out by factions of his own *lema*, especially members of List 14. This leader's strong personality has kept this group more close-knit than the other factions and also made it the biggest of the Colorado Party's *sublemas*. However, this unity was severely compromised by Luis Batlle's death; three groups now dispute the ascendancy within List 15: Unidad y Reforma led by Jorge Batlle (son of the dead leader), which seems likely to win the contest; the Por la ruta de Luis Batlle group led by Amilcar Vasconcellos; and the Frente Colorado de Unidad. The relations between these three groups are currently being exacerbated by the present election campaign. Furthermore, the rivalry between their respective leaders is endangering *sublema* 15's traditional pre-eminence in the party. List 15 has a daily newspaper, *Acción*, founded in 1948 by Luis Batlle Berres.

 – List 99, formed in October 1962 by Zelmar Michelini after his break with List 15, and Renán Rodríguez, a dissident from List 14. This group represents the left wing of the Colorado *lema*. *Sublema* 99 places the main emphasis on two points: defence of the country's economic independence, and a more equitable distribution of the national wealth. This faction is practically the only one to put forward a coherent plan of government in which the land problem and agrarian reform occupy a central place; even so, the solutions proposed to this problem are relatively moderate (expropriation with compensation over a long period, a struggle against internal monopolies and middleman speculation, development of trade circuits). So far as external trade is concerned, *sublema* 99 advocates a protectionist policy for Uruguay, and generally wishes the government to take a more independent line towards the International Monetary Fund.

Sublema 99 obtained encouraging results in its first encounter with the electorate in November 1962; although it was outpaced by the two other *sublemas* in the Colorado Party, it still managed to come well in front of the smaller parties, the Christian Democrats, Socialists and Communists. It seems that it was able to take advantage of the internal divisions in the left and attract a proportion of its voters. This *sublema* has not been in existence long enough to judge with certainty the social composition of its following; however, the 1962 results show a clear predominance of urban voters, with the department of Montevideo alone providing 70 per cent of the votes won by the faction over the whole country. At the time of the 1966 election campaign the question of constitutional reform caused some difficulties within the *sublema*, with some of its members refusing to vote for a reform which they considered too conservative, while others (notably Renán Rodríguez) joined with A. Vasconcellos (15) and List 14 in defence of the collegial principle. At the present stage of its development an internal split would have rather serious consequences for the Michelini group, which because of the present disarray in List 15 might hope to improve its position in the elections of November 1966. Following the failure to establish a united front with the Independent Colorados, List 99 decided to present its own candidates for the presidency and vice-presidency, in the person of its two main leaders, Zelmar Michelini and Aquiles Lanza. The election campaign is conducted on their behalf by *Hechos*, the group's daily paper.

– One further group of Batllists should be mentioned, small in numbers but influential because of the composition of its following. This is List 10, led by Justino Jiménez de Aréchaga, which falls somewhere between the Independents and List 14. This group is supported chiefly by executives and businessmen, and is practically confined to Montevideo.

The Colorado Party's Impact on the National Life

It is clear from the foregoing that the *sublemas* considered together have a number of features in common, over and above their differences, which enable us to gain an impression of the general physiognomy of the Colorado *lema*. It is a party with a left-wing slant, but belonging to the very moderate left and disinclined to consider radical reform. At the moment it evinces some anti-clericalism, especially the Batllist sector, traditionally attached to the secular principle incorporated in the Constitution since 1918 thanks to José Batlle. Its electoral following is drawn largely from the urban middle class (small industrialists and merchants), with the qualification that the independents attract more executives and 'technocrats' while the Batllists have a more popular following. However, these distinctions are only of relative value, in that family tradition continues to play a major part in the voter's choice.

The party's *sublemas* have all adopted similar forms of organization; their basic structural unit is the committee, the local delegates of which form the *sublema*'s general assembly. The organizational structure is more close-knit in the case of the Batllists than with the independents. Likewise rank-and-file participation is more advanced in Michelini's *sublema* 99 than in the others. At *lema* level, coordination between the various groups is fairly loose, depending as it does on the leaders or delegates (who have no decision-making powers) of each *sublema*. The lack of homogeneity in the party that results from this mode of organization may be considered one of the reasons for its election defeat in 1958. At that time the struggles between factions, and sometimes indeed between smaller groups within those factions, had reached crisis proportions and paralysed the party, rendering it utterly incapable of producing any remedy for the economic crisis that gripped the country. Those sectors of the population most directly affected were precisely the lower middle class and the workers, the Colorados' traditional following; their discontent was further augmented by that of part of the rural population, the farmers around Montevideo and the small stock-farmers of the interior, who had been forgotten in the series of reforms introduced and whose votes went to a peasant league allied to the National Party.

In 1962, however, the National Party achieved only a very narrow victory over its Colorado rival, the difference between the two parties being no more than 23,798 votes (out of more than one million), and the Colorados headed the poll in five counties, including Montevideo. They seem to have been the main beneficiaries of the great increase in the number of voters registered for that election.

Colorado Party – Election Results (1950–62)
Distribution of Votes and Seats between the Sublemas

	Total for the party	Indepen-dents	List 14	List 99	List 15
1950					
Votes obtained[9]	433,454	120,949	150,930	161,262	—
Deputies' seats	53	12	19	22	—
Senators' seats	17	abst.	6	6	—
1954					
Votes obtained	444,429	9,292	180,164	254,648	—
Deputies' seats	51	3	15	33	—
Senators' seats	17	1	6	10	—
1958					
Votes obtained	397,062		154,110	215,881	—
Deputies' seats	38	abst.	12	26	—
Senators' seats	12	abst.	5	7	—
1962					
Votes obtained	521,231	167,085		277,259	76,510
Deputies' seats	44	9		28	7
Senators' seats	14	4		8	2

9. The number of votes obtained in elections to the executive. Only since the 1951 Constitution have elections to all posts been on a single list.

Sources : Election results from 1950 to 1958 : Fabregat, Julio T., *Elecciones uruguayas*, vols. II–V, Montevideo, Corte Electoral, quoted by Taylor, Philip B., in *Government and Politics of Uruguay*, Tulane University, New Orleans, 1960. Election results for 1962 : *Carta de Montevideo*, 21 November 1966.

Partido Nacional

Historical Background

The Blanco Party did not officially adopt the name National Party until 1872, having used it unofficially since 1857 (although the term Blanco continued to be used in common parlance to refer to it).

Having ruled the country on several successive occasions, amid numerous civil wars, the National Party underwent a very long eclipse, since it was kept out of power from 1865 to 1958. During this period it was the victim of numerous internal disputes, especially after 1920, when some groups even refused to add their votes to those of the other *sublemas*. This fragmentation was to continue until 1956, at which time the National Party decided to regroup in order to challenge the Colorados effectively for power. Thanks to this move it was victorious in November 1958, and repeated its success in November 1962, although by a rather narrow margin.

The National Party and its Sublemas

Despite the great multiplicity of groups and factions coming under the National label, there are, as in the case of the Colorado Party, a number of general features common to all which make it possible to draw an outline of the National Party.

On the Uruguayan political scene, it emerges as a conservative party. It should however be emphasized that this conservatism is manifested principally on the economic plane, and has little effect on political or ideological issues. In fact although some sectors of the party proclaim themselves anti-Communist and anti-Castroist they do not call for the prohibition of the Communist Party, unlike other party groups of similar tendencies in Latin America. Likewise although the National Party finally resigned itself to breaking off diplomatic relations with Cuba after the 1964 Washington conference, when it was still in power, it refused to adopt the economic sanctions against Cuba advocated at that conference. Moreover, although its voters are avowedly Catholic, the party has rarely presented itself as the defender of the Catholic faith, wishing, like the Colorados, to keep such questions out of the political field. Nationalism is also a characteristic feature of this party's ideology, to a more or less marked degree, depending on the *sublemas* (and not without occasionally assuming contradictory forms).

In the political field, the Nationalists are supporters of a strong executive, of the presidential type, and they have not ceased to criticize the collegial executive system [10] since its introduction in 1951. Their refusal to condemn the Axis or the regimes of Franco and Perón, which they explained at the time as a desire to respect the principles of neutrality and non-interference, made them appear to some extent favourable to regimes of the fascist or neo-fascist type; and indeed tendencies of this kind did make their appearance from time to time at the very heart of the party.

But the fact that the National Party's conservatism tended to manifest itself principally in the economic and social fields may be explained by the social composition of its following. The interests it represents are chiefly rural (wealthy landed proprietors and cattle-farmers in the interior), together with urban merchants engaged primarily in the commercial exploitation of agricultural products. This party is the champion of economic liberalism. It is concerned particularly to promote free exchange and looks forward to the relaxation or relin-

10. It should, however, be noted that on two separate occasions, in 1917 and in 1951, substantial sectors of the National Party supported constitutional reform in favour of a collegial executive and the sharing of power.

quishing of state control over a number of enterprises (especially commercial outlets for the products of the agricultural and cattle-farming sector). In the financial field it advocates devaluation of the currency and the abolition of variable exchange rates. These measures, taken together, tend to favour the big landowners, because most of them in effect increase land values.

Despite this common ground, there are serious differences between the two *sublemas* that make up the National Party – the *sublema* Herrerista and the Unión Blanca Democrática. The conflicts between them are to some extent due to purely political questions, such as differences in interpretation or execution of pre-election pacts; they do also go deeper than this, however, and stem from more or less firmly held ideological convictions and differences in the recruitment of their respective followings.

a) The sublema *Herrerista.* This group is to the National Party what Batllism is to the Colorado Party, expressing as it does the traditional position of the Blancos both with regard to its programme and its political following. It, too, was marked by the exceptionally powerful personality of its old leader, Luis Alberto de Herrera, who died in April 1959.

The *sublema* Herrerista is itself far from united. A number of small groups have sprung up within the *sublema* whose opposition to one another rests largely on personality conflicts, a fact which does not prevent them from taking advantage of the electoral system to put forward their own lists. The choice of a successor to L. A. de Herrera at the head of the *sublema* provoked a severe crisis; the eventual victor was Martín Echegoyen.

Disputes between various leader-figures tend especially to highlight the opposition between two principal groups: a moderate wing, led by Echegoyen, and a more extreme wing (calling themselves orthodox) led by Eduardo V. Haedo. Some

individuals in the *sublema,* such as Hector Payssé Reyes and
Alberto Heber Usher, have made repeated attempts to restore
unity, but without success, especially since the approach of
an election always revives old rivalries and old grudges by
presenting the delicate problem of choosing candidates. It
may be said that the complex web of alliances concluded and
subsequently broken by rival Herrerist groups was one of the
main causes for the paralysis of the executive during the
eight years of Blanco government.

The *sublema*'s main source of funds consists of voluntary
grants and contributions. Its leaders are drawn from a very
narrow sector of society; this is illustrated by the fact that the
candidate in an election must pay a contribution proportional
to his rank number on the list of the *sublemas* and to the re-
muneration he would derive from the corresponding post if
elected. The Herrerista *sublema* owns the daily paper *El
Debate.*

b) *The* sublema *Unión Blanca Democrática* (UBD). This
sublema is of more recent creation. It was set up in November
1956 through the union of three groups which had broken
away from the Herreristas at different times, all through opposition to L. A. de Herrera. These three groups were the
Partido Blanco Independiente (founded around 1926), the
Movimiento Popular Nacionalista (MPN), set up in 1953,
and Reconstrucción Blanca.

In its following and political attitudes, the UBD differs
quite sharply from the Herreristas, which introduces an additional element of instability into the *lema.* Its electoral support comes more from the towns than from the countryside,
and consists chiefly of business people from the upper middle
class. The UBD also enjoys the support of recent peasant
arrivals in the towns, who continue to vote Nationalist out of
pure reflex-action. Its intermediate position, between the orthodox members of the National Party and of the Colorado

Party, also enables it to benefit from time to time from shifts in the floating vote. This happened for example in 1958, when part of the urban middle class gave it its vote; the UBD thus won control of the Montevideo County Council, and on the national level the Herrera *sublema* only retained the upper hand by dint of the majority it enjoyed in the country areas. This situation was reversed after the 1962 elections, thanks to the Union's alliance with the Herrerista group Azul y Blanco, led by Haedo and Heber.

The UBD represents the more progressive wing of the national *lema*. It supports, rather half-heartedly, the proposed reform of the executive, when no major factions within the group come out against it. Its attitude to economic affairs is quite far removed from that of the Herrerista *sublema*, because the interests of their supporters differ. Thus until 1962, it opposed the austerity measures and monetary reform envisaged by the government. However, once it had won a majority on the National Council, it applied these same measures with energy and ruthlessness, which upset a large number of its electors. Although it is in some ways a supporter of liberal principles, the UBD favours the maintenance of state control over state enterprises with autonomous management boards.

The UBD is no more noted for its unswerving unity than any other *sublema*. Until the departure of its leader, Daniel Fernández Crespo, in 1964, internal divisions within the group seemed less virulent than in the case of the Herreristas. The situation became somewhat more complicated when it came to choosing a successor; the mantle finally fell upon Carlos M. Penadés.

The three movements from which the *sublema* was originally constituted kept different lists within the UBD, and the two biggest of these are List 51 (the old MPN), led by Carlos M. Penadés, Fernando Dardo and F. R. Camusso, and List 400, the majority group of which is led by Washington

Beltrán. Rivalry between these two lists for the leadership of the *sublema* is an additional factor of internal disturbance. The old Independents are collected together in List 97, the leader of which is Eduardo Rodriguez Larreta.

The UBD controls three newspapers, *El País*, directed principally at business and professional people, *El Plata*, with much the same clientele, and *El Nacional*, which follows the line laid down by List 51.

c) These two *sublemas* of the National Party have recently been supplemented by a third group, the Liga Federal de Acción Ruralista (Peasants' Federal Action League), a typical example of the politicization of a pressure group. Until March 1964 this League was led by Benito Nardone. The movement was of the type which might be termed 'Poujadist', with all the demagogic and fascistic overtones of that movement. Its following is recruited chiefly from the small farmers of the coast and the interior. A charismatic leader, Nardone attracted the peasant masses and the marginal population of the cities. He kept up the pretence of apolitical objectives until 1954, and then, after abortive overtures to the Colorados, he allied himself with the Herreristas, supporting Herrera in 1958 and Echegoyen in 1962. The League forms the extreme right wing of the National Party; both intransigent and opportunist, it has contributed greatly to the exacerbation of inter-factional disputes. The ephemeral alliances which Nardone's ambition led him to conclude with various party factions in turn make it difficult to define the true position of this movement with any accuracy. Some basic attitudes do emerge, however. In the political field, the Ruralists advocate a return to the presidential system; in economic affairs, they press for the abolition of exchange control and import restrictions; they also want the autonomous state corporations to be denationalized.

The League has lost a great deal of influence since Nardone's death. It is at the moment split into two groups, one of which is led by Nardone's widow, who continues his own policy, while the other, under Juan B. Bordaberry, is tending to dissociate itself from the National Party and seems to be devoting itself to trade-union action.

The Party's Role in the Life of the Nation

1946 marks the beginning of the National Party's recovery in the electoral field. After that time, it made steady progress, culminating in a clear victory in 1958. However, this date seems to represent the high-water mark of the party's advance; although it was successful again in 1962, a study of the percentage of votes it obtained by comparison with the number of registered voters and the number actually going to the polls reveals a distinct drop in its electoral support. The gap separating it from the Colorado Party seems to be narrowing (see table, p. 492).

The Blancos are assured of maintaining their dominance over the countryside for a long time to come, because of the type of relationships that still predominate in rural society. But its economic power is the decisive factor, one that gives it a great deal of weight. The products of stock-farming and agriculture still constitute the country's main source of wealth. The big landowners, most of whom live in Montevideo, have organized very powerful lobbies there, and control substantial pressure groups, notably the Asociación Rural and the Federación Rural, established at the end of the last century.

However, the National Party suffers even more from its lack of unity and coherent structure than its Colorado rival; disputes occur inside the party not only between the *sublemas,* but between the various groups that have been set up within them. As the last few years have shown, this total absence of internal discipline may have serious consequences

when the party is in power; it tends to hamper, if not paralyse, the workings of the executive, the majority *sublema*
being a prey to a fluctuating majority, which sometimes
drops to well below the danger level or even disappears altogether.

National Party: Electoral Results 1954–62
Distribution of Votes and Seats between the Sublemas

	Votes cast	Deputies' seats	Senators' seats
1954			
Herrerists	160,738	—*	—
UBD	112,124	—	—
Total for the party	309,818	35	11
1958			
Herrera-Nardone	241,939	24	9
UBD	230,649	25	8
Total for the party	499,425	51	17
1962			
UBD-Haedo	316,533	28†	9‡
Echegoyen-Nardone	227,205	20	6
Total for the party	545,029	48	15

NOTE: It is fairly difficult to indicate the exact distribution of
votes between the different *sublemas* as some of the groups form
links and put forward common lists at the elections. In 1958, for
example, Herrera joined with Nardone and left the UBD to fight
alone; in 1962 Haedo (Herrerist) joined with the UBD and Echegoyen
(Herrerist) with Nardone (Peasants' Federal Action League).

Sources: Fabregat, J. T., op. cit.; Taylor, P. B., op. cit.; *Carta de
Montevideo*, 21 November 1966.

The results of the eight years of Blanco government cannot
in all objectivity be considered as positive, at least not on the
economic level. It would seem that the measures it introduced, far from remedying the economy's problems, only increased them. The acceptance, in December 1959, of the pro-

* 1954 figures for distribution of seats not available.

† 22 for UBD, 6 for the Haedo group.

‡ 7 for UBD, 2 for the Haedo group.

Electoral Results of the Colorado and National Parties Compared: 1950-62

Date	Total registered electors	Total votes cast	Colorado Party			National Party		
			Number of votes cast	% of total votes	% of registered electors	Number of votes cast	% of total votes	% of registered electors
1950	1,168,206	823,829	433,454	52·6	37·1	254,834	30·9	21·8
1954	1,295,502	879,242	444,429	50·5	34·3	309,818	35·2	24·7
1958	1,410,105	1,005,362	379,062	37·7	26·9	499,425	49·6	35·4
1962	1,519,648	1,171,120	521,231	44·5	34·3	545,029	46·5	35·8

Source: *Marcha* (Montevideo), 25 November 1966.

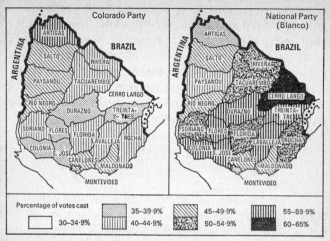

Figure 22. Distribution of Colorado and National Votes
in 1962

posals of the International Monetary Fund – abolition of
import restrictions, abolition of the system of multiple exchange rates, and devaluation – was especially damaging to
the nation's industry, while the policy of austerity affected a
major proportion of the population, because of the large
number of state employees. Since the national price index
quadrupled between 1959 and 1966, strikes and wage demands greatly increased. Now the boot seems to be on the
other foot: like the Colorado Party in 1958, the National
Party may well find itself in 1966 the victim of the continuing economic crisis and the unpopularity of its policy.

The Smaller Parties

The smaller Uruguayan parties, which happen at the same
time to be the parties termed 'ideological', also have in common the fact that they are very much marginal parties: in
1962 the Catholics, Socialists and Communists only managed

to muster 6.8 per cent of the electorate, taken together. This gives an indication of the importance which these formations must necessarily give to their programme, the only factor by means of which they can hope to attract voters. Like most parties condemned for one reason or another to remain in opposition, they have never succeeded either in joining forces, although attempts have been made, or in avoiding internal splits provoked by tactical disagreements.

The Catholic Parties

The political situation is different in Uruguay from almost all other Latin American countries in that religion does not interfere with politics and the Catholic Church plays practically no part at all in political affairs.

It is certainly true that in contrast to the National Party the Colorado Party has traditionally professed to be anti-clerical, and controversies arise from time to time, but they rarely become at all virulent. This is partly due to the fact that the problem of relations between Church and State was settled at a very early date, since the principle of separation was written into the Constitution in 1918; moreover, although Catholicism is the dominant religion in Uruguay, many surveys have revealed that there is a high proportion of non-practising Catholics and fairly widespread indifference towards religion.

Uruguayan Catholics long hesitated (and the debate is still going on) over what tactics to follow in order to get themselves heard. Two possibilities presented themselves: either to vote 'usefully' and work within one of the dominant parties, in this case the National Party which was well-disposed towards them; or work from the outside by creating their own party. The supporters of the second course were behind the formation in 1872 of the Unión Católica del Uruguay, which subsequently became the Unión Cívica del Uruguay. This party made strenuous efforts to penetrate the trade-union movement; in order to extend its influence in that field it set up a Christian trade-union federation in the 1920s, the SCU (Christian Trade Unions of Uruguay), which never managed to grow to any size.

At first strongly influenced by the European Christian parties, the Unión Cívica eventually followed the same course of development as most of the other Christian Democratic groups in Latin America, and under the influence of Dardo Regules, the party's leader and chief ideologist until his recent death, adopted the line called the 'third course': it defined itself as being neither capitalist nor communist, but 'communitarian' with regard to labour relations and property rights. From that moment, the risk of conflict between the party's conservative and more progressive wings grew. The first crisis was provoked in 1961 by the signing of an anti-Castro declaration (adopted by one hundred and sixty votes to seven, with seven abstentions) and resulted in the expulsion of the members opposed to this step. In the hope of reducing the disagreements between the two wings of the party and attracting a larger number of voters by profiting from the successes scored in some other countries of the continent by Christian Democratic parties, the Unión Cívica decided in 1962 to amalgamate with a small group of Catholics with no precise political affiliations, and the new formation took the name of Christian Democratic Party (PDC). Daniel del Castillo became president of the PDC's national committee.

However, against the expectations of its leaders, the PDC actually lost votes in 1962, instead of gaining them, and the internal tensions in the party were accentuated. This finally culminated in 1964 in the inevitable split: the party's old guard, led by Venancio Flores and Dr Tomás Brena, withdrew and formed the Movimiento Cívico Cristiano, while the progressive wing, led by Américo Plá Rodríguez and Daniel Sosa Díaz, remained in the Christian Democratic Party.

Party Programme. The 1966 election campaign provided the two parties with the opportunity of publishing their respective points of view. From the evidence of their election manifestoes, it would seem that they are not divided by any fundamental ideological disagreement. The PDC follows a more radical line than the Civic Movement, and seems willing to make an alliance with the whole of the left, without exception; the Civic Movement on the other hand is unenthusiastic about any agreement that would include groups more radical than the Socialists.

The Christian Democratic Party's programme is more precise and better set out than that of its rival. With regard to political institutions, the PDC does not attach any great importance to the form of the executive; on the other hand, it advocates the abolition of the law of the *lemas*, the re-establishment of separate lists for local elections, and the depoliticization of the governing boards of large administrative bodies. In the economic field, it underlines the urgent need to reform the system of land tenure. In this respect it is violently opposed to the amendment of Article 32 of the Constitution, proposed by the two big parties, which provides for 'just compensation *in advance*' in case of expropriation; instead, it advocates the expropriation and redistribution of the big estates, with repayment extended over a long period, and an all-out effort with maximum mobilization of resources to improve the standard of living of the peasantry. This interest in land problems is one of the constant features of the party, already evident at the time of the Unión Cívica. In foreign affairs, the PDC emphasizes the need to achieve political and economic integration of the countries of Latin America to enable the continent to escape from foreign influence of whatever kind or origin.

Electoral Following and Election Results. (See table, p. 505.) The Catholic parties have made efforts to entrench themselves both in the countryside and in towns. They seem to have had more success in this than the other small parties : in the 1962 elections, Montevideo and Canelones, the two most densely populated and industrialized regions, only provided 57·2 per cent of their electorate, as against 76·3 per cent in the case of the Socialist Party and 83·6 per cent for the Communist Party. However, it would seem that the bulk of the Christian Democrat electorate consists of intellectuals and professional people.

Having progressed slowly but steadily from 1938 onwards, the Catholic parties' electorate has fallen away since 1954. In fact the voting figures for 1958 and especially 1962 were hardly any better than those in the 1946 election (a year when the small opposition parties scored one of their major successes). It is unlikely that the Christian Democrats will succeed in reversing the trend in 1966, and their recent split seems likely to weaken them still further.

The Socialist Parties

Historical Background. Socialist ideas were introduced very early into the River Plate area : in 1837, Esteban Echevarría published *La dogma socialista*, and founded in Uruguay the Sociedad de Mayo. The working-class movement made fairly rapid progress : the first trade union, of typographers, was founded in 1865, and ten years later the first Uruguayan section of the 1st Socialist International was set up. In 1905 the anarcho-syndicalist Federación Obrera Regional Uruguaya (FORU) made its appearance – the ancestor of the present-day trade-union federations.

The various political groupings with socialist leanings that existed in the country united in 1910 to form the Socialist

Party, under the leadership of Emilio Frugoni. Rejecting an
alliance themselves with José Batlle, who was trying to create
a Batllist Workers' Party, from that time on they presented
their own candidates at elections. The Socialist Party had not
been in existence many years when it experienced a serious
crisis brought about by the formation of the Third International. At its eighth congress in 1921 the majority of the delegates came out in favour of joining the Communist International (by 1,267 votes to 175, with 275 abstentions) despite
the opposition of Frugoni. He then withdrew from the party
and set up a new Socialist Party. In the 1922 elections, this
party only obtained 997 votes (compared with 3,179 for the
Communist Party), but gradually won back its original
electoral support after 1928.

The Socialists' Place in the Political Life of the Nation.
– Difficulties. While the growth of all the political formations was affected by the existence of two major, dominant
parties, the Socialist Party undoubtedly suffered most. Its
natural electorate, the working class, in fact votes Colorado:
the social reforms introduced by José Batlle represented the
transposition to the legislative plane of the minimum programme put forward by the Socialists, so that Batllism became identified with Socialism and working-class loyalty to
the Colorado Party was assured. The Socialists' actual electorate is composed primarily of intellectuals, professional people
and part of the lower middle class. It is recruited almost entirely in the towns, so that in 1962 the department of Montevideo alone represented 72·8 per cent of the total votes obtained by the Socialists in the country. It is true that the
Socialists have managed to preserve their position in the trade
unions, where they control about 20 per cent of the membership, but Uruguayan trade unionism's preoccupation with
economics does not allow them to derive any real political
advantage from this.

– Tactics and divisions. The main difficulties in the Socialist Party have arisen out of the problem of electoral tactics, and more particularly out of the question of a possible alliance with the Communist Party. Several of its leaders have opposed Emilio Frugoni (who is against such an alliance) on this point. In 1962, having once more refused to set up a united front with the Communist Party but aware of the necessity of enlarging its electoral base, the Socialist Party joined with certain left-wing intellectual groups and even with some refugees from the National Party (List 41 led by E. Erro, a dissident Herrerist) to form the Unión Popular. The failure of this somewhat unnatural union (and the contrasting success of the Communists in a similar experiment) poisoned relations between the two wings of the party and increased the opposition to Frugoni, who was accused of conservatism. Breaking point was finally reached in 1963 when Frugoni, who had accepted the formation of the Unión Popular only with reluctance, withdrew from it and set about organizing a new Socialist Party.

At the moment the socialists are therefore divided between the Frugoni group (the Movimiento Socialista) and the old Unión Popular, which has taken over the name of Socialist Party. They will fight the election of November 1966 under the *lema* of Partido Socialista (to which both claim to have an exclusive right), but with their own separate lists.

The differences between these two movements are not in fact as great as their leaders claim. The most that could be said is that the Movimiento Socialista (List 3,000) represents the more moderate tendency, social democrat in tone and bearing some resemblance to European parties of the same type. In its declarations of principle it advocates the nationalization of all large fortunes, state planning and control over the economy, and condemns the policy of foreign loans on a bilateral basis; trade-union liberty, secular education and land reform have not been forgotten, and the subjection of the

American continent to United States imperialism is denounced. All these economic and social changes are to be carried out gradually and with the assent of a democratic majority, as the Movimiento formally rules out the use of violence. List 3,000's national executive committee is chaired by Dionisio Pizzolanti, its general secretary is Edgardo Guigo and its honorary president E. Frugoni; other important figures include E. R. Jaurena and Andrade Ambrosoni.

The Partido Socialista (List 90), led by Vivián Trías, José P. Cardoso and José E. Díaz (general secretary), regards itself as revolutionary and refuses to confine the struggle to the electoral field only. It has broken with the Socialist International to follow an 'independent anti-imperialist line'. More eager for union with the Communist Party in the political and trade-union fields, it endeavours to appear as the representative of a *national* Marxist left. It puts forward the same claims, by and large, as the Movimiento, but expresses them with greater intransigence: for example, it is not content to denounce the policy of foreign loans, but demands a complete break with the International Monetary Fund. List 90 has one immediate advantage over its rival – it has retained most of the officers of the old party, and also its journal, *El Sol.*

– Election results. (See table, p. 505.) In absolute terms, the votes won by the socialists increased regularly, if not substantially, between 1942 and 1958. However, this increase, due principally to the increase in the national electorate, does not indicate an advance but near-stagnation in the party's electoral support. It is true that in the elections of 1954 and 1958 it experienced a distinct improvement in its fortunes each time; it would seem, however, that this was due largely to 'borrowed' votes, as it is extremely likely that the Socialist Party benefited from the disaffection of some left-wing Colorado voters. This view seems to be confirmed by the collapse of the Socialist Party in 1962, coinciding with the spectacular recovery by the Colorados, and more especially the success of Michelini's newly-formed List 99. The tactical error of setting up the Unión Popular was a further reason for this grave setback, which sank the party to a level below that which it had reached in 1946.

The Communist Party

Historical Background. The Communist Party in Uruguay has enjoyed an exceptionally privileged position : it has never been banned, even under dictatorships – except that of Gabriel Terra, between 1933 and 1935, but then all the political parties found themselves in the same boat.

As has already been mentioned, Uruguay and Chile are the only countries in Latin America where the Socialist Party itself joined the Third International. Since the trade-union wing of the party had been one of the chief architects of this affiliation, it is not surprising that the Communist Party has from its foundation shown great interest in trade-union affairs. (The future leader of the Communist Party, Eugenio Gómez, had at the time been head of the Federation of Seamen.) It therefore made considerable efforts to control the whole of the trade-union movement, but with only partial success.

Electorally the party made even slower progress, without gaining ground at all until the Second World War, after which it benefited from the prestige won by the USSR. In 1946, therefore, it reached the height of its power, both in the trade-union field (where it controlled the UGT – the General Union of Labour) and in Parliament, where its 32,677 votes (about 5 per cent of the total cast) gave it five seats in the Chamber of the Senate. However, the truce was brief, and at the beginning of the Cold War the Communist Party lost again the ground it had won electorally (in 1950 and 1954 its results were appreciably lower than they had been in 1942) and in the trade-union field (with the dissolution of the UGT in 1954).

Nevertheless, after 1958 the Communists began to win wider sympathy because of the country's economic difficulties, the rise of anti-Americanism and the sympathy felt by a large number of Uruguayans towards Cuba. The reconquest of the footholds it had lost was achieved through a change of tactics on the part of the Communist Party, which after 1961 posed as the champion of left-wing unity. This was, of course, no new departure, since the party had tried several times to set up a popular front with the Socialist Party, without success. The repetition of this failure in 1961 finally drove it to act independently of the Socialists; in 1962, in conjunction with a number of other left-wing groups and left-wing dissidents from the two big parties (mostly Batllists), it created the Left Liberation Front (Frente Izquierda de Liberación, or FIDEL). The Front's success in 1962 and the parallel failure of the Socialists' experiment (Unión Popular) encouraged the Communist Party to maintain and expand this formation, which it completely dominated and which was joined by numerous other left-wing groups, including Movimiento Revolucionario Oriental (MRO), led by Ariel Collazo and A. Cuervo.

Programme and Organization. The Communist Party and FIDEL programmes concentrate on two main points: the struggle for national liberation, and land reform. Defence of national independence on the economic plane entails a struggle against internal enemies by nationalization of the private banks and the biggest private companies (especially the meat-packing industry), and against external enemies (primarily American interests) by similar but even more radical means – by a complete breach with the International Monetary Fund and the denunciation of the activities of the Alliance for Progress, the Inter-American Development Bank and other organizations of the same sort. The party demands national-ization of foreign trade and state control of the merchant navy. Politically it calls for the renunciation of all pacts which subject Uruguay to the domination of politico-military blocs, and for an independent foreign policy. The Communist Party claims both to be internationalist and deeply conscious of the nation's interests, and to underline its patriotism it makes frequent reference to the heroes of the independence struggle.

In order to achieve its objectives, the Communist Party proposes a flexible strategy combining direct action with parliamentary activity, while denouncing the small left-wing extremist groups (like the Trotskyists and Anarchists) who advocate violent action as the only remedy.[11] In the present Sino-Soviet dispute it seems to have plumped for the USSR, but has so far succeeded in avoiding a split in the party.

It should be pointed out that in their attacks on the other parties the Communists, while reserving their worst venom for the National Party, are hardly any easier on the Colorad-os, but they do treat the Christian Democrats with a little more indulgence.

We shall not go into the structure and organization of the Uruguayan Communist Party, which is similar to that of its sister parties in other countries. Its ruling echelons have not changed much over the years; until 1955, when he was ex-pelled on a charge of Stalinism, Eugenio Gómez led the party. At the moment, the party's first secretary is Rodney Aris-mendi, assisted principally by E. Rodríquez, José Luis Mas-sera, E. Pastorino, A. Suárez, J. Pérez and Alberto Altesor.

Until 1947 the party's daily paper was called *Justicia,* succeeded by *El Diario popular* and then in 1957 by *El Popular,* whose editor in chief Eduardo A. Viera is a member of the Central Committee.

11. More particularly, the Movimiento Revolucionario Oriental organized on the Cuban model and advocating armed struggle.

The Communist Party and the Elections. (See table, p. 505.) The Communist Party recruits its following chiefly among the urban working class; in 1962 the department of Montevideo alone provided 79·8 per cent of its voters. In an endeavour to improve its position over the rest of the country, the Communist Party has in recent years launched a major propaganda campaign in the countryside, which does not so far seem to have had any great success. It takes a relatively moderate attitude towards the other small parties, especially the Christian Democrats (and even Michelini's *sublema* of the Colorados), in the hope of winning over some of their supporters, intellectuals and members of the middle class. Despite all its other activities, however, the party's chief strength lies in the domination it exercises over the trade-union movement, many of whose leaders are also leading members of the Communist Party.

In the 1962 elections, the Communist Party took the lead over all the other small opposition parties; it overtook the Christian Democrats for the first time, and recovered its lead, temporarily lost in 1954 and 1958, over the Socialists. The failure of the attempt to form a united electoral front with the Socialists has been skilfully exploited to the latter's detriment; moreover the current division of the Socialists and the Christian Democrats will no doubt enable the Communist Party to mobilize some of the left-wing electorate to its own advantage, especially those sympathetic to its desire to unite the forces of the opposition and attracted by its new-found dynamism. Finally, the continuing economic crisis and the manifest inability of either of the two big traditional parties to do anything about it is liable to bring a growing number of discontented voters over to its side.

Election Results Obtained by the Small Parties[12]

Years	Registered voters	Votes cast	Unión Cívica PDC	% of votes cast	Socialist Party Unión Popular	% of votes cast	Communist Party FIDEL	% of votes cast
1950	1,168,206	828,403	36,093	4·35	17,400	2·1	19,026	2·29
1954	1,295,502	879,242	44,255	5·03	28,704	3·26	19,541	2·22
1958	1,410,105	1,005,362	37,625	3·74	35,478	3·52	27,080	2·69
1962	1,519,648	1,171,020	35,703	3·04	27,041	2·3	40,886	3·49

12. Source: *Marcha* (Montevideo), 9 December 1966.

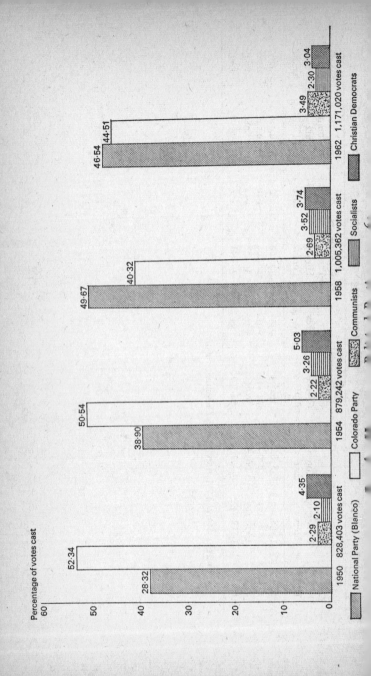

Percentage of votes cast

National Party (Blanco) Colorado Party Communists Socialists Christian Democrats

1950 828,403 votes cast
52·34
28·32
2·29
2·10
4·35

1954 879,242 votes cast
50·54
38·90
2·22
3·26
5·03

1958 1,005,362 votes cast
49·67
40·32
2·69
3·52
3·74

1962 1,171,020 votes cast
46·54
44·51
3·49
2·30
3·04

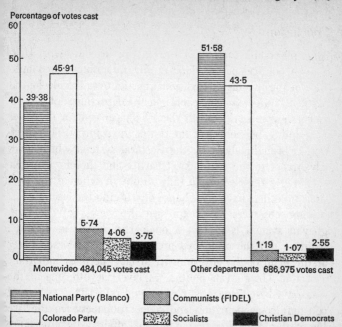

Figure 24. *Results of the 1962 Elections in Montevideo and the Rest of Uruguay*

Standing of the Smaller Parties in Relation to the National Electorate[13]

Years	Percentage of number registered	Percentage of number voting
1950	6·18	8·75
1954	7·13	10·52
1958	7·09	9·96
1962	6·81	8·84

13. Source: *Marcha* (Montevideo), 25 November 1966.

Conclusion

Some observable facts emerge from this brief study of Uruguayan political parties. First of all, the absolute predominance of the two major traditional parties over the ideological parties is quite unmistakeable: in the department of Montevideo they collect between them 85.3 per cent of the votes cast, and 95 per cent over the rest of the country. This situation is brought about by the electoral system, which gives advantages to the two biggest parties and therefore further encourages the electors to rally to one or other of the two, since no others have any chance of winning the elections.

Some observers have expressed the view that the Uruguayan system is in fact a one-party system in disguise, pointing out the prolonged presence of the Colorado Party at the helm of the government. In fact the most important aspect of Uruguayan politics, as Pivel Devoto, one of the country's best historians, has pointed out, is the system of constant co-participation and cooperation between the two big parties in the direction of national affairs. The importance attached to this system and, more particularly, its extension to the form of the executive, have led people to make the observation that Uruguay has pressed the application of the democratic principle to the ultimate. However, a problem arises in this connection: how is it that it is precisely the question of the collegial executive which has aroused the most controversy both inside and outside the country? Where has the practical application of the system broken down?

Liberal parliamentary democracy is a game with rules: it entails the existence of protagonists, generally speaking organized political groups, possessing a minimum of common aims and discipline. This definition, which fits the modern conception of the political party, can hardly be applied in Uruguay except to the small parties, forced by their weakness and their position of permanent opposition to be more rigorous. In fact, the two big *lemas* correspond to an older form of political party; they are more like coalitions of groups, often heterogeneous, with a very loose overall organization and sometimes contradictory aims. An excessively loose internal structure prevents the establishment of a common discipline and facilitates the proliferation of factions within the *lema*, and even inside the *sublema*; these factions enter into alliances with one another, mostly transitory, because they are more concerned with questions of personality than with programmes. As a result, the operation of the organs of the executive, already made difficult by the latter's collegial form, is paralysed by incessant conflicts between factions inside the victorious *lema*. These sometimes take the form of a veritable parliamentary opposition conducted against the dominant *sublema* by the other factions of the same party. In these circumstances the allegation, common in the current election campaign, that the collegial principle alone is responsible for all present political ills misses the point.

At all events, the priority given to the question of constitutional reform in this campaign has had the effect of bringing out a new reason for conflict in the parties, and at least in the case of the two big groups to push the question of a programme of government into the background. This is all the more serious for the fact that Uruguay is going to be faced with a difficult situation, both internally and externally. The political and economic crisis it is currently going through, and the growth in social agitation, have not gone unnoticed by Uruguay's two powerful neighbours, Brazil and Argentina, both with a traditional interest in Uruguayan affairs; and at the present time that country's neutral approach to the political attitudes prevalent in Washington, Brasilia and Buenos Aires arouses distrust, even irritation, in these capitals. In 1965, the Argentinian and Brazilian chiefs of staff went so far as to speculate, as a thinly veiled threat, on the possibility of intervention beyond their own frontiers; the fact that one of them subsequently became the head of the military regime established in Argentina was hardly calculated to allay Uruguayan apprehensions.

In 1966 elections were held and yielded the following results:

– Approval of the constitutional reform re-establishing presidential rule.

– Victory of the Colorado Party, and accession to the presidency of General Oscar Gestido, candidate of the Unión Colorado y Batllista which won a majority within the Colorado *lema*. In December 1967, after General Gestido's death, the Vice-President, Dr Pacheco Areco, succeeded him in office.

Election Results of 27 November 1966[14]

Registered electors: 1.658,368
Votes cast: 1,231,762

Parties	Number of votes obtained	% of registered electors	% of votes cast	Seats in Parliament	
				Deputies	Senators
Colorado	607,633	36.64	49.33	50	17
Nacional	496,910	29.96	40.34	41	13
FIDEL	69,750	4.20	5.66	5	—
PDC	37,219	2.24	3.02	3	1
Socialistas	11,559	0.69	0.93	—	—
Movimiento Cívico Cristiano	4,230	0.25	0.34	—	—

July 1966

14. Source: *Marcha* (Montevideo), 17 February 1967.

1966–71

Return to the Presidential System

The National Party's defeat in the 1966 election clearly came as no surprise. Out of office, it found itself divided into three groupings, as a result of splits in both main *sublemas* during the campaign. Opposition to the constitutional reform had produced an alliance between Echegoyen's Herrerista group and List 51 of the UBD under Dardo Ortiz. The other two groups had supported the return to presidential government: the Movimiento de Rocha under Carlos Julio Pereira with the remainder of the UBD led by Washington Beltrán (List 400), and Herrerismo de Heber.

In the Colorado Party too were new alignments. Rallying to a return to the presidency and Gestido (the Independent Colorados' candidate) were List 15, with Jorge Batlle now its undisputed leader (see p. 480), together with the Frente Colorado de Unidad, but the issue had separated Amilcar Vasconcellos from List 15 and Renán Rodríguez from List 99 (see p. 481). The election result signified a defeat in terms of internal party politics for the orthodox *colegialistas*. It now appears that *colegialismo*, a long-standing bone of contention within the Colorado Party (see p. 475), no longer exists as an issue in Uruguayan politics.

Gestido's rise to power had been less as a career politician than as a skilled administrator who had rationalized certain state enterprises. His integrity and the unipersonal executive seemed to counter the lack of leadership which had characterized the previous regime, but he died on 6 December 1967 before making a definitive mark.

The political stance of his successor, Jorge Pacheco Areco, was somewhat obscure; director of a Montevideo newspaper, he had not been publicly prominent in politics. However, his government's objectives and methods caused new divisions within his party. Faced with acute problems of economic decline and rapid inflation, Pacheco aimed to achieve stabilization at all costs, and his methods placed him well to the right of mainstream Colorado orientation. The brunt of hardships entailed by his wage and price freeze fell on the low-income groups traditionally protected by the Colorados. He showed a new intolerance towards the ideological parties, closing their newspapers on various occasions. He implemented unpopular measures by means of emergency powers, first invoked on 13 June 1968, on which occasion they remained in force for nine months.

After his cabinet resigned in May 1968 over the Legislature's censure of two ministers, Héctor Luisi and Guzmán Acosta y Lara, he sought to widen support by assembling a team of more neutral political complexion, including a member of the Movimiento Cívico Cristiano, Venancio Flores. A considerable body of normally moderate opinion approved: Pacheco's departure from liberal principles at first aroused little protest because of a widespread sense that a national crisis did indeed exist, and strong, non-factional government seemed apt in this context.

Seldom is the executive assured of a smooth ride with the legislature, however. The *Lema* Law unites a party to win an election, not to support a government. Between elections the pattern of factional behaviour is of shifting alliance whose permutations are rarely confined within a single *lema*. Predictably, supporting factions gradually defected, ministers were censured or resigned entailing cabinet reshuffles, and Pacheco had to seek new allies. By mid-1968, led by Vasconcellos, three Colorado factions were consistently opposing Pacheco: List 315, List 99, and Agrupación Pregón. Unidad y Reforma (List 15) voted to censure Jorge Peirano Facio in June 1969, and thereafter their support of the government became increasingly selective.

Pacheco could count on some Nationalist support. The

Herrerista group, Por la Unión del País, led by Alberto Gallinal Heber, usually voted with the government. Indeed, the emphasis on strong government, repression of trade-union activity, and cooperation with the IMF made common ground with Nationalist orientation. In August 1969 Pacheco had to approach Echegoyen in order to avoid personal censure in the Legislature. The manoeuvre exacerbated Colorado discontent. Apart from his tactics, his policies created resentment: the business community disliked the recession, and a crop of strikes in the winter of 1969 expressed labour's sufferings under the austerity programme. The Pacheco administration became widely disliked. His predilection for rule by decree greatly irritated the Legislature and the protracted impositions of security measures became a particular *casus belli*. Pacheco narrowly escaped censure in July 1971, when for the second time he reimposed the measures by decree after a legislative resolution had lifted them.

The Election Campaign of 1971

The further Pacheco departed from liberal democratic modes, the more vocal and active opposition from the left-wing ideological parties and trade unions became. His repressive and intolerant measures in dealing with them in turn strengthened their case against him. The old Colorado–National dichotomy blurred as the growth of left-wing opinion created a new polarization in which the traditional parties appeared to cluster on the right as defenders of an inegalitarian *status quo*. The activities of the Tupamaros, highly organized urban guerrillas, helped to discredit the Uruguayan establishment by exposing its corruptions and inefficiencies. The revitalized left, sensing their increased popular support, hoped to produce in Uruguay some echo of recent successes elsewhere in Latin America, particularly the victory of Allende in Chile. The problem of translating this climate of opinion into electoral terms was solved by the creation of the Frente Amplio de Izquierda in October 1970, a coalition of which Communists, Christian Democrats and Socialists formed a nucleus, and into which disaffected splinters of the traditional parties could be drawn.

Elections were due on 28 November 1971, Pacheco's fixed term expiring in March 1972. One issue dominated the campaign – for or against Pacheco. The Frente Amplio's open air rally of 26 March 1971 had a massive attendance; in an IUDOP poll the same month, 35 per cent of voters intended supporting the Frente. Their presidential candidate, General Liber Seregni (an ex-Colorado), running with Dr Juan José Crottogini, ex-Rector of the University, declared a programme of agrarian reform, takeover of private banks, active state participation in industry, takeover of most export business, re-establishment of relations with Cuba and a break with the IMF. By presenting a single slate, the Frente was the only party to offer a clear alternative to Pacheco.

An attempt to unite the traditional parties against this challenge failed. The Nationalist paper *El País* called for an inter-party coalition behind Alberto Gallinal Heber, but important factions of both parties rejected the suggestion, and Gallinal declined to stand. The Nationalists tried to reduce internal disunity by instituting a single party executive, under Dr Justo Alonso, in place of the 'official' board of Alberto Heber Usher and Echegoyen's 'parallel' board; but the UBD and Herreristas were still unable to agree on a single slate of electoral candidates. Gallinal's decision prompted General Mario Aguerrondo, a former police chief, to stand for president with Alberto Heber Usher, looking for support to Echegoyen's Alianza Nacionalista, Movimiento Herrera-Heber, and Gallinal's Por la Unión del País. This old guard team was opposed within the Nationalist Party by Wilson Ferreira Aldunate and Carlos Julio Pereira, leaders respectively of Por la Patria and Movimiento Nacional de

Rocha who were supported by a third *ubedista* group, Washington Beltrán's Unión Nacional Blanca. Ferreira looked a strong contender: basically a conservative Nationalist, he had established some common ground with the Frente by consistent opposition to Pacheco, hounding of business and police scandals, and a promise to nationalize the banks and re-establish relations with Cuba.

The Colorados faced the election deeply divided over *continuismo* – amending the Constitution to allow Pacheco a second term. Although a petition for the amendment in June 1971 received only 402,000 signatures, in August Pacheco announced his candidacy, and the Unión Colorada y Batllista became the Unión Nacional Reeleccionista. Commentators speculated that the election might not take place.

Pacheco faced a strong Colorado competitor. Jorge Batlle, List 15 leader, having supported Pacheco selectively, could expect a dual following of those preferring a more moderate policy, and those who broadly upheld Pacheco's policy but opposed his *continuismo*. With Batlle stood Renán Rodríguez. A third Colorado slate, entirely *anti-pachequista*, consisted of two ex-ministers, Vasconcellos and Manuel Flores Mora. Michelini and another ex-minister, Alba Roballo, left the *lema* and, like the Nationalist Rodríguez Camusso, joined forces with the Frente Amplio.

To strengthen his bid, Pacheco decreed a wage increase of 27 per cent in the private sector effective from 1 October 1971, and an interest-free loan to state employees.[15] He named as running-mate his Minister of Agriculture, the Ruralista Juan María Bordaberry, with Augusto Legnani as alternate candidate should the constitutional amendment fail. An opinion poll in October 1971 put the Colorados in the lead with 24 per cent compared with 21 per cent to the Frente and 15 per cent to the Nationalists.

15. Wage increases in the public sector are illegal in the year preceding an election.

The Results of the 1971 Election

From the standpoint of the traditional parties, the *Lema* Law was vindicated. On the first count,[16] Colorados aggregated 595,570 votes, Nationalists 585,974, and the Frente Amplio 276,636. Wilson Ferreira Aldunate received the biggest personal vote, but most-voted within the winning *lema* was the Pacheco-Bordaberry slate. As the constitutional amendment was not endorsed, Bordaberry was declared President-elect.

The Frente's 18 per cent share of the vote is remarkable compared with the showing of minor parties in previous elections (see p. 507), but disappointed their expectations particularly in Montevideo, where the mayoral victory went to the *pachequista* incumbent, Oscar Rachetti.

The result underlines the firm entrenchment of the two major parties. Traditional loyalties are difficult to erode – Uruguayans inherit Colorado or Nationalist allegiances – and voting patterns are strongly rooted too in the patron-client relationship which makes a voter's allegiance his guarantee of a smooth passage in the bureaucratic procedures which permeate so extensively the Uruguayan citizen's daily life.

Election Results of 28 November 1971
Votes cast 1,477,570

Parties	Number of votes obtained	% of votes cast
Colorado	595,570	4·20
Nacional	585,974	2·24
Frente Amplio*	276,636	0·69
Unión Radical Cristiano	7,402	0·25

*Frente Amplio used the *lema* Partido Demócrato Cristiano, to comply with the *Lema* Law.

January 1972

16. At the time of writing, January 1972, a recount is in progress.

LESLIE F. MANIGAT

Venezuela[1]

The existence of modern political parties, within the framework of a fair and well-regulated competition for power, is a
fairly recent phenomenon in Venezuela's political development. The homeland of the Libertador in fact experienced
throughout the nineteenth and for the first third of the
twentieth century a succession of military dictators, the last
few of whom all came with singular consistency from the
same part of the country – the Andean state of Tachira. The
era of modern political parties goes back no further than 1928,
when the struggle against Juan Vicente Gómez (1908–35),
one of the three dictators of the Tachira[2] 'old school', was intensified and properly organized. The creation of a Venezuelan Revolutionary Organization (ORVE) in opposition to

1. I should like to express my thanks to those Venezuelans in
public life who have been kind enough to give details, in private
conversation, of various aspects of Venezuelan party politics and
provide some useful biographical data. I should like to make an exception to the rules of discretion which I have generally observed in
respecting their anonymity, to express my gratitude to my friend
Boris Bunimov-Parra who was good enough to read through this text
and suggest corrections, without which a number of regrettable
errors of fact might have been overlooked, besides any such in-
voluntary mistakes which might remain, and for which I am of course
solely responsible.
2. In point of fact Tachira provided five successive strong men for
the country, but only three of them are considered by the Venezuelans to be true dictators.

the dictatorship marks the beginning of a new arrangement of the political chess-board. To this extent, the years 1928 to 1936 mark a turning point in the development of Venezuelan politics.

Until then, the country had been given over to pressure groups and action groups who competed with one another under the judicious eye of a 'soldier' who generally proved a worthy successor to Bolivar by fulfilling the latter's prophecy that after him the country would be 'delivered up to unscrupulous and narrow tyrants', although it must be said that while all lacked scruple, some of them were not so narrow, notably Guzmán Blanco and Juan Vicente Gómez, who died a septuagenarian in his bed, in the twenty-eighth year of his 'reign'. The process of modernization of the country really began under Gómez, thanks to the return of peace and the discovery of petroleum. Before him, politics were the affair of traditional political forces, usually in the service of the oligarchy and supported by landowners, professional groups, the clergy and above all the Army, or rather the praetorian guard which did duty for an army. Venezuela was not only the classic example of a country of social contrasts, it was also the country of military *pronunciamentos*. Even today, when parties exist and a new era in the history of political institutions has been inaugurated in the country, political life is still marked by the stigmata of the past. The parties are far from having exhausted the springs of political dynamism, and despite their existence the struggle for power still shows the signs of a taste for violence and of rivalry between individuals, a propensity towards dissension within political families and an exclusivist fervour on behalf of interest groups and individual personalities, who play just as important a part as ever in the conquest, preservation and transfer of power.

The development and full flowering of the political parties went hand in hand with the economic development of the country, based on its oil resources, in the first instance, and secondarily on iron. The new Venezuela with its political parties is therefore a Venezuela which has developed a new economy, based primarily on petroleum but to an increasing extent on iron, which has brought about a rapid growth along the Caribbean coast. This area includes the federal district which contains, in Caracas, the capital, and its surrounding area, almost one fifth of the entire population of the country. It also provides, around Lake Maracaibo, a second economic pole and centre of population responsible for two thirds of the country's petroleum production. On this same coast, to the east, facing Trinidad, is a third centre of the petroleum industry, comprising the states of Anzoategui and Monagas. The interior of the country, however, including most of the twenty states, is noticeably backward by comparison with this dynamic coastal area; this goes both for the *llanos* of the interior and the mountainous areas of the Andes.

Party politics have also developed in accordance with the results of this economic change, which have been twofold: on the one hand there has been a considerable expansion of the urban sector, which has had difficulty in absorbing the great population influx resulting from rural migration, and secondly the cost of living has greatly increased, so that Caracas now holds the record in this respect for the whole of the continent. The orientation of these parties has also been influenced by a dual external influence: on the one hand, the magnitude of foreign investments, mostly American, in the key oil sector, where total incomings (including royalties) account for two thirds of the government's income, and on the other hand Fidel Castro's Cuban revolution and the various attitudes taken towards it.

But the origins and explanation of the birth of the political parties must be sought in internal political developments. The students' strike which broke out in February 1928, and the period of political ferment which followed it from 1928 to 1936, brought the ORVE, the organization from which three

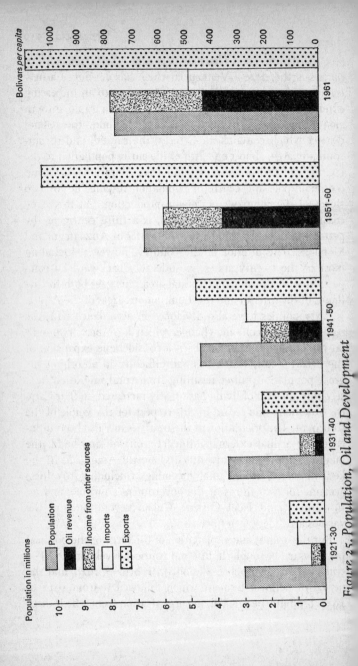

Figure 25. Population, Oil and Development

of Venezuela's biggest parties were born, to the forefront of the open struggle against the dictator Gómez. The men responsible for 1928 were to animate the country's political life, with various interruptions, up to the present day. This was the 'generation of 1928', with leaders such as Rómulo Betancourt and Raúl Leoni, founders and leading lights of the future Acción Democrática (AD), Jovito Villalba, founder and leading activist of the future Unión Republicana Democrática (URD) and, with reservations, since he does not belong properly speaking to the generation, Gustavo Machado, founder and chief of the future Partido Comunista Venezolano (PCV).

It should be pointed out at once that the most successful of the new parties set up were primarily those of the left and the centre, since the clientele of the right usually defends its interests directly at the level of government and administrative decision-making centres, through the medium of pressure groups such as the Fedecámaras (Association of Chambers of Commerce), the most powerful businessmen's organization in the country, and above all through traditional political forces and their connections with the higher clergy and the Army. It feels no need to provide itself with a party organizational structure, and in any case is unable to do so. In fact, faced with the success won by the new parties and the centre, the right itself attempted to set up left-wing parties, but these grand schemes did not bear the expected fruit. In 1958, for example, a group of businessmen and executives set up a group called Integración Republicana which has been referred to as a political party.[3]

The existence of political parties is considered in Venezuela as a victory for democracy. The parties do in fact enjoy legal recognition and have on several occasions formed a united front against dictatorship by temporarily sinking their dif-

3. It has since disappeared as a formal association, but its influence can still be felt in the person of some of its one-time members.

ferences. Until 1958, for instance, a Junta Patriótica was set up against the dictatorship of Pérez Jiménez, comprising Acción Democrática (AD), the Unión Republicana Democrática (URD), the Communists and the Christian party COPEI. Similarly the acute rivalry between the parties during the election campaign did not prevent the drafting of a plan for a coalition government with the object of preventing a return to dictatorship after the elections: this was the pact of Punto Fijo, drawn up in December 1958 between the three presidential candidates of the AD, the URD and the COPEI. But these frequently stormy coalitions did not long survive the pressures of power.

In reality, the political stability of the country is insecure: the problems facing this population of nine million (more than half of them under twenty-five years old and more than two thirds now living in cities) are multiplying. It is true that after a century of uneven development, Venezuela enjoys the highest income per head of the population of any country in South America, the biggest reserve of foreign exchange per head of any country in the world after Kuwait, thanks to its oil and iron, and has now had its currency, the bolivar, accepted by the International Monetary Fund as an international medium of exchange; but rural illiteracy is far from being eradicated, more than 13 per cent of the work force is unemployed, and the country comes a close second in the South American population-explosion table. All this gives considerable cause for concern, especially since Venezuela's self-imposed role as a counterweight to Castro's Cuba brings its own problems. It is hardly easy to safeguard representative democracy in such conditions. The AD in power has, however, attempted to preserve it, while ready to suspend constitutional guarantees and progressively outlaw, between 1962 and 1965, the Communist Party and the Movement of the Revolutionary Left (MIR), and to face up to the reappearance of urban 'terrorism' and the resurgence of the revolutionary guerrilla movement. Nevertheless, President Betancourt's achievement in handing over power, for the first time in Venezuelan history, at the end of his term to a successor regularly elected by direct universal suffrage, like himself, will not easily be repeated. If the political parties were to break the rules of the constitutional game and interrupt the normal functioning of constitutional institutions with violence, a sector of the Army might be tempted to forestall them in this and take over power itself. Four attempts at military uprisings in the last eight years, two 'conservative' and two 'progressive', are unequivocal signs of the precariousness of the current political regime.

Yet the party system continues to survive, and to help it to take root in the life and political customs of the Venezuelans and make identification easier for the electors, the law obliged each party to adopt an official colour during the period when all still enjoyed legal recognition: white for the AD, green for the COPEI, brown for the URD up till 1952, then yellow, and red for the PCV. Today, the fragmentation of these parties has brought more than a dozen parties and organizations into being, and all the colours of the rainbow would not suffice to represent every shade of the political spectrum.[4]

Until 1964, the bigger Venezuelan parties in the political arena could be broadly classed into three categories: (1) the parties of the government coalition: Acción Democrática (AD) and the Comité de Organización Política Electoral

4. As early as 1963 ballot papers carried a 'carnival of colours': black for the AD, yellow for the URD, green for the COPEI, a horse on a silver ground for the AD *en la oposición* which was to become the PRN (now superseded by the PRIN), navy blue and white for the FDP, blue for the Venezuelan Socialist Party, yellow and brown for the PAN, a Santiago cross on a white ground for the MAN, etc. The edition of 3 May 1967 of *El Nacional* had counted thirty-five parties and political groups intending to take part in the forthcoming elections of 1968.

Independiente (COPEI); (2) the parties of the so-called 'democratic' opposition, i.e. those accepting the rules of the parliamentary game, and regarding elections as the only legitimate means of achieving power: the Unión Republicana Democrática (URD) and the Acción Democrática en la oposición (ADop.) which was to become the Partido Revolucionario Nacionalista (PRN); (3) the parties of the revolutionary opposition doctrinally committed to violence as a means of acceding to power: the Partido Comunista Venezolano (PCV) and above all the Movimiento de la Izquierda Revolucionária (MIR), the group which first initiated guerrilla warfare.

It is doubtless significant that these parties should for some time have remained so distributed into groups with different approaches and attitudes. But this distribution no longer reflects contemporary realities, the political chess-board having been completely overthrown in the last two years. The first significant event in this respect was the break-up of the AD–COPEI coalition, with the latter organization taking up a tactical position of 'constructive opposition' following the victory of the AD candidate, Raúl Leoni, over the COPEI candidate Rafael Caldera in the 1963 presidential elections. Since then the AD has governed some of the time alone (from March to October 1964), some of the time with the URD and a recently formed political group, the National Democratic Front (FND), and then with the URD alone after the FND's withdrawal in March 1966. The comings and goings of supporting groups between the government and the opposition clearly make nonsense of any attempt at classification within the three general groupings mentioned above. The revolutionary opposition, for its part, has been divided on the tactical question of the usefulness of opportunity and necessity for rural guerrilla warfare. The dispute over Douglas Bravo, a dissident guerrilla commander expelled from the PCV, and the split in the MIR concerning the resistance fighters set one faction against the other in roughly equal proportions in both the Venezuelan revolutionary movements. On top of this, within the government coalition and in the ranks of the various opposition fronts, each party jealously preserves its own individuality. There can therefore be no substitute for a separate study of each.

Acción Democrática (AD)

Acción Democrática is the most powerful political party in Venezuela. It has provided a major stimulus to political life by institutionalizing the parties, and its own emergence provoked the formation of rival or hostile parties as a reaction.

Foundation

The origins of the AD go back to the revolutionary students' movement of the generation of 1928, later to become part of the Venezuelan Revolutionary Organization (ORVE) in opposition to the dictatorship. The first direct forerunner of the AD, however, was the National Democratic Party (PDN), born out of the ORVE after the break with the Communists. It is often said, indeed, that the AD is simply the PDN under a new name and in new format. It may be of interest to observe at this point that the AD is a left-wing party in origin, more precisely a revolutionary party with social-democratic leanings. Its founder and leader, Rómulo Betancourt, had been involved in the Communist movement before 1933, but broke with his erstwhile comrades at that time.

The AD was first constituted in 1940 and achieved legal recognition in September 1941, under the regime of President Medina Angarita. This is its official date of birth.

History

The history of the party was shortly to become one with the history of modern Venezuela. From 1941 to 1945 the AD grew rapidly, but the regime of Medina Angarita presented an obstacle to its accession to power, and even to its full expansion. In 1945, therefore, the AD took part in a coup d'etat together with young liberal army officers organized in the Patriotic Military Union. This was the AD's first experience of power, and its leader Betancourt presided over the half-civil, half-military junta from October 1945 to February 1948. This experience of power from 1945 to 1948, sharing responsibility with a faction of the younger officers in the Army – some of them active liberals – is of capital importance in the history of the AD. The party served its apprenticeship in practical administration, organized itself effectively and became known among the population while creating a democratic interlude in the succession of Venezuelan dictatorships. The party defined its position as 'to the left of the British Labour Party, but to the right of the Communists'. The elections organized by the junta ended in the victory of the great novelist Rómulo Gallegos, the AD's candidate; but he was overthrown and removed from power nine months later by that faction of the Army that was unhappy with the new direction in which the country was moving.

From 1948 to 1958, therefore, the AD was in opposition, and having been banned by the military junta was forced underground. It suffered merciless persecution from the junta, and then from the dictator Pérez Jiménez: two of its general secretaries were killed, a third died in prison, a fourth was arrested and incarcerated until the fall of the regime. The effects of this period of suppression also included the disorganization of the party and its loss of ground among the working class and the student population, wooed by other influences which had managed to get themselves accepted by the reigning power. On the other hand, persecution made the party more dynamic and combative and marked it out as the dictatorship's number one adversary, together with its then ally the URD.

The elections of 1958, held after Pérez Jiménez's overthrow, brought to power the AD's leader Rómulo Betancourt, victorious over his great left-wing rival, Rear-Admiral Wolfgang Larrazabal, a leading figure in the provisional government. After 13 February 1959 the AD was in power, first under Rómulo Betancourt's presidency, which lasted until 1964, then under his successor Raúl Leoni (1964–9). The exercise of power left its mark on the AD, which became recognizably a government party. Its opponents claim, not without justice, that the AD in power was an entirely different animal from the AD of before 13 February 1959.

Organization and Recruitment

From the first, the AD was a party of personalities. Great names could be found in the upper echelons of the party and its governing bodies, such as the writer and ex-President Rómulo Gallegos; the founder of the Organization of Oil-Exporting Countries (OPEC), Dr Pérez Alfonso; the Chairman of CEPAL (Economic Commission for Latin America), José Antonio Mayobre; the poet Andrés Eloy Blanco; the majority party leader in Parliament and party chairman Gonzalo Barrios; and the architects of AD policy on education, Luis Prieto Figueroa, economics and finance, Carlos d'Ascoli, and internal affairs, Luis Augusto Dubuc – not to mention Rómulo Betancourt, the party's founder, hero, and chief theoretician. As a government party, the AD had a strong organizational structure and most public officials belonged to it, which ensured it a powerful representation in the provinces. The rank and file was recruited primarily from among the peasants, the AD's staunchest supporters; the working class, amongst whom its position, once preponderant, remained very strong outside the Marxist unions; and finally from progressive circles in the middle and upper class.

Through its period in exile (1948–58) the AD became accustomed to operating inside the country from two types of base: firstly it possessed basic units or cells, organized with considerable audacity even in the prisons (*grupos de cárceles*), and secondly it was able to rely on the authority of its organizers, the initiative of its officers, and the dynamism of its leaders. These are two primary characteristics of the party organization – the democratic nature of discussion and decision-making procedure within the AD, and the important part played by the leadership in the actual taking of decisions. This is doubtless also a legacy of the party's original Marxist training and inspiration. Moreover, the period of exile helped the AD to establish useful international contacts and set up centres of activity in Buenos Aires, in Mexico (under Rómulo Gallegos), in Santiago, in New York, in San Juan de Puerto Rico, in Havana (where Rómulo Betancourt lived until the fall of Prío Socorras in 1952), and above all in San José de Costa Rica where the External Coordination Committee had its headquarters. The party was even able to hold a general assembly of its leaders in exile in Puerto Rico – the 1956 Conference of Exiles.

The emphasis placed on the need for organization was expressed in the directive of 'a branch of the party in every village and every hamlet'.

There can be no doubt that the party organization, together with the personality of Rómulo Betancourt, was the chief architect of the AD's election victories. The party organization adapted itself to the administrative structure of the country, divided into twenty states (plus two federal territories), one hundred and fifty districts and six hundred and fifty parishes; the Federal District of Caracas, the capital, is a separate entity. The organigram of the AD broadly conforms to this administrative pattern, pairing the party's regional institutions with national bodies, with a deliberative assembly, an executive body and a disciplinary body at each level. This organizational structure is fairly flexibly articulated: the deliberative Assembly, which has general responsibility, by comparison with the two permanent but more specialized bodies, is the supreme authority at its level, while still permitting consultation with or appeal to the superior level, so that the district organization includes and governs the parish organization, that of the state includes and governs that of the district, and finally the national organization includes and governs that of the states.

The smallest unit in the party is the 'basic group' including a maximum of one hundred active members divided into sectors of twenty members each. The group meeting, which takes place two or four times per month by statute, is the fundamental base of the party (Article 86 of the party Statutes). The permanent organization at local level consists of a local committee of at least three members, one of whom is concerned with organization and propaganda, the second with industrial and agricultural labour, and the third with finance. The 'basic group' is the party cell which, as has been mentioned, continued in clandestine existence under the dictatorship, even in the prisons.

The cells of each parish are grouped together at municipal level. The party's organization at this level consists of a municipal assembly, which is the ruling body at this level, the municipal committee, which is the executive body, and the municipal disciplinary commission, which is self-explanatory. The members of these bodies are elected by a general assembly consisting of delegates from all the basic groups.

The pattern is the same at district and state level, as has been seen, with a general assembly or convention, an executive committee and a disciplinary commission. Each state has a section of the AD, as does the federal district and the federal territories. One special feature should be noted, however, concerning liaison between the bodies: at state level, the section holds a convention once a year, consisting of three delegates per district, plus two delegates of the party's national office. It sits two or three months before the national general assembly of the party, and lays down the state party's policy and organization for the national assembly.

There are four national bodies, comprising the party's superior authorities: the national convention, the national steering committee, the national executive committee and the national disciplinary tribunal. At this level, the object seems to have been, apart from ensuring party unity and the smooth functioning of the apparatus, to enable the wishes of the rank and file to reach the leadership easily, by emphasizing the three social groups which the AD is eager to encourage, notably the rural sector, the trade-union sector, and the youth sector, all of which also have their own assemblies. Besides these, certain states are over-represented on some specialized bodies, to take account of real disparities in size and importance by comparison with the others. These are the Federal District of Caracas and the states of Libertador and Miranda. The administrative machine is consequently complex and clumsy.

According to Article 24 of the party Statutes, the national convention meets once a year in ordinary session. It may, if necessary, hold an extraordinary session at the request of a majority of the sections or on the initiative of the national steering committee or the national executive committee. This national convention is the party's supreme authority: it defines party doctrine, programme and general strategy and appoints the members of the national executive committee and the national disciplinary tribunal. It consists of delegates from the local parties (one delegate to every two thousand members), and also the party's national and regional officers, i.e. the members of the national steering committee (one hundred and twenty), those of the national disciplinary tribunal (ten) and the secretaries of section executive committees (sixty, or three per section).

The national steering committee (see Articles 28–34 of the Statutes) is the supreme authority in the interval between sessions of the national convention. It defines tactics and makes any readjustments that may be necessary. It meets at least twice a year, but extraordinary sessions may be convoked by the national executive committee or at the written request of seven sections. The national steering committee has one hundred and twenty members, including the chairman of the disciplinary tribunal, the members of the national executive committee and the representatives of two other committees, the committee for trade-union and peasant affairs and the national youth committee. Most of the members of the national steering committee, however, come from the states, each of which contributes two members, i.e. the section general secretary and a permanent delegate elected by the section.

The national executive committee (NEC) is the responsible body in the interval between sessions of the national steering committee (Articles 35–61). Its members are elected by the national convention. The NEC is a full-time body, which meets twice a month in full session. It includes the chairman, the two vice-chairmen, the general secretary and the assistant general secretary of the party, four political secretaries and fourteen administrative secretaries. The general secretary of the executive committee for the federal district and his colleague representing the department of Libertador also participate in the work of the NEC, which indicates the preponderance of these regions in the life of the country and of the party.

The NEC itself covers several specialized bodies: the national political committee, the national secretariat and the three working bureaux.

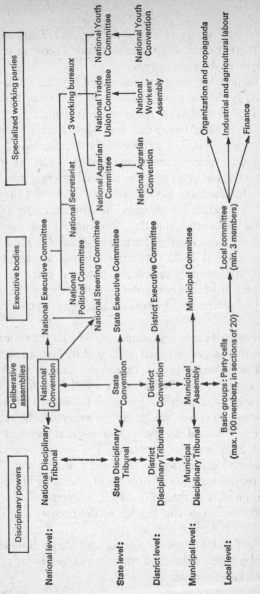

Figure 26. Organigram of the AD in 1966

The national political committee (eleven voting members) is the core of the party leadership, comprising the chairman, the two vice-chairmen, the general secretary, the four political secretaries and the three secretaries for organization, labour and agriculture. The political bureau meets once a week (usually on a Tuesday at four in the afternoon), but may be convoked more often by the chairman, the general secretary, or at the request of three members.

The role of the national secretariat (sixteen members) is primarily administrative. It includes the general secretary, the assistant general secretary and the fourteen administrative secretaries, and forms the nucleus of the party bureaucracy. It meets once a fortnight, or is convoked specially by the general secretary or at the request of three members. The fourteen administrative secretaries deal with party affairs in connection with youth, agriculture, public relations, education and culture, international affairs, the press, propaganda, finance, Parliament and local government, political studies and doctrine, economic and technical affairs and community development.

Within this complex web, the make-up of the three working bureaux is rather special. The national trade-union committee, which meets once a fortnight, includes sixteen members: the secretary for labour and his assistant, the secretary for labour of the department of Libertador, one of the political secretaries and the twelve national labour leaders appointed by the party's workers' assembly, the Pleno Sindical Nacional. The national agrarian committee, which also meets once a fortnight, includes nine members: the secretary for agriculture and his assistant, a political secretary, the agrarian secretary of the state of Miranda and five agricultural leaders chosen by the party's agrarian convention, the Pleno Agraria Nacional. Finally, the national youth committee has eleven members: the youth secretary and his assistant, a political secretary, the youth secretary for the department of Libertador and seven youth leaders appointed by the youth convention of the party, the Pleno Juvenil Nacional.

The AD's fourth national body is the national disciplinary committee, the members of which are appointed by the national convention. The NDC consists of five judges and five assistants. They make the final decision on when and whether to apply the following sanctions: censure and general warning; temporary suspension; removal from office; and finally expulsion.

In practice, the AD has from time to time found it necessary to create new extra-statutory *ad hoc* national bodies, like the 'Commando electoral' that operated during the 1958 and 1963 elections as a central coordinating body controlling all matters relating to the conduct of the elections (financing the campaign, propaganda material, political education of the electorate, organizing the selection of candidates and choosing observers for the elections).

The AD keeps close links with the other Latin American parties of a similar political colouring, which together make up the political family of socially reformist and politically liberal democrats of Latin America: José Figueras's Liberación Nacional in Costa Rica, Muñoz Marín's Partido Popular Democrático in Puerto Rico. They have a common press mouthpiece, the weekly *Combate*. In Caracas itself, the AD publishes or controls the daily *La República* and the monthly review *Política*. Finally, the periodical publication *Acción Democrática* informs the membership on the party's activities and current watchwords.

Doctrine

The AD has had the opportunity of defining its doctrine in the various fields of Venezuelan public life and applying its ideas when in power. Its ideology does seem to have evolved from the militant left towards the centre left, or at any rate in the direction of restraint, moderation and realism. At first the socialist emphasis was very marked. Today, the AD has a doctrinal platform which amounts to a liberal and progressive reformism. It likes to call itself 'social' and 'democratic', but there is no lack of advocates of a 'return to the grass roots' in its ranks.

On the political level, the AD is a supporter of liberal democracy and repudiates all personal autocratic power. A party that has fought against dictatorship, the AD extended its anti-fascism to the international plane by its hostility to the regime of Franco in Spain and Trujillo in the Dominican Republic. Its political liberalism is of the nineteenth-century European type, upholding political liberties (freedom of the press, of speech, of assembly and of religion) and civil rights (such as habeas corpus, voting rights) within the framework of a regime that ensures the rule of law. The AD's ideal is therefore 'representative democracy' in the sense understood in the Inter-American Declaration of Santiago de Chile. Generally speaking, moreover, the AD proclaims its fidelity to the principles of the OAS. This doctrinal position goes hand in hand with a militant anti-Communism, sharpened by the spectacular and unremitting duel with the Cuban revolution. It is alleged by its adversaries that anti-Castroism has led the AD to move closer to those conservative positions against which it once fought. At all events, the AD in power outlawed the Venezuelan Communist Party and the Castroist-inspired MIR, in reaction against the waves of terrorism and armed uprisings unleased by the extreme left. These two parties were declared unqualified to operate legally, a euphemism equivalent in practice to a legal prohibition.

Being a liberal organization, the AD wanted to abolish the anomaly of an army effectively constituting a state within a state. Hence its early anti-militarism, as some people have termed it, underlined on the political plane by the Betancourt doctrine of non-recognition of regimes resulting from military coups. The AD has in practice been primarily concerned to emphasize the need for army loyalty to the constitutional government, and has assigned it a useful practical role in the construction of a democratic Venezuela.

In the field of economic affairs, the AD supports the mixed-economy system, that is to say an economy with strong public and private sectors. Its programme is designed to safeguard the rights of free enterprise generally. It therefore encouraged the formation of the Cavendes (CA Venezolana de Desarrollo), a private development fund for Venezuela. The AD is not in principle hostile to foreign investment, quite the contrary. Nevertheless, its doctrine shows signs of its dual preoccupation with nationalism and interventionism. Its nationalism is expressed in terms of tariff protectionism, and through the fifty-fifty system by which foreign oil companies may never receive a share of the annual profits greater than that received by the Venezuelan state. Its interventionism is revealed in the growth of state control over the economy and the creation of national corporations like that for oil, or the Orinoco Steelworks and the Venezuelan Petrochemical Institute, all owned by the state.

To pull the country out of its under-development, the AD advocates diversification of the economy, notably by industrialization. Besides the oil industry, other industries have begun to emerge, such as the iron and steel industry, for example, controlled and guided by the Corporación de Fomento, which has now become the Corporación de Guayana. At the same time, the AD has made efforts to improve agricultural machinery and techniques in order to increase peasant productivity, as a corollary to land reform.

Finally, in the social field the AD has set itself up as the champion of land reform on the basis of the principle of 'the land to those who work it'. The sharing-out of the *latifundia* was to be accomplished by the extension of rural credit facilities. This mode of land reform, entirely reformist in conception, included compensation for the big dispossessed landowners, the whole operation being financed by petroleum royalties. The AD also supported the recognition of social rights for workers (education and professional training, trade unions, the right to strike), and an advanced social legislation providing a fully-fledged welfare state. In practice, however, it has often been accused of sacrificing the rights of the workers to the need to protect and encourage foreign investment. Above all, it has been reproached for its movement towards a technocratic, pro-American attitude, and for having abandoned its original anti-imperialist position. At all events, land reform, costly and incomplete, does not seem to have given the expected results, except that 80,000 families have received 1,500,000 hectares from the National Agrarian Institute since 1959. As for its attitude towards the USA, the AD has declared it to be 'patriotically firm, but free from aggressiveness or mindless hostility'.

Electoral Strength

The AD remained for a long time at the top of the list in the various election battles, but its percentage of the vote has steadily fallen since 1946. It is true that this falling-off has coincided with an increase in the number of Venezuelan political parties and with a series of splits within the AD itself. In elections during the period 1946–8, it alone obtained between 70 and 78 per cent of the votes. In 1958, it obtained 49·45 per cent of the votes cast, and in the presidential elections of December 1963 32·81 per cent of the votes cast, or 957,699 votes.

The party's electoral support is drawn chiefly from the rural areas, where it controls the Peasants' Federation, even after the defection, in 1962, of some of the federation's leaders. The AD also controls a number of important labour unions. It has strong support in intellectual and professional circles and organizes a majority of minor officials and civil servants in both the central and local administrations. On the other hand, it is in a minority in the universities, among the more conservative sectors of the population, and in general in the federal district and the surrounding states. It is also weak in the Andean states. Its two great bastions are the Maracaíbo region and the *llanos*.

The AD has been weakened by a series of splits on the left. The breakaway tendency in the party has generally been conditioned by a threefold set of differences: generation conflicts, personality conflicts, and ideological conflicts. The split which gave birth to the Revolutionary Nationalist Party was the result of a generation and personality conflict. A conflict of generation and ideology explains the split which gave birth to the Movement of the Revolutionary Left (Movimiento de la Izquierda Revolucionária, or MIR).

Until 1968, the AD was still in power, under President Raúl Leoni, whose policy was to ensure continuity with the preceding government of Rómulo Betancourt. His general secretary was Jesús Pazgalarraga, but the man chosen to bear the party's standard in the 1968 elections was Gonzalo Barrios, ex-General Secretary of the AD, and ex-Minister of the Interior from 1964 to mid-November 1966. His candidature was in rivalry with that of Luis Beltrán Prieto Figueroa, who was even more of an organization man than he was himself. It would seem that behind this personal rivalry a real political and ideological gap has developed, for the left wing of the party supported Luis Beltrán Prieto, who was more firm in his intention to explore new avenues in the field of social advance and economic and political nationalism.

Comité de Organización Política Electoral Independiente (COPEI)

The Comité de Organización Política Independiente (COPEI) is a Christian Democratic party which became Social Christian as a result of a very marked slide towards the left, especially among the younger members of the party.

Foundation

The origins of the COPEI go back to 1936 with the establishment of a Catholic student association, following a dispute in the Federation of Venezuelan Students. The occasion for this dispute was the debate over the expulsion of Venezuelan Jesuits, against which the Catholic youth protested. The idea then took shape of forming an organized political force, a notion already entertained by some Catholics in 1928, hostile to the predominant left-wing group in the ORVE, and on an international level hostile (after 1936) to the Spanish Republic.

Originally a conservative and clerical party, the Venezuelan 'Catholic party' called itself Electoral Action under Medina Angarita, and then National Action up until 1946. It was at that time a party said to be inspired by the Spanish Falange, and certainly supported by the Andean landowners.

The official date of birth of the COPEI was the year 1946. Under its founder Rafael Caldera, the party developed fairly rapidly towards a left-wing Christian position, while still bearing the marks of its conservative origins, which today it would like to forget. Its first political bureau was presided over by Pedro del Corral, but the real power behind the scenes was Caldera.

History

From 1946 to 1948, the COPEI at first represented the conservative opposition to the AD, which it accused of Marxist tendencies. It is therefore not surprising that some members of the party collaborated, between 1948 and 1950, with the military regime which took over power by a coup d'etat against the new president Rómulo Gallegos. This is indicative of the party's position at that time.

In 1950, the COPEI joined the opposition to Pérez Jiménez. It was one of the first, and one of the few, parties to denounce the regime of Pérez Jiménez, in an open letter on 20 June 1952, for its totalitarian nature and concentration-camp methods. Nevertheless in at least three states, those of Tachira, Aragua and Yaracuy, the party organization continued to support Pérez Jiménez until the end of his regime. This ambiguity seems to be due rather to the opposing trends in the party's ideology and support than to a political accident. At all events, the majority of the party became progressively more radical in its opposition to the dictatorship, and its adoption of a resolutely left-wing position resulted in the desertion of those conservative elements attracted by the early collaboration with the regime of Pérez Jiménez.

From 1958 to 1963 the COPEI supported and collaborated with the Betancourt government. This constancy in its collaboration with the AD, up to 1964, has indeed operated in its favour. It maintained and nurtured this collaboration not only because it shares common principles with the AD in the field of basic reforms, to be put into effect by democratic means, but also through its concern to contribute to the stabilization of democratic political life in Venezuela. This is also the policy advocated by the World Christian Democratic Congress held in August 1964 in Santiago de Chile, which recommended alliances with Social Democratic parties. The tactical split in 1964, however, resulted in a general slide in COPEI doctrine and activity towards an increasingly militant left-wing position, which went as far as reproaching the AD for timidity in its social policy.

Organization and Recruitment

The COPEI is subject to the authority of one undisputed leader, its general secretary and founder Rafael Caldera. The party is clearly more close-knit than the AD. Since the departure of the conservatives, it has maintained and reinforced its own unity, and while there are shades of opinion and even factions within the COPEI, it has never suffered from the fragmentation which has been a feature of the AD's history. It has moreover adopted the latter party's structure and rules more or less exactly, in order to be in a better position to measure up to it. Like the AD, it also profited by the influence and patronage conferred by power to extend and consolidate its bases in the hinterland.

The party, which is still progressing from strength to strength, has taken trouble to train young leaders from the rural and industrial working class. The rank and file is recruited chiefly from student circles, which provide the most dynamic party militants; the peasant masses of the Andean states, where the COPEI is strongly entrenched; the lower and middle bourgeoisie which provide the party officers; and from some working-class sectors responsive to the 'Christian' label, although the party is weakly represented in the trade unions. In expectation of an electoral victory, which the party's strategists consider to be close, the emphasis has been placed on the need to strengthen the party's organization, from the basic cells right up to the summit of the hierarchy, and to widen the base of the party in the working class not only by increasing its influence in the Confederación de Trabajadores del Venezuela, where the

COPEI is represented by three members on the executive committee, but by consolidating its hold on the trade-union confederation CODESA, affiliated to the Confederación Latino-Americana de los Sindicatos Cristianos (CLASC).

The COPEI runs several publications. The most important, entitled simply *COPEI*, is the party's official journal. It also keeps very closely in touch with other democratic and social Christian parties on the continent, and is an important link in the International set up by Social Christian Democracy.

Doctrine

The COPEI programme has become steadily more radical, evolving hand in hand with its general position on the Venezuelan political chess-board. It is significant that it first called itself Christian Democrat, and now prefers the title Social Christian. Its current pogramme may be summarized in the formula 'basic reforms with democracy', which calls to mind President Frei's slogan of 'revolution with liberty'. In fact, in the political field the COPEI, like the AD, wishes to promote a libertarian ideal. It is a democratic party, firmly anti-totalitarian, and determined to combat all forms of dictatorship. It is also resolutely anti-communist. It is true that there is a faction in the COPEI, influenced by the position taken up by its Chilean and Dominican counterparts, which today regards itself as anti-imperialist. At all events the party considers itself nationalist with regard to the United States and socialist with regard to the spokesmen of Venezuelan big capital, the Mendozas and Vollmers.

In the economic sphere, the COPEI's development has brought it close to the positions cherished by the AD: mixed economy (joint public and private sectors), within which the state plays the general role of guide and controller, increase of productivity and diversification of production in accordance with the methods of the Alliance for Progress, protection of natural resources and defence of the national interest.

In the social sphere, the COPEI has come out against the oligarchy and in favour of more vigorous implementation of land reform. Its social doctrine is based on the protection of marriage and the family, the development of community spirit, the extension of education, and accelerated modernization of the transport and communications network to the benefit of the interior. Being a social Christian party, the COPEI emphasizes the dignity of the person, and the social function of property. It is in this spirit that it advocates structural reforms to bring about, in Caldera's words, the disappearance of social stratification through class collaboration. Is this perhaps a sign of a search for a doctrinal 'third course'? It is interesting to note the close links being forged between the COPEI and the Latin American Confederation of Christian Trade Unions (CLASC), which has its headquarters in Caracas and proclaims itself positively anti-imperialist, and even anticapitalist.

Finally, as a Christian Party the COPEI advocates harmony between State and Church in mutual respect and liberty. To sum up, the COPEI has the reputation of being relatively more moderate than its Chilean and Dominican counterparts, and its alliance with the AD has often been held responsible for the latter's general change of course towards centrist if not conservative positions. At the moment, however, under the influence of the younger party workers and even of Caldera himself, the party strategist and theoretician, the great mass of the party seems strongly to favour development towards a form of socialism inspired by Christian ideals.

Electoral Strength

Between 1946 and 1947, the party won 13 per cent of the votes. These were modest beginnings by comparison with the results obtained by its then adversary, the AD, but nevertheless promising. In 1958, it won 15.2 per cent of the total vote. The COPEI is the only one of the big Venezuelan parties to have increased its electoral strength between 1958 and 1963. In the 1963 presidential elections, its founder, then a candidate for the presidency, won a total of 588,372 votes, or 20.19 per cent of the votes cast. It thus became the second largest political party in the country.

The COPEI has always enjoyed stronger support in the country than in the towns. Its bastions, from the beginning, were the three Andean states, especially Tachira and Merida. In 1958 it only had candidates returned to Parliament in four non-Andean states; outside the Andes, therefore, it was weak. By 1963, however, it managed to get Deputies elected in fourteen non-Andean states. The party has made marked progress since 1958.

Apart from the peasantry, a large proportion of the middle classes and professional people generally support it, and it has won a dominant position in the universities. Seven years of power shared with the AD do not seem to have brought about even a gradual erosion of its voting strength. This is the party for foreign observers to watch, if no major obstacles arise before the Venezuelan presidential elections of 1968, to determine the successor to Raúl Leoni, who, as we have seen, has not enjoyed the COPEI support granted to Rómulo Betancourt.

However, the COPEI's position is not entirely free from difficulties. In spite of the pressures placed on it, the party refused to join a grand anti-AD front, promoted by Uslar Pietri (FND), W. Larrazabal (FDP) and a recently formed group, the PRIN, but supported most significantly by the

Marxist parties, who would like, if not to control the Front at least to provide its driving force. The reason for this refusal is that the Social Christians would like to preserve the candidature of their leader, Rafael Caldera, in the race for the 1968 presidential succession. It is known that the opposition parties consider Caldera's candidature to be 'divisionist', but the COPEI leader is convinced that the natural operation of the system should ensure that it will soon be 'his turn', given the steady drop in the AD's popularity, whittled away during its years in power, and the continuous rise of the COPEI, which came second to the declining AD in the last elections. Even the offer of a pact according to which the party which gained the largest number of votes in the forthcoming parliamentary elections, out of all the parties in the broad front set up to dislodge the AD from power, would nominate the Front's single candidate in opposition to the AD in 1968 does not seem to have overcome Caldera's fears, since he is inclined to view this as a manoeuvre to oust him from a candidature of which he is assured as long as he keeps the COPEI on its present course.

Unión Republicana Democrática (URD)

In 1958 the URD was the second biggest of the major Venezuelan political parties.

Foundation

The origins of the URD go back to the Venezuelan Democratic Party (PDV) set up during Medina Angarita's presidency, and which was the 'official' party until Medina's fall in 1945. Since the PDV had acquired a good deal of discredit through its close association with the fallen regime, the liberal faction in the party reorganized and on 18 December 1945 took the name of Unión Republicana Democrática, which shortly came under the leadership of Jovito Villalba. The latter, one of the generation of 1928, made an explosive entry into Venezuelan politics at the time of the students' strike against Gómez, and was president of the Venezuelan Students' Federation in 1936. The leadership of the new party included a defector from the AD, Inocente Palacios, and men like Isaac Pardo and Elías Toro.

Having started life as a simple political pressure-group, the URD became a new political party in two months, and in February 1946 it applied for legal recognition as such. This was its official date of birth. The object of the URD's foundation was to combat the hegemony of Democratic Action. It acquired the support of a number of well-known public figures such as J. M. Domínguez Chacín, Ignacio Luis Arcaya, Humberto Bartoli, Luis Hernández Solis and Alfredo Tane Murzi. The latter was soon to leave the party and enter his name in the electoral list of the AD.

History

The history of the party may be summarized as a gradual evolution from the centre towards the left. From 1945 to 1948 the URD was in opposition to the junta presided over by Rómulo Betancourt. In 1948 it therefore supported the military government which overthrew President Rómulo Gallegos, and participated in that government until the assassination of Delgado Chalbaud. This political crime, which paved the way to open military dictatorship, drove the URD back into opposition. From this time on, the party joined wholeheartedly in the merciless struggle against the dictatorship of Pérez Jiménez. As the AD was outlawed, the URD in fact benefited from the tactical support of that party's clandestine organization, which gave it the mass of its voting support in the 1952 elections. On the first ballot, the URD won 54 per cent of the votes. To prevent it enjoying the fruits of its victory, Pérez Jiménez annulled the elections and embarked on a campaign of arbitrary arrest, imprisonment and persecution of URD members, ending up by banning the party altogether.

In 1958, the party put forward Rear-Admiral Wolfgang Larrazabal, the dominant personality in the government junta supported by the Communists, as its candidate, as the only possible counter-attraction to the personality of Rómulo Betancourt. The results of the elections placed the URD second after the AD in the order of the political parties, classified according to the number of votes cast.

As a result of the anti-dictatorship Pact of Punto Fijo between the candidates of the AD, the COPEI and the URD, signed in December 1958, the latter party became a member of the government coalition and received the portfolios of Foreign Affairs, Labour and Communications and Transport. The party's collaboration with the AD had its conflicts, in particular with regard to the distribution of key posts in the administration and the balance of influence among the three parties of the coalition.

The break came during the seventh conference of Western Foreign Ministers, held in San José de Costa Rica, on the Cuban question. The chancellor Ignacio Luis Arcaya refused to sign the San José Declaration, and was replaced by Falcón Briceno. Arcaya's resignation finally brought the URD into opposition, because it refused to associate itself with an anti-Cuban government policy.

The party has continued to harden its line since 1960, and its verbally violent hostility to government policy has brought it closer to the MIR and the PCV, although an ideological gulf still separates them from these avowedly Marxist and revolutionary parties, which both support the use of violence. However, the expulsion of its left wing in

1964 was the outward manifestation of a pendulum effect by which the URD has moved towards a more conciliatory attitude to the government coalition since that date.

Organization and Recruitment

The URD is often represented as a party of personalities. Its chairman is Dionisio López Orihuela. But the most striking personalities in its leadership are Jovito Villalba, the party's general secretary, and the former chancellor, Ignacio Luis Arcaya. The URD is strongly represented throughout the country, and it is impossible to pick out any one particular social milieu from which it draws its support.

After 1960, the party gained reinforcements from the Venezuelan left, especially from the Proletarian Revolutionary Party (PRP). The leaders of these new recruits made their presence felt by a more systematic approach to organization with the object of creating a mass party, but after a power-struggle with the moderate wing for control of the party machine, which they hoped to influence towards a radical left-wing approach, they were defeated and expelled in 1963 and 1964. Among the victims were Fabricio Ojeda, one of the heroes of the militant struggle against Pérez Jiménez's dictatorship, Luis Miquelena, José Herrera Oropeza and José Vincente Rangel.

The URD has won a following among the workers and peasants on the one hand, and the progressive middle class on the other. In 1958, the impressive results obtained in the presidential elections gave it the reputation, until 1963, of being the biggest party after the AD. Its main strongholds then were the Federal District of Caracas and the surrounding states, where the party won a comfortable majority. This might have been ascribable to a close-knit organization with a full network of branches in the poorer areas, particularly since the party adopted the same organizational pattern as the AD to make it more competitive with the latter. But in 1963 the URD proved impotent even to retain control of Caracas. The great swell of support in 1958, far from being due to an exceptionally efficient organization, seems more rationally imputable to the personality of Larrazabal. At all events, the URD seems to have lost considerable impetus in electoral terms. The party has now been taken in hand again by Jovito Villalba and given a new direction, after the departure of the wing that sympathized and even wanted to collaborate with the extreme left-wing parties, the PCV and the MIR, which called itself the party's Young Avant-Garde. The URD is now placing its stake on its participation in the government to increase its influence in the country. The problem is to decide whether the accusation of opportunism will have tarnished its image in the eyes of the electors, and especially with the working class, whose old soft spot for the party still ensures it two seats on the executive committee of the CTV.

Doctrinal Position

The political credo of the URD has undergone a marked evolution during the party's existence. Initially, it represented itself as a nationalist and democratic party. It advocated constitutional reform to have the President elected by the people, and to adopt proportional representation in parliamentary elections. It regarded itself as belonging to the moderate left, proposed rational industrialization with greater national control of oil resources, expansion of education among the poorer classes, and social welfare to be made the concern of the state. At the same time, however, it did not mince words in its criticism of what it considered to be the 'socialist' programme of the AD, and declared itself opposed to the class struggle and in favour of national reconciliation. It was at that time therefore a 'liberal' organization.

Before long the URD found itself adopting positions on a variety of subjects that were close to those of the AD, but this only accentuated its rivalry with the dominant party. The turning point came in 1958, when the URD put forward the candidature of Wolfgang Larrazabal, in alliance with the Communists. The party's revolutionary radicalism became more and more marked. The Cuban question provided an opportunity of making a resounding contribution to the cause, predictably enough in view of its nationalist outlook and its firm attachment to the principles of non-intervention and anti-imperialism. From that time on, the logic of its opposition to the Betancourt government, which it considered subservient to the United States, forced the URD to make a systematic analysis of its anti-imperialist position. The activist wing of the party, as we have seen, almost openly espoused Marxist principles. Recent developments have put a brake on this hardening of the party's ideological line. The URD is intent on staying part of the non-Marxist left. Its return to the government is in blatant contradiction to the professions of faith made by Arcaya after San José. It was at this time that the party's left-wing dissidents formed the Popular Nationalist Avant-Garde, whose loss to the party weakened the URD's position among young people and in the proletariat.

The URD backs or owns a few newspapers, including URD, its official journal, and *Clarín*, which disappeared with the expulsion of Miquelena.

Electoral Strength

The URD's beginnings, from 1946 to 1948, were humble. It hardly managed more than 3 per cent of the votes cast. Then came the great period of struggle against the Jiménez dictatorship, followed by the support for Larrazabal: this was when the party was at its height. Until 1963, as has been indicated, the URD was considered the second largest political party in Venezuela. It has since suffered a distinct drop in popularity, even in the federal capital where it got most of its votes. In the 1963 presidential elections, its general secretary received 551,120 votes, or less than 19 per cent of the total number of votes cast. However, the URD, still fired by its old ambitions, will not readily resign itself to playing second fiddle to the AD for ever.

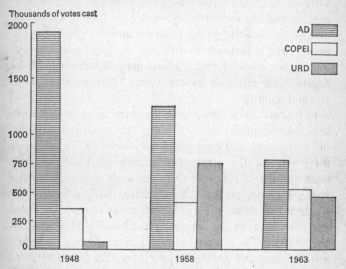

Figure 27. Votes Cast for the Main Parties 1948–63

Partido Revolucionario Nacionalista (PRN)

The Revolutionary Nationalist Party, the result of an internal split in the AD, has had a very brief history. It has now ceased to exist, most of its support going to make up the following of the PRIN, a very recent political formation. All the same, it is of interest to consider its brief intervention in Venezuelan politics.

Foundation and History

The PRN owed its origins to a faction in the AD hostile to the 'Old Guard'. First and foremost, the problem presented itself as a generation conflict for the control of the party : the 'Young Turks' protested against the annexation of all key positions by the generation of 1928. This generation conflict, however, disguised a real conflict of principle. Initial expulsion, in 1948, was shortly followed by reunification in the struggle against the military dictatorship. However, the old wound was imperfectly healed, and another break came in 1961, when the AD was in power under Betancourt, whose reforms were criticized by the Young Turks for their tardiness and timidity.

In January 1962, two national conventions of the AD were held, one organized by the Young Turks and the other by the Old Guard, and each group announced the expulsion of the leaders of the other, each considering itself the only representative of AD orthodoxy and authenticity. What the younger group, or ARS, held against the Old Guard was its departure from the 1958 programme, and it criticized the alliance with the conservative Christian Democrats of the COPEI. The national electoral court delivered a judgement of Solomon on the dispute : the Old Guard retained the right to use the label AD, adding the abbreviation Gob., which signified the AD in power, while the ARS were also granted the right to use the AD label if they added Op., meaning the AD in opposition. This was on the understanding that the 1963 elections would determine which faction should resume the exclusive title to the initials AD.

In February 1964, the ARS (or the old AD Op.) officially adopted the label PRN, or National Revolutionary Party. The split became final. The breakaway group attracted a large number of remarkable personalities, grouped around the figure of Raúl Ramos Jiménez, including some twenty deputies.

Organization and Recruitment

After the split, the PRN seemed to have taken with it most of the AD's dynamism. Dominated by the personality of its president Raúl Ramos Jiménez, it was based largely upon the full-time officers of the old guard AD, so that it possessed a considerable talent for leadership and a fine selection of the most competent elements in the AD. Of the most striking members of the PRN leadership, mention may be made of Ramón Quijada, founder and president of the Peasants' Federation, and Cesar Rondón Lovera, a politician enjoying considerable notoriety.

The parliamentary group of the AD Op. (subsequently PRN) was even strong enough to secure the Speakership of the House.

The party's rank and file support was much the same as that of the Old Guard : peasants and workers. However, in the struggle for the loyalty of the party following, the PRN proved less successful than the AD, in the final analysis. In particular, the PRN's influence among the peasants declined when Ramón Quijada left the party to support Arturo Uslar Pietri's presidential campaign in 1963, and its influence over the industrial working class also fell when the AD recovered control of the powerful Venezuelan Workers Confederation (CTV).

Party Programme and Doctrine

The PRN claimed to represent a return to the original principles of the AD, the principles which led to its foundation. In doctrinal terms, it was therefore to the left of the Old Guard, demanding oil nationalization, a more understanding attitude towards Cuba, and the dissolution of the AD–COPEI alliance. In agriculture, the PRN was critical of the rate of reform and the conditions with which it is hedged about. At the same time, it was hostile to left-wing extremism. The faction from which it originated, the AD Op., was the most active in demanding the expulsion of young Castroist enthusiasts in the party, the *muchachos*. In fact, the PRN's differences with AD were more a matter of tactics and personalities than general ideology. Its philosophy called for a return to the doctrinal springs of the AD, or in other words to a clearly more 'left-wing' position.

Voting Strength

The PRN's voting strength is difficult to assess, because it was not really properly organized as a party until after the 1963 elections. However, in the presidential election the AD Op. candidate obtained 66,837 votes, or less than 3 per cent of the total. The PRN was represented in Parliament by four deputies and two senators, until its final dissolution.[5]

5. The PRIN (Partido Revolucionario de la Izquierda Nacionalista) was born of an amalgamation between the left-wing parties hostile to the dominant position held by the three big traditional parties (AD, COPEI and URD) in Venezuelan politics. These left-wing groups included, principally, the PRN (created, as we have seen, out of a left-wing breakaway from the AD), the Popular Nationalist Avant-Garde, a left-wing breakaway group from the URD, the 'legalist' sectors of the MIR and other members from various quarters of the independent left. The founders of this party were Raúl Ramos Jiménez and Domingo Alberto Rangel. The PRIN's immediate objective, however, is to provide a rallying-point for PCV and MIR voters and act as a temporary stand-in for the two banned organizations.

The PRIN was the first to put out the call for a general anti-AD front (*ancha base*) dedicated to the goal of a left-wing government brought to power by democratic means. Contacts and discussions were arranged to this end with other parties, and even with Rafael

Movimiento de la Izquierda Revolucionária (MIR)

The Movement of the Revolutionary Left, or MIR, is the Venezuelan exemplar of a new family of Latin American parties, with a Marxist credo, Castroist in type, and with a form of organization differing from the traditional communist parties.

Foundation

The origins of the MIR can be traced back to the dissatisfaction of the AD's left wing with Rómulo Betancourt's cautiously reformist policies. From the beginning, the conflict was deeper and more fundamental than that between the ARS and the Old Guard. As early as the AD convention held in August 1958, Domingo Alberto Rangel emerged at the head of the movement of young, impatient militants termed the *muchachos*. In April 1960, the collective resignation of the *muchachos* from the AD marked the official inauguration of a new party. This was first called Izquierda de Acción Democrática, then took the name MIR.

The split was occasioned by a dual disagreement. In

Caldera (and the COPEI) and Uslar Pietri (and the FND). The failure of this broad anti-AD front did not prevent the PRIN from playing a major, if not a decisive part in the close struggle between Gonzalo Barrios, Luis Beltrán Prieto and Rafael Caldera. While it had no real chance of putting forward a candidate of its own with any hope of success, the PRIN found itself in a position to tip the balance in favour of the candidate it eventually decided to support, as long as it was able to carry all its voters with it. The PRIN was in favour of the legal recognition and rehabilitation of the PC and the MIR, and according to informed sources Raúl Ramos Jiménez recently had a series of meetings of great political significance in Moscow with Jesús Faria, leader of the PC in exile in the Soviet capital after his liberation.

The activists and suporters of the old PRN can nearly all be found in the ranks of the PRIN today.

domestic affairs, it arose out of the discussions surrounding a new oil contract. In foreign affairs, the dispute was over the Cuban question, and was rendered irremediable by the Conference of San José de Costa Rica in the summer of 1960. Consequently the MIR is labelled 'Fidelist'. In fact, the *muchachos*' collective resignation merely forestalled certain expulsion.

History

The MIR's history is brief and uncomplicated. It held its first national convention in July 1960 and immediately embarked upon energetic opposition to the Betancourt government. It rapidly developed towards a violent form of opposition, which earned it 'suspension' by the government following a revolt by a battalion of marines at Carupano in May 1962. The MIR, an ardent advocate of direct action, first organized terrorist attacks and then revolutionary guerrilla war. The leaders of the party were arrested in September 1963 and Betancourt demanded the proscription of the MIR, which he finally secured in December 1963.

In 1966 the MIR, while distinct from the Venezuelan Communist Party, was allied with the Communists in the National Liberation Front and had participated in the armed struggle against the government. However, Domingo Alberto Rangel left the party in mid-January 1965 to organize the Popular Nationalist Avant-Garde, born as has been mentioned from a left-wing breakaway from the URD.

Organization and Recruitment

The MIR's principal leader was its founder, Domingo Alberto Rangel, but the leadership of the party also included men like Fabricio Ojeda,[6] Simón Sáez Mérida, general

6. Found hanged in his cell after having been captured in early June 1966 as a guerrilla leader.

secretary of the AD during its clandestine period, who had since moved to militant Marxism, Jorge Dager who withdrew from the party in 1962 to form the Popular Democratic Front, and Jesús María Casals, arrested and imprisoned in 1963, freed in 1966.

It was first and foremost a party for young people, enjoying some support in the towns. It made its chief appeal to the trade unions – the party's founders were for the most part trade-union leaders – and to students, notably those at the University of Caracas. It operated as a clandestine organization. The striking-force of their urban organization was the UTC (Tactical Combat Units), and in the countryside they had guerrilla groups in the bush in Falcón and the Cordillera, led notably by Douglas Bravo and Napoleón Loyo. But the MIR was torn between a sector which favoured the continuance of the guerrilla war and a sector which agreed with the PCV in preferring a tactical return to peaceful action.

Party Programme and Doctrine

The MIR was a socialist party of the people, inspired by 'Fidelism' and independent of the PCV. It denounced liberal democracy as being purely formal and unreal. It looked forward to a social democracy that would benefit the working class, and it worked for the installation of a 'national democracy' in Venezuela. It favoured radical land reform, accelerated industrialization, nationalization of key industries and an end to the power of North American monopolies in the country. One of the party's leaders wrote:

We have turned to Marxism-Leninism because we have recognized the ideological bankruptcy of social democracy and experienced its opportunism; also we have been the victims of its unprincipled alliance-making and exercise of power. We have built our party on a Marxist-Leninist base, the only valid one and the only one capable of assisting progress, explaining the causes of the under-development of our country and pointing the way towards national liberation.

The MIR was in favour of a Castroist-type revolution in Venezuela. Its theoretical journal was *Pensamiento revolucionário*. Its chief ideologist was Américo Martín, one of the leaders of the Armed Forces of National Liberation organized in conjunction with the communists.

Electoral Strength

The MIR repudiated formal democracy and denounced the imposture of the AD regime, and it recommended abstention in the December 1963 elections. In fact it never took part in an election. It is therefore difficult to assess its electoral potential statistically, but at all events it does not appear to have been very strong in numbers. It was divided, as indeed is the Communist Party, between those who wanted to end guerrilla warfare and terrorism and work in depth with the masses, and those who advocated a relaunching of revoltionary violence in a kind of 'long march', at the end of which the proletarian revolution would defeat national capitalism and American imperialism. This second faction appeared to be a clear reflection of the Chinese line; in fact, it was close to the official Cuban line, and indeed Cuba provided open encouragement and assistance to the supporters of revolutionary guerrilla warfare.

Partido Comunista Venezolano (PCV)

The Venezuelan Communist Party is one of the oldest parties in modern Venezuela. It has been outlawed for most of its existence.

Foundation

The origins of the PCV go back further than those of the COPEI and even of the AD. Its early years were difficult, and its influence was small. The Venezuelan Communist Party was founded in 1931 from a number of different Marxist groups, including that of Juan Bautista Fuenmayor, on the initiative of Gustavo Machado. It was shortly outlawed by the dictator Gómez, and the cycle of persecution began. The communists then joined forces with the ORVE, and subsequently with Rómulo Betancourt's PDN.

In 1938 they withdrew from the PDN to reconstitute an independent working-class party with an orthodox Marxist ideology, under the leadership of Gustavo Machado. The Communist Party then won legal recognition under the Medina Angarita regime, but under the name Acción Municipal, and subsequently Unión Popular Venezolana (UPV).

History

The history of the Venezuelan Communist Party is a history of persecution, dating from its very inception, and of factional struggle between rival groups that found it very difficult to maintain unity under one banner. Two main factions emerged after Gómez's fall, when the party was legalized once more: one led by Gustavo Machado and the other by Juan Bautista Fuenmayor. The opposition between the two factions even led to the operation of two rival organizations, with the two hostile camps calling themselves respectively Venezuelan Communist Party and Revolutionary Proletarian Party. While one supported the Medina government, enjoyed the complicit tolerance of Pérez Jiménez but subsequently opposed the AD government, the other took a precisely opposite line. This duplication of the parties lasted practically until 1953, with the supporters of the Popular

Union being called the 'Reds' while those of the Revolutionary Proletarian Party were classed the 'Blacks'. Finally, the latter announced their own dissolution in 1958. Unity was re-established, and the united Venezuelan Communist Party was able to put forward the candidature of Wolfgang Larrazabal. From the accession of Betancourt, normal political life had hardly begun before the PCV went into opposition. The only occasion on which it consented to a truce was in 1959, under the threat of a right-wing coup d'etat: it answered the call to unity in the defence of the constitutional government.

From 1958 to the present day, the PCV has thus been opposed to the policies of the AD, an opposition which has been as much a matter of principle as of tactics, and which has covered internal and foreign affairs.

Shortly afterwards it made the important strategic move of joining the MIR in the insurrectional movement of the FALN, or Armed Forces of National Liberation. The party was suspended in May 1962, its leaders were arrested in September 1963, and finally the PCV was outlawed by the Betancourt government. In foreign affairs, it has often been obliged to engage in violent polemical erchanges with Fidel Castro, who singled it out for particular abuse.

Organization and Recruitment

The Venezuelan Communist Party has not succeeded in acquiring the powerful structure and homogeneous composition characteristic of the Leninist model. The number of its supporters is unstable, and it has not been able to escape from the consequences of the law which seems to govern the existence and operation of other political parties throughout Latin America, namely the tendency towards disintegration or at least fragmentation.

Its leaders, individually remarkable, each had his own

loyal following within the party, which helped to aggravate the tendency towards schism: on the one hand stood Gustavo Machado, veteran of the struggle for communism, with his following, the Reds, faced by Luis Miquelena, Cruz Villegas and Rodolfo Quintero, leaders of the Black communists. The latter managed to build up a solid base for the party in the Federation of Workers of the Federal District. Moreover, the PCV generally speaking managed to extend its influence in the labour movement with a fair degree of success. In 1958, the party was second only to the AD in its influence over the trade-union movement, and controlled a number of influential unions, such as the petroleum workers, the automobile workers, textile workers, chemical workers, and workers in the rubber industry. Its general secretary, Jesús Faria, was also secretary of the petroleum workers' union. Its policies are generally supported by the central Confederation of Venezuelan Workers.

The PCV has also succeeded in winning control of a large sector of the press, radio and television, with the support of certain groups of editorial staffs and reporters (for instance in the big Capriles chain). It publishes a number of newspapers itself, such as *Tribuna popular, Gazeta, Tiempos, Qué pasa en Venezuela?* and a monthly theoretical journal, *Principios*. The PCV is also firmly entrenched in the universities, especially the University of Caracas where it has numerous militant student supporters, organized in the Venezuelan Communist Youth (JCV). It has also managed to extend its influence in intellectual circles, especially in the legal profession. Its membership is estimated at 40,000, to which should be added some 35,000 sympathizers.

The party leadership has not been able to prevent a split in its membership, and especially in the ranks of party officials, between supporters of Chinese communism and those loyal to the Soviet version. Despite this, the party has since 1961 been organized to prepare for the phase of armed action, and one of its leaders, Guillermo García Ponce, was able to announce at the end of the party's twenty-fifth congress that the call for the overthrow of the government – a call entailing the preparation of the party's forces, propaganda and agitation – could be changed into a call for action within a matter of hours. Recourse to violent methods was moreover the subject of lively debate at the PCV national conference in January 1963, where some of the members opposed participation in guerrilla action and in the MIR's terrorist movement. With a swing of the pendulum at the end of 1965 and in 1966, the party entered into negotiations with the government for the cessation of violence and a return to legality, following the victory of the supporters of the soft line (*línea blanda*) over the hard line (*línea dura*), although the latter included the general secretary of the party, Pompeyo Marques. The government had meanwhile released a number of the former persuasion that it had arrested in 1963, including the brothers Eduardo and Gustavo Machado, who returned to swell the ranks of supporters of the *línea blanda*.

Party Programme and Doctrine

The PCV professes the doctrine of Marxism-Leninism, and applies it to its programme in Venezuela while emphasizing the following points: seizure of power by revolutionary violence, nationalization of oil and iron, revolutionary land reform, solidarity with the Cuban revolution, national democracy as a first step towards socialism, continuation of the anti-imperialist struggle in accordance with the general line of the international communist movement. The PCV's allegiance is to Moscow, and it has very serious differences with Castroist communism, both in matters of theory and even more on tactics.

For the PCV, in fact, the revolutionary struggle is not

simply reducible to armed struggle, and the latter in turn does not consist purely of rural guerrilla warfare. For instance, it has opposed Douglas Bravo and his group, which it accuses of divisive and anti-party behaviour, regarding his guerrilla activities as action for action's sake and adventurism, to the extent that the 'true communists', as they call themselves, no longer feel any affinity with the 'Party in the hills'. The PCV stresses the fact that 'the motive force of the Venezuelan revolution is in the big towns' and that the metropolitan area is the 'epicentre of the revolution'. The condemnation of this attitude by the Cuban newspaper *Granma* and by Fidel Castro himself has led the PCV to clarify the position by announcing that after March 1961 the party had indeed adopted the road of armed insurrection to seize power, but that this insurrection needed to be prepared by degrees, and that an analysis of local conditions demonstrated the need for a broad movement of national liberation as a first step in the march towards socialism. At all events, at the September plenary session of the PCV in April 1965, after the failure of the first wave of guerrilla attacks, the party embarked on a policy of a 'democratic peace line' to enable it to 'bury its dead, heal its wounds, and prepare for future combat'. Visibly piqued by Fidel Castro's jibes, the Venezuelan Communist Party emphasizes the specific conditions affecting the revolutionary struggle in the country; rejects all outside interference, declaring that it is not a satellite of any power; and underlines at the same time the collective nature of the party leadership, free of any taint of the cult of personality, and the loyalty to Leninism demonstrated by its approach and its tactical methods.

Voting Strength

In 1958 the PCV, supporting Larrazabal, received a total of 150,791 votes, which earned it seven deputies' seats and two senators. This was an appreciable improvement over the elections during the 1945–8 period, when it won hardly more than 3 per cent of the votes cast. In 1963, the party recommended abstention from the presidential elections. The call does not seem to have been heeded very widely. At all events the PCV did not take part in the 1963 elections.

Its voting strength is drawn largely from the urban sector – trade unions, students and university teachers, journalists, intellectuals – and hardly at all from the country, where it is very weak. In the federal district, the PCV pulled up to second place in December 1958. The majority of its active members and sympathizers are still concentrated in Caracas and its surroundings. Its weakness stems primarily from its failure to acquire a foothold in the countryside.

Fuerza Democrática Popular (FDP)

The Popular Democratic Force is one of the latest left-wing formations to have emerged in Venezuela.

Foundation

This party's origins may be found in the very lively discussions within the MIR over the tactics adopted by the party in the struggle against the government, and in its collaboration with the Communist Party, especially during 1961 and 1962. The disagreement, which broke out into the open in July 1962, became official in 1963 with the foundation of a new party, called the Popular Democratic Force, under the leadership of Jorge Dager, erstwhile leader within the MIR of the faction opposed to the insurrectional line of that party and favouring action independent of the Communist Party.

History

The FDP published its decision to follow its own path with something of a splash, by presenting as its candidate for the 1963 presidential elections the retired Vice-Admiral Wolfgang Larrazabal, Betancourt's defeated rival in 1958. The FDP tries to provide a rallying-point for those sectors of the left opposition with reservations about terrorist violence and guerrilla war.

Organization and Recruitment

The party is organized around the figure of its president Jorge Dager, and is working hard to extend its influence in the country. It would seem that it has had some temporary success in taking root among the underprivileged sectors of the urban proletariat, particularly in Caracas and the federal district. It has certainly benefited from the recruitment of Larrazabal, whose personal vehicle it has become. It has one representative on the executive committee of the CTV.

Party Programme and Doctrine

The FDP has announced its support, in domestic policy, for political and social democracy, specifically demanding in its programme the legalization of the banned parties, an end to the state of emergency, and an improvement in the conditions of the working class and the more underprivileged sectors of the population. It is avowedly democratic socialist. In foreign policy it supports 'positive neutralism', in other words non-alignment hand in hand with a distinct anti-Americanism.

Voting Strength

It is still too soon to give an accurate assessment of the FDP's voting strength, which seems to be concentrated chiefly in the poorer quarters of the big towns. Its national support still seems limited, to judge from the results of the 1963 presidential elections, when its candidate, despite his personal popularity (going back to the 'emergency plan' put into effect in 1958 to help the unemployed), only obtained 275,309 votes, or less than 10 per cent of the total cast.

Frente Nacional Democrático (FND)

Only the future will tell whether the National Democratic Front is merely an alliance of convenience, created in the special circumstances of the 1963 presidential elections, or whether the gathering of a number of personalities and political groups around the candidature of the writer Arturo Uslar Pietri has provided the point of departure for a new viable and strong political party.

The National Democratic Front was created in 1963 out of a grand alliance between various political movements behind a famous name of Venezuelan letters and politics, its president Arturo Uslar Pietri, one-time minister to presidents López Contreras and Medina Angarita, and an intellectual of high standing. Its first general secretary was Ramón Escobar Salom, leader of the biggest of the constituent groups of the FND, the Progressive Republican Movement (MRP).[7] The FND is in fact a loose confederation with a wholly heterogeneous structure. It is somewhere on the centre-right of the political spectrum, although some of its demands have a left-wing tinge.

7. The MRP has since dissociated itself from the FND, still with Escobar Salom as its leader. It is currently considered an autonomous political organization.

In the 1963 presidential elections, the party immediately proved a major political force in the country, winning 469,240 votes, or 16 per cent of the total cast, which earned it eighteen seats in the Chamber of Deputies.

Its support comes from businessmen and the urban middle class, as well as the lower middle classes and part of the proletariat. It has also won the support of the old instigator of the peasant leagues, Ramón Quijada, a defector from the Nationalist Revolutionary Party ARS.

The party's programme has endeavoured to take account of the wide variety of trends represented in this vast conglomeration: effective democracy, national reconciliation with an amnesty for the rebels, tax reform, although combined with a pragmatic policy very friendly to foreign capital, and defence of national sovereignty within the framework of the western world.

The National Democratic Front entered the government in October 1964, following the working out of a joint programme in September. However, it left the government coalition in March 1966, considering that the Leoni government had not respected the agreement of September 1964 in the two key sectors of petroleum policy and fiscal reform. However, its leader, Arturo Uslar Pietri, announced that the FND would not oppose the regime on all issues as a matter of policy.

The Small Extreme Right-Wing Parties

Finally, some mention should be made of the extreme right-wing organizations, which only enjoy limited support. Two in particular have made efforts to concentrate the votes of conservatives and anti-progressives: the Movement for National Action (Movimiento de Acción Nacional, or MAN) and the Authentic Nationalist Party (Partido Auténtico

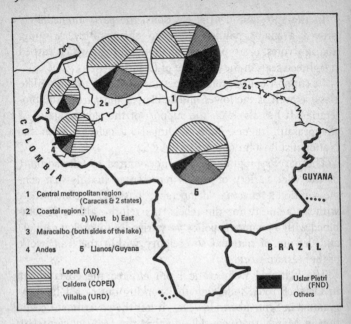

1 Central metropolitan region
   (Caracas & 2 states)
2 Coastal region:
      a) West   b) East
3 Maracaibo (both sides of the lake)
4 Andes   5 Llanos/Guyana

Leoni (AD)
Caldera (COPEI)
Villalba (URD)
Uslar Pietri (FND)
Others

Figure 28. Results of the 1963 Presidential Elections: By Main Regions

Nacionalista, or PAN). The latter, whose general secretary is Enrique Parra Bozo, has been characterized as 'Catholic, anti-communist and an admirer of the regime of Francisco Franco'. The PAN is also favourable to the ex-dictator Pérez Jiménez, and even tried to put him forward as its candidate in the 1963 presidential elections. Curiously Pérez Jiménez's own party, the National Civic Crusade, enjoys some popularity in certain poor quarters and among specific categories of workers, such as Caracas taxi-drivers. It puts out a violently anti-Yankee publication, *Polémica*, which runs to three thousand copies. United States agreement to the deportation of the ex-dictator explains this attitude.

In the same vein, the Independent Venezuelan Association may be mentioned, founded in 1962 by a group including Rafael Tinoco, president of the National Banking Association. This organization consists largely of industrialists and financiers. The AVI is not a political party properly speaking, but a pressure group wielding a degree of power and influence far beyond the numerical strength of its support.

Venezuela has therefore developed towards a multi-party system which has only created confusion on the political scene.[8] Alliances form and break up again, and progressive fragmentation continues to eat away at the parties. Nevertheless, the hardening of the extreme left has brought about some clarification of the situation, with a redistribution of parties into conservative right, the ruling reformist centre and the revolutionary left, the usual criterion determining a party's position being its attitude towards the United States, the dominant power on the continent. With the advent of guerrilla warfare and the bitter struggle between

8. Besides the parties considered in this chapter, mention should be made of the existence of political formations whose strength, support and durability are in doubt because they have but recently appeared. Most of them are for the time being mere 'mini-parties', whose electoral behaviour is awaited with curiosity by observers. The following are just a few of these parties: AFN (Amplio Frente Nacional); CCN (Cruzada Cívica Nacional); PL (Partido Liberal); AVI (Acción Venezolana Independiente); OPINA (Opinión Nacional); ORI (Organización Regional Independiente); PSV (Partido Socialista Venezolano); MAP (Movimiento Alianza Popular); MICO (Movimiento Independiente Campesino Obrero); MENI (Movimiento Electoral Nacional Independiente); PSN (Partido Socialista Nacional); FEI (Frente Electoral Independiente); ACI (Agrupación Cívica de Integración); FUN (Frente de Unificación); MDI (Movimiento Democrático Independiente); UNIR (Unión Nacional Independiente Regional); API (Alianza Popular Independiente); BIN (Bloque Independiente Nacional); FPN (Frente Político Nacional); BV (Buena Vecindad); VPN (Vanguardia Popular Nacionalista), etc.

the AD in power and the communists in opposition, Venezuela has become a sensitive area in the western hemisphere, and will provide a touchstone for the whole of Latin America. The country of representative democracy is a prey to the twin dangers of left-wing subversion and renewed militancy on the part of those who have not forgotten the strength of the army or the grand old traditions of dictatorship. The least we can say is that the survival of the party system will be a never-ending battle.

1967

Christian Democracy in Power

The presidential elections of December 1968 took place in an atmosphere of increasing tension. Rumours of an impending military takeover spread throughout the country. Apprehension continued to mount during the week as it became apparent that no single candidate would receive a clear majority. Eventually the victor was declared. COPEI's Rafael Caldera had defeated AD's Gonzalo Barrios by the narrowest of margins, 32,000 votes out of a total of 3·7 million. Caldera had obtained 29·08 per cent to Barrios's 28·24 per cent. They were followed by: Dr Miguel Angel Burelli Rivas of the Frente Victoria (URD, FND, FDP, MENI) with 22·27 per cent, Dr Beltrán Prieto Figueroa (MEP, PRIN, OPINA) with 19·32 per cent, Alejandro Hernandez (PSD) 0·71 per cent and German Borregales (MAN) 0·34 per cent.

In Congress, however, AD retained a small majority with 19 senators and 66 deputies. COPEI received 16 and 59. The remainder were as follows: MEP 5, 25; CCN 4, 21; URD 3, 18; FDP 2, 10; FND 1, 5; UPA/PCV 1, 5.

Slowly fears of the *golpe de estado* subsided and Venezuela found itself with yet another coalition government. The election seems to have marked the beginning of a new, somewhat less promising future for the country. First AD, under whose guidance the nation had been for over a decade, was defeated. The immediate cause undoubtedly was the pre-election split which saw its former president, Prieto Figueroa, form his own party, the Movimiento del Pueblo (MEP).

The significance of the departure of Figueroa's social reformist group is that AD is now a centre party with growing right-wing tendencies. It has, therefore, become increasingly difficult to differentiate the two major parties on an ideological level. Nevertheless, the victory of Caldera's Christian Democrats suggests that the electorate is seeking an alternative to the worn out social democratic solutions, however limited this alternative may turn out to be in reality.

Far more interesting was the striking success of the ex-dictator, Pérez Jiménez. Not only did he personally win a senatorial seat without leaving Madrid but his party, CCN, emerged to become the country's fourth largest. The implications of this will be discussed below.

During the first year the new government abandoned AD's 'Betancourt Doctrine' which refused diplomatic recognition to communist and Latin American dictator-dominated countries. Relations were established with several eastern European countries as well as with the military governments in Argentina and Peru. At home, the Communist Party was legalized and an amnesty offered to certain guerrillas as part of a 'pacification' programme. The latter was fiercely opposed by AD who advocated the suspension of constitutional rights and imposition of martial law. The most explosive issue faced by the government in its early days was its confrontation with students of the University of Caracas. Long a centre of radical activity, it appeared as though Caldera had earmarked it for a change. COPEI and AD joined against the remaining coalition parties to promulgate the University Reform Law which, in effect, destroyed the university's autonomy and placed it under government surveillance. Towards the end of 1972 Caldera's attitude seemed to be softening, but it is clear that 'ideological' subversion is being dealt with along the lines followed during the 1960s by Brazil, Argentina, Peru and Mexico.

Soon, more pressing problems had to be tackled. The coalition government took over a dependent economy distinguished by the following characteristics:

– 63 per cent of the government's income and 90 per cent of its foreign exchange were derived from petroleum exploitation, which, along with iron ore, is almost entirely in the hands of American companies.

– An import substitution process which, although initiated and implemented by the reformist AD, had ground to a halt, bringing in its wake a new type of dependency. The import of raw materials, semi-finished goods and foreign technology was increasing so rapidly that the foreign exchange provided by the oil industry was not growing fast enough to cover the country's needs. In addition, the number of subsidiaries of US multi-national firms had risen from 120 to 213, thus effectively denationalizing the meagre native industry that existed previously.

– Balance of payments problems had risen. A current account surplus of $390 millions became a deficit of $360 millions in 1969.

– On a different level, the inability of a capital-intensive manufacturing sector to absorb the fast growing population could be seen in the level of unemployment which stood at 8·4 per cent officially and 18 per cent unofficially. Underemployment in the mushrooming 'marginal' sector was last estimated at 60 per cent.

– An agrarian sector where reform had, for all practical purposes, ended in 1966 with the *latifundia* structure still intact. Consequently the flow towards the cities of hungry, jobless, landless peasants continued unabated. In short, the government faced problems similar to most Latin American governments. Its attempt to deal with these problems was hardly unique.

The nationalist response became apparent in late 1970 with the new banking law. Under the law, foreign ownership in commercial banking operations was reduced to 20 per cent. This was followed by a bill raising the income tax rate on oil company profits from 52 per cent to 62 per cent. It was proposed by AD as an alternative to widening the tax base (latifundists, for example, pay no land tax) illustrating the real basis of its increase in nationalism. In July 1971, URD and MEP presented the Oil Reversion Bill which stipulated that in 1983–4, when seventy-five of the existing oil concessions expire, the companies would have to surrender without compensation their concessions, areas, equipment and installations. Finally, in late 1971, a thirty-five man commission was set up to examine the whole question of foreign investment. They will probably recommend the nationalization of banks and iron ore as well as the limitation of foreign investment to certain sectors that the government will designate.

The present coalition is in reality another step towards the disintegration of representative democracy in Venezuela. During the past decade innumerable divisions, regroupings and realignments have occurred against a background of persistent if limited guerrilla warfare. A situation has been created where no political party is able to play a dominant role. Moreover, nearly half of the electorate continue to vote 'anti-government'. On the left, these parties once again are hoping to form a united front to combat the AD–COPEI axis at the next election. On the extreme right is the growing threat of the CCN indicative of the instability and explosive potential of the petit bourgeois and 'marginal' classes. AD is currently working on a bill to prevent those associated with Pérez Jiménez's government from taking part in the

1973 elections. The point, however, has been made that the social basis for neo-fascist politics exists in present-day Venezuela.

The main elements of the political system then are as follows :

– a tendency towards radicalization (to the left or right) by important sectors of the petit bourgeois, salaried middle classes and the 'marginal' class.

– a socialist-oriented guerrilla movement.

– ruling class parties which are no longer assured of their former basis for consensus *vis-à-vis* the masses.

– armed forces whose 'institutionalization' is tenuous at best.

– lastly, a government whose right-wing and reformist parties are about evenly divided creating an immediately dangerous political equilibrium, itself a reflection of a deep rooted structural crisis. Thus, the stage is set for Caesar. The uncertainty seems to lie mainly in the hour of his arrival.

February 1972

More about Penguins and Pelicans

Penguinews, which appears every month, contains details of all the new books issued by Penguins as they are published. From time to time it is supplemented by *Penguins in Print*, which is a complete list of all available books published by *Penguins*. (There are well over four thousand of these.)

A specimen copy of *Penguinews* will be sent to you free on request. For a year's issues (including the complete lists) please send 30p if you live in the United Kingdom, or 60p if you live elsewhere. Just write to Dept EP, Penguin Books Ltd, Harmondsworth, Middlesex, enclosing a cheque or postal order, and your name will be added to the mailing list.

Note: *Penguinews* and *Penguins in Print* are not available in the U.S.A. or Canada

The Pelican Latin American Library

Sven Lindqvist

The Shadow: Latin America faces the Seventies

'This book is a classic,' writes Richard Gott in his foreword. 'It is a must for anyone concerned with Latin American affairs.'

Sven Lindqvist, who has written extensively on third-world problems, spent two years in Latin America to gather material for this book. He talked to landowners and peasants, government officials and slum-dwellers; witnessed corruption at all levels, police brutality and the reprisals that await the politically active; and checked the facts behind the stories he was told and the official figures he was given.

His account of the common problems which face each country in the seventies is as readable as it is scholarly. Drawing on anecdotes, recorded conversations and personal impressions, it sets the political upheavals of contemporary Latin America in their social context.